Pricing Strategies

To my parents

Pricing Strategies

A Marketing Approach

Robert M. Schindler

Rutgers University–Camden

Los Angeles | London | New Delhi
Singapore | Washington DC

Los Angeles | London | New Delhi
Singapore | Washington DC

FOR INFORMATION:

SAGE Publications, Inc.
2455 Teller Road
Thousand Oaks, California 91320
E-mail: order@sagepub.com

SAGE Publications Ltd.
1 Oliver's Yard
55 City Road
London EC1Y 1SP
United Kingdom

SAGE Publications India Pvt. Ltd.
B 1/I 1 Mohan Cooperative Industrial Area
Mathura Road, New Delhi 110 044
India

SAGE Publications Asia-Pacific Pte. Ltd.
33 Pekin Street #02-01
Far East Square
Singapore 048763

Acquisitions Editor: Lisa Cuevas Shaw
Associate Editor: Megan Krattli
Editorial Assistant: Mayan White
Production Editor: Eric Garner
Copy Editor: Megan Markanich
Typesetter: C&M Digitals (P) Ltd.
Proofreader: Wendy Jo Dymond
Indexer: Marilyn Augst
Cover Designer: Anupama Krishnan
Marketing Manager: Helen Salmon
Permissions Editor: Karen Ehrmann

Printed in the United States of America

Library of Congress Cataloging-in-Publication Data

Schindler, Robert M.

Pricing strategies: a marketing approach / Robert M. Schindler.

p. cm.
Includes bibliographical references and index.

ISBN 978-1-4129-6474-6 (hardback)

1. Pricing. 2. Marketing. I. Title.

HF5416.5.S38 2012
658.8'16—dc23   2011031174

This book is printed on acid-free paper.

11 12 13 14 15 10 9 8 7 6 5 4 3 2 1

Brief Contents

Detailed Contents

11 Time as a Price-Segmentation Fence

12 Place as a Price-Segmentation Fence

13 Pricing of Interrelated Products

Preface

I first became interested in pricing about 30 years ago, while I was working as a marketing research analyst at AT&T Long Lines. One of our research projects was to investigate why AT&T was rapidly losing market share to the upstart competitor, MCI Communications, whose rates were only a few cents cheaper than those of AT&T. Customer focus groups, backed up by survey research, determined the answer: Customer perceptions were greatly exaggerating the difference between AT&T and MCI's rates. Consumers had formed their impressions of AT&T's rates during the decades when AT&T was the high-priced monopoly provider in a regulated market. When MCI entered the long distance calling market, AT&T's actual rates were only a fraction of what most consumers thought they were.

As someone with academic training in the field of cognitive psychology, I was impressed by such enormous business consequences that arose from the consumer's perceptions, rather than the reality, of marketplace prices. I returned to academics and began to carry out research on behavioral pricing topics, such as the effects of the use of 9-ending prices in retailing and the reasons why framing a price as a discount can so powerfully stimulate sales.

As I became involved in the teaching of pricing as well as the research, I began to appreciate that a business school pricing course is as important to students as it is fun to teach. This book is an attempt to make basic pricing concepts more accessible to business school students, at both the undergraduate and MBA levels. It is also intended to serve as a useful handbook for the thoughtful business manager, who may not have had the opportunity to take a college course in pricing. There are several aspects of this book that help support these goals.

A Simple, Unified System. I have made an effort in the book to present a sensible and consistent system for the setting and management of prices. The basic tasks are to set initial prices, improve existing prices, consider different prices for different market segments, and to consider the effects of product interrelations. In spelling out this simple framework, I have applied the idea of a price-change breakeven analysis along with many other insightful and elegant concepts from Thomas Nagle's influential contributions to the teaching of pricing.

Intuitive Mathematical Techniques. In several ways, I have worked to make it clear to students that they *can* do the math necessary for making effective price-related decisions. First, I have used in the book only a small number of formulas and mathematical concepts.

Several of these—breakeven analysis, expected value, and multiple regression—are applied in several places in the text to show their relevance to different aspects of pricing and to reinforce the student's understanding. Second, no mathematical knowledge beyond high school algebra is assumed. Everything necessary for carrying out each mathematical analysis is presented in the text. Third, I make an effort to demystify the formulas used in pricing. In particular, I show that the formula for a price-change breakeven analysis is nothing more than a general form of the simple breakeven formula that most business students already know.

Focus on Customer Needs and Behavior. The marketing approach to pricing involves more than recognizing how pricing relates to the other three of the "four Ps" of the marketing mix. A theme of this book is that the practice of pricing will benefit from an attentiveness to customer needs and sensitivities as much as will marketing practices such as advertising or product design. Further, in this book I work to demonstrate that psychological factors, rather than being a footnote on the limits of "rational" pricing, are central to core pricing questions. The issues and findings of consumer behavior research are integrated into the text, for example, in the discussions of assessing value to the customer, communicating value to the customer, predicting price-change response, and selecting an appropriate price-segmentation fence.

Small-Business Friendly. I have worked to choose business examples and illustrations that demonstrate that the basic pricing principles discussed in this book are applicable to all types of businesses. However, I have also tended toward examples involving retail business—which students can readily relate to—and have written many discussions with small businesses in mind. Small businesses are relatively easy to understand and thus serve well to illustrate basic pricing principles. But also within virtually every small business lies the entrepreneurial spirit—the dream of becoming a larger business. Many business students cherish such entrepreneurial dreams, and orienting pricing discussions toward easily understandable businesses encourages students to think about the pricing aspects of their dreams, thus motivating study and perhaps even someday helping such dreams become reality.

Grounding in Practical Theory. Throughout the book, I have tended to make repeated use of a small number of key concepts (such as the concept of price segmentation) and have favored descriptions in simple terms that seem likely to endure (such as organizing legal issues into four categories: price fixing, inappropriate price levels, inappropriate price differentials, and inadequate price communication). To the extent that these practices are considered to be bringing theory into the text, I would note that good theory is practical. The practical benefits of using a small number of concepts expressed in simple terms are that it facilitates both the ability to learn basic concepts and the ability to keep them in mind so that they can actually be used. Indeed, as the digital revolution throws more and more product categories into "price consternation," we don't really know how things will turn out. This uncertainty makes mastery of simple principles, expressed in basic terms that are unlikely to change, all the more important.

ACKNOWLEDGMENTS

In the writing of this book, I have benefitted from the help of many people—many more than I can list. Simply invaluable has been the contribution of my students, the hundreds of undergraduates and MBA students who have taken my class, "Pricing Strategies." My ambition to create a simple, organized, and comprehensive set of pricing principles was forged in the crucible of their feedback. To the extent that this book is effective, it is a reflection of my students' unceasingly holding me to the highest standards of clarity, consistency, and organization.

I owe a great debt to my colleague and outstanding teacher, Alok Baveja. His help with the material on revenue management and other topics has made a substantial difference in the text. My thanks also go to David Vance, Allie Miller, and Ivo Jansen for their help with accounting-related material and to Vinay Kanetkar for his help with the discussion of conjoint analysis. Over the years, conversations with H. G. Parsa, Eric Anderson, Kent Monroe, John Deighton, Franklin Houston, Carol Kaufman-Scarborough, Maureen Morrin, Briance Mascarenhas, Gerald Haubl, Manoj Thomas, Vishal Lala, and many more of my academic colleagues have clarified my understandings and enhanced the discussions in this text.

I very much appreciate my conversations with Keith Spirgel, Maurice Herrara, Richard Wallin, Edward Janes, Eric Naiburg, Richard Clements, Thomas Magoffin, Jonathan Lane, and the many other businesspeople who took the time to talk with me about the pricing practices in their industries. Also, I thank Stephanie Capps, whose research assistant work provided many useful pricing examples.

Thanks also go out to Al Bruckner, Lisa Shaw, Deya Jacob, Megan Krattli, Eric Garner, Megan Markanich, Maggie Stanley, and the others at SAGE who have been involved with this book. They have been outstanding in their helpful expertise and supportiveness. I deeply appreciate the feedback and input from the following manuscript reviewers:

Wasim Azhar, University of California, Berkeley

Ann Barker, University of Colorado

Randolph E. Bucklin, UCLA Anderson School

Anthony Dukes, University of Southern California

Hooman Estelami, Fordham University

Eugene Jones, Ohio State University

P. K. Kannan, University of Maryland at College Park

Dmitri Kuksov, Washington University in St. Louis

Yunchuan Liu, University of Illinois

Preethika Sainam, Indiana University

Gerald Smith, Boston College

Catherine Tucker, Massachusetts Institute of Technology

Tuo Wang, Kent State University

I have been able to incorporate many reviewer suggestions, and the text is far better because of their efforts.

To my Rutgers–Camden colleagues, as well as to the administration and staff of the School of Business, my thanks go to you for your help in making the school a supportive and stimulating intellectual environment. To my wife, Jean, and our sons, Eric and Kevin, I express my deepest appreciation for your patience with the many hours I have spent working on this book and for your creating a supportive home—one full of life, love, and joy.

ANCILLARIES

The password-protected instructor's site at www.sagepub.com/schindler contains PowerPoint presentations, teaching tips, answers to the end-of chapter exercises, and SAGE Journal Articles for use in the classroom.

About the Author

Robert M. Schindler is professor of marketing at Rutgers University in Camden, New Jersey. He has carried out numerous studies of consumer perception and motivation, especially concerning the effects of price endings and price promotions. His work has appeared in publications such as the *Journal of Consumer Research*, the *Journal of Marketing Research*, the *Journal of Retailing*, the *Journal of Advertising*, and the *Journal of Consumer Psychology*. He has been ranked among the most published researchers in the area of pricing and has received a Lifetime Achievement Award from the Fordham University Pricing Center.

Professor Schindler received a BA in biochemistry and psychology from the University of Pennsylvania and an MS and PhD in cognitive psychology from the University of Massachusetts. He has been teaching courses in marketing, consumer behavior, and pricing at Rutgers–Camden since 1989 and is a recipient of the Chancellor's Award for Teaching Excellence.

Introduction: Pricing as an Element of the Marketing Mix

Anytime anything is sold, there must be a price involved. The focus of this book is to present concepts, principles, and techniques that provide guidance to help a seller set the best price.

Our study of how to set the best prices will take the marketing approach. In this chapter, we will describe the business context for pricing and provide an overview of how the basic principles of marketing can guide effective price setting.

THE COMMERCIAL EXCHANGE

Although people often think of marketing as synonymous with advertising or salesmanship, it is actually much broader. Marketing consists of the full range of activities involved in facilitating commercial exchanges and having all of these activities be guided by a concern for customer needs.

The central idea here is that of the commercial exchange (see Figure 1.1). This is where a seller provides a product to a buyer in return for something in exchange (usually an amount of money). The product could be something tangible, which is referred to as a good, or the product could be the result of human or mechanical effort, which is referred to as a service. The buyer could be a consumer—an individual who purchases a product for his or her own use—or the buyer could be a business customer—an individual or group who purchases the product in order to resell it or for other business purposes.

One aspect that makes the commercial exchange a very important idea is that it describes an interaction that is voluntary. Both the buyer and seller participate in the exchange voluntarily because the exchange will lead them *both* to be better off. For example, consider the vending machine in the office lounge. You put in your dollar and get a large package of M&M's. You do that voluntarily because you would rather have the bag of candy than that dollar. On the other hand, the Mars company, which produces M&M's, also

Figure 1.1 The Commercial Exchange

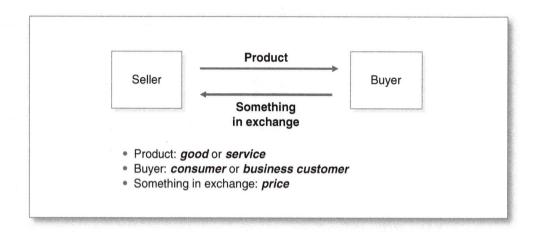

Source: Adapted from W. M. Pride and O. C. Ferrell, *Marketing: Concepts and Strategies* (Boston: Houghton Mifflin Co).

engages in this transaction voluntarily. As we know, the company would rather have your dollar than that extra package of candy.

Although we tend to take commercial exchanges for granted, we shouldn't forget that there is something very important and wonderful involved here. Because both parties to the exchange are better off after the exchange than before, one could say that the exchange makes the world a just a little bit better place. There is a little more happiness after the exchange than before it. Although there may be only a tiny bit of increased happiness from any one commercial exchange, these little pleasures can quickly mount up. In a society where the distribution of most goods and services is governed by a free-market economy, every person engages in numerous commercial exchanges every day. Each little increase in pleasure that a commercial exchange brings is then multiplied many times, and the societal benefits can become considerable.

In all of this, it must be recognized that there are degrees of voluntariness, and that choices may be so limited for some buyers that they may not *feel* much better off after an exchange. Also, it is possible that a product purchased voluntarily could fail to perform as expected or that a third party (other than the buyer and seller) may be harmed by an exchange. These illustrate the need for some governmental regulation—a free-market economy cannot be entirely free. Nevertheless, in modern free-market societies, people experience the pleasures of choice and are energized by entrepreneurial possibilities. The commercial exchange is at the heart of the free-market economic system, which, as we have seen in recent years, has become more and more widely adopted among the various nations of the world.

WHAT IS A PRICE?

From this understanding of the commercial exchange, we are now able to give a formal definition of a price: that which is given in return for a product in a commercial exchange.

This essential role of price in commerce is sometimes disguised by the use of traditional terms. If the product in the commercial exchange is a good, then the product's price will most likely be called "price." However, if the product is a service, then the product's price may well go by one of a variety of other possible names (see Figure 1.2).

Figure 1.2   Some Terms Used to Mean "Price"

Alternative Terms	What Is Purchased
Price	*most goods*
Tuition	*college courses, education*
Rent	*use of a place to live or use of equipment for a period of time*
Interest	*use of money*
Fee	*professional services: for lawyers, doctors, consultants*
Premium	*insurance*
Fare	*transportation: air, taxi, bus*
Toll	*use of a road or bridge, or long-distance phone rate*
Salary	*work of managers*
Wages	*work of hourly workers*
Commission	*sales effort*

Source: Adapted from Thomas C. Kinnear and Kenneth L. Bernhardt, *Principles of Marketing,* 2nd ed. (Glenview, IL: Scott, Foresman and Company, 1986), 546.

"Price" Versus "Cost"

Although a price may go by many names, one name it should not go by is cost. This is because, in this book, we will usually be taking the viewpoint of the seller.

If we were taking the viewpoint of the buyer, this would not be an issue. Buyers, particularly consumers, will typically use the terms *price* and *cost* synonymously. For example, a woman could tell her friend, "The price of this sweater was only $30." Or she could just as easily say, "This sweater cost me only $30."

However, from the viewpoint of the seller, the difference between prices and costs is quite important. A price is what a business charges, and a cost is what a business pays. Thus, a grocery manager may set a price of $3.79 for a 17-ounce box of Honey Nut Cheerios, may price large navel oranges at 3 for $1.99, or may sell ground chuck at the price of $3.49 per pound. But the manager must also attend to his costs. These costs include, for example, what he pays the wholesaler per case of Cheerios, what he pays employees to stock it on the shelves, what he pays for the building, for heat and lights, for advertising, and so on.

PRICING AS A MARKETING ACTIVITY

Marketing activities are those actions an organization can take for the purpose of facilitating commercial exchanges. There are four categories of marketing activities that are particularly important, which are traditionally known as the four elements of the marketing mix:

- *Product*—designing, naming, and packaging goods and/or services that satisfy customer needs
- *Distribution*—efforts to make the product available at the times and places that customers want
- *Promotion*—communicating about the product and/or the organization that produces it
- *Pricing*—determining what must be provided by a customer in return for the product

If you use the term *place* for the activities of distribution, the four elements of the marketing mix can be referred to as "the four Ps," a mnemonic that has proved useful to generations of marketing students.

Note that there is an important way in which pricing differs from the other three elements of the marketing mix. This is illustrated in Figure 1.3. Product, distribution, and promotion are all part of the process of providing something satisfying to the customer. Product activities concern the design and packaging of the good or service itself, distribution involves getting the product to the customer, and promotion involves communicating the product's existence and benefits to customers and potential customers. All three of these types of marketing activities contribute to the product being of value to customers. In this book, the term value will refer to the benefits, or the satisfactions of needs and wants, that a product provides to customers.

Figure 1.3   Pricing Harvests the Value Created by the Other Three Marketing Mix Elements

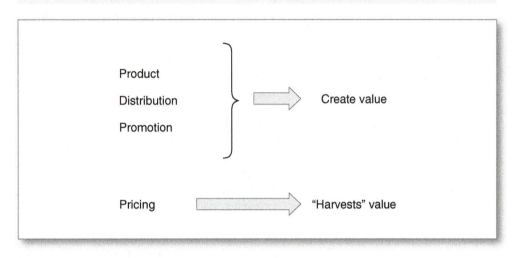

Product

Distribution   } ⇨   Create value

Promotion

Pricing   ⇨   "Harvests" value

Source: Based on Nagle (1987).

Pricing, on the other hand, is not primarily concerned with creating value. Rather, it could be said to be the marketing activity involved with capturing, or "harvesting," the value created by the other types of marketing activities.[1] In the words of Philip Kotler, "Price is the marketing-mix element that produces revenue; the others produce costs."[2] Because it is a marketing activity fundamentally different than the others, it is important that the implications of pricing's uniqueness be fully understood. This is one of the reasons that a course in pricing is an important part of a business education.

The Marketing Concept

The marketing approach to business involves not only engaging in a variety of marketing activities but also having these marketing activities be guided by the marketing concept. The marketing concept can be expressed as follows: The key to business success is to focus on satisfying customer needs.

What this means is that an organization that works toward satisfying customer needs in every feasible way when carrying out marketing activities is likely to see more long-run success than a company that does not have such a customer focus. Sellers who rely only on their own opinions and ignore those of their customers or sellers who view their customers as "marks" to be tricked or manipulated may do well at a particular time but are unlikely to be able to sustain whatever short-term success they may have. The marketing concept is a modern form of the philosophical viewpoint known as "enlightened self-interest": One's self-interest is best served by focusing one's attention on the needs of others.

Pricing and the Marketing Concept

It is clear how product, distribution, and promotional activities can be guided by the marketing concept. Through marketing research (which, by the way, is a fifth important category of marketing activities), a personal computer manufacturer can learn, for example, the features and styling consumers want and then build machines to satisfy consumer preferences. A bank could determine the hours consumers would prefer walk-in service and could arrange to have those services available during those hours. A cell phone service provider may find out that many consumers are unaware of all of the convenient features of their service and may design a promotional program to communicate this information.

However, it is less clear how pricing activities can be guided by the marketing concept. Certainly, customers would prefer paying less. In fact, paying nothing at all might well be their first choice! But it is simply not feasible to "give away the store." An organization that gives away the value it creates will soon cease to exist, and thus the value it creates will disappear. This does not serve customers well. Rather, it is in the customer's interest for an organization that creates customer value to set prices that maximize the organization's profitability, since that would give the organization the greatest possible chance of continuing to create that value.

Lest this endorsement of profit maximization sound somewhat extreme, rest assured that in a free-market system, competition will tend to keep maximum profits modest. Nothing attracts competitors more quickly than a highly profitable product. Further, the marketing concept points the price setter to consider not only the customer value that can be harvested but also the customer's feelings about the price that is being charged. Examples of such price feelings that need to be considered include the following:

- The feeling of a price being substantially higher than the customer's expectations (sometimes referred to as "sticker shock")
- The feeling that a price is unfair or is higher than can be justified
- Customers perceiving they are receiving a discount, or a price lower than their expectations

It is important to note that both identifying the value that the product represents to the customer and considering customers' price expectations and feelings depend on understanding and attending to customer needs. Both of these aspects of the marketing approach to pricing will be discussed in detail in later chapters.

EARLY PRICING PRACTICES

As you might imagine, the practice of pricing has a very long history. Consider the following:

> The oldest records of prices ever found are clay tablets with pictographic symbols found in a town known as Uruk, in what was ancient Sumer and what is now southern Iraq. These price records are from 3300 BC—they've survived 5,300 years. The documents—records of payment for barley and wheat, for sheep, and for beer—are really receipts. "Uruk was a

large city, at a minimum 40,000 people," says UCLA professor Robert Englund, one of the few experts on the Uruk documents. "So some of the quantities are very high—hundreds of thousands of pounds of barley, for instance."

But here's the really remarkable thing. The earliest Uruk tablets aren't just the oldest pricing records ever found. They are the oldest examples of human *writing* yet discovered. In other words, when humans first took stylus to wet clay, the first things that they were compelled to record were . . . prices.[3]

In the earliest commercial exchanges, goods or services were exchanged for other goods or services. For example, the price that a farmer might pay for a bolt of cloth could be a bushel of corn. This practice, termed barter, still goes on today, especially in less developed countries. Barter occurred in recent years when Shell Oil purchased sugar from a Caribbean country by giving in return one million pest control devices.[4] Although barter is still used, it can make exchange difficult. For example, what if the seller of the bolt of cloth had no need for the farmer's bushel of corn? Because of such inefficiencies of barter, almost all modern commercial transactions use a medium of exchange—something that is widely accepted in exchange for goods and services in a market.[5]

A medium of exchange could be anything that the buyers and sellers in a society agree upon. In the past, items such as cattle, seashells, dried cod, and tobacco have been used as a medium of exchange. However, many of these presented certain difficulties. In his book *The Wealth of Nations,* Adam Smith gives an example of this:

> The man who wanted to buy salt, for example, and had nothing but cattle to give in exchange for it, must have been obliged to buy salt to the value of a whole ox, or a whole sheep, at a time. He could seldom buy less than this, because what he was to give for it could seldom be divided without loss. . . . [6]

Over time, it became clear that the best medium of exchange is one that is finely divisible, such as the metals of various weights used in coins. This use of coins and notes to represent them led to national systems of money, such as dollars, yen, or euros. It is prices expressed in such monetary terms that will be considered in this book.

THREE CATEGORIES OF PRICING ISSUES

As the use of prices in monetary terms proliferated among human societies, various questions that required pricing decisions began to arise. Most of these issues fall into one of the following three categories: (1) buyer–seller interactivity, (2) price structure, and (3) price format.

Buyer–Seller Interactivity in Determining Prices

Throughout most of history, prices were not the fixed amounts displayed in stores and advertising that are so familiar today. Rather, prices were negotiated during an interaction between the buyer and the seller. The basic elements of price negotiation can be illustrated by imagining how, for many centuries, the price determination process typically occurred:

> A customer arrives at the seller's stall in the local marketplace and examines the merchandise. When he finds something he wants, the customer asks the seller, "How much?" The seller then states an asking price, which is higher than his reservation price, the lowest price at which he would sell the item: "23 ducats." The customer then states his initial offer. This, of course, is lower than the *customer's* reservation price (the highest price that the customer would pay for the item): "I can't pay more than 14."
>
> The seller and the customer would then try to arrive at an amount they can both agree on by haggling, a process involving some number of prices and offers and statements supporting the validity of each. "This item is really of the very highest quality," the seller might argue, "but since I'm in a good mood today, I'll let you have it for 21." The customer might respond, "I've seen items at least as good as this in other shops, but since I'm here, I'll give you 16."

If there is overlap between the reservation price of the seller and that of the customer, then they could be successful in arriving at a negotiated price—that is, one that is agreeable to both. In that case, the object's price would have been the number that resulted from an interaction between the buyer and seller. A price arrived at by the buyer–seller interactions of negotiation or the interactions of auction bidding would be referred to as an interactive price.

If you find yourself a little uncomfortable with the deception involved in the process of price negotiation, you are not alone. Religious leaders were among the earliest critics of this type of business practice. In fact, it was George Fox, the founder of the Society of Friends (often called the Quakers), who first suggested that an alternative was possible. He led his followers to carry over to their businesses the principle of total honesty that they adhered to in their personal lives. As a result, Quaker merchants adopted the practice of stating to the customer the price that they actually expected to receive and sticking to it. Such a price is referred to as a fixed price.

It is interesting that, rather than hurting their competitive position, the use of fixed prices actually tended to help the Quakers in their businesses. Customers appreciated the quicker and less stressful buying process associated with fixed prices and often tended to feel more trusting of Quaker merchants. The use of fixed prices spread steadily and was strongly stimulated by the development, in the middle of the nineteenth century, of new types of retailing designed to serve mass markets. In particular, fixed prices helped make possible the large department store (pioneered by entrepreneurs such as F. W. Woolworth, John Wanamaker, and J. L. Hudson), which depended on a large number of quick transactions and staffing by low-paid, relatively unskilled clerks. In an 1859 advertisement for his growing New York department store, Rowland Macy claimed, "Best products, and same prices for all customers!" Also, the use of fixed prices enabled the growth of mail-order sales and the development of large catalog companies such as Sears Roebuck.[7]

During the twentieth century, the use of fixed prices became predominant in retail pricing throughout the developed world. Although we take fixed prices for granted when we shop, for example, in department stores, grocery stores, drugstores, hardware stores, or bookstores, the purchase of expensive items such as automobiles or real estate still usually involves price negotiation. Also, in contrast to most retailers (companies that sell directly to consumers), companies that sell to business customers are likely to make heavy use of price negotiation. The issues involved in buyer–seller interactivity in pricing will be discussed in more detail in a later chapter.

Price Structure

Although there are benefits to moving from negotiated prices to fixed prices, there are also disadvantages. One strength of interactive pricing is that it makes it easy for the seller to charge different prices to different buyers. For example, when prices are negotiated individually, a customer willing to pay a particularly high price could be charged, say, $200 for an item without interfering with the seller's ability to charge more typical customers a lower price, say, $125 for the same item. The practice of charging different customers different prices for the same item is known as price segmentation.

In order to accomplish price segmentation with fixed prices, it is necessary to have more than one price for a single product. For example, a product may have one price when purchased alone and another price when purchased in large quantity or when purchased along with other items. The product may have one price when purchased during the week and another when purchased on a weekend. It may have one price when purchased in the city and another when purchased in a rural area. These numerous prices for an item are part of the pattern of the seller's prices. In general, the pattern of an organization's prices is known as its price structure.

The price structure of a seller involves more than the array of prices that can be charged for the same item. Most organizations sell more than one product, and the pattern of prices across these different products is another component of the organization's price structure. Often the various products are interrelated such that the price charged for one item should take into account the prices charged for other items sold by the organization.

Price Format

The third category of pricing issues involves how a price is expressed when it is communicated to potential customers. For example, early fixed prices tended to be round numbers, such as $1.00, $5.00, or $2.50. However, by 1880 retail advertisements began to appear showing items priced at a penny or two below the round number (see Figure 1.4). The practice of pricing an item just below a round number does not substantially affect the level of a price, but it does affect how that price level is expressed. The form of expression of a price is known as the price format.

Expressing a price in a "just-below" format often has the effect of lowering the price's leftmost digit. This may make the price level appear lower than it actually is and have a positive effect on sales. It is sometimes suggested that early retailers used this technique as a means of reducing dishonesty among clerks. For example, a price such as $1.99 would oblige employees to use the cash register to make change and thus reduce their opportunity to

Figure 1.4 Macy's Ad From 1880, Showing 9-Ending Prices

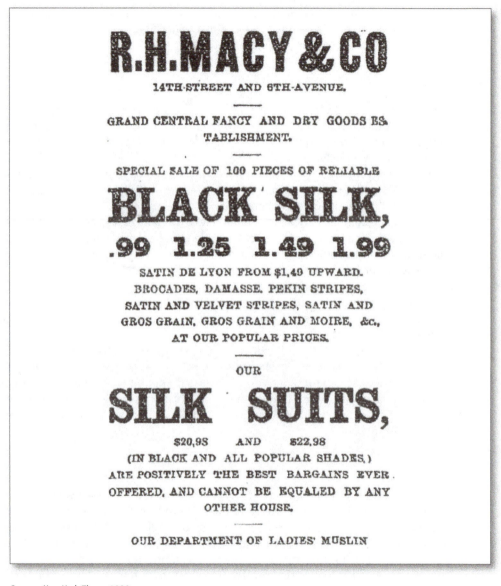

Source: New York Times, 1880.

pocket the payment. However, research on early price advertising has indicated that just-below prices were more likely to be used when the advertised item was claimed to be a discount or an otherwise low price. This suggests that the use of the just-below price format was, from the start, motivated by managerial intuitions about its effects on the perceptions of the consumer.

Price format also involves the question of how many numbers are required to express an item's price. For example, a price advertisement could directly show the price of a mushroom and pepperoni pizza, or it could express that price as a base price plus an additional amount for the two toppings (see Figure 1.5). The price of a lamp in a home furnishings catalog might be expressed as a price for the lamp that includes shipping or as a price for the lamp alone along with a separate price for the shipping of the lamp to the purchaser. The question of whether a price should be expressed as a single number or as the sum of more than one number is the issue of price partitioning.

Figure 1.5   Alternative Price Formats for a Mushroom and Pepperoni Pizza

THE PRICING ACTIVITY
================================

The marketing activity of capturing the value created by the other marketing activities is obviously of essential importance to a business organization. One could imagine an organization failing to carry out distribution or promotion activities and still be in business. But if there is no attention to pricing, a business organization cannot be viable.

The activity of making decisions about prices consists of two general components. One component is price setting, which consists of decisions about individual prices. These decisions concern the price of a specific item to a specific customer or market in the current marketing environment or situation at hand. The other component of the pricing activity is establishing pricing policy, which involves decisions that guide and regulate the setting of individual prices. This guidance could be general, such as a "fixed-price policy," which would require the organization to maintain fixed prices. It could also be more specific, such as indicating the situations when it would be permissible for the organization to offer volume discounts. Broadly, pricing policies are the organization's rules that govern particular price-setting decisions.

Participants in the Pricing Activity

In a small business organization, the owner/manager will be heavily involved in, and most responsible for, pricing activities. In a large business organization, it is likely that many people within the organization will play a role in pricing activities.

Some of the individuals in a large organization who play a role in pricing will have very direct pricing involvement and responsibility. Here are some examples of such direct roles:

- In a department store, it is usually the merchandise buyer who will do most of the price setting for the items he or she buys to be sold in the store.
- In many large consumer products organizations, a brand's product manager will have much of the responsibility for setting the prices of a brand.
- In companies that sell to business customers, salespeople and their managers play a crucial role in the negotiation processes by which prices are determined.
- In service industries, such as airlines and hotels, there will often be pricing departments with specialists trained in revenue management, a set of complex price-setting techniques that are frequently used in these industries.[8]

There are also likely to be many people in a large organization who participate in pricing activities but who do so in a way that is less direct. For example, employees in the accounting department often provide information about the costs of products and of the operations involved in getting products to the customer; accurate cost information is essential for effective price setting. Lawyers and others in the legal department could establish legal and ethical guidelines for pricing and could adjust proposed prices to comply with relevant laws and contracts. Analysts in the finance department may be involved in assessing the degree to which pricing schedules developed by product or sales managers are consistent with the profit goals of the organization. In many large business organizations, higher-level managers are involved in approving, and perhaps revising, proposed price schedules.

Organization of Pricing Activities

Particularly because of the likely involvement in pricing activities of many people within different parts of a large business organization, it is somewhat surprising that many companies do not have a means to effectively coordinate pricing-related decisions across departments in the company.[9] For pricing decisions to be made effectively in a large organization, it is important that these decisions either involve high-level management in the organization or use some other means to centrally coordinate and constrain the many pricing-related decisions that are likely to be made by many different people throughout the organization.[10] There are at least three reasons why such organization of pricing activities is important.

First, it is possible for a large company to experience problems in the effective implementation of pricing decisions. For example, the product manager of a manufacturing company that sells to distributors and retailers may set an item's invoice price—the price of the item that will appear on the customer's bill. However, a large or longtime customer may be able to convince his or her sales representative into offering a small off-invoice discount—say, an annual volume rebate. Further, the customer may contact the company's advertising department and arrange a small discount for, say, displaying the product in the customer's flyers. The accounts receivable department may be convinced to give this good customer more favorable payment terms, the transportation department might give this customer a break on shipping costs, and the account services department could allow this customer a more generous return policy. Employees in each part of the company might be assuming that it makes sense to give a break to such a good customer. However, together, all of these actions may substantially reduce the item's pocket price—the amount that's actually left in the company's pocket after the transaction. Without central pricing coordination, such revenue "leaks" could be as high as 20 percent of invoice prices.[11]

Second, a business organization should take steps to help insure that everyday pricing decisions fit with the organization's strategies and long-term interests. As will be seen in later chapters, pricing decisions made for immediate purposes can have consequences that are far-reaching. For example, price cutting done in response to competition can lead to price warfare and serious erosion of profits. Recent financial difficulties among companies in the U.S. airline industry may be, at least partly, a consequence of such price warfare. On the other hand, small price increases, it they continue to occur, could eventually have the effect of leading customers to find alternative types of products to serve their needs. Kellogg's, General Mills, and other breakfast cereal manufacturers made continual small price increases for many years until, eventually, sales in the entire cold cereal category began to decline as more consumers switched to bagels, muffins, and other breakfast alternatives. It is important that a person or a group with a broad view of the selling organization consider the possibility of such long-term effects of pricing decisions.

Third, for a business organization to follow the marketing concept and effectively focus on satisfying customer needs, marketing activities need to be well-coordinated with each other and with the other functions of the organization. Having pricing activities managed by a central authority can help accomplish this coordination. For example, if a price decrease is expected to lead to a sales increase, then it is useful to make sure that production, procurement, customer service, and other functions of the organization are prepared to handle this price decrease. Or if new cost economies are achieved by some aspect of the company's operations, rapid knowledge of this could contribute to more efficient pricing decisions. In addition, new possibilities, such as lowering costs by purchasing a component in an Asian country, could be more effectively evaluated with the combined input of marketing research and centrally coordinated pricing decision makers.

Relevance of Studying Pricing

It is hoped that the previous discussion helps make clear that pricing is a relevant topic to study even if you do not expect to be directly involved in the pricing activities of an organization. Pricing is so critical to a business organization that it affects, and is affected by, virtually every function of the organization. Thus, for example, if you are interested in advertising, keep in mind that the pricing of a product affects how it should be promoted—a product's pricing influences what is said about the product and to whom. Correspondingly, what is effectively communicated about the product can strongly affect the price that can be charged.

In addition, price setting is relevant to our personal lives. Even if we do not sell things at garage sales or on eBay, we are almost all marketers of our professional services. Our compensation—salary, bonuses, and benefits—constitutes the price we charge employers for our services. As managers of what is most likely, over the course of our careers, a multimillion-dollar product, it makes good sense for us to be familiar with the principles of effective pricing.

PLAN OF THE BOOK

We will begin our study of pricing with the situation where an organization is offering a product, or form of a product, that it has not sold before. What should its price be? Focusing on this relatively well-defined situation will enable us to introduce some basic pricing principles and procedures.

Of course, setting an initial price is not the most commonly occurring situation. More often than not, the manager is faced with an existing product that already has a price. The question then would be, is this existing price the *best* price? If it were higher, or lower, would more profits be likely to result? We will introduce a breakeven formula that can be of considerable help in decisions about modifying existing prices.

However, this breakeven formula alone does not make effective pricing decisions possible. What is needed also is some ability to predict (and perhaps even influence) how the customers in the market will respond to the product's price change. In order to gain this predictive ability, we will focus on understanding four types of factors that determine the market's price-change response: (1) economic, (2) competitive, (3) cognitive, and (4) emotional. The latter two types of factors will also shed light on issues of price format. Following discussion of these four types of price-response factors, we will discuss market-research procedures for directly measuring the market's price-change response.

At this point, we will have a basic ability to set a price: We will be able to set the price of a newly offered product, and we will be able to effectively modify the price of a product that is currently being offered. We then expand our focus to the design of an organization's price structure. We first discuss the use of price structure to accomplish price segmentation. We then discuss how a product's price may need to be adjusted because of interrelations with the other products that are being sold by the organization.

The last section of the book addresses several other pricing issues of importance. We will discuss some of the special challenges involved in managing interactive prices, such as prices arrived at through negotiation and auctions. Auction pricing has taken on a renewed importance with the rise of the Internet. We will become familiar with some of the basic ideas involved in considering the social and societal consequences of pricing decisions. Better understanding of these issues can not only help price setters avoid legal pitfalls but can also help us all better exercise our civic responsibilities to help make pricing policies maximally beneficial to society. Finally, we will return to the importance of a business organization having an integrated, centrally managed pricing policy and will discuss how the many pricing considerations covered in the book can be put together in constructing an overall pricing strategy.

SUMMARY

A price is what is given in a commercial exchange in return for a good or service. A price can have many names, such as "fee" or "rent" but should be not be confused with a company's "costs." Pricing is one of the four activities of the marketing mix; it is the marketing activity involved in capturing the value created by the other three marketing activities. Early commercial transactions involved barter, but the advantages of using a medium of exchange soon became evident and modern prices are typically expressed in terms of money.

Issues that arise in the setting of prices can be divided into three categories: (1) the question of interactive versus fixed prices, (2) the pattern of an organization's prices, and (3) how a price can be expressed when communicated to potential buyers.

The pricing activity consists of setting specific prices and developing the rules that govern price-setting decisions. In large organizations, many people play a role in the organization's pricing activities and central coordination of these price activities is important. Given that all businesses are involved in pricing and that pricing is part of managing one's career, the study of pricing is an important part of one's business education.

The book begins with the setting of an item's initial price and continues with the modifying of existing prices to increase profits. Key in effectively modifying a price is understanding the factors that determine the market's price-change response. The focus of the book is then expanded to the pattern of prices set by a selling organization and to considering interactive prices, societal consequences of pricing, and the integrated management of pricing activities.

KEY TERMS

price	marketing mix	interactive price
price setting	value	fixed price
commercial exchange	marketing concept	retailers
product	barter	price segmentation
good	medium of exchange	price partitioning
service	price structure	pricing policy
consumer	price format	revenue management
business customer	asking price	invoice price
free-market economy	reservation price	pocket price
cost	initial offer	
marketing activities	haggling	

1. Describe the two parties in a commercial exchange and what is given and received by each party.

2. How is the voluntary nature of the commercial exchange related to its potential for creating benefits for society?

3. Give some terms other than "price" that are commonly used to refer to prices.

4. In a business organization, describe how what a manager is referring to when speaking of "prices" differs from what a manager is referring to when speaking of "costs."

5. What are the four categories of marketing activities, usually referred to as the marketing mix? In what important way does pricing differ from the other three categories?

6. What is the marketing concept? How can pricing activities be guided by the marketing concept?

7. What is barter? Give an example of barter, either from your reading or from your own experience.

8. What is a medium of exchange? What is most commonly used in our society as a medium of exchange?

9. Describe the basic elements of price negotiation. Why is a price arrived at through negotiation referred to as an "interactive price"?

10. What are fixed prices? What do customers like about fixed prices? What do retailers like about fixed prices?

11. What is price segmentation? Why might a seller want to engage in price segmentation?

12. Give an example of how different numbers could be used to express what would be substantially the same price.

13. What is the difference between price setting and pricing policy?

14. Give some examples of job titles of those in a large organization who are likely to have direct responsibility for making pricing decisions.

15. What are some of reasons that a item's pocket price may not be the same as the item's invoice price? What could be done about this?

16. Give an example of a way that everyday pricing decisions could work against a company's long-term interests.

17. Describe some benefits of coordinating pricing activities with the other functions of a business organization.

18. Why might the study of pricing be relevant to a student who does not plan to ever set prices within a business organization?

EXERCISES

1. The CEO of a large company selling seeds and garden supplies to consumers and businesses through catalogs and the Internet is unhappy with its overall profitability. He feels that part of the solution is to be more professional in price setting, and he asks the director of marketing to hire an experienced person for a new position of pricing manager. While interviewing one candidate, the marketing director explains that the company has been advised to listen more to customers and respond to their needs and asks the candidate how he would implement this advice in the area of pricing. The candidate responds as follows:

   "It's great to listen to the customer when you are designing your product, but it's just not practical in pricing. All the customers have to say is that they want lower prices. If you want me to increase profits, I can't very well listen to that!"

   a. What should the marketing director make of this response?

   b. If you were the candidate, how would you have responded to this question?

2. An entrepreneur is starting a business selling decorative items, such as vases, wall hangings, and prints (framed or unframed) over the Internet. She is aware that she needs to make a number of pricing decisions.

   a. Describe a decision that the entrepreneur must make that would be an example of price setting. Describe a decision that she would have to make that would be an example of pricing policy.

   b. Describe a decision that she would need to make regarding price format, and describe one regarding price structure.

3. As the marketer of your own professional services, you are responsible for price setting. Thus, it is necessary that you think about your pricing policy.

   a. Describe how a business professional might implement the following pricing policies in the pricing of his or her services: negotiated price policy and fixed price policy.

   b. Give and justify your views as to which of these pricing policies would be more appropriate in an individual's professional services pricing.

4. Identify someone you know who works in a business organization. Talk with that person to learn about the individuals in the organization who are involved in the setting of prices.

   a. Describe the job of a person within the organization who plays a direct role in price setting.

   b. Describe the job of a person within the organization who plays an indirect role in price setting. What is the information or expertise provided by that person? When during the price-setting process does that person interact with an individual who has a more direct role in price setting?

5. The marketing manager of a large truck manufacturer was surprised to learn that the price lists generated by his department had little relation to the prices that were actually charged to customers. The company's finance department often changed the prices to conform to profit goals before the prices reached the company's sales force. The salespeople often gave customers discounts to increase their sales volume. The operations manager made price adjustments to accommodate delays in promised shipping times.

    a. Why is this situation undesirable for the company?

    b. What can be done about this situation?

NOTES

1. Thomas T. Nagle, *The Strategy and Tactics of Pricing* (Englewood Cliffs, NJ: Prentice Hall, 1987), 1.
2. Philip Kotler, *Marketing Management,* 10th ed. (Upper Saddle River, NJ: Prentice Hall, 2000), 456.
3. Charles Fishman, "Which Price Is Right?" *Fast Company* 68 (March 2003): 92–102.
4. Roger A. Kerin, Eric N. Berkowitz, Steven W. Hartley, and William Rudelius, *Marketing,* 6th ed. (Boston: McGraw-Hill Irwin, 2000), 363.
5. Jack Hirshleifer and David Hirshleifer, *Price Theory and Applications,* 6th ed. (Upper Saddle River, NJ: Prentice Hall, 1998).
6. Adam Smith, *The Wealth of Nations,* Modern Library Edition (1776; repr., New York: Random House, 1994), 26.
7. David J. Schwartz, *Marketing Today: A Basic Approach* (New York: Harcourt Brace Jovanovich, 1981), 306.
8. Jeffrey I. McGill and Garrett J. Van Ryzin, "Revenue Management: Research Overview and Prospects," *Transportation Science* 33 (May 1999): 233–256.
9. Kent B. Monroe, *Pricing: Making Profitable Decisions,* 3rd ed. (Boston: McGraw-Hill Irwin, 2003), 19.
10. Robert J. Dolan, "How Do You Know When the Price Is Right?" *Harvard Business Review* (September–October 1995): 174–183.
11. Michael V. Mam and Robert L. Rosiello, "Managing Price, Gaining Profit," *Harvard Business Review* (September–October 1992): 84–94.

PART I

Setting of Initial Prices

The Starting Point in Setting an Initial Price

There are many situations when a seller must come up with a price for a product that does not already have a price. This occurs when an organization develops a new product or begins to offer a new version of an existing product. It also occurs for existing products when an organization introduces a product into a new market or begins selling an existing product that the organization has not previously sold. In all of these situations, management must arrive at an initial price for the item that is being sold.

Where would one start in setting an item's initial price? Surveys of price setters of both goods and services have found that the most commonly used starting point for an item's price is its cost. The second most commonly used starting point is the price of similar items sold by one or more competing companies.[1] In this chapter, we will first discuss how an item's costs and competitors' prices can serve as starting points for determining an item's initial price. Then we will discuss an alternative place to begin—the value of the benefits that the item creates by satisfying the needs of the customer.

COST-BASED PRICING

When the setting of an item's initial price begins with a consideration of the item's costs, the process is known as cost-based pricing. The logic of cost-based pricing is very simple. An item's selling price should be greater than what it costs to produce or acquire that item. Thus, the price can be calculated by adding an amount of money to the item's costs. There are many ways in which this could be done.

Perhaps the simplest form of cost-based pricing is the procedure referred to as cost-plus pricing. This pricing method involves determining the amount to be added to an item's cost and then adding that amount to arrive at the item's price. If C is an item's cost, then its price (P) is calculated as follows:

$$P = C + \text{added amount}$$

Cost-plus pricing is particularly common among companies that sell customized products.[2] For example, a construction company asked to give a price estimate for a job might calculate that its costs to do the job would be $35,000. The construction company might then determine how much should be added to this cost by considering factors such as the number of such jobs it is likely to do in a year, its overhead costs, and its desired final profits. If these factors indicated that $20,000 would have to be added to the job's cost, the company would set the price of doing that job at $55,000.

Markup Pricing

Some organizations sell such a large number of different products that it becomes difficult to determine the added amount separately for each product. In particular, organizations that buy goods and resell them, such as wholesalers and retailers, may carry tens of thousands of separate items and are constantly dropping items and adding new ones. Such companies often will set the price of an item by adding to the item's cost some standard percentage of that cost.[3] The percentage used could be the same for all of the company's products or there could be a separate standard percentage for each type of product sold by the company. This type of cost-based pricing is known as markup pricing.

The standard percentage used in markup pricing is called the markup. It is the amount added to an item's cost (C) expressed as a percentage of that cost. A markup (M will be used in to represent *markup* in the equations) could be calculated as follows:

$$M = (\text{added amount}/C) \times 100$$

To determine a price based on a markup, the markup must first be converted into a proportion (by dividing it by 100) and then multiplied by the cost. The result of this multiplication is then added to the cost. This method of calculating a price is expressed symbolically as follows:

$$P = C + [(M/100) \times C]$$

For example, to set initial prices on its line of portable audio devices, a consumer electronics retailer might apply a 150 percent markup. If the retailer pays $50 for a particular MP3 player, it would use the following calculations to set a $125 price for that item:

$$P = \$50 + [(150/100) \times \$50]$$
$$P = \$50 + (1.5 \times \$50)$$
$$P = \$50 + \$75$$
$$P = \$125$$

What determines the markups that companies use? For many wholesalers and retailers, the markup levels tend to be governed by tradition or simple rules of thumb. In wholesaling, a typical markup on merchandise costs would be 20 percent.[4] In retailing, sellers of clothing, gifts, and other items have traditionally used what is called keystone pricing (or "keystoning")—doubling an item's cost to arrive at its price (i.e., applying a 100 percent markup).[5] In the restaurant industry, the typical guidelines are that the prices of menu items should be determined by tripling an item's food costs (i.e., applying a 200 percent markup) and quadrupling the costs of served alcoholic beverages (i.e., applying a 300 percent markup).[6]

Note that when a good changes hands more than once before reaching the consumer, successive markups are applied. In Figure 2.1, you can see a typical distribution channel for a consumer good. If the manufacturer's selling price for the good is $5, then that amount is the wholesaler's cost. A 20 percent markup makes the wholesaler's price for the good to be $6. That becomes the retailer's cost. The retailer's 100 percent markup makes the good's retail price—that is, the price charged to consumers—to be $12.

Figure 2.1   Typical Distribution Channel for a Consumer Good

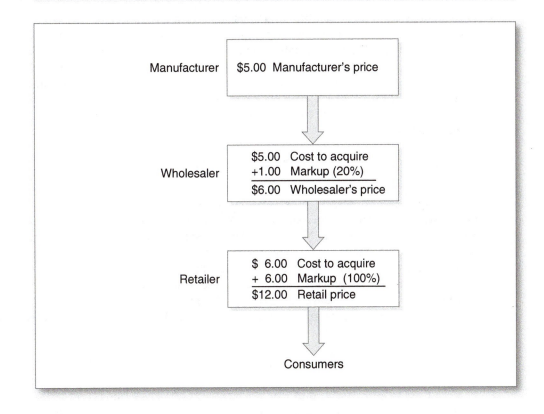

Gross-Margin Pricing

The process of determining the amount to be added to a product's costs to arrive at its price is often heavily influenced by the profit goals of the organization. A company's profit goals can be expressed in many forms, but they are commonly expressed in terms of gross margins. A gross margin is the amount of a company's sales revenue that remains after subtracting the "cost of goods sold," a standard accounting measure of the costs of manufacturing or acquiring the items that are sold. The percent gross margin is the gross margin as a percentage of the sales revenue. An example of the use of gross margins for pricing was described by researchers who interviewed executives of a company that built automated workstations for businesses. One of the company's managers explained that a 50 percent gross margin is "the guideline we generally expect prices to conform to."[7]

A percent gross margin can provide helpful guidance in setting price levels, but note that it cannot be used by a price setter as easily as can a markup. In contrast to a markup, which is the amount added to an item's cost as a percentage of that cost, a percent gross margin is the amount added to an item's cost expressed as a percentage of the item's price. In symbols, a percent gross margin (%GM) could be written as follows:

$$\%GM = (\text{added amount}/P) \times 100$$

Computationally, there are two ways to use a percent gross margin to set a price. The first method is to convert the percent gross margin to the more intuitive markup percentage (M). Because an item's price is a higher number than the item's cost, the result of dividing an added amount by the item's price (which will result in a %GM) will be smaller than the result of dividing the same added amount by the item's cost (which will result in the equivalent M). Thus, to convert a percent gross margin to a markup, we must do something to increase the %GM side of the equation that relates the two. The formula that accomplishes this is as follows:

$$M = \%GM \times [100 / (100 - \%GM)]$$

For example, the 50 percent gross margin of the automated workstation company previously described would correspond to a 100 percent markup, the result of multiplying 50 by 100/(100 − 50), or by 2. Note that because costs are greater than zero, the percent gross margin must always be less than 100. This causes the 100/(100 − %GM) factor to be greater than 1, which leads it to increase the %GM side of the equation. A table illustrating some equivalent percent gross margins and markups can be seen in Figure 2.2.

The second method of using a gross margin for price setting is to compute the product's price directly from the gross margin percentage. The formula for doing this is as follows:[8]

$$P = C / [1 - (\%GM/100)]$$

It can be seen from this formula that when %GM is small, very little is subtracted from 1 in the denominator, and the item's price is only a little above the item's cost. By contrast, when %GM is large, a large amount is subtracted from 1 in the denominator, and the item's price becomes considerably above the item's cost.

For an example of these two methods of using a gross margin to set a price, say that the consumer electronics retailer described in the previous section used a 60 percent gross

Figure 2.2   Gross Margin–Markup Equivalents

Percent Gross Margin	Markup
10	11
20	25
30	43
40	67
50	100
60	150
70	233
80	400
90	900

margin as a guide to the initial pricing of its line of MP3 players. The retailer could convert the 60 percent gross margin to a markup percentage and then apply the resulting 150 percent markup:

$$M = 60 \times [100/(100 - 60)]$$
$$M = 60 \times (100/40)$$
$$M = 60 \times 2.5$$
$$M = 150$$

Or the retailer could calculate prices directly from the 60 percent gross margin. For the MP3 player that cost the retailer $50, the $125 retail price would be calculated as follows:

$$P = \$50 / [1 - (60/100)]$$
$$P = \$50 / (1 - 0.6)$$
$$P = \$50 / 0.4$$
$$P = \$125$$

Note that the 60 percent gross margin produces the same $125 price as applying the 150 percent markup. Calculating a price from a percent gross margin may be less intuitive than applying a markup, but the use of gross margins in price setting helps bring to pricing the influence of the selling organization's profit goals.

Determinants of Gross Margin Goals

For many companies, gross margin goals, like markups, are based on tradition and rules of thumb. However, it is also possible to look to industry norms for this type of guidance. A

Figure 2.3 Form 10-K for the J. C. Penney Company, Inc.

CONSOLIDATED STATEMENTS OF OPERATIONS			
($ in millions, except per share data)	**2009**	**2008**	**2007**
Total net sales	$ 17,556	$ 18,486	$ 19,860
Cost of goods sold:	10,646	11,571	12,189
Gross margin	6,910	6,915	7,671
Operating expenses:			
Selling general and administrative (SG&A)	5,382	5,395	5,402
Pension expense/(income)	337	(90)	(45)
Depreciation and amortization	495	469	426
Pre-opening	28	31	46
Real estate and other, net	5	(25)	(46)
Total operating expenses	6,247	5,780	5,783
Opreating income	663	1,135	1,888
Net interest expense	260	225	153
Bond premiums and unamortized costs	–	–	12
Income from continuing operations before income taxes	403	910	1,723
Income tax expense	154	343	618
Income from continuing operations	249	567	1,105
Income from discontinued operations, net of income tax expense/(benefit) of $1, $(3) and $4	2	5	6
Net income	$ 251	$ 572	$ 1,111
Basic earnings per share:			
Continuing operations	$ 1.07	$ 2.55	$ 4.96
Discontinued operations	0.01	0.03	0.03
Net income	$ 1.08	$ 2.58	$ 4.99
Diluted earning per share:			
Continuing operations	$ 1.07	$ 2.54	$ 4.90
Discontinued operations	0.01	0.03	0.03
Net income	$ 1.08	$ 2.57	$ 4.93

Source: From U.S. Securities and Exchange Commission.

source of this information are the publically available reports, such as the Form 10-K, that every company must file with the U.S. Securities and Exchange Commission (SEC).[9] For example, a recent operating statement from the Form 10-K of the J. C. Penney Company, Inc., a major U.S. retailer, can be seen in Figure 2.3. The line labeled "Gross Margin" is Penney's sales revenues minus its cost of goods sold. Dividing this gross margin in dollars by Penney's dollars of sales revenue gives Penney's average gross margin—39.4 percent in 2009.

In Figure 2.4, you can see the recent average gross margins for some well-known U.S. companies that were calculated from SEC 10-K forms. It can be seen that pharmaceutical manufacturers tend to have higher gross margins than do consumer goods manufacturers and that department stores (such as Macy's) tend to have higher gross margins than do discount department stores (such as Walmart). However, note also that there may be unexpected differences, such as the higher gross margins for the "low-end" 99¢ Only Stores than for the "high-end" Neiman Marcus Group. The presence of such unexpected patterns suggests that it would be wise for a company to use some caution when drawing on gross margin data from other companies to determine the company's pricing-related profit goals.

Advantages and Disadvantages of Cost-Based Pricing

One advantage of cost-based pricing is its simplicity. The idea of starting with costs is intuitive, and cost-based prices are relatively easy to calculate. Such simplicity is particularly important in situations where there are large numbers of prices to determine on a continuing basis. This is often the case among product resellers, which at least partly explains why cost-based pricing is particularly widespread in wholesaling and retailing.

A second advantage of cost-based pricing stems from the common practice of using standard markup or margin levels in an industry or for a particular type of product. Because per-item costs are often similar among competitors, applying a standard markup or margin reduces the need to carry out research on competitors' prices. Use of such cost-based standards could serve as an economical means of keeping one's prices from being substantially out of line with those of competitors.

A major disadvantage of cost-based pricing is perhaps related to what is often considered an advantage. There is frequently the presumption that by looking first at costs and then setting the price sufficiently above those costs that one can insure a good profit on what one sells. Although this might be so for each item sold, it is not so for the far more important measure of *total* profits.

This disadvantage of cost-based pricing, then, is that it turns out to not be particularly useful in efforts to maximize total profits. For example, a markup set to yield a good profit on each item might result in a price so high that few items are sold. The total profits made from that item might then be quite disappointing. Alternatively, a markup set to yield a good profit on each item could result in a price that is substantially lower than customers would be willing to pay. The result of this could be a level of total profits far lower than could otherwise have been made.

Figure 2.4   Average Gross Margins of Selected U.S. Companies

2008 Annual data (or latest year available in 2008)—Numbers in millions of dollars (as reported)			
Company Name	**Sales**	**Cost of Goods Sold**	**Gross Margin**
Pharmaceutical manufacturers			
Pfizer Inc	48,296	8,112	83.2%
Merck & Co., Inc	23,850	5,583	76.6%
Johnson & Johnson	63,747	18,511	71.0%
Consumer packaged goods manufacturers			
Coca-Cola Co.	31,944	11,374	64.4%
Procter & Gamble Co.	83,503	40,695	51.3%
3M Co.	25,269	13,379	47.1%
Campblell Soup Co.	7,998	4,827	39.6%
Kraft Foods, Inc.	42,201	28,186	33.2%
Retailers			
Macy's Inc.	24,892	15,009	39.7%
99 Cents Only Stores	1,199	738	38.4%
Penney (J.C.) Co., Inc.	18,486	11,571	37.4%
Kohl's Corp.	16,389	10,334	36.9%
Neiman-Marcus Group, Inc.	3,822	2,494	34.7%
Dollar Tree, Inc.	4,645	3,053	34.3%
Home Deport Inc.	71,288	47,298	33.7%
Target Corp.	62,884	44,157	29.8%
Wal-Mart Stores, Inc.	401,244	306,158	23.7%
Costco Wholesale Corp.	70,977	63,502	10.5%

COMPETITION-BASED PRICING

When the setting of an item's initial price begins with the examination of competitors' prices, the process is known as competition-based pricing. When a seller's intent is to match the levels of competitors' prices, the pricing method is often referred to as parity pricing.[10] A seller may also make note of the prices charged by competitors and then choose to set prices lower or higher than these competitors' prices.

Complexities of Competition-Based Pricing

Typically, a look at the competitive marketplace will show the existence of different prices for a particular product, perhaps many different prices. One comparative price study found a considerable amount of price dispersion even among neighboring retail stores. For example, among ten competing retailers, a particular item—Neutrogena Body Emulsion, 5.2-ounce pump-top package—was being sold at seven different prices, ranging from $4.61 to $5.99.[11] Moreover, the multitude of online sellers of virtually any item can substantially increase the complexity of competitive price information.

A competition-based method of setting a product's initial price could deal with this complexity by focusing on only the highest marketplace prices, on only the lowest, or on only prices in the middle of the competitive price range. Alternatively, attention could be focused on the prices of one particular competitor, perhaps the one that is largest, the one showing the fastest growth, the one that is most prestigious, or the one considered most similar to the company that is setting an initial price.

In business markets, a further difficulty of competition-based pricing involves determining competitors' actual prices. In many business markets, prices are not publicly posted either because they are determined by a bidding process or because they are determined by private negotiations between the buyer and seller. Sometimes the publicly available posted prices are not the prices at which products are actually sold because of subsequent private discounts or negotiations. In such situations, a seller may be able to draw on reports from salespeople concerning what customers have told them about the prices of their competitors. In most cases, useful estimates of competitors' prices would require supplementing such information from customers with information about competitors' likely costs, strategies, profit levels, and other elements of "competitive intelligence."[12]

Advantages and Disadvantages of Competition-Based Pricing

Despite the complexities of multiple competitive prices and, in business markets, the possible difficulties of determining competitors' actual prices, competition-based pricing shares with cost-based pricing the advantages of being intuitive and relatively easy to carry out. However, it also shares with cost-based pricing the disadvantage of producing prices that may not be helpful to efforts toward maximizing total profits. In focusing on the prices of competitors, a seller might ask what these competitors focused on when setting their prices. If the seller's competitors set prices by looking to *their* competitors, the seller might wonder how long this has been going on. Has anyone ever considered a rationale for the pricing of these products?[13]

A BETTER ALTERNATIVE: CUSTOMER-BASED PRICING

In most companies, there is an appreciation that pricing by the simple application of standard markups or margins or by following the prices of competitors is not really adequate. Often managers using cost- or competition-based pricing will try to improve outcomes by making adjustments to those prices that don't seem to be working, or "just don't look right." However, such trial-and-error processes tend to be haphazard, stopgap measures. The more basic solution to the inadequacy of cost- and competition-based pricing is to use a different starting point for setting an initial price. Rather than starting with costs or competitors' prices, the price-setting process can begin with thinking about the customer's needs and, especially, about the ability of the seller's product to satisfy those needs. This is known as customer-based pricing.

Starting the initial price-setting process by considering the customer's needs makes possible a rational basis for price setting. As we discussed in Chapter 1, the role of price in the commercial exchange is to capture the value created by the other three elements of the marketing mix. Because this value consists of the satisfactions of customer needs and wants that are provided by the product, careful consideration of each of the ways a product satisfies, fails to satisfy, or could be made to satisfy these customer needs and wants provides essential guidance. Such consideration places at the starting point of the initial price-setting process a measure of the value that the product's price could potentially capture.

Estimating the Value to the Customer

This value created by the product, distribution, and promotion elements of the marketing will be known as the product's value to the customer (VTC).[14] A key technique of customer-based pricing is to be able to arrive at an estimate of this value in monetary terms (such as dollars). The process of estimating your product's VTC can be broken down into four steps (see Figure 2.5).[15]

Figure 2.5   Four Steps of Value to the Customer Estimation

1. Identify the price of the competing product that the customer views as the best substitute. This is the *reference value.*

2. Identify all factors that differentiate your product from this competing product. These are the *differentiating factors.*

3. Determine the monetary value to the customer of each of these differentiating factors. These are the positive and negative *differentiation values.*

4. Sum the reference value and the differentiation values to determine the total *value to the customer (VTC),* the maximum that someone fully informed of the product's benefits would be willing to pay for the product.

The first step is to identify what the customer perceives as the next closest substitute for your product. In other words, if the customer were not to buy your product, what competing product would the customer be likely to buy? The price of this alternative product could be referred to as the reference value of your product.

The second step is to identify all of the differentiating factors, the factors that differentiate your product from this next closest substitute. There are numerous ways in which products could differ. A product could be more effective in accomplishing its principle function than its next closest substitute. For example, a new window cleaning liquid could produce fewer streaks than the largest selling window cleaner currently on the market. Or a product could be effective for a longer time, as with a window cleaning product that keeps windows clean for longer than competing products. A product could have capabilities or features not present in its likely substitutes, it could be more attractive, it could be sold in a more convenient package, it could include better support services, and so on. Because an understanding of possible differentiating factors is such an essential component to estimating a product's VTC, we will further discuss these factors later in this chapter and again, in more detail, in Chapter 3.

The third step in VTC estimation is to determine what is, for the customer, the monetary value of each of these differentiating factors. If your product is superior to the next closest substitute on a factor, then this differentiating factor's monetary value is a positive differentiation value. If your product is inferior to the next closest substitute on a factor, then this differentiating factor's monetary value is a negative differentiation value.

The fourth step in this process is to sum the reference value and the differentiation values. Each positive differentiation value would be added to the reference value. Each negative differentiation value would be subtracted from the reference value. The resulting total, your product's VTC, is a monetary representation of the value created by the product for that customer. It is the maximum amount that the customer, when fully informed of the product's benefits, would be willing to pay for the product.

Value to the Customer Estimation: An Example

For an example of this estimation process, consider the case of Station Auto Service, Inc. This is a car repair shop in a town that is a suburb of a large city. The town is served by an efficient commuter rail line and many of the residents of the town use this rail line to go to work in the city. Station Auto Service is located across the street from the town's train station for this commuter rail line.

Let's say that the managers of Station Auto Service are using a VTC analysis to help them decide on the price of an automobile tune-up (see Figure 2.6). They conduct some market research on car owners in town and find that their closest substitute is Joe's Texaco, located about two miles away, in a direction away from the train station. The price of a tune-up at Joe's Texaco—$80—then becomes the reference value in their analysis. The managers' market research also enables the identification of three differentiating factors. The first is that a customer using Station Auto Service can leave his or her car there in the morning and walk to the train station across the street to take the rail line to work. At the end of the day, the customer can get off the train, walk across the street, and pick up his or her car. This is a considerable convenience that Joe's Texaco does not provide. Joe's customers must arrange their own transportation to and from the repair shop. With the help of the market research, the managers estimate the positive differentiation value of this factor is about $20.

The second differentiating factor is also a positive one. A local consumer magazine surveyed the reliability of auto repairs done at local shops and rated the work of Station's mechanics as the most reliable in the area. The managers' research suggests that the positive differentiation value of this factor is about $15. The third differentiating factor is a

Figure 2.6   Value to the Customer for a Tune-Up at Station Auto Service, Inc.

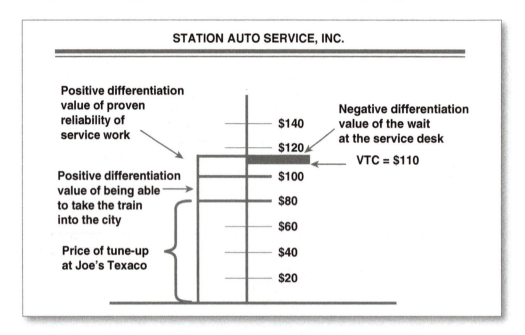

negative one. Because most of Station's customers come in to pick up their cars at around the same time at the end of the workday, they often experience a wait at the service desk to get their cars. There is usually no wait at Joe's Texaco. The managers' research suggests that the negative differentiation value of this factor is about $5.

Summing these elements—the $80 reference value, plus the positive differentiation values of $20 and $15, minus the negative differentiation value of $5—results in a tune-up at Station Auto Service having an estimated VTC of $110.

Translating a VTC Estimate Into a Price

If a product's VTC is the maximum amount that the customer, when fully informed, would be willing to pay, is that what the product's price should be? The answer, in general, is no. Even if customers are fully informed of a product's value, it is a good idea to set the product's price at a level *below* the product's VTC.

The reason for this is simple. Assuming that the product's VTC is assessed accurately, then a price equal to that value would put the customer in a situation where there is no net benefit for purchasing the product. The costs and benefits would be totally balanced. To avoid having a large number of potential customers pass up the product, it is generally wise to tip that balance by setting the price below the product's VTC. How much below the VTC should a product's price be set? The answer concerns how fast you want the item to sell. This is an issue that we will examine in some detail in Chapter 4.

Identification of the Reference Value

It is important to keep in mind that a product's reference value is the price of the closest substitute product. Because this alternative product is usually one sold by a competitor, the use of an item's reference value in VTC analysis provides a means of combining information about competitors with the customer-need information involved in estimating a product's VTC.

To identify the reference value of a product, it makes sense to consider a similar quantity of the closest substitute product. For example, if a new dishwashing detergent comes in a 10-ounce box and the next closest substitute comes in a 20-ounce box, then the new dishwashing detergent's reference value should be equal to half of the price of a box of the substitute detergent. If the new dishwashing detergent is so powerful that one ounce of it accomplishes the same cleaning as 2 ounces of the substitute in the larger box, then the reference value of the new dishwashing detergent's 10-ounce box should still be equal to half the price of the 20-ounce box. The greater per-ounce capability of the new dishwashing detergent should be considered one of its differentiating factors. An example of such a differentiating factor can be seen in the ad shown in Figure 2.7 in which a product's greater per-item capability is used to communicate its value to potential customers.

Figure 2.7   Example of a Product's Greater Capability Being Used to Communicate Its
Value to the Customer

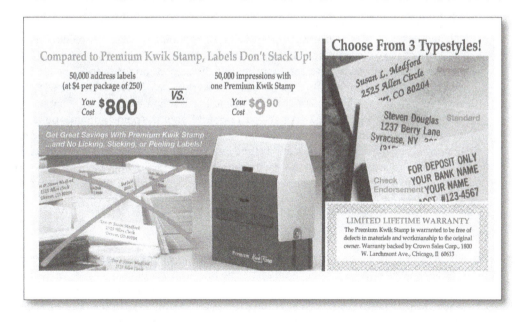

In addition, because a product's reference value is the price of an alternative product, it should not include the prices of items that may be used along with the alternative product but that are actually separate products. For example, suppose the formulation of the new dishwashing detergent was such that it removed the necessity for the consumer to use a rinse agent. Because the rinse agent would be considered a separate product, saving the money that would have been spent on the rinse agent should be considered a differentiating factor of the new dishwashing detergent and not part of its reference value.

Two Approaches to Determining Differentiation Values

Broadly, there are two approaches that can be taken to develop a monetary estimate of the degree to which a customer values a differentiating factor. The first is to translate the factor into monetary terms by identifying additional expenditures and/or savings that result from the factor. The second approach is to use market research to estimate how customers weigh money against their preferences and feelings for the differentiating factor. This can be accomplished through systematic observation of past customer choices or through use of customer surveys. A survey method for estimating how consumers trade off product benefits against price will be discussed in Chapter 3.

Both of these approaches can be seen in the VTC analyses carried out routinely by real estate agents to help their clients set a price for their homes or other properties (real estate agents often refer to these as "market analyses"). To illustrate the expenditures-savings approach, say a real estate agent has identified a recently sold house that is comparable to his client's house except that the recently sold house had a newly remodeled kitchen. To estimate the customer value of this differentiating factor, the agent might consider the price that a consumer would have to pay for each element of a remodeled kitchen—new refrigerator, new countertops, new cabinets, and so on. For customers who require an up-to-date kitchen, the total of the necessary remodeling expenditures would provide a reasonable estimate of the differentiation value of this factor.

The market research approach to estimating differentiation value could be illustrated by supposing that the comparable house was located on a cul-de-sac, while the client's house was located on a through street. The real estate agent might carry out the market research using his own records, by looking at the past price differentials paid for houses on cul-de-sacs versus similar houses on through streets. The agent might also draw on market research conducted by outside sources, such as trade associations. These sources would be likely to have a much larger past-purchase database to study and would be likely to have sufficient resources to survey consumers as to their preferences for different housing alternatives.

Importance of Understanding Customer Needs

Often the key to effectively estimating differentiation values is to understand the customer's needs well enough to fully appreciate the implications of differences between a product and its next closest substitute. For example, a classic marketing case involves Dewey & Almy, a firm that sold supplies to companies that used offset printing presses.[16] One such supply item was the "blanket" that was placed behind the printing plate and kept the plate at the right tension for making clear print images.

The major reason that a printing blanket would need to be replaced was the occurrence of a "smash"—a piece of foreign matter or a creased sheet of paper passing through the press and causing a depression in the blanket surface. When a smash occurred, all work had to stop, and the press had to be dismantled so the blanket could be replaced. Dewey & Almy had developed a more resilient printing blanket that could resist many smashes. On average, it lasted twice as long as any of the printing blankets that were currently being sold. Because current available blankets were priced at $100, the company priced its new blankets just below $200.

Very soon after the introduction of this product, Dewey & Almy's salespeople informed management that the price of the new blankets would have to be lowered. Customers considered the almost-$200 price tag just way out of line. Management hired a consultant to help deal with this problem. The consultant, along with a salesperson, visited some of Dewey & Almy's customers. He listened carefully to their price concerns but also probed in detail to better understand how these companies used printing blankets.

What the consultant found was that one new blanket being equivalent to two current blankets (the $200 reference value) was not even the largest component of the new blankets' value to customers. The differentiating factor of the new blankets resulting in half as many press smashes as current blankets had numerous value implications. For instance, fewer press smashes resulted in the following:

- Less wasted printing crew time
- Less maintenance crew time needed
- Less need for blanket replacement-related repair materials
- Less wear on the presses (and thus longer life of these expensive machines)
- Lower inventory costs of repair materials
- Fewer job-deadline disruptions

Tallying all of these consequences of a press smash, the consultant determined that avoiding a single smash saves a printing company around $300. Because, by lasting twice as long, each new blanket can be expected to avoid one smash that otherwise would have occurred, $300 is the differentiation value of the new blanket's greater resiliency. Adding this $300 to the new blanket's reference value of $200 leads to a VTC of $500. Needless to say, after being trained in presenting this VTC analysis to customers, the salesforce no longer had any trouble selling the new blankets for just under $200.

The lesson of this example is not only the importance of understanding customer needs well enough to fully appreciate the implications of differentiating factors. It also reminds us that when customers are not fully informed, providing meaningful information is a clear alternative to lowering price as a means of dealing with customer price resistance.

THE POTENTIAL OF CUSTOMER-BASED PRICING

This discussion of how a product's VTC can be estimated and how such an estimate can be used as a means of capturing a larger amount of a product's value illustrates an important benefit of customer-based pricing. However, this is certainly not only way that customer-based pricing can be used. Starting the pricing process with a consideration of customer needs has a much wider range of potential benefits.

When a Product's VTC Is Lower Than Its Reference Value

It is generally a happy situation when a VTC analysis indicates that your product is worth more to customers than the products of your competitors. You can work to meet the challenge of effectively communicating to customers the extent of this value and then harvest the profits from the value that you have created.

But what if the VTC analysis indicates that your product is worth less to customers than the products of your competitors? For example, say you are a small-appliance manufacturer and your market research indicates that your new hair dryer model is perceived by customers to have similar features to a popular Conair model selling for $35. The research further indicates that your hair dryer has no positive differentiating factors over that Conair model and has two negative ones: Your lack of a well-known brand name has a negative differentiation value of $5 and the slightly less attractive styling of your hair dryer has a negative differentiation value of $3. This analysis would then indicate that the total VTC of your hair dryer is $27.

So long as your costs are below your product's VTC, this could also be a happy situation. Setting your hair dryer's price below its VTC, say at $22, would give customers an incentive to buy and could result in a profitable product. The use of customer-based pricing helps avoid the temptation of parity pricing, which, for this hair dryer, would have probably led to very low sales and discontinuation of the product. Basing the initial price on an evaluation of customer needs confirms that a lower price is required in this case and gives management a reference point for deciding how much lower this price might be.

Using Price to Guide Product Development

Up to this point, our discussion of setting initial prices has assumed the existence of a finished product that needs a price. But what if price-related customer needs are considered early in the product development process? An outstanding example of what becomes possible is illustrated by the story of the Ford Mustang.

In 1960, the newly promoted general manager of the Ford Division of the Ford Motor Company noted the forecasts that there would be an increasing number of youthful car buyers who would find a stylish sports car appealing but who were unable to afford the prices of the current sports cars, such as Ford's Thunderbird or General Motor's (GM's) Corvette. He also noted indications that consumers would value a car with sporty styling even if it did not have features of sports car performance, such as a large engine.

Thus, the manager began the process of developing a new sports car that could be sold at a low price. To make the low price possible, the manager designed sporty styling features over the engine, transmission, and axles of Ford's existing compact car, the Falcon. When the prototype was complete, what had been referred to by the engineers as the "Special Falcon" was given the name, Mustang. The manager then,

> . . . had his staff invite fifty young, middle-income couples to the Ford Styling Center as a means of confirming consumer reactions to the Mustang. They came in small groups, then looked and admired. Almost to a couple their only negative reaction was to what they believed such a fine car would cost. Their estimates ranged from $4,000–$7,000, hardly practical for middle-incomes of the time. When they heard that the base price was somewhat under $2,500, they expressed amazement and disbelief. At such a price, all agreed, Mustang was a car that they would like to own.[17]

Ford sold over 400,000 Mustangs in the first year after its introduction, and within two years, it made over $1 billion in net profits from the car. The Ford Division general manager, Lee Iacocca, went on to become CEO of Chrysler and one of the most well-known marketers of his time.

The consideration of customer needs in this case told Ford that customers in the large middle-income market did not value all of the aspects of a sports car enough for them to pay what it would cost Ford to provide these aspects. By considering these price-related customer needs early in the product development process, the Ford designers were able to look for, and include, the aspects that customers most wanted (e.g., styling) and to cut costs on the other aspects (e.g., engine, transmission).

In other words, starting the pricing process with the consideration of customer needs rather than product costs helped lead the company to start the pricing process before any cost commitments were made. This made it possible to substantially reduce those costs and achieve a highly profitable product.

Different Customer Values for Different Market Segments

So far, our discussion of customer needs has not considered differences between customers. As will be noted in Chapter 10, dealing with different market segments is an important aspect of pricing strategy. An additional benefit of VTC analysis is that it helps the price setter identify possible pricing-related differences between market segments. As an illustration, consider again the situation of Station Auto Service. If the estimated VTC of Station's tune-up for those town residents who commuted to the city by train was $110, what would be the VTC for those residents who did not take the train to work? For those residents, there would be no station-location differentiating factor, so their estimated VTC would become $90 (plus $15 for the added reliability and minus $5 for the wait).

Further, within those town residents who do not take the train, there may be other distinctions possible. For example, it may be that groups such as parents with young children or seniors may find the prospect of breaking down in their car particularly aversive and thus place greater value on the increased reliability of Station Auto Service's repair work. This could indicate the presence of at least three segments of Station's market with differing VTCs for the shop's car maintenance services (see Figure 2.8). Methods for acting on such market segment information—charging different prices to different market segments—will be covered in Chapters 10 through 12.

Customer Needs as the Drivers of Initial Price

When setting a price for a product that does not already have a price, there is no question that all three types of information—(1) costs, (2) competition, and (3) customer needs—are relevant. The distinction that is being made here concerns the type of information that the price setter should attend to first.

If the price-setting starting point is a consideration of customer needs, there are substantial benefits possible. As illustrated in the Dewey & Almy example, focusing on understanding customer needs in order to estimate a product's VTC can help make possible a price

Figure 2.8   Value to the Customer of Station Auto Service's Tune-Up for Different Market Segments

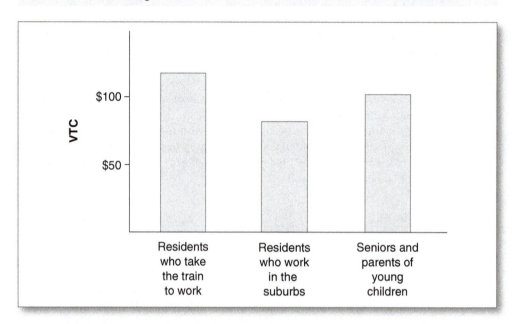

higher than one that might be suggested by a typical markup on costs or the prices of competing products. As illustrated in the Ford Mustang example, understanding customer needs in order to identify product characteristics that are not sufficiently valued can make possible a price lower than one that might be arrived at from starting with costs or the prices of other products in the category. Further, both of these types of benefits of customer understanding could occur for the same product and make possible different initial prices for different market segments.

The use of customer-based pricing is suggested by, and is a key element of, the marketing approach to pricing. There is research evidence that focusing on the customer first in price setting can pay off, for example, by increasing the likelihood of success in new product introductions.[18] Further, starting the price-setting process with consideration of customer needs has been widely advised by both consultants and academics.[19] One prominent business theorist and consultant, Peter Drucker, has even put cost-based pricing on his list of "The Five Deadly Business Sins."[20]

These considerable benefits to customer-based pricing raise the question of why it is not more commonly used. It is sometimes suggested from studies of industry practice that there is justification for the pricing procedures common to certain industries or certain conditions. For example, it has been suggested that when costs are high, cost-based pricing is favored in order to make sure that profitability can be achieved.[21] Although this managerial focus on costs is understandable in such a situation, it could also be noted that a customer-based pricing process might reveal that prices could be substantially higher than even these high costs, at least for a particular segment of the market.

No doubt a major reason that customer-based pricing is not more often used is that it requires research on customer needs rather than only an estimate of one's incurred costs or the prices of competing products. Although such investigation can involve expensive market research studies, it is also possible to gain some preliminary ideas of how one's product creates value, or could create value, by more informal conversations with consumers and observations of the marketplace. Indeed, as advances in information technology make collecting information about customer behavior more inexpensive, the use of customer needs as the starting point in the pricing process becomes less a matter of what can be afforded and more a matter of whether the price setter has the will to do it.

SUMMARY

When an organization sets an initial price for an item, the process may begin with the item's costs (cost-based pricing), the prices of competing products (competition-based pricing), or the benefits that the item creates by satisfying customer needs (customer-based pricing).

Cost-based pricing could involve adding a specific dollar amount to the product's costs or adding a standard percentage of the product's costs. Gross margins are often used in cost-based pricing to bring in consideration of the organization's profit goals. Cost-based pricing is widely used because it is intuitive and relatively simple to operationalize, but it is not particularly useful in efforts to maximize total profits.

Competition-based pricing could involve matching competitors' prices or choosing to set prices higher or lower than these prices. Although there are often many competitive prices and such prices are sometimes difficult to identify, competition-based pricing shares with cost-based pricing the advantage of being intuitive and relatively simple. However, it also may not be helpful in efforts to maximize total profits.

A key component of customer-based pricing is the estimation of a product's VTC. This is assessed by determining the price of the product's next closest substitute and then adding or subtracting the value of each factor that differentiates the product from this next closest substitute. A VTC analysis can help a seller use a high price to capture a large amount of a product's value or can help guide the setting of a low price that will help the product achieve sales success. Customer-based pricing also facilitates the consideration of price while it is still possible to substantially reduce costs, and it is useful in identifying differences in the degree to which different market segments value a particular product.

KEY TERMS

cost-based pricing	retail price	value to the customer
cost-plus pricing	gross margin	reference value
markup pricing	competition-based pricing	differentiating factors
markup	parity pricing	positive differentiation value
keystone pricing	customer-based pricing	negative differentiation value

REVIEW AND DISCUSSION QUESTIONS

1. What are the three possible starting points for the process of setting an initial price that are described in this chapter?

2. Suppose that you have a service business such as house painting. Describe how you would use cost-plus pricing in developing an estimate for a potential customer.

3. If an item costs $10 and you apply a 60 percent markup, what would be the item's price? If you used keystone pricing in this case, what then would be this item's price?

4. If management's profit guidelines mandate gross margins of 25 percent, calculate the markup percentage that would be equivalent to this gross margin.

5. If an item will be priced according to a 55 percent gross margin and the item costs $20, use that gross margin percentage to directly calculate the item's price.

6. Describe how you would research industry norms on gross margins to inform your company's decisions regarding pricing-related profit goals.

7. Cost-based pricing is sometimes justified by arguing that it ensures that a company receives a good profit on the products that it sells. Describe a problem with this justification. What does this problem have to do with the main disadvantage of cost-based pricing?

8. Given that there is a serious disadvantage to cost-based pricing, how would you account for its widespread use in retailing and other businesses?

9. What is parity pricing? How does it differ from other forms of competition-based pricing?

10. Describe some ways that a seller using competition-based pricing could deal with the presence in the marketplace of a variety of prices for an item.

11. What might make it difficult to determine the prices of one's competitors? When such difficulties occur, what could be done to surmount them?

12. Describe one advantage and one disadvantage that competition-based pricing has in common with cost-based pricing.

13. How is customer-based pricing related to the role of price in the commercial exchange versus the role of the other three elements of the marketing mix?

14. Describe the concept of a product's VTC. Why is the monetary estimation of this value important for price setting?

15. Describe the concept of a product's reference value. How would you calculate the reference value for a consumer product whose package size is different than the package sizes of all of its competing products?

16. Consider a familiar product, such as Apple's iPhone. What would you consider to be its next closest substitute? Describe two factors that would differentiate the iPhone from its next closest substitute.

17. What is the difference between a positive differentiating factor and a negative one? Is it possible for an item to simultaneously have both positive and negative differentiating factors?

18. Which would be more prudent: pricing an item above its VTC, exactly at its VTC, or below its VTC? Explain your reasoning.

19. If a salesperson tells a manufacturer that the machine the salesperson is selling is better than competing machines because it will last longer, what approach should be used to estimate the value of this differentiating factor?

20. If an item is particularly valuable to a customer, using customer-based pricing might suggest a price that is higher than the one that would be indicated by use of a standard markup. Describe a situation where the use of customer-based pricing would suggest a price that is lower than the one that would be indicated by use of a standard markup.

21. Explain how an openness to customer-based pricing helped contribute to the outstanding success of the Ford Mustang.

22. Describe a situation where different market segments would have different VTCs for the same product.

23. If a company uses customer-based pricing, does that mean that costs and the prices of competing products are not taken into account?

24. What is the most likely reason that customer-based pricing is not more often used? What do you think of this reason?

EXERCISES

1. A well-known local wine shop uses keystone pricing for its line of modular wine racks.

   (a) Given this pricing practice, use the cost information here to calculate the retail prices for the following items. Show your calculations:

12-bottle rack, natural finish	Per-item cost:	$22.50
12-bottle rack, mahogany finish	Per-item cost:	$26.25
24-bottle rack, natural finish	Per-item cost:	$36.00

   (b) What is the markup percentage being used for these wine racks?

   (c) If these wine racks are sold at the prices you calculated in Part (a), what would be the shop's percent gross margin for these items?

2. You are the manager of a successful gift shop. After a meeting with her accountant, the owner of the shop has told you that the shop's cost of goods sold should be about 30 percent of total sales revenue and that the price of each of the items that the shop sells should be in line with this.

   (a) Based on the owner's instructions, give the price you would set for the following items. Show the formula(s) you used in your calculations:

Item A	Per-item cost:	$26.00
Item B	Per-item cost:	$9.25
Item C	Per-item cost:	$103.60

   (b) Is the owner using cost-based, competition-based, or customer-based pricing? What are the pros and cons of the owner's pricing procedure?

3. The manager of a local convenience store is expanding his line of small toy items. To price these new items, the manager is looking at the prices being charged by competing retailers in his area. For the popular "Titan Joe Action Figure," he has observed the following prices:

Downtown department store:	$14.00
Chain drug store:	$11.99
Well-known local variety store	$10.99
Large discount department store:	$9.97
Discount toy store	$9.55

   If the manager is inclined to use parity pricing, what price should he set for the Titan Joe Action Figure? Explain your reasoning.

4. A homeowner has asked a local real estate agent for advice on the price he should set for his house. The real estate agent notes that the only comparable house in the neighborhood that is currently for sale is asking $350,000. Both houses are on a hill that overlooks a beautiful lake, but the owner's house is forty feet farther up the hill than the comparable house. The agent estimates that, in this area, customers will pay an additional $10,000 for a house for each ten added feet of elevation associated with the house's location. The owner's house has an old, outdated kitchen, but the sellers of the comparable house have just spent $24,000 to remodel their kitchen.

   What is the selling price that the real estate agent should recommend?

5. Lincoln Manufacturing has just developed a more durable commercial carpeting. It has all the advantages of the currently available commercial carpeting and lasts twice as long. Lincoln's materials and labor costs for producing this new carpeting are $14.50 per square yard. Buyers of commercial carpeting must have it installed by independent contractors whose installation charges for this new carpeting average $10 per square yard.

   The price of the currently available commercial carpeting averages $12 per square yard. Independent contractors charge $8 per square yard for installing the currently available commercial carpeting.

(a) Use VTC analysis to calculate the VTC for commercial buyers of a square yard of Lincoln's new carpeting.

(b) Recommend a price for a square yard of Lincoln's new carpeting, and justify your recommendation. Your justification should make use of your estimate of the VTC of Lincoln's new carpeting.

NOTES

1. Peter M. Noble and Thomas S. Gruca, "Industrial Pricing: Theory and Managerial Practice," *Management Science* 18, no. 3 (1999): 435–454. Also see George J. Aylonitis and Kostis A. Indounas, "Pricing Objectives and Pricing Methods in the Services Sector," *Journal of Services Marketing* 19, no. 1 (2005): 47–57.

2. Lawrence A. Gordon, Robert Cooper, Haim Falk, and Danny Miller, *The Pricing Decision* (New York: The National Association of Accountants, 1980).

3. Barry Berman and J. R. Evans, *Retail Management: A Strategic Approach,* 7th ed. (Upper Saddle River, NJ: Prentice Hall, 1998), 431.

4. Charles M. Futrell, *Fundamentals of Selling: Customers for Life Through Service,* 10th ed. (Boston: McGraw-Hill Irwin, 2008), 209–210.

5. Robert L. Steiner, "The Inverse Association Between the Margins of Manufacturers and Retailers," *Review of Industrial Organization* 8 (1993): 717–740.

6. Charles L. Ilvento, *Profit Planning and Decision Making in the Hospitality Industry* (Dubuque, IA: Kendall/Hunt Publishing Company, 1996), 154.

7. Thomas V. Bonoma, Victoria L. Crittenden, and Robert J. Dolan, "Can We Have Rigor and Relevance in Pricing Research?" in *Issues in Pricing: Theory and Research,* ed. Timothy M. Devinney (Lexington, MA: D.C. Heath and Company, 1988).

8. The formula for calculating a price from %GM can be derived by expressing the amount to be added to an item's cost in terms of %GM—that is, $P \times (\%GM/100)$—and then adding it to the item's cost. The result is $P = C + [P \times (\%GM/100)]$. Rearranging the terms gives $P - [P \times (\%GM/100)] = C$. Pulling out the common factor gives $P \times [1 - (\%GM/100)] = C$. Solving for price then gives the %GM formula, $P = C / [1 - (\%GM/100)]$.

9. SEC 10-K forms for all U.S. public companies are publically available at http://www.sec.gov.

10. Michael H. Morris and Roger J. Calatone, "Four Components of Effective Pricing," *Industrial Marketing Management* 19 (1990): 321–329.

11. Robert M. Schindler, "Relative Price Level of 99-Ending Prices: Image Versus Reality," *Marketing Letters* 12, no. 3 (2001): 239–247.

12. Daniel Rouach and Patrice Santi, "Competitive Intelligence Adds Value: Five Intelligence Attitudes," *European Management Journal* 19 (October 2001): 552–559.

13. Jagmohan Raju and Z. John Zhang, *Smart Pricing: How Google, Priceline, and Leading Businesses Use Pricing Innovation for Profitability* (Upper Saddle River, NJ: Pearson Education, 2010), 7.

14. John L. Forbis and Nitin T. Mehta, "Value-Based Strategies for Industrial Products," *Business Horizons* 24, no. 3 (1981): 32–42. Shortened from their "economic value to the customer."

15. Thomas T. Nagle and Reed K. Holden, *The Strategy and Tactics of Pricing,* 3rd ed. (Upper Saddle River, NJ: Prentice Hall, 2002), 75.

16. Example is adapted from "Dewey & Almy Chemical Division," Harvard Business School Case 9-506-084, Boston: Harvard Business School Publishing.

17. David Adodaher, *Iacocca* (New York: Macmillan Publishing Co., 1982), 126.

18. Paul Ingenbleek, Marion Debruyne, Ruud T. Frambach, and Theo M. M. Verhallen, "Successful New Product Pricing Practices: A Contingency Approach," *Marketing Letters* 14, no. 4 (2003): 289–305.
19. Andreas Hinterhauber, "Value Delivery and Value-Based Pricing in Industrial Markets" in *Creating and Managing Superior Customer Value,* ed. Arch G. Woodside, Francesca Golfetto, and Michael Gibbert (Bingley, UK: JAI Press, 2008).
20. Peter F. Drucker, "The Five Deadly Business Sins," *Wall Street Journal,* October 21, 1993.
21. Thomas V. Bonoma, Victoria L. Crittenden, and Robert J. Dolan, "Can We Have Rigor and Relevance in Pricing Research?" in *Issues in Pricing: Theory and Research,* ed. Timothy M. Devinney (Lexington, MA: D.C. Heath and Company, 1988).

CHAPTER 3

Assessing Value to the Customer

As we have seen, knowing a product's value to the customer (VTC) can provide important guidance for setting an initial price for the product. The first step in our four-step method for assessing a product's VTC is to determine a reference value—the price of the item that the customer perceives as the next closest substitute of the product. The second step is to identify all of the factors that differentiate the product from this next closest substitute. The third step is to determine the monetary value to the customer of each of these differentiating factors. The fourth step is to take all of these differentiation values (some of which may be negative) and add them to the reference value. This results in an estimate of the product's VTC.

In this chapter, we examine in greater detail the second and third steps in VTC estimation. For the second step, we present a framework to help the price setter identify the full range of a product's differentiating factors. For the third step, we cover some concepts and methods for determining the monetary value that customers place on a differentiating factor. We discuss a means to quantify uncertainty when estimating the monetary consequences of a differentiating factor and describe a survey method to measure how customers trade off product benefits against price.

A FRAMEWORK FOR IDENTIFYING DIFFERENTIATING FACTORS

To carry out the second of the four steps to estimating a product's VTC, it is important to consider the widest array of potential differentiating factors. Doing this is often very difficult, because there are a great many aspects of a product that could potentially differentiate it from its substitutes. In fact, the possibilities are probably endless. A checklist could provide the price setter with useful assistance in thinking of these possibilities. A framework is described that can serve as such a checklist. Because this framework is based on types of product characteristics and types of customer needs that these product characteristics could help satisfy, it could be referred to as a "product-needs framework."

Types of Product Characteristics

Traditionally, marketers have considered the characteristics of products by grouping them into categories such as product quality versus product feature characteristics[1] or core versus augmented benefits[2] and by describing the various aspects of brand equity.[3] These considerations could be integrated to produce three broad categories of product characteristics.

The first category consists of a product's core-quality characteristics. These are characteristics that affect the product's ability to accomplish what is considered by customers to be its primary purpose, or function. For example, the primary function of a window cleaning liquid would be to get a window clean. If one window cleaning liquid were formulated to produce fewer streaks than another, then this formulation would be a core-quality characteristic that could serve as a differentiating factor. Core quality also includes characteristics that affect how consistently the product performs its primary function and for how long. For example, a car repair shop may employ mechanics with more expertise so that the shop can diagnose a car's problem more consistently than do its competitors. A hair spray product may contain an ingredient that enables it to hold one's hair in place for a longer period of time than its next closest substitute.

The second category consists of a product's features and styling characteristics. These characteristics contribute to benefits beyond the product's primary function. This category includes aspects sometimes referred to as "bells and whistles." For example, a cell phone could also have the capacity to take photographs, an orange juice product could have added calcium, or a soft drink at a fast-food restaurant could come in a reusable cup. This category of product characteristics also includes characteristics related to a product's packaging and appearance. If appearance is intimately associated with a product's primary function, such as is the case with men's suits or designer clothing, then appearance characteristics would be considered in the first category, core quality. However, when appearance characteristics are viewed by customers as secondary to a product's main function, they then fall into this second category. For example, the unusual styling of Apple's iMac personal computer or the attractive appearance of a JanSport backpack would most likely constitute differentiating factors in this second category.

The third category consists of reputation and support service characteristics. These include characteristics that support a product's primary and secondary benefits and that could be characteristics of the selling company rather than only of the product itself. In this category are aspects of the product that communicate its brand and/or the name of the company that produced it. This category also includes the seller's services related to the customer's acquisition of the product—selecting, ordering, delivering, and installing the product—and services related to the customer's use of the product—operating, maintaining, repairing, and even disposing of the product when its useful life is over. Such product support services are a rich area of possible differentiating factors. It has been noted that even generic commodity goods, such as common industrial chemicals, can be differentiated through product support services.[4] For example, one chemical provider could offer customers an easier ordering process or faster delivery times. A software product could offer better technical support than its competitors do or an automobile manufacturer could offer a longer and more comprehensive warranty than others do.

Although these three categories are very broad, they help make possible a framework that can provide structure for the process of identifying a product's differentiating factors. What needs to be added is how these product characteristics may serve to satisfy customer needs.

Types of Customer Needs

A product characteristic is relevant to the product's VTC only to the extent that the characteristic has an effect on how well the product satisfies the customer's needs. It is a basic tenet of the marketing approach to pricing that the product value that can be captured by the product's price can be appreciated only by considering the customer's needs. It should be noted that the term need is used here broadly, to include a customer's wants, preferences, desires, enjoyments, satisfactions, and so on. In everyday speech, needs that are strong or essential are referred to as needs, and needs that are weaker or more discretionary are referred to as "wants." In this book, all forces within a person that could attract that person to a product will be referred to as needs.[5]

Just as it is useful to have categories of product characteristics, it is also useful to have categories of product-related customer needs. In the study of consumer behavior, there is a long-established distinction between product needs and benefits that are functional or utilitarian and those that have to do with the consumer's hedonic or aesthetic experience.[6] Even older is the recognition that people can use products as a means of showing social status.[7] There has also been work on the importance of the perceived risks concerning product performance[8] and recognition that customers often prefer to minimize the effort involved in making purchases.[9] For the purposes of identifying a product's VTC, these observations are combined to divide customer needs into five broadly defined types. Because each of these five types of needs could potentially be addressed by each of the three types of product characteristics, these two dimensions can be crossed to produce the fifteen-cell framework shown in Figure 3.1. This figure also

Figure 3.1   Framework for Identifying Differentiating Factors (With Examples)

	Core-Quality Characteristics	Features–Styling Characteristics	Reputation–Support Characteristics
Objective performance needs	ingredient leading to fewer streaks	more effective nozzle	detailed installation instructions
Hedonic/aesthetic performance needs	recipe leading to enjoyable taste	fun shoelaces	favorable brand associations
Social performance needs	design allowing it to go in snow	sleek, trendy styling	prestige brand
Performance reliability needs	effective quality control processes	tracking number	warranty protection
Product convenience needs	design requiring less maintenance	spring-loaded retractable cord	24-hour help

provides examples of how each type of need could be satisfied by each type of product characteristic.

Need for Objective Performance

For a large number of consumer products (products purchased by consumers) and for virtually all business products (products purchased by business customers), the product performance that is important to the buyer is objectively measurable. This will be referred to as a product's objective performance because it involves results that are a matter of observable facts, as opposed to a matter of opinion. For example, a consumer needs a dishwashing detergent to help get the dishes clean, needs an air conditioner to keep a room cool, and needs an airline ticket to accomplish getting to a faraway destination. A manufacturer might purchase plastic in order to make a children's toy that retailers will buy and a retailer may purchase the toy in order to be able to sell it at a profit. The needs buyers have for this objective product performance can be referred to as the buyers' objective performance needs.

Product characteristics in each of the three categories can contribute to improving a product's objective performance. For core-quality characteristics, a dishwashing detergent could contain a substance that helps keep spots from forming on dishes. A computer could use a more advanced microprocessor to achieve greater computing speed. A toy manufacturer could incorporate a character licensed from a popular children's television show to make the toy more likely to sell rapidly. For features and styling characteristics, a bottle of liquid window cleaner could be equipped with a powerful spray nozzle, which could increase the cleaner's ability to remove dirt from the window. For reputation and support characteristics, a room air conditioner could come with detailed installation instructions and a support telephone number to help the buyer to fit it tightly into the window—the tighter its fit, the better would be its cooling performance.

That a product's objective performance involves observable facts does not necessarily mean that these facts are easy to observe. For example, it might be difficult to measure precisely the amount of foreign substances that remain on dishes after they have been washed. However, the possibility of such objective measurement distinguishes a product's objective performance from its subjective performance. A product's subjective performance involves results that can be directly evaluated only by the person consuming the product. This distinction is important because when a product's performance can be measured objectively, it presents the possibility that there can also be an objective determination of the value of that performance to the customer.

Need for Hedonic and Aesthetic Performance

There are many consumer products that are purchased not for their objective performance but rather for their subjective performance. Very often, this subjective performance is based on what the consumer experiences as he or she consumes the product. For example, food, beverages, music, art, movies, TV shows, games, plays, poetry, and the styles of clothing, furniture, and automobiles are appreciated largely for the feelings of pleasure they create in the consumer. The more sensual pleasures, such as for food and drink, are often referred to as "hedonic" pleasures, while the pleasures of music, art, literature, and the performing arts are often referred to as "aesthetic." Products and product characteristics that are valued for the hedonic and aesthetic pleasures they create could be said to satisfy the consumer's hedonic/aesthetic performance needs.

Core-quality characteristics can often help satisfy hedonic/aesthetic performance needs. For example, Papa John's claims that better ingredients create better tasting pizza. Movies, plays, and concerts will often advertise widely recognized performers as evidence of having a greater likelihood of satisfying the consumer's hedonic/aesthetic performance needs. When movie theaters offer particularly comfortable seats or outstanding sound systems, these could be considered product features that enhance the consumer's hedonic and aesthetic satisfaction. It is also possible to enhance a product valued primarily for its objective performance by adding features that satisfy needs for hedonic/aesthetic performance. A clock radio could have a sleek, modern design, or a pair of children's shoes could have "fun" shoelaces showing small pictures of popular cartoon characters. Reputation–support characteristics that enhance hedonic/aesthetic performance needs would include favorable brand associations, such as the good feelings one might experience from a familiar can of Campbell's soup.

Need for Social Performance

In addition to hedonic/aesthetic performance needs, an additional area of a product's subjective performance is the degree to which it leads the buyer to experience increased social acceptance or respect from others. Consumers may purchase an automobile or a fashion accessory such as a watch or a handbag not so much for its objective performance or for the pleasure of experiencing it but rather for the effect it is intended to have on the opinions and attitudes of people toward the buyer. Product characteristics valued by a customer for their expected effects on the customer's social image are said to satisfy social performance needs.

Core-quality characteristics can enhance the satisfaction of social performance needs by enabling a product to outperform most others in a way that is visible to the people in the customer's social environment. Thus, an automobile with characteristics that allow it to accelerate faster than others or more effectively negotiate snow or other bad road conditions could lead its customers to feel a pride of ownership. Visible product features could have similar effects. For example, power sliding doors and an on-board television could be prestigious or stylish minivan features. A prestigious automobile brand name could help a customer feel respected by his friends or family members and thus experience greater social performance satisfaction in product ownership.

Need for Performance Reliability

If a product that is purchased to accomplish a particular function fails to perform that function, the failure creates a disruption in the life or business activity of the customer. Such a disruption might be expensive, as was seen in the case of Dewey & Almy in Chapter 2. In addition, such disruptions, or the fear of them, might create anxiety among managers and consumers. The customer's desires to avoid the expenses and anxieties of product inconsistency or failure could be referred to as the customer's performance reliability needs.

Core-quality characteristics can help satisfy customers' performance reliability needs by increasing the consistency and/or duration of the product's performance. Using highly durable materials for product components or instituting more effective quality control processes would decrease the risk that the product will fail. Adding a feature that shows the customer how the product is performing can be effective in minimizing the customer's anxieties. The ability to track online the progress of a package shipped by FedEx is an example of such a feature. A feature such as a tightly reclosable package could enhance the shelf life of a food product and thus help satisfy performance reliability needs. A warranty is an example of a reputation–support characteristic that would help protect buyers against the consequences of a product failure.

Need for Product Convenience

Customers who are interested in the benefits of a product tend to prefer to expend as little effort as possible to receive these benefits. Customers would prefer a product be easy to select, easy to obtain, easy to assemble or install, easy to use, easy to maintain, easy to store, and easy to dispose of when they are finished with it. Product characteristics that reduce the effort involved in receiving the product's benefits are satisfying the customer's product convenience needs.

Core-quality characteristics that lead a product to function with less routine maintenance would help satisfy product convenience needs. Products often have features that make them more convenient to use. For example, a vacuum cleaner could have a spring-loaded retractable power cord, which would make it easier to use than a model where the cord must be wrapped by hand. A product with a familiar brand name could satisfy product convenience needs by making possible an easier product decision process. The availability of 24-hour live customer service for a bank or a large online retailer would be a service support characteristic that would satisfy the customer's product convenience needs.

Framework for Identifying Differentiating Factors

Each of the fifteen cells in the product-needs framework shown in Figure 3.1 illustrates a potential differentiating factor for a product that might need to be priced. Whether the product is being newly developed or modified or is simply new to the organization, this framework can serve as a checklist for identifying possible sources of value to the customer. It is important that the VTC analysis include consideration of all of the customer benefits that can potentially be captured in the product's price.

It should be noted that a particular product characteristic could contribute to satisfying more than one need. For example, superior telephone customer service could impact objective performance, performance reliability, product convenience, and perhaps even social performance needs. Recognizing the full range of needs that could be served can help the seller avoid underestimating the value produced by such a characteristic.

UNDERSTANDING THE INDIVIDUALS
INVOLVED IN THE CUSTOMER'S BUYING DECISION

Because the nature of the customer's needs is so important in identifying differentiating factors and estimating their value, it is important to also understand the various individuals who may be involved in the customer's purchasing decision. Each of these individuals may have different needs, and thus each may differently value any particular differentiating factor. In some cases, it might even be worthwhile to consider the product-needs framework shown in Figure 3.1 separately for each person involved in a purchase decision. In such a case, the set of individuals involved could be considered a third dimension of the framework.

When the customer is a business, there is almost always more than one member of the business organization involved in the decision process. The set of people in the buying organization involved in a business-to-business purchase decision is referred to as the organization's buying center. To help identify these people, it is useful to consider the decision process roles that have been described.[10]

- *User*—those in the organization who use the product
- *Influencer*—specialists, such as engineers, financial analysts, or legal advisors, who have input on the purchase process
- *Gatekeeper*—those who control the flow of information to other members of the purchase process, such as those who decide which companies are invited to submit proposals
- *Decider*—managers, who rule on whether or not the purchase should take place
- *Purchaser*—those in the organization who carry out the purchase

Asking questions, such as who are the users or who are the influencers, helps identify people whose needs should be considered. For example, when Aluminum Corporation of America (Alcoa) was offering to General Motors (GM) a new lighter and stronger aluminum alloy, it recognized that a design engineer in the GM organization (an influencer) would value the new alloy more than GM's production manager (user). For the engineer, proposing the new alloy meant an opportunity to show his resourcefulness. For the production manager, using the new alloy meant changes that could produce problems. By appealing first to the design engineer, Alcoa was able to help the GM organization more fully appreciate the value of the new alloy.[11]

When there is more than one person involved in a consumer purchase, the people involved are usually members of the same household. For example, a wife may be the decider on a new set of dining room furniture while the husband might be an influencer, perhaps pointing out the importance of durability given how the kids (users) tend to treat furniture. General Mills may have considered the differing needs of family members when introducing a new candy product called Fruit by the Foot. Recognizing that kids (users) would appreciate the product's value by experiencing it when sharing snacks with other kids (influencers), it positioned the product as containing fruit, apparently in an attempt to convince moms (deciders) that the product had some benefits over a typical candy.

DETERMINING A DIFFERENTIATING FACTOR'S VALUE BY CONSIDERING MONETARY CONSEQUENCES

Once a differentiating factor has been identified, the next step—the third step in assessing a product's VTC—is to determine the value that the customer places on this differentiating factor. Because this differentiation value will be used to set a price, it needs to be expressed in monetary terms. As mentioned in Chapter 2, there are two approaches to determining the value of a differentiating factor in monetary terms. The first is to identify the monetary consequences of the factor for the customer, such as additional savings, profits, and/or expenditures caused by the factor. The second approach is to use market research to measure how customers trade off product benefits against price. A commonly used market research technique to measure such trade-offs—conjoint analysis—is discussed in the next section.

To identify the monetary consequences of a differentiating factor, it is important to consider and explore the customer's needs relating to the product. If a product has a characteristic not possessed by its next closest substitute that results in a customer benefit, then it is useful to consider the question, "What money would be gained by the customer from receiving this benefit?" The Dewey & Almy case discussed in Chapter 2 illustrated how understanding the cost-saving consequences of their printing blanket's greater resiliency could make possible a monetary estimation of the value of that benefit.

The question of what money would be gained by the customer from receiving a differentiating benefit can also be useful in determining differentiation values for consumer products. For example, if the more effective cleaning mechanism of a home carpet shampoo steamer enables the product to remove types of carpet odors that cannot be removed by the product's next closest substitute (such as odors from pet "accidents"), it could be asked why this differential odor removal ability is important to consumers. Suppose that interviews with consumers indicated that the persistence of unwanted odors leads many consumers to have their rugs cleaned by a professional carpet cleaning service, at an average price of $250 per cleaning. Suppose further that these interviews indicated that the home carpet shampoo steamer would save these consumers an average of three such professional cleanings over the life span of the product. With such understanding of the consumer's monetary savings, the positive differentiation value of the shampoo steamer's more effective cleaning mechanism could be calculated: $3 \times \$250 = \$750$.

Quantifying Uncertainty

It is often the case that there is uncertainty involved in the monetary consequences of a differentiating factor. To estimate such monetary consequences, it is helpful to quantify this uncertainty. A probability is a means of quantifying uncertainty. It is a measure of the likelihood of an event expressed as the ratio of the number of occurrences of the event to the number of instances when the event could have occurred. For example, if a coin comes up heads fifty times in a set of one hundred flips, then our measure of the probability of a flip of that coin coming up heads would be 0.5. Because it is a ratio, a probability will always be a number ranging between zero and one. However, in common speech, probabilities are often referred to in the form of percents, such as "there is a 50 percent chance of the coin flip coming up heads."

To illustrate how probabilities could be useful in estimating the monetary consequences of a differentiating factor, consider the price-setting task of a clothing manufacturer who must set the price of a basic cotton–acrylic sweater being offered to clothing retailers for the winter selling season. The manufacturer's competitor offers the next closest substitute, a sweater priced at $10 per unit. The manufacturer not only recognizes that $10 is his reference value but also notes that efficient production processes enable him to offer a clothing retailer a very short order lead time. Order lead time is the duration between when an order is placed and when the merchandise is received. The manufacturer can offer clothing retailers a five-week lead time, whereas his competitor's lead time is fifteen weeks. The manufacturer knows his shorter lead time is a positive differentiating factor and would like to assess the value of this factor.

The manufacturer's sales force provides input to this value assessment process by explaining to management what they have learned about the needs of the customers they call on—mostly large retail chains. The typical clothing retailer values a shorter order lead time because of the uncertainty of product demand. If a retailer would like to sell a sweater during the winter selling season (November through January), then a fifteen-week lead time would mean that the retailer would have to place the order by mid-July, well before the retailer would know the particular sweater colors, fabrics, and patterns that will be popular in the coming season.

In terms of the manufacturer's sweaters, this demand uncertainty is illustrated in Figure 3.2. If a retailer estimates that consumer demand will be 130 sweaters per store and plans a $20 selling price for the sweaters purchased at a cost of $10 per unit, then the retailer's gross margin on the sweaters would be $1,300 per store. Recognizing the uncertainty of consumer demand, the retailer might judge that there is a 0.4 probability of the 130-sweater estimate being correct, a 0.3 probability that demand for the sweaters would be half-again higher (i.e., 195 sweaters), and a 0.3 probability that demand would be half-again lower (i.e., 65 sweaters).

In the case of the fifteen-week order lead time of the manufacturer's competitor, the higher demand scenario would lead to a stock-out situation, and the per-store profit would still be only $1,300. The lower demand scenario would lead to sixty-five unsold sweaters—if (for simplicity) it is assumed that the extra costs of handling the those sweaters would balance the revenue from a postseason clearance sale, the per-store profit in that situation would be $0.

However, the manufacturer's five-week order lead time would allow the retailer to order only sixty-five sweaters for the start of the season and then consider further purchases after observing the first few weeks of consumer demand. If early demand were half-again higher than estimated, 130 additional sweaters could be ordered and sold, resulting in a per-store profit of $1,950. If early demand were half-again lower, then only sixty-five sweaters per store would have been purchased, resulting in a per-store profit of $650.

Figure 3.2 Determining the Monetary Consequences to a Clothing Retailer of a Shorter Order Lead Time

Lead Time	Consumer Demand	Number Bought	Cost	Selling Price	Gross Margin	Probability	Gross Margin × Prob.	Number Bought × Prob.
15 weeks	Higher	130	$10	$20	$1,300	0.3	$390	
	As estimated	130	$10	$20	$1,300	0.4	$520	
	Lower	130	$10	$20	$0	0.3	$0	
Expected value							*$910*	
5 weeks	Higher	195	$10	$20	$1,950	0.3	$585	58.5
	As estimated	130	$10	$20	$1,300	0.4	$520	52
	Lower	65	$10	$20	$650	0.3	$195	19.5
Expected values							*$1,300*	*130*
5 weeks	Higher	195	$13	$20	$1,365	0.3	$409.50	
	As estimated	130	$13	$20	$910	0.4	$364	
	Lower	65	$13	$20	$455	0.3	$136.50	
Expected value							*$910*	

Translating Probabilities Into Profits

Applying this type of detailed understanding of customer needs to arrive at an estimate of monetary consequences requires the concept of the expected value of a variable, often known simply as expected value. The expected value of a variable is the long-run average of the variable. It is equal to the sum of each possible value of the variable multiplied by the probability of that value occurring.

As an example, consider the coin mentioned previously that we measured as having a 0.5 probability of coming up heads. Suppose the variable of interest is what you will receive from a flip of this coin. If you get $10 when a flip comes up heads and $0 when it comes up tails, then the expected value of what you will receive from a flip of this coin equals the outcome of the flip coming up heads (gain $10) times the probability of this outcome occurring (0.5) plus the outcome of the flip coming up tails (gain $0) times the probability of that outcome occurring (0.5). Thus, the expected value of what you will receive from a coin flip would be $5 [($10 × 0.5) + ($0 × 0.5)]. You could conclude from this that paying any price below $5 for a flip of this coin would lead you to benefit in the long run.

In this discussion of the use of expected values in determining differentiation values, it is helpful to keep in mind that the word *value* is being used here in two different senses. In expected values, the word *value* means what a variable could equal. In differentiation values, the word *value* means the customer benefits (or lack of them) associated with a differentiating factor.

In the case of the sweater manufacturer who can offer clothing retailers a shorter order lead time, the use of expected values enables the profit advantage of the five-week lead time to be represented by a single number. The column in Figure 3.2 labeled "Gross Margin × Prob." shows the profit at a particular level of consumer demand multiplied by the probability that such a demand level occurs. Adding these for each of the three possible levels of consumer demand gives the expected value of the retailer's profits from buying the sweaters for $10 per unit from a particular vendor. If the sweaters were purchased from the competitor with a fifteen-week order lead time, the clothing retailer's expected profit would be $910 per store. If the sweaters were purchased from the manufacturer with the five-week order lead time, the retailer's expected profit would be $1,300 per store. The difference, $390, is an estimate of the monetary consequence—and thus the differentiation value—of the shorter lead time differentiating factor.

To use the per-store differentiation value for setting a per-sweater price, it is necessary to know how many sweaters would be purchased by a store. Although with the five-week order lead time the number of sweaters purchased would depend on consumer demand during the first few weeks of the selling season, the expected value of the number of sweaters that the retailer would purchase can be calculated (see the rightmost column of Figure 3.2). This calculation indicates that with the five-week lead time, the manufacturer could expect, on average, the purchase of 130 sweaters per store. Dividing the $390 of added profit among these 130 sweaters gives a positive differentiation value of $3 per sweater.

To check this calculation of the positive differentiation value of the shorter lead time, the lower section of Figure 3.2 shows what would happen if the manufacturer took the entire added value to the retail customer in the form of a higher price. By selling the sweaters at $13 per unit, the retailer's expected profit would then be, not $1,300, but the same $910 per-store profit that the retailer could expect if the sweaters were purchased from the vendor with the fifteen-week lead time. This analysis is useful only as a check of logic and calculations. As mentioned in Chapter 2, it is not advisable to try to capture the entire amount of the customer value created by an offered product.

DETERMINING A DIFFERENTIATING FACTOR'S VALUE BY MEASURING CUSTOMER TRADE-OFFS

Although considering monetary consequences is useful for determining the value of differentiating factors that satisfy objective performance needs, many differentiating factors satisfy subjective needs (such as needs for hedonic/aesthetic or social performance) or involve the customer's subjective perceptions of product risk and effort. In these cases, it is usually difficult or impossible to determine the monetary consequences of the differentiating factor. For such differentiating factors, it is often more appropriate to determine their value by measuring how customers trade off product benefits against price. As mentioned in Chapter 2, this can be done through systematic observation of past customer choices or through survey methods.

Conjoint Analysis

Perhaps the most commonly used of the survey methods is conjoint analysis, which is also known as trade-off analysis.[12] Conjoint analysis involves carrying out a study where a set of possible alternative products are presented or described to respondents and the respondents are asked to rate, rank, or choose among these alternative products. The alternatives could be real competing products or fictitious alternative products developed for the purpose of the study.

Each of the alternative products in a conjoint analysis is defined by two or more attributes, which serve as variables in the study. In fact, the term *conjoint* comes from the alternative products being defined by several attributes *"considered jointly."* When conjoint analysis is used to measure the value of differentiating factors, one of these attributes must be price.

Each attribute used to define an alternative product has at least two levels. Each level is a specific example of the attribute. Thus, in a study of laundry detergents, the product attribute of the detergent's formulation might have these levels: "contains enzymes" and "does not contain enzymes." The product attribute of the detergent's brand in such a study might have three levels, say, "Tide," "Bold," and "President's Choice" (a retailer brand). The price attribute may have the two levels: $2.49 and $2.99 (see Figure 3.3).

A key advantage of conjoint analysis is that it presents respondents with relatively realistic trade-off scenarios. Asking respondents directly how much they would pay for enzymes in their laundry detergent is a difficult question. It is not the type of judgment people usually make, and it tempts the respondent to understate what they would pay, since one's preference would always be to pay less rather than more. By contrast, a conjoint study asks respondents to compare alternative products. Comparing products is a familiar task that most people can do easily, and it is more difficult for a respondent to purposely manipulate his or her responses. If the set of alternative products in the study is properly designed and analyzed, the respondents' choices can reveal subjective judgments such as the amount of money that they would trade off for the inclusion of enzymes in their laundry detergent.

Figure 3.3   Set of Alternative Products for Laundry Detergent Conjoint Study

Formulation	Brand	Price
No enzyme	Tide	$2.49
No enzyme	Tide	$2.99
No enzyme	Bold	$2.49
No enzyme	Bold	$2.99
No enzyme	President's Choice	$2.49
No enzyme	President's Choice	$2.99
Enzyme	Tide	$2.49
Enzyme	Tide	$2.99
Enzyme	Bold	$2.49
Enzyme	Bold	$2.99
Enzyme	President's Choice	$2.49
Enzyme	President's Choice	$2.99

Designing the Alternative Products

In the simple form of conjoint analysis that we will discuss here, the set of alternative products in a study will be those necessary for including every combination of the levels of every attribute in the study. Thus, for the laundry detergent study previously mentioned, the set of alternative products that includes every combination of levels of every attribute would be the twelve alternative products shown in Figure 3.3. In general, the number of alternative products that include all combinations can be calculated by multiplying the number of levels of each of the attributes. In this study,

2 levels of formulation × 3 levels of brand × 2 levels of price = 12 alternative products

Fielding the Research Questionnaire

When the set of alternative products has been identified, a questionnaire is developed to present these alternatives to respondents. Each alternative could be described in words, or the alternatives could be illustrated by drawings. In elaborate studies where prototype products have been constructed, each alternative product is actually presented to the respondents. The respondents could be asked to rate the alternative products, to rank them, or to choose among each possible pair of alternative products. It is generally best to present the alternative products to respondents in a random order.

The questionnaires should be administered to a sample of respondents who will be considered to represent the customers in the market or market segment of interest. Thus, for the laundry detergent study, the questionnaire might be administered to several hundred homemakers across the United States selected by one of several possible random sampling techniques.

Analyzing the Responses

In the simple form of conjoint analysis that is being presented here, the respondents will respond by providing a preference ranking for each of the alternative products in a set. To help keep the analysis simple, the highest number rank will represent the *most* preferred alternative product in the set, and the lowest number rank will represent the *least* preferred alternative.

These rankings can then be analyzed using multiple regression, a statistical procedure for examining the relationships between variables in a data set. In multiple regression, the variable we want to explain is known as the dependent variable (DV). In this case, the respondents' preference rankings of the alternative products would be the DV. A variable that may affect the DV is known as an independent variable (IV). When the regression technique is referred to as "multiple" (as it is here), the analysis considers more than one IV. In this case, the IVs would be formed from price and the product attributes investigated in the study.

The multiple regression procedure requires the construction of a rectangular array of numbers, which is referred to as a data matrix. In the conjoint analysis being presented here, there is one row in the data matrix for each preference ranking that is given by a respondent. Thus, if 100 respondents each ranked the twelve alternative products, there would be 1,200 rows in the data matrix. Each column in the data matrix contains a variable in the study. In this case, the rightmost column in the data matrix will contain the DV. All of the other columns in the data matrix will contain the study's IVs.

Coding refers to how the variables in a study are converted into numbers. For the analysis to be done correctly, it is important that each of the variables in the study be coded correctly. This study's DV, the preference rankings, can be entered into the data matrix without any coding. The level of an alternative's price attribute can be entered as an IV into the data matrix. Because price is expressed in meaningful units—that is, dollars—it can also be entered into the data matrix without coding.

The two product attributes in this study, formulation and brand, will require some coding. To make the results easy to interpret, these are best coded using only 0s and 1s. This is known as dummy-variable coding; 1 indicates that an attribute of interest exists, and 0 indicates that it does not exist. The formulation attribute has two levels: (1) enzymes and (2) no enzymes. If we assume that having enzymes (as opposed to not having them) is the differentiating factor of interest, then it would make sense to code the formulation IV so that having enzymes = 1 and not having enzymes = 0. With this coding, we could estimate the value consumers place on a laundry detergent having enzymes rather than not having them.

The brand attribute has these levels—Tide, Bold, and President's Choice. To use dummy-variable coding for this three-level attribute, it is necessary to use two IVs to include the attribute. The first of the two IVs would be whether the brand is Tide (coded as 1) or not Tide (coded as 0). The second of the two IVs would be whether the brand is Bold (coded as 1) or not Bold (coded as 0). Since an alternative product cannot be both Tide and Bold, the Tide and Bold variables will never both be coded as 1 on the same data line. With this coding, we could estimate the value consumers place on a laundry detergent being Tide (versus Bold or President's Choice) and being Bold (versus Tide or President's Choice).

With this coding, there would be five variables in the data matrix: four IVs (Tide, Bold, enzyme, price) and the DV (preference rank). An example of how the first few data lines might look can be seen in Figure 3.4. These data would indicate that the respondent in this example gave Tide with enzymes priced at $2.49 the rank of 11 (second best), gave President's Choice with enzymes priced at $2.49 a rank of 8, and gave Bold with enzymes priced at $2.49 a rank of 10.

Figure 3.4   Example of First Few Lines of Laundry Detergent Conjoint Study Data Matrix

Tide	Bold	Enzyme	Price	Respondent's Preference Ranking
1	0	1	$2.49	11
0	0	1	$2.49	8
0	1	1	$2.49	10
1	0	1	$2.99	7
0	0	1	$2.99	1

There are a number of software packages that can run a multiple regression. Perhaps the most accessible is Excel. To use regression to analyze conjoint data in Excel 2007, bring the data matrix into the spreadsheet. On the Data tab, select Data Analysis (if Data Analysis does not appear as a choice, select Add-Ins under Excel Options and under Manage Excel Add-ins, check Analysis ToolPak). When the Data Analysis dialog box appears, select Regression. For the "Y range," enter the endpoints for the column in the data matrix that contains the DV (the preference rankings in this case). For the "X range," enter the endpoints for the rectangle containing the IVs (in this case, the columns containing the variables Tide, Bold, enzyme, and price). It is handy to also include the column labels in the Y and X ranges and then check "Labels." When the ranges are entered, click on OK to actually carry out the regression.

As an example, part of a data matrix and an Excel regression dialog box can be seen in Figure 3.5. In this example, fifteen respondents each ranked the twelve alternative products to produce a data matrix with 180 rows. Because the DV (rankings) is in column F, the Y range would be F1:F181 (the first row contains the column labels). Because the IVs are in columns B through E, the X range would be B1:E181. The column labeled "Line" contains the data matrix line numbers. Strictly speaking, such line numbers are not part of the data matrix and should not be included in the regression analysis.

Figure 3.5   Example of Regression Dialog Box for a Conjoint Analysis Using Excel 2007

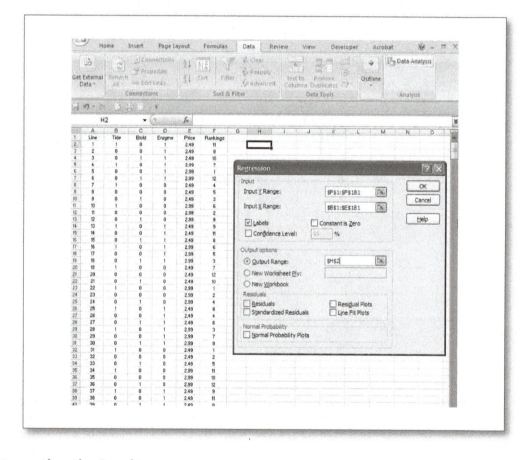

Interpreting the Results

In Figure 3.6, you can see the Excel regression output of the data matrix and dialog box shown in Figure 3.5. Pay particular attention to the coefficients of this study's four IVs, Tide, Bold, enzyme, and price. The regression coefficient for each of these variables represents a measure of the relative utility, or benefit, of that variable.

Figure 3.6   Excel 2007 Output for Regression Analysis

SUMMARY OUTPUT

Regression Statistics	
Multiple R	0.691
R Square	0.478
Adjusted R Square	0.466
Standard Error	2.529
Observations	180

ANOVA

	df	SS	MS	F	Significance F
Regression	4	1025.511	256.378	40.077	0.000
Residual	175	1119.489	6.397		
Total	179	2145.000			

	Coefficients	Standard Error	t Stat	P-value	Lower 95%	Upper 95%
Intercept	29.745	2.100	14.162	0.000	25.600	33.890
Tide	1.500	0.462	3.248	0.001	0.589	2.411
Bold	-0.100	0.462	-0.217	0.829	-1.011	0.811
Enzyme	1.044	0.377	2.770	0.006	0.300	1.789
Price	-8.844	0.754	-11.729	0.000	-10.333	-7.356

The positive sign of the Tide coefficient indicates that the presence of the Tide brand was preferred over its absence. The positive sign of the enzyme coefficient indicates that the enzyme formulation was preferred over the formulation without enzymes. Although the Bold coefficient is negative, note that the lower 95 percent and upper 95 percent range of that coefficient includes 0. This indicates that this conjoint study failed to provide evidence of a preference either in favor of, or against, the Bold brand.

The negative sign of the price coefficient indicates that the lower price ($2.49) was preferred over the higher one ($2.99). Further—and this is what makes conjoint analysis well-suited for measuring the value of a differentiating factor—the size of each coefficient is a measure of the size of the customer's preference. Thus, the price coefficient being a larger size than the enzyme coefficient indicates that the respondents valued a price lower by one unit (i.e., by $1) more than the presence of enzymes. We can conclude from this that the presence of enzymes is worth less than $1 to customers. In fact, with the coding used in this example, we can get a precise measure of the value of including enzymes (or the value of any product attribute) by using the following formula (the vertical lines indicate the absolute value; a number's absolute value is its value with any negative signs ignored):

$$\text{Value of a product attribute} = \frac{|\text{coefficient of that product attribute}|}{|\text{coefficient of price}|}$$

For the enzyme variable in this study, its value to customers would be $0.12 ($ = 1.044/8.844$). Thus, these results would provide a measure in monetary terms of the value of the presence of enzymes as a differentiating factor in a laundry detergent.

Although the accuracy of this estimate would depend on the realism of the alternative products used in this study (as well as on other factors), the ability to arrive at a monetary value estimate based on customer perceptions makes conjoint analysis an important tool for determining the value of a differentiating factor.

ASSEMBLING THE VALUE-TO-THE-CUSTOMER ESTIMATE

One of the main benefits of the framework for identifying differentiating factors that is proposed in this chapter is that it helps the price setter keep in mind that there are likely to be not just one or two but many factors that differentiate his or her product from the product's next closest substitute. Although the examples in this chapter have emphasized positive differentiating factors, it will frequently be the case that in one or more ways, the price setter's product will present the customer with disadvantages, rather than benefits, over competing products. As was mentioned in Chapter 2, the identification of negative differentiating factors can be as important for effective price setting as the identification of positive ones. Also, it is important to note that the methods for determining a factor's value are as appropriate for negative differentiating factors as for positive ones.

Further, the likely involvement of many differentiating factors in any one VTC estimate suggests that more than one value estimation method would often be involved. For those differentiating factors that satisfy objective performance needs, some efforts to estimate monetary consequences would be appropriate. For those differentiating factors that satisfy subjective performance needs or subjective perceptions of product reliability and/or convenience, then some measurement of customer trade-offs—whether by looking at past customer choices or survey responses—would be useful. The importance of assessing a product's VTC when setting an initial price suggests that it would be worthwhile to invest both careful thought and organizational resources into accomplishing this assessment.

SUMMARY

Identifying a product's differentiating factors and estimating the monetary value of these factors to customers are essential steps in assessing a product's VTC. To identify differentiating factors, it is helpful to have a framework to suggest the range of factors possible. One such framework crosses types of product characteristics—core quality, features–styling, and reputation–support—by types of customer needs—objective performance, hedonic/aesthetic performance, social performance, performance reliability, and product convenience. These two dimensions result in a fifteen-cell framework that can serve as a checklist for identifying possible sources of value to a customer.

The usefulness of this framework can sometimes be enhanced by considering it separately for each of the individuals involved in the purchase process. For business customers, such involved individuals could be users, influencers, gatekeepers, deciders, and purchasers. For consumer purchases, each member of the household may be involved in the purchase process.

The value of a differentiating factor can be determined by identifying the factor's monetary consequences or by measuring how customers trade off the factor's benefit against price. Monetary consequences include the additional savings, profits, and/or expenditures caused by the differentiating factor. Probabilities and expected values are often useful in estimating these monetary consequences.

Conjoint analysis is a widely used method to measure how customers trade off a differentiating factor's benefits against price. In a conjoint analysis study, respondents are given descriptions of products showing price and several product attributes and are asked to rate, rank, or choose among these product descriptions. The product attributes are chosen so that the respondent must make trade-offs between, say, higher prices and the presence of desirable product attributes. Statistical analysis of the respondent's preferences using multiple regression makes it possible to assign a dollar value to the respondents' interest in each of the product attributes studied.

KEY TERMS

core-quality characteristics	subjective performance	attributes
features and styling characteristics	hedonic/aesthetic performance needs	levels multiple regression
reputation and support service characteristics	social performance needs performance reliability needs	dependent variable independent variable
need	product convenience needs	data matrix
consumer products	buying center	coding
business products	conjoint analysis	dummy-variable coding
objective performance	probability	
objective performance needs	expected value	

REVIEW AND DISCUSSION QUESTIONS

1. Describe the three types of product characteristics discussed in the chapter. Give some examples of each type.

2. Human needs are very diverse. Why is it useful to classify product-related needs into a small set of categories?

3. What is the difference between objective performance of a product and the subjective performance of a product? What are the implications of this difference for the measurement of the value of a performance difference between two products?

4. Give some examples of products valued mostly for their hedonic and/or aesthetic performance.

5. A cell phone is a product that helps people interact socially with other people. Does that mean that a cell phone is a product that will always satisfy consumer needs for social performance? Explain your reasoning.

6. Give an example of both monetary costs and emotional costs related to the possibility of a product failing to perform as expected.

7. A product can satisfy customers' convenience needs by being easy to purchase. What are some other ways that a product could satisfy customers' need for product convenience?

8. Choose a particular consumer product that you are familiar with and use the fifteen-cell product-needs framework described in the chapter as a checklist to indicate ways this product may differ from its next closest substitute.

9. What is an organization's buying center? Describe the five main buying-center roles that have been identified.

10. Explain how awareness of an organization's buying center or the involvement of household members in a consumer decision could affect the process of estimating a product's VTC.

11. Describe the two general approaches to determining the value of a differentiating factor in monetary terms.

12. The chapter gives the example of a shorter order lead time being a clothing manufacturer's differentiating factor. In terms of the product-needs framework described in the chapter, what type of product characteristic is this? In the example, what type of customer need is involved?

13. If there is a 25 percent chance that a new machine would save a business customer $24 per day in labor costs and a 75 percent chance that the new machine would save the customer $12 per day, use the concept of expected value to estimate the per-day monetary consequences of this new machine for the business customer.

14. What aspect of conjoint analysis makes it a more effective means of determining the value of a product feature than directly asking respondents how much they would pay for the feature?

15. If a conjoint study of a food product involves three levels of price, two levels of brand, and three levels of fiber content, what is the total number of product descriptions that could be rated by respondents in the study?

16. For the conjoint study described in the previous question, identify the IVs. Give an example of what could be used as a DV in the study.

17. If each respondent in a conjoint study rated sixteen products and there were 200 respondents in the study, how many rows would there be in the data matrix resulting from the study?

18. What is dummy-variable coding? Would it be appropriate to use dummy-variable coding to code the price variable in a conjoint study designed to estimate the monetary value of a product attribute?

19. If the regression output of a conjoint analysis indicates that the regression coefficient for presence of Feature A is 2.46 and the regression coefficient for price (coded in dollars) is −1.23, what would be the estimate of the monetary value of the presence of Feature A?

EXERCISES

1. Imagine that you are a member of a new-project team of a large appliance manufacturer. Your team is given the task of designing a new refrigerator for the U.S. consumer market.

    (a) For each of the five types of consumer needs discussed in this chapter, give a suggestion for how a new refrigerator could satisfy that need better than most currently available refrigerators.

    (b) For two of the suggestions you made in Part (a), discuss which of the three types of product characteristics might best accomplish this better satisfaction of the consumer need.

2. In 2010, the Center for Science in the Public Interest reported a study on the popular 100-calorie packs of branded snack foods, such as Doritos, Cheez-Its, and Oreos. They found that the per-ounce prices of these 100-calorie packs were 16 to 279 percent higher than the per-ounce prices of the regular-sized packages of these products. Use the product-needs framework described in this chapter to suggest the differentiating factors that could have created sufficient customer value to make these higher prices possible.

3. The Loctite Corporation, a large adhesives producer, makes a wide variety of products for both industrial and consumer markets. One of Loctite's industrial products is Quick Set Instant Adhesive. It is described in their catalog as follows:

    A particularly powerful instant adhesive especially suited for equipment maintenance and repair. Typical applications include rubber belts, bumpers and O-rings; metal handles, parts and wires; plastic nameplates, signs and trim.

    (a) Give the title of the person in a manufacturing company (that would be a potential Loctite customer) who would be most likely to value Quick Set Instant Adhesive. What role is that person likely to play in the adhesives purchase process? How might knowing that role affect Loctite's efforts to price Quick Set Instant Adhesive so as to capture a large portion of its VTC?

    (b) One of Loctite's consumer products is Loctite Super Glue Liquid. It is described as follows:

    Uses a new formulation that affords super glue users increased working time, eliminating the need to rush and reducing the risk of mistakes when gluing. This allows for repositioning and precision alignment of surfaces, making it ideal for use on items such as porcelain dolls, china, and jewelry.

Who in a consumer household would be most likely to value Loctite Super Glue Liquid? What role is that person likely to play in the adhesives purchase process? How might knowing that role affect Loctite's efforts to price Super Glue Liquid so as to capture a large portion of its VTC?

4. A large information technology (IT) company sells a software product designed to help protect an organization's data. The company's market research has determined that hospitals and other medical organizations in its market area have a 1.3 percent chance of losing some of a patient's data over a five-year period. With the IT company's software, the chances of patient data loss for a five-year period are reduced to 0.12 percent.

Further, the market research has determined that, when patient data loss occurs, there is a 15 percent chance that the organization will lose the patient's business and a 0.75 percent chance that a lawsuit will result. The average cost of losing a patient's business is $600 in promotion expenses and other start-up costs to acquire a new patient. The average cost of a lawsuit is $100,000.

Given these research findings, calculate the value of this data-protection benefit of the IT company's software product to a medical organization that keeps data records on 20,000 patients.

5. The marketing manager of an automobile battery manufacturer is considering the prices that should be set for some new additions to the company's product line. The Basic is the standard model, which sells to consumers for $54. The Security is a new model that features power drain protection—the ability to turn off sources of excessive battery drain, such as headlights left on when the vehicle is parked. The Security Plus is a new model that features not only power drain protection but also includes a small backup battery that will start a car three to five times if the primary battery goes dead for any reason.

The manager commissioned a conjoint study in which 300 automobile owners were asked to rank their preferences among a set of alternative batteries, each containing different features and prices. Dummy-variable coding was used for the power-drain protection and backup battery variables. The price variable was coded in dollars. A regression analysis on the responses of these consumers produced the following regression coefficients:

Variable	Coefficient
Presence of power drain protection	11.31
Presence of backup battery	23.08
Price	−0.82

(a) Based on this data, calculate an appropriate price to retailers for the Security model. Assume that retailers take a 40 percent gross margin on car batteries.

(b) Based on this data, calculate an appropriate price to retailers for the Security Plus model. Again, assume that retailers take a 40 percent gross margin on car batteries.

NOTES

1. William M. Pride and O. C. Ferrell, *Marketing,* 14th ed. (Boston: Houghton Mifflin, 2008), 338–341.
2. Philip Kotler, *Marketing Management,* 10th ed., (Upper Saddle River, NJ: Prentice Hall, 2000), 394–395.
3. David A. Aaker, *Managing Brand Equity* (New York: The Free Press, 1991).
4. Theodore Levitt, "Marketing Success Through Differentiation—of Anything," *Harvard Business Review* (January–February 1980).
5. The conception of a need as a force is based on Henry A. Murray, *Explorations in Personality* (New York: Oxford University Press, 1938), 123–124.
6. Morris B. Holbrook and Elizabeth C. Hirschman, "The Experiential Aspects of Consumption: Consumer Fantasies, Feelings, and Fun," *Journal of Consumer Research* 9 (September 1982): 132–140.
7. Thorstein Veblen, *The Theory of the Leisure Class* (1899; repr., Boston: Houghton Mifflin, 1973).
8. Ivan Ross, "Perceived Risk and Consumer Behavior," ed. Mary Jane Schlinger, Association for Consumer Research, *Advances in Consumer Research* 2, (1975): 1–20.
9. Judith Lynne Zaichkowsky, "Measuring the Involvement Construct," *Journal of Consumer Research* 12 (December 1985): 341–352.
10. Frederick E. Webster and Yoram Wind, "A General Model for Understanding Organizational Buying Behavior," *Journal of Marketing* 36 (April 1972): 12–19.
11. Kenneth R. Davis (1981), "Case 4-2: Aluminum Company of America," *Marketing Management: Text and Cases,* 4th ed. (New York: Wiley, 1981), 161–182.
12. Phillipe Cattin and Dick R. Wittink, "Commercial Use of Conjoint Analysis: A Survey," *Journal of Marketing* 46 (Summer 1982), 44–53.

CHAPTER 4

Basic Pricing Strategies and the Use of Breakeven Analysis

In the marketing approach to setting an initial price, customer needs, and in particular the product's value to the customer, should start the price-setting process. Although this information should be considered first, it is not the only type of information that needs to be considered. In this chapter, we discuss how to combine customer-need information with considerations of product costs, marketplace pricing strategies, and factors that drive these pricing strategies. Following that, we discuss the use of breakeven analysis in evaluating an initial price.

CONSIDERING COSTS IN SETTING INITIAL PRICES

Although we introduced the discussion of product costs when we covered cost-based pricing in Chapter 2, our further consideration of costs requires making the important distinction between fixed and variable costs. An organization's fixed costs are those that do not vary with changes in the number of product units that are sold (see the first graph in Figure 4.1). Examples of fixed costs include executives' salaries, depreciation on the plant and equipment, interest on debt, rent for facilities, insurance, general administration costs, and advertising costs. An organization's variable costs vary directly with the number of product units that are sold (see the second graph in Figure 4.1). Examples of variable costs include direct labor costs, costs of materials, shipping costs, and sales commissions. Note that, for price-setting purposes, the identification of costs as fixed or variable depends on how they behave with respect to changes in the number of product units that are sold.

Calculating Per-Unit Costs

A product's price is typically expressed as a per-unit quantity. For example, a bakery's price for bread will usually be an amount per loaf, a gasoline retailer will display a price per gallon, and an appliance store will charge a certain amount per washing machine or refrigerator.

Figure 4.1   Fixed Costs and Variable Costs Are Distinguished By Their Behavior With Respect to Unit Sales

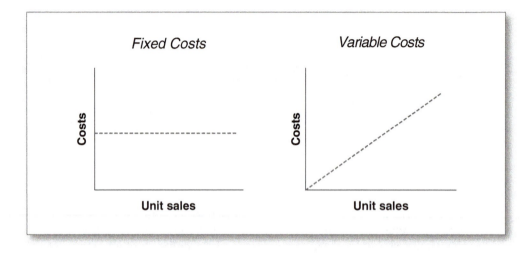

The units used might vary—a lawyer might charge a certain fee per hour or be on retainer for a certain amount per year—but either way, prices are expressed per unit.

Given the per-unit nature of price, managers responsible for considering costs when setting prices tend to find it desirable to have a per-unit measure of costs. This is not a problem for variable costs. Since they vary directly with the number of units sold, their per-unit values can be calculated easily. For example, if a workshop that sells 600 units of a product per week incurs $12,000 per week in material and labor costs, then the variable costs for that product would equal $12,000/600, or $20 per unit.

Fixed costs, on the other hand, are often more difficult to translate into per-unit values. One could always simply divide, say, the costs of the head office staff by the number of items the company sells. But if the company sells both paper clips and large copying machines, it would seem that each copying machine should be given a larger amount of the office staff costs than each paper clip. Accountants, of course, have developed numerous cost allocation methods that attempt to minimize arbitrariness. However, the allocation of fixed costs among the individual items sold is not necessary for price-setting purposes—nor is it even desirable.

The Advantage of Leaving Fixed Costs Out of Per-Unit Costs

Consider the case of the electrical parts manufacturer who tried to enter the market for compact power supplies for computers. He developed a line of high-quality power supplies and priced them at a very modest markup over his fully allocated costs. In other words, each item's price was determined by applying the markup to the total of the item's variable costs and the item's share of the company's fixed costs. When the manufacturer investigated why his power supplies were not selling well, he discovered that his main competitor, who also produced high-quality products, was underselling him by a considerable amount. This puzzled the manufacturer because he knew that his competitor's costs were similar to his own.

The mystery was solved a few months later when the manufacturer hired one of the managers of the competing company. The manager explained that the competitor's CEO also favored modest markups but ended up with low prices because he applied the markup percentages to only the product's variable costs. He believed that as long as a product's price was higher than its variable costs, the product was contributing something to covering fixed costs. If he could sell enough of the product, these contributions would mount up and eventually more than cover fixed costs to produce a bottom-line profit. At the competitively low price he was charging, the CEO easily was able to sell enough power supplies to accomplish this profitability.

There is of course no guarantee that leaving fixed costs out of a product's per-unit costs will eventually result in profitability. However, this story illustrates that leaving fixed costs out of management's conception of per-unit cost increases management's pricing flexibility. If properly used, this flexibility should increase the likelihood of setting profit-maximizing prices.

BOUNDS OF THE TYPICAL PRICE

We are now in a position to identify the range within which a price should normally be set. The high end of this range is the product's value to the customer (VTC), determined from consideration of the customer's needs. Because the VTC is the maximum amount that the buyer, when fully informed, would pay, one can expect that sales will amount to zero if a price exceeds the product's VTC. A price equal to a product's VTC is simply the highest practical price.

What, then, should be the lower end of the range within which a price should be set? It makes sense for this lower bound to be the product's variable costs. As was the view of the CEO of the successful power supply competitor, any price above a product's variable costs will contribute to covering the organization's fixed costs. If enough of the product is sold, any level of contribution could be sufficient to first cover fixed costs and then go on to produce net profit. Thus, any price above the product's variable costs could be a viable price. This, then, is a way that costs can start to be considered in the pricing decision.

To say that a product's variable costs comprise the lower bound of its price is not to say that there are no circumstances when a manager might consider setting a price below that bound. It is just to say that the level of a product's variable costs is the lower end of its price range that should be considered under typical circumstances. Setting a price below a product's variable costs means that the seller will lose money on every item that is sold. This can work only if there is some benefit that can make up for these losses. One such benefit can arise if a company's products are interrelated such that sales of one will cause sales of another. If money is lost on sales of the first product, it could be more than made up by profits on the second product. A second benefit that could make up for losses on every item sold is the possibility that such a low price will deter or drive out competition and enable later prices to be higher than otherwise would have been possible. These concepts will be discussed in later chapters (Chapters 13 and 15) but for now should be considered exceptions to typical circumstances.

A product's VTC forms the upper bound of its price, which can be referred to as its price ceiling.[1] In typical situations, the level of a product's variable costs forms the lower bound of its price, which can be referred to as its price floor (see Figure 4.2). The product's price should be set somewhere in between these two bounds. Simply knowing this is a step forward in the pricing process. For example, if there turns out to be very little space between these bounds, then the product's price should be set right in that spot. In such a case, the process of setting the product's initial price is largely done! However, when there is a substantial range between these bounds, then simply knowing them leaves open the important question of where within these bounds should the price be initially set. This decision is largely dependent on pricing strategy considerations, which is discussed next.

Figure 4.2   Bounds of the Typical Price

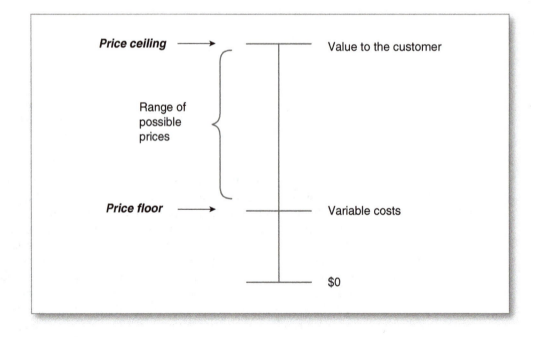

BASIC STRATEGIES FOR SETTING AN INITIAL PRICE

In a classic paper first published in 1950, Joel Dean described two basic strategies for the pricing of newly developed products.[2] The skimming strategy involves setting a price so high that most potential customers will decline to buy the new product. Although unit sales of a skim-priced item will be low, the high per-item profits involved make skimming a potentially viable strategy. The product's high price attempts to make a profit by appealing to those few customers willing to pay a lot, thus "skimming the cream of the market."

By contrast, the penetration strategy involves setting a price so low that the new product sells briskly in the market. Although the per-item profits will tend to be low, it is the likelihood of selling a large number of items that makes penetration a potentially viable strategy. The product's low price enables it to rapidly "penetrate the market" and thus generate the large number of sales that could result in an overall profit even though only a small amount is made on each unit sold.

Application to Setting a Price Within Its Typical Bounds

Although a newly developed product is only one of the many situations when an initial price is needed, these two basic new-product pricing strategies can be applied to the general question of where an initial price should be set within the bounds of a typical price. In practice, determining the upper bound of the range—the value to the customer—involves deciding on a product's target market (or market segment) and measuring the product's VTC among the potential customers in that target market. Inevitably, there will be customers in this target market whose valuation of the product will be less than the measured VTC. This is both because of individual variation in needs and preferences and because the process of measuring a product's VTC tends to occur under conditions of particularly high levels of product information.

In this target market, setting the product's price close to its VTC would constitute a skimming strategy. Those customers who fully appreciate the product's value would be "the cream" of this target market. The high skim price would be attractive to these customers and would be likely to involve a relatively high per-unit profit. The disadvantage is that only a limited number of the customers in the target market would buy the product at that price.

Setting the product's price close to its variable costs would constitute a penetration strategy. A large proportion of the customers in the market would perceive the value of the product to be considerably higher than its low penetration price. Thus, although the penetration-priced product would involve small per-unit profits, it would be likely to quickly achieve a high level of unit sales within the market.

By applying the skimming and penetration strategies to the task of determining where a price should be set within the range of its typical bounds, we are establishing these strategies as a form of customer-based pricing. Neither strategy can be used without there first being an estimate of the product's VTC.

In this context, we can describe a third basic initial-pricing strategy—the in-line strategy. Rather than setting a price so high as to deter customers or so low as to attract customers, this strategy involves setting the price to be "in line with" the prices of competing offerings.[3] This does not usually mean that in-line prices will be the same as the prices of competing products, but it does mean that they will be relatively close. This closeness results from the price setter selecting no more than one differentiation value (or even only part of one) to add to or subtract from the price of the item's next closest substitute. Thus, like skimming and penetration (but unlike parity pricing), in-line pricing is also customer-based—it starts with an understanding of the product's value to the customer.

Initial-Pricing Strategies as Customer-Based

Each of these three basic initial-pricing strategies has implications as to where within the typical bounds of variable costs and VTC a price should be set (see Figure 4.3). These implications can be illustrated in the Dewey & Almy example described in Chapter 2. The consultant's research indicated that the new printing blanket's VTC in the offset printing market was around $500. A skim price, such as $450, would give Dewey & Almy a high per-unit profit but relatively few customers. A penetration price, such as say $120, would lead the product to sell briskly but leave Dewey & Almy with a low per-unit profit.

Figure 4.3   The Three Basic Initial-Pricing Strategies

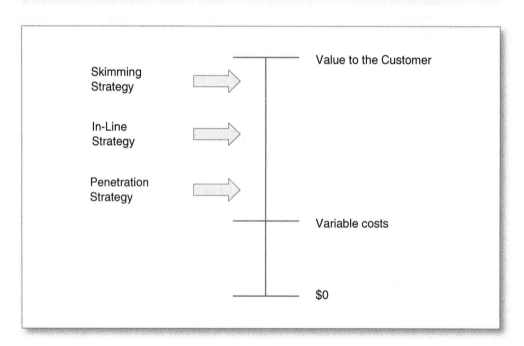

Dewey & Almy's decision to leave their new printing blankets priced at $200 indicates that they chose an in-line strategy. Dewey & Almy arrived at a price of $200 by considering that the blanket lasts twice as long as competing blankets, so its price should be twice as high. Although saving the purchase of a $100 printing blanket captured only part of the differentiation value of the new printing blanket's greater resiliency, it simplified what the customer needed to understand. At a price of $200, Dewey & Almy needed to communicate to its potential customers only the value of the blanket purchases saved. The value of the blanket replacement expenses saved—somewhat more difficult to quantify—was left as an incentive to purchase.

Because initial-pricing strategies are described here in terms of the estimated value to the customer, skimming and penetration prices may not necessarily map onto what one might consider a high or a low price. For example, if the single-pack roll of Bounty paper towels priced at $1.79 is targeted at the mass market but gets only a small fraction of that market, then that $1.79 price could be considered a skim price. The price might be high relative to the single roll's VTC to most members of the market. On the other hand, if the Toyota Prius priced at $25,000 is targeted at the North American market for hybrid cars and has a high market share, then its $25,000 price could be considered a penetration price. The price might be low relative to the car's value to the customers in this market.

Which Differentiation Value Should Be Included in an In-Line Price?

The in-line pricing strategy involves the recognition that product benefits often differ greatly in the degree to which they are apparent to potential customers. In an influential paper published in 1970, Philip Nelson pointed out that a product characteristic that a customer can examine before purchase—a search characteristic—is easier to appreciate than a product characteristic that can be observed only after purchasing and using the product—an experience characteristic.[4] It has also been noted that some product characteristics cannot be observed by customers even after product purchase and ordinary use—such as the health benefits of a daily vitamin pill.[5] Such characteristics require customer belief or faith, so they have been referred to as credence characteristics.

A positive differentiation value based on a product's search characteristics can usually be incorporated into a price without leading customers to perceive the price as out of line. For example, if customers can observe for themselves that one car has more legroom than another or that one copier can make clear copies faster than another, then they would be willing to pay for such differentiating factors. Correspondingly, if customers can observe negative differentiating product characteristics, such as the use of thinner metal supports or a smaller display screen, the in-line price for the product would tend to be a price lower than customers' reference values.

A positive differentiation value based on a product's experience or credence characteristics typically presents sellers with more of a communications challenge. Although factors such as a company's reputation or endorsements by experts are sometimes persuasive to a large proportion of the market, it is more often the case that there are practical limits to a seller's ability to communicate to most customers a differentiation value resulting from experience or credence characteristics. These communication limits could involve seller costs, such as the cost of the salesperson's time, the costs of collecting and reporting evidence, or the costs of media advertising. Further, even if a seller is willing to incur such costs, persuasive communication about some differentiating factors may be impractical because the potential buyer may have only a limited amount of time to listen.[6]

An in-line pricing strategy could involve selecting a differentiation value based on experience or credence characteristics that could be communicated within these practical limits. Or an in-line strategy for an initial price could be based on search characteristics entirely. One study of business customers in the health care industry found that most of them would readily pay half of the claimed cost savings of a product if these cost savings could be convincingly demonstrated to them before purchase.[7] This might provide a useful rule of thumb for an in-line strategy for the initial pricing of a business-to-business product.

STRATEGIC FACTORS IN SETTING INITIAL PRICES

When are each of these three basic initial-pricing strategies most appropriate? In this section, we review a sampling of factors that should be taken into account when making strategic choices (see Figure 4.4).

Figure 4.4   Strategic Factors in the Setting of Initial Prices

- Factors supporting skimming
  — New product perceived as risky
  — Presence of protection against competitive products

- Factors supporting penetration
  — Ability of low price to serve as an incentive to buy
  — Protection against competitive price matching
  — Market conditions favoring a pioneer advantage

- Use in-line pricing when market conditions do not support skimming or penetration.

Factors Supporting Skimming

One factor that supports a skimming strategy in setting an initial price is the degree to which customers perceive the product as risky. This is particularly likely to be important for products that are new to the market, as opposed to being a new version of an existing product or new only to the company that is selling it. New-to-market products are referred to as innovations.[8] There are at least three types of risk that might be involved in an innovative product:[9]

- Economic risk, such as the risk that a consumer product involving a large expenditure may not perform as expected or the risk for a business customer that a new product's failure might cause costly disruptions in the company's operations

- Physical risk, such the chance that a new recreational product could lead to accidents or that a new medical procedure could have serious unforeseen side effects

- Social risk, such as the possibility that a new clothing style or automobile body design could lead to negative reactions among one's peers

For the initial pricing of risky new products, there are two main reasons why a skimming strategy, rather than penetration or in-line pricing, is more likely to be appropriate.

The first reason is that the riskiness of the new product is likely to overwhelm customers' concern about price. For the small group of potential customers who like innovations and are less sensitive to risk—the "early adopters"—the excitement of the product's new capabilities and perhaps the pleasures of the social attention of being among the first to own a new product tend to lead them to accept high prices. For the larger group of potential customers, a cautiousness about new-product risk leads them to decline such products, even if the products are offered at very low prices. The second reason that new-product riskiness supports skimming is that risky new products are likely to require substantial resources for promotion, to educate the market about how to use the product and its benefits. A high price would help finance such promotional efforts.

A second factor supporting a skimming strategy is the presence of protection against competitive products. Although (as will be seen in Chapter 11) a high skim price need not last forever, there does need to be sufficient time for the "cream skimming" to be complete. If the entry of lower-priced competition is an immediate threat, then a skimming strategy becomes nonviable. Protection against such competition need not be airtight and can take many possible forms. For example, competitive protection could include a patent on a product or process, control of limited natural resources, ownership of choice retail locations, unique design or production expertise, a prestigious brand image, or a superior company reputation.

Factors Supporting Penetration

A key factor supporting the use of a penetration strategy is the ability of a price that is low with respect to the product's VTC to serve as an incentive for the customer to buy. A penetration strategy depends on a large market response to a low price. One way such a large market response might occur is if the low price leads customers to find new uses for the product. For example, DuPont's decision in the 1940s to sell the synthetic fiber nylon at a relatively low price led to its use in automobile tires and other products besides women's hosiery, which greatly increased sales of nylon.[10] Another way a strong response to a low price might occur is if the price is so low that it removes much of the economic risk of the new product. This may have been the case when Procter & Gamble introduced the Crest Spinbrush, a battery-powered electric toothbrush, at the price of $5.00[11] or when Apple's iTunes business introduced virus-free, legal music downloads for $0.99 per song.

There are a number of situations that could erode the ability of a low price to be an incentive to buy. If a low price leads customers to question the quality of a product or the degree to which it carries a prestige image, then that low price may not lead to a high level of sales. For example, when the Omega brand of prestige watches introduced low-priced watches, it lost more from damage to its brand image among upscale buyers than it gained in increased sales.[12] Or the problem may be that the amount of money involved is too small; a product such as a jar of mustard may involve so small an expenditure and be so infrequently purchased that even a price that is low relative to the product's VTC may not motivate most customers.

A penetration strategy may tempt competitors to match the low prices, so a second factor supporting a penetration strategy is protection against competitive price matching.

Such protection could be conferred by being an exceptionally low-cost producer (which would create an advantage in a price war) or being so small relative to the competition that it would not be practical for the competition to match low prices.

Under some market conditions, a company can develop an advantage over competition as a result of being first to sell to customers in a market. Such a benefit of being first is known as a pioneer advantage.[13] The market conditions that make possible a pioneer advantage are an important third factor supporting a penetration pricing strategy. This is so because the low penetration price can enable the product to be the first sold in its category to a large number of customers. If the market conditions for a pioneer advantage exist, then penetration pricing could create protection against competition where such protection did not already exist.

The market conditions making possible a pioneer advantage could concern the product's costs. If there are large economies of scale in producing the product, then the first company to sell a large amount of the product will attain low production costs that may be hard for later competitors to match. Texas Instruments benefitted from such economies of scale in the 1980s when it introduced its handheld calculators at penetration prices.

The market conditions making possible a pioneer advantage could also concern the product itself. For example, being first may give the seller's product a favorable image ("We're the original"), or customers may simply find it safer or more convenient to stick with the brand that they know from experience that they can trust. These are product benefits that could be hard for later competitors to duplicate. Further, such product loyalty can be very long lasting. One study found that a majority of 25 brands that were market leaders in 1923 were still the brands with the largest market shares 60 years later.[14]

Importance of "Being Strategic"

In considering an initial-pricing strategy, it is important also to be "strategic" in the way in which the decision is made. Strategic thinking involves careful consideration of supporting factors and the longer-term implications of an action, as opposed to thinking that is reactive or short term. Although there may be factors that support skimming or penetration in addition to those discussed here, it is important that a skimming or penetration strategy be chosen only if one or more such supporting factors are present. If market conditions support neither skimming nor penetration, then the in-line strategy serves as a reasonable default.

An example of nonstrategic thinking would be to set a new product's initial price high (i.e., a skimming strategy) just to see if such a high price would work. The thought would be that if the high price didn't work one could always lower it. The problem with such thinking is that there may not be time to subsequently lower the price. Your high price might attract lower-priced competitors who might not have otherwise entered that market, and you could be pushed out. Even if you were to survive, to the extent that there are market conditions favoring a pioneer advantage, you could forfeit to others the opportunity of obtaining enduring competitive benefits.

EVALUATING THE INITIAL PRICE

By determining a product's VTC and its variable costs and by choosing an appropriate pricing strategy, a manager can arrive at a tentative initial price for the product. The next step is to carry out some evaluation of this price. An important means of doing this is to make a judgment as to whether offering the new product at this price is likely to increase the company's profits. A breakeven calculation is a valuable aid in making this judgment.

Contribution Margin

As we saw earlier in this chapter, selling a product at any price above the product's variable costs will contribute toward covering the organization's fixed costs and producing net profits. Because of this, the amount of a product's price that remains after subtracting the product's variable costs is known as its contribution margin (in equations that appear in this book, contribution margin will be represented by CM). The concept of contribution margin is essential to a breakeven calculation.

In dollar terms, a product's contribution margin is equal to its price (P) minus its per-unit variable costs (VC):

$$CM = P - VC$$

It is sometimes useful to talk about the contribution margin as a percent of the product's price (%CM). This is calculated as follows:

$$\%CM = [(P - VC)/P] \times 100$$

For example, say you are considering opening a discount dry cleaning shop. Based on your VTC analysis and strategic considerations, you are planning to charge customers $1.79 per garment. If you expect your variable costs (e.g., direct labor costs and costs of materials such as cleaning fluids) to be $1.27 per garment cleaned, then the contribution margin would be $0.52 per garment ($1.79 − $1.27). The percent contribution margin would be 29.1 percent ([$0.52/$1.79] × 100).

A product's contribution margin is a measure of its profitability that is alternative to the gross margin measure described in Chapter 2. The difference between the two measures is that contribution margin is defined by a product's variable costs, but gross margin is defined by the standard accounting concept "cost of goods sold," which is not the same as a product's variable costs.[15] Because a product's price affects its sales, defining the product's profits in terms of costs that vary with sales (i.e., variable costs) is considerably more useful for pricing than defining costs in terms of a standard accounting measure not closely tied to the number of units sold. Thus, although we discussed gross margins in Chapter 2 in the context of cost-based pricing, our focus in this book is on the contribution margin measure of product profitability.

Despite the important difference between them, the concepts of contribution margin and gross margin are similar in that they are both measures of *gross* profitability. In other words, they both refer to the whole realm of potential profits as opposed to actual profits, or *net* profits. Given our focus on contribution margin as the measure of gross profitability more useful for managerial pricing decisions, we will in this book break slightly from accounting tradition and use the term *gross profits* to refer to the dollars of a product's contribution margin.[16]

Breakeven Analysis

A breakeven analysis is the determination of the number of units of a product that must be sold so that the organization's profit after a managerial decision is equal to that before the decision. This number is termed the breakeven units or breakeven sales level. Sometimes it is referred to as just "the breakeven," and it may be further shortened in this book to BE.

In the case of a new product whose initial price is above its variable costs (as it generally will be), selling only one unit of the product will yield some contribution toward increasing the organization's net profits. If that is the whole story, then the breakeven for that new product would be zero; the company would be ahead profitwise if even one unit is sold. However, that is typically not the whole story. Usually, the decision to offer a new product involves a commitment to carry out research and development activities, hire new managers, construct or modify production equipment, implement an advertising campaign, and so on. The costs of these activities are fixed costs, because these costs will not vary directly with changes in the number of units of the new product that are sold. However, because these fixed costs will be incurred (i.e., will be increments to costs) only if the decision is made to offer the new product, they are incremental fixed costs (ΔFC).[17] They equal the change in the organization's level of fixed costs (new fixed costs minus old fixed costs) that is due to the decision to offer the new product.

Since it is usually the case that the decision to offer a new product involves at least some incremental fixed costs, then each unit of the new product that is sold provides "a chunk" of contribution dollars toward covering these fixed costs. Thus, the breakeven units—the number of units that must be sold to not change an organization's net profit—would be equal to the number of contribution "chunks" that would be required to totally cover the product's incremental fixed costs. This is expressed in the breakeven formula:[18]

$$BE = \Delta FC/CM$$

If we return to the discount dry cleaning example, say that the decision to open the shop would involve incurring fixed costs (for facilities, equipment, etc.) of $7,000 per month. Dividing these incremental fixed costs by the per-garment contribution margin of $0.52 (calculated earlier) indicates that the breakeven for this shop would be to clean 13,462 garments per month. This tells us that, at the price of $1.79 per garment, we would have to clean 13,462 garments per month to have the same amount of net profit from this project as we have before we start—that is, zero dollars of profit.

Note that the logic of breakeven analysis can be thought of as involving a balance scale, such as the one illustrated in Figure 4.5. On the left side of the scale are the incremental fixed costs that would be incurred by offering the new product. On the right side of the scale are the chunks of contribution dollars that will be returned from each product sale.

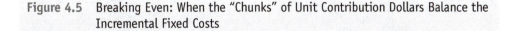

Figure 4.5   Breaking Even: When the "Chunks" of Unit Contribution Dollars Balance the Incremental Fixed Costs

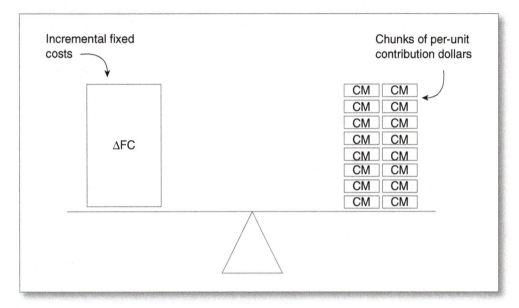

Note: CM = contribution margin dollars; ΔFC = change in fixed costs.

The breakeven sales level is reached when sales of the product produces enough chunks of contribution dollars to balance the product's incremental fixed costs.

Use of Breakeven Analysis

How then can a breakeven calculation help the manager evaluate an initial price? The answer is that it specifies the sales level that would have to be exceeded for the new product offer to increase the company's net profits. If the company's managers estimate that actual sales of this new product are likely to exceed this necessary level, then that would support the appropriateness of the initial price used in the breakeven calculation. If it seems unlikely that actual sales would exceed this necessary level, then it should lead to a reevaluation of the initial price used in the breakeven calculation.

Although the failure of a product's sales estimate to surpass the breakeven sales level should lead to reevaluation of the initial price, it should also lead to the reevaluation of estimates of the product's costs. As was illustrated by the Ford Mustang story in Chapter 2, sometimes it is desirable and possible to lower costs rather than to rethink the initial price. However, when a new product doesn't pass its breakeven test, it is probably the case that all of the factors that go into the breakeven calculation—fixed costs, variable costs, and price—will be reconsidered. If it is not possible to find an acceptable combination of these three factors that leads to a breakeven sales level that can be surpassed, then it would make sense to drop the idea of offering the new product.

Benefits of Breakeven Analysis

It is important to remember that the breakeven sales level does not provide a sales prediction. In fact, accurate specific predictions of future sales levels are usually very difficult to obtain. What makes a breakeven calculation so useful is that it reduces the amount of such predictive information that is necessary for making a well-reasoned pricing decision (or other business decision). Rather than having to know how many units will be sold at a particular price, a breakeven calculation makes a business decision possible knowing only whether or not a critical sales level will be exceeded. This critical sales level is the number of units that must be sold for the net profit after the decision to be the same as that before the decision.

To illustrate how a breakeven calculation can reduce the amount of information needed for a decision, let's return to the discount dry cleaning example. The breakeven calculation indicated a breakeven sales level of 13,462 garments per month. If there are 5,000 households in what would be the dry cleaning shop's market area and each household dry-cleaned an average of four garments per month, then there would be a total market potential of 20,000 garments per month. If there are already three dry cleaners in this area, then the likelihood of any new shop achieving a sales level of 13,462—over two-thirds of the market—seems remote. Without even having all the information necessary for an accurate sales prediction, it can be seen that product's initial price and/or the shop's costs would need to be reworked or the idea of locating the shop in that market area would have to be abandoned entirely.

In real business situations, it is often the case that a decision must be made with only very limited information. That reality makes methods such as breakeven analysis extremely valuable. We've seen here how it can be useful in setting a product's initial price. In the next chapter, we will show how a more general form of the breakeven formula can make it possible to use this type of analysis in the far more common task of considering price modifications.

SUMMARY

When setting an initial price, consideration of customer needs should be followed by consideration of costs and pricing strategies. To consider costs, it is important to distinguish between fixed costs (which do not change with the number of product units sold) and variable costs (which vary directly with the number of product units sold). Putting aside fixed costs when setting a product's price increases management's pricing flexibility.

Under typical circumstances, a product's price should be below its VTC (its price ceiling) and above its variable costs (its price floor). When there is a substantial range between these bounds, consideration should be given to the choice of initial-pricing strategy. Skimming involves setting a product's price close to the product's VTC, and penetration involves setting a price close to the product's variable costs. In-line pricing involves adding or subtracting no more than one differentiation value to competitors' prices. It is helpful if that differentiation value is based on search characteristics rather than experience or credence characteristics.

Choice of initial-pricing strategy should involve consideration of product and marketplace factors. New product risk and protection against competitive products support skimming. Ability of price to motivate customers to buy, protection against competitive price matching, and market conditions favoring a pioneer advantage support penetration. When market conditions support neither skimming nor penetration, then an in-line strategy should be used.

A tentative initial price can be evaluated through a breakeven calculation. The amount above what's necessary to cover the product's variable costs is the contribution margin associated with the price. Dividing a product's incremental fixed costs by this contribution margin gives the breakeven sales level. High likelihood of sales exceeding this breakeven sales level would support the product's tentative initial price. Making pricing decisions from a breakeven sales level criterion reduces the amount of predictive information necessary.

KEY TERMS

breakeven analysis	in-line strategy	social risk
fixed costs	search characteristic	pioneer advantage
variable costs	experience characteristic	contribution margin
price ceiling	credence characteristics	breakeven sales level
price floor	innovations	incremental fixed costs
skimming strategy	economic risk	breakeven formula
penetration strategy	physical risk	critical sales level

REVIEW AND DISCUSSION QUESTIONS

1. Describe the difference between fixed costs and variable costs.

2. What makes it difficult to allocate a portion of fixed costs to individual products? Why is it useful to consider only variable costs when making price-setting decisions?

3. What is meant by a price ceiling? Describe the logic of considering a product's VTC to be its price ceiling.

4. What is meant by a price floor? Describe the logic of considering a product's variable costs to be its price floor.

5. If there is little space between a product's price ceiling and price floor, what, then, should be its price? If there is substantial space between these two quantities, then what pricing-related factors should be considered next?

6. Describe the skimming strategy. Where within the bounds of a typical price is a skim price likely to fall?

7. Describe the penetration strategy. Where within the bounds of a typical price is a penetration price likely to fall?

8. Describe the in-line strategy, and indicate where within the bounds of a typical price an in-line price is likely to fall. Explain how an in-line price for an item could be different than the price of competing items.

9. Explain how a brand of a commonly purchased consumer packaged good, such as toilet tissue, could be skim-priced.

10. How does a search characteristic differ from an experience or credence characteristic? Why might product benefits based on search characteristics be particularly useful for in-line pricing?

11. Which initial-pricing strategy would be most appropriate for a risky innovative product? Explain your reasoning.

12. Explain how protection against lower-priced competition supports a skimming strategy. Give examples of factors that might offer such protection.

13. Give an example of a situation where a price that is low with respect to the product's VTC would not serve as an incentive to buy. What would be the implications of this for the use of a penetration strategy for pricing this product?

14. Explain how protection against low-price matching could support a penetration strategy. Give examples of factors that might offer such protection.

15. What is a pioneer advantage? Describe some examples of market conditions that would make a pioneer advantage possible. Why does a pioneer advantage support a penetration strategy?

16. Explain the concept of contribution margin. How is a contribution margin calculated?

17. If offering a new product would involve $10,000 in incremental fixed costs and variable costs of $3 per unit, what would be the breakeven sales level if the product were priced at $5? How can knowing this breakeven sales level facilitate the evaluation of this possible price?

18. Given that a breakeven sales level is not a sales prediction, explain why it is so widely used in business situations where accurate sales predictions would be helpful.

EXERCISES

1. A new product has per-unit variable costs of $15 and an estimated value to the customer of $45 per unit. Products in this category have been selling at around $35 per unit. Describe the three basic initial-pricing strategies, and give the approximate price for this product that would be suggested by each of these three strategies. For each price, explain your reasoning.

2. In 1999, Sony introduced a new product into the U.S. market. It was Aibo, the first interactive robot dog. It was able to learn its name, respond to commands, dance, and be programmed to perform a variety of actions.

   Assume Sony's variable costs for producing this product were around $700, and market research indicated that the VTC of this product was around $1,400. Recommend a price that consumers should be charged for this product, and explain how you considered the factors determining initial-pricing strategy in making your recommendation.

3. A manufacturer is considering incurring $60,000 in research and development costs in order to produce a more sensitive electronic thermostat. The materials and labor costs for the production and sale of this product are $1.60 per unit.

(a) Calculate the breakeven sales level for this product if it is priced at $2.20 per unit.

(b) Calculate the product's breakeven sales level if it is priced at $4 per unit.

(c) Explain the implications of the difference between these two breakeven sales levels.

4. Optical Distortion, Inc. (ODI) is about to introduce its new product: contact lenses for chickens.[19] Unlike contact lenses for humans, which are designed to improve sight, these contact lenses for chickens are designed to distort images so that the chickens become half-blind. This is desirable to poultry farmers because chickens whose vision is impaired will exhibit significantly less fighting (i.e., establishing of a pecking order). This will reduce flock mortality from 25 percent to 4.5 percent (each chicken killed through this fighting costs the farmer $2.40).

The typical poultry farm consists of 10,000 to 50,000 birds. Currently, poultry farmers deal with deaths due to fighting by debeaking the chickens. Debeaking reduces flock mortality from 25 percent to 9 percent but is so traumatic to the chickens that they stop laying eggs for a week after the operation (a chicken lays an average of five eggs per week and the farmer sells eggs for an average price of $0.53/dozen). Moreover, debeaked chickens have difficulty eating feed from a trough. The resulting spillage causes increased feed costs to the farmer that amount to $0.084 per chicken per year (the normal life span of a chicken is approximately one year).

The ODI lenses do not cause the chickens to become traumatized, and since it enables them to keep their beaks, it does not cause any eating difficulties. A three-person crew, which is able to debeak 250 chickens per hour could, after training, install contact lenses in 225 chickens per hour. The average labor costs for this crew is $36 per hour. ODI's materials and manufacturing costs are $0.035 per pair of lenses.

ODI is aware that promoting their new product will not be easy. Many poultry farmers consider the idea of contact lenses for chickens to be ridiculous and complain that their workers are unfamiliar with the lens insertion procedure. However, ODI's immediate question is what price to charge for a pair of lenses.

(a) What is the low end of the price range that ODI should be considering?

(b) What is the high end of the price range that ODI should be considering?

(c) What price within this range should ODI use for its new contact lens product? Justify your answer, making use of what you know about the basic initial-pricing strategies.

(d) Assume the contact lens price that you recommended in Part (c). If first-year fixed costs are $68,000, how many pairs of contacts lenses would ODI have to sell during the first year to breakeven? How does this number affect your confidence in the price you recommended in Part (c)?

NOTES

1. Alfred R. Oxenfeldt, *Pricing Strategies* (New York: Amacom, 1975), 164.
2. Joel Dean, "Pricing Policies for New Products," *Harvard Business Review* 18 (November 1950): 45–56.
3. C. Merle Crawford, *New Products Management,* 2nd ed. (Homewood, IL: Irwin, 1987), 429.
4. Phillip Nelson, "Information and Consumer Behavior," *Journal of Political Economy* 78, no. 2 (1970): 311–329.
5. Michael R. Darby and Edi Karni, "Free Competition and the Optimal Amount of Fraud," *Journal of Law and Economics* 16 (April 1973): 67–88.
6. James C. Anderson, James A. Narus, and Wouter van Rossum, "Customer Value Propositions in Business Markets," *Harvard Business Review* 84 (March 2006): 90–99.
7. James C. Anderson, Marc Wouters, and Wouter van Rossum, "Why the Highest Price Isn't the Best Price," *MIT Sloan Management Review* 51 (Winter 2010): 69–76.
8. Everett M. Rogers, *Diffusion of Innovation,* 5th ed. (New York: Free Press, 2003), 12.
9. William L. Wilkie, *Consumer Behavior,* 3rd ed. (New York: Wiley, 1994), 333.
10. Peter F. Drucker, "The Five Deadly Business Sins," *Wall Street Journal,* October 21, 1993, A18.
11. Charles W. Lamb, Joseph F. Hair, and Carl McDaniel, *Marketing,* 9th ed. (Mason, OH: Thomson South-Western, 2008), 570.
12. Ibid., 571.
13. William T. Robinson and Claes Fornell, "Sources of Market Pioneer Advantages in Consumer Goods Industries," *Journal of Marketing Research* 22 (August 1985): 305–317.
14. *Advertising Age,* "Study: Majority of 25 Leaders in 1923 Still on Top," September 19, 1983, 32.
15. A product's cost of goods sold is different than its variable costs because the cost of goods sold may include fixed costs (such as a share of factory overhead) and may exclude some of a product's variable costs (such as commissions paid to salespeople).
16. Accounting textbooks usually use the term *gross profit* to refer to gross margin. See, for example, Karen W. Braun, Wendy M. Tietz, and Walter T. Harrison, Jr., *Managerial Accounting,* 2nd ed. (Upper Saddle River, NJ: Prentice Hall), 258.
17. Note that the Greek letter Δ indicates "change."
18. In this formula, ΔFC is often written without the Δ, which is understood.
19. Adapted from Darrel G. Clarke and Randall E. Wise, "Optical Distortion, Inc. (A)," Harvard Business School Case 9-575-072, Boston: Harvard Business School Publishing.

PART II

Modification of Existing Prices

Development and Use of the Generalized Breakeven Formula

$\mathbf{I}$n Chapters 2 through 4, we focused on how to set the initial price for a product. After that initial price has been set, the question arises whether it can be improved. An improvement in a price consists of a modification, up or down, that leads to an increase in the company's gross profits (i.e., contribution dollars). The goal of these modifications is to arrive at the product's best price—the price that results in more profits than prices that are higher or lower.

Because there is only one initial price but an unlimited number of potential modifications of that price, modifying prices is a much more common pricing activity than setting initial prices. Thus, procedures for effectively modifying a price will be given considerable attention in this book. In this chapter, we introduce the application of breakeven (in the formulas, we refer to breakeven with BE) analysis to the task of optimally modifying a product's price.

APPLYING BREAKEVEN ANALYSIS
TO THE EVALUATION OF EXISTING PRICES

In Chapter 4, we introduced the use of breakeven analysis for evaluating an initial price. The breakeven formula, $BE = \Delta FC/CM$, is used to calculate the number of units of the product that need to be sold at the tentative initial price in order to cover the incremental fixed costs associated with producing the product. A manager's estimate that the product's sales would surpass this critical sales level would support the tentative initial price. A manager's estimate that the product's sales would not surpass the critical sales level would suggest that the tentative initial price should be reconsidered.

To understand how breakeven analysis could be used for evaluating the modification of a price, it is helpful to first look at how the breakeven formula could be used to help evaluate the existing price of a product in the absence of a price modification.

Consider, as an example, a situation where a toy company has been selling 12,000 units per year of a particular educational toy at $30 per unit. The company's variable costs for manufacturing this product are $10 per unit, so the product's unit contribution margin (in the formulas, we will refer to contribution margin with CM) is $20 (= $30 – $10). If a manager is considering spending an additional $45,000 to advertise the toy, he could use the breakeven formula to evaluate the ability of the existing $30 price to support this expenditure:

$$BE = \$45,000/\$20 = 2,250 \text{ units}$$

This application of the breakeven formula tells us that the critical sales level for the incremental advertising fixed cost is 2,250 units. This means that the additional advertising would have to lead to sales of 2,250 units over what would otherwise have been sold to support the ability of the existing price to handle the additional advertising. The number of units that would otherwise have been sold will be referred to as the level of base sales (in the formulas, we refer to base sales with BS).

The critical sales level of a breakeven analysis is always the number of units sold over and above the base sales level. For a breakeven analysis on an existing product, the sales level in the previous period can be used as an estimate of base sales. In the educational toy example, the base sales level could be estimated at 12,000. If sales had been at that level during the previous years, it is reasonable to estimate that sales would continue to be at 12,000 units during the upcoming year if the additional advertising expenditure were not made. Thus, at the price of $30, the total sales level of the toy would have to surpass 14,250 units (= 12,000 + 2,250) for the additional advertising to increase the company's profits.

For a breakeven analysis on a new project, such as in the use of the breakeven formula to evaluate an initial price, the number of units that would be sold if the project is not undertaken would be zero. In this case then, the base sales level is zero, and the breakeven units provided by the application of the breakeven formula is the total sales level that would need to be surpassed.

THE GENERALIZED BREAKEVEN FORMULA

The breakeven formula is useful for evaluating a tentative initial price as well as for evaluating the ability of an existing price to support a change in fixed costs. As was discussed in Chapter 4, the breakeven formula involves determining the number of "chunks" of contribution dollars that balance the incremental fixed costs (see Figure 5.1).

Certainly, the breakeven formula is well-known and has long been widely used as a business decision-making tool.[1] However, to adapt breakeven analysis to the modification of existing prices, the breakeven formula is inadequate.

Effects of Price Modification on Profit From Base Sales

To understand why the breakeven formula is inadequate for a price-change decision, consider the situation in which the manager of the toy company mentioned above is considering a price modification. He is evaluating whether or not to decrease the educational toy's

Figure 5.1 Breaking Even With an Existing Price: When the "Chunks" of New Per-Unit Contribution Dollars Balance the Incremental Fixed Costs

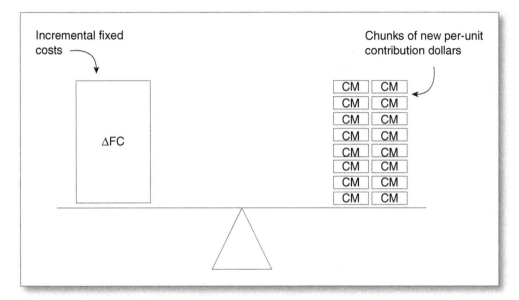

Note: CM = contribution margin dollars; ΔFC = change in fixed costs.

price from $30 to $25 per unit and focus the additional $45,000 advertising expenditure on communicating this price decrease to consumers. Use of the breakeven formula here would suggest that the breakeven sales level for this prospective price decrease would be $45,000/($25 − $10), which equals 3,000 units.

The problem with this breakeven level is that it fails to take into account that it is not just the new unit sales generated by the price decrease that will determine the profitability of this price change. Modifying an existing price affects *all* of the product's sales. Thus, if the price of the toy is decreased by $5 per unit, then the sales of the toy that would have occurred even if the price had not decreased—the base sales—will have a contribution margin that is $5 lower. To be appropriate for decisions concerning the modification of existing prices, a breakeven calculation must take into account changes in profit from base sales.

Taking Changes in Profit From Base Sales Into Account

For a price-change breakeven calculation to take into account the effect of the price change on profit from base sales, it is necessary to calculate the change in total contribution dollars that results from changing the price on these base sales. When this change in total contribution dollars is an *increase,* then it needs to be subtracted from the incremental fixed costs (see Figure 5.2). Those "new" contribution dollars from base sales would reduce the amount that would need to be covered in order to break even. When this change in total contribution dollars is a *decrease,* then it needs to be added to the incremental fixed costs (see Figure 5.3). The contribution dollars lost on base sales would increase the amount that would need to be covered in order to break even.

Figure 5.2 Price Increase Involves a Profit Gain on Base Sales That Reduces What Needs to Be Covered by "Chunks" of Contribution Dollars

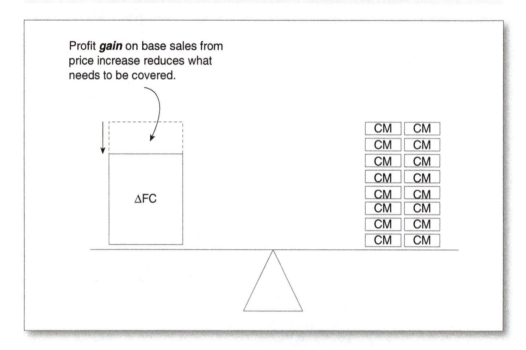

Computing the change in total contribution dollars due to the effect of the price change on profit from base sales involves identifying the change in contribution margin (ΔCM). The contribution margin that would result from the price change taking place will be referred to as the new contribution margin. From here on, the symbol CM without a subscript will refer to the new contribution margin. The contribution margin that would result if the price change did not take place will usually be the contribution margin that existed before the price change was considered. Thus, it will be referred to here as the old contribution margin (CM_o). Because change equals new minus old,

$$\Delta CM = CM - CM_o$$

Since the change in contribution margin is the change in contribution dollars per unit, the change in total contribution dollars due to the effect of the price change on base sales can be arrived at by multiplying this per-unit quantity by the number of units comprising the base sales level. In other words, it can be obtained by multiplying ΔCM by BS.

Figure 5.3   Price Decrease Involves a Profit Loss on Base Sales That Adds to What Needs to Be Covered by "Chunks" of Contribution Dollars

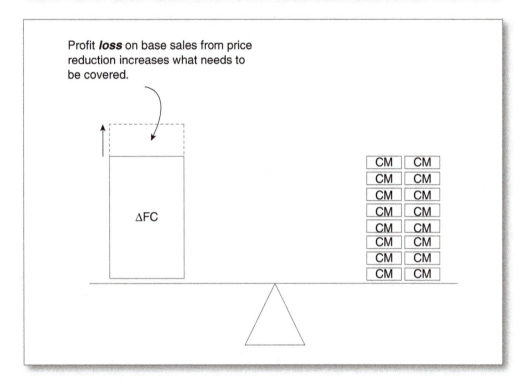

To take this change in total contribution dollars into account in a breakeven calculation, it needs to be subtracted from the incremental fixed costs. When it is a positive change—an increase in contribution dollars—subtracting it reduces the amount that needs to be covered in order to break even. When it is a negative change—a decrease in contribution dollars—subtracting it adds to the amount that needs to be covered because, as you recall, a minus times a minus equals a plus. Thus, the formula for taking base sales into account in a breakeven calculation is as follows:

$$BE = \frac{\Delta FC - (\Delta CM \times BS)}{CM}$$

This will be referred to as the generalized breakeven (GBE) formula.

To illustrate the use of the GBE formula, let's return to the example of the educational toy. The breakeven formula indicated that the incremental fixed costs associated with the $5 per unit price decrease could be covered by 3,000 units of additional sales. However, this did not take into account that the $5 price decrease would also apply to existing sales, which would have the effect of increasing the number of additional units that must be sold to break even. Using the GBE formula to take this effect into account:

$$BE = \frac{\$45,000 - \{[(\$25 - \$10) - (\$30 - \$10)] \times 12,000\}}{\$15}$$

$$= \frac{\$45,000 - [(\$15 - \$20) \times 2,000)]}{\$15}$$

$$= \frac{\$45,000 - (\$5 \times 2,000)}{\$15}$$

$$= \frac{\$45,000 - (-\$60,000)}{\$15}$$

$$= \frac{\$45,000 + \$60,000}{\$15} = \$105,000 / \$15 = 7,000 \text{ units}$$

This, then, indicates the correct breakeven sales level for the price change. For a $5 decrease in the toy's price to increase the company's gross profits, the additional annual sales resulting from that price decrease would have to exceed not 3,000 units, but rather 7,000 units.

The GBE formula is very useful for the task of modifying existing prices to achieve greater profitability, and we will make extensive use of it in this book. To help you remember it, you should note how it relates to what you already know. Note that when the pricing task is to set an initial price, the GBE formula can still be used. In that case, the product in question is not yet being sold, so there are no base sales. This makes BS equal to zero, which makes the entire term ΔCM × BS equal to zero. Thus, the GBE formula becomes the breakeven formula. The GBE formula is called "generalized" because it is useful in a wider range of pricing situations than the breakeven formula that is usually used. In a sense, the ΔCM × BS term was always there—just not needed. The GBE formula is simply the usual breakeven formula written in a more complete form.

USE OF THE GENERALIZED BREAKEVEN FORMULA WHEN COSTS DO NOT CHANGE

The next step is to examine in detail how the GBE formula can be used. In beginning to do this, we will assume that the price modification is being considered in a situation where the price change will not cause, or be associated with, any changes in either fixed costs or per-unit variable costs. Both will be at the same level after the price change as before it.

When it is the case that neither fixed costs nor per-unit variable costs change, the GBE formula becomes somewhat simpler. With no change in fixed costs, the ΔFC term becomes zero and thus could be left out. With no change in per-unit variable costs, the ΔCM factor becomes the change in price (ΔP). To make explicit how this is so, consider the definition of change in contribution margin written so as to show the definition of contribution margin (i.e., $P - VC$). The symbol P stands for the new price, and VC stands for the new variable costs; P_o stands for the old price, and VC_o stands for the old variable costs:

$$\Delta CM = (P - VC) - (P_o - VC_o)$$

If the variable costs do not change (i.e., $VC = VC_o$), then ΔCM becomes equal to ΔP,

$$\Delta CM = P - P_o = \Delta P$$

In this simpler situation where neither fixed costs nor per-unit variable costs change, the breakeven sales level calculated from the GBE formula will be affected by three factors: DP, BS, and CM_o. We will examine each of these factors in turn.

As we illustrate these factors, it will be seen that the unit breakeven sales level can often be more easily evaluated when thought of as a percent of base sales. As you would expect, this involves simply dividing the breakeven sales level by the base sales level and multiplying by 100:

$$\% BE = (BE/BS) \times 100$$

The Prospective Price Change

Sam's Janitorial Services is a small company that provides office cleaning services for local businesses. Sales have been fairly constant at 1,000 hours per month, so the proprietor, Sam Millstone, expects that sales will continue at that level next month if he does not change his price. Sam's current price is $40 per hour, his variable costs are $28 per hour, and his monthly fixed costs are $2,400.

Sam first wondered if he might be able to increase profits by lowering price. He used the GBE formula to calculate the breakeven sales level for a price reduction of 20 percent, to $32 per hour:

$$BE = \{0 - [(\$32 - \$40) \times 1,000 \text{ hours}]\} / (\$32 - \$28)$$

$$= -(-\$8,000) / \$4$$

$$= 2,000 \text{ hours}$$

Sam felt that there was some price sensitivity in the market; decreasing his price would definitely result in an increase in sales. But the breakeven computation indicates that his sales level would have to increase by more than 2,000 hours per month before his profits would start to increase. In other words, if his sales jumped by 200 percent, to 3,000 hours per month, he would just break even—that is, have as much gross profit as he has now. He would have to exceed that sales level of 3,000 hours per month for his profits to begin to increase. Sam felt sure that there was not *that* much price sensitivity in his market. A 200 percent sales increase seemed completely impossible.

Sam next wondered if a smaller price decrease would be more realistic. He used the GBE formula to calculate the breakeven sales level for a price reduction of 10 percent, to $36 per hour:

$$BE = \{0 - [(\$36 - \$40) \times 1,000 \text{ hours}]\} / (\$36 - \$28)$$

$$= -(-\$4,000) / \$8$$

$$= 500 \text{ hours}$$

This breakeven sales level meant that once his sales level surpassed 1,500 hours per month, a 50 percent increase, then his profits would begin to increase. This seemed within the realm of reason, but Sam still felt uncomfortable. A 50 percent sales increase seemed like a lot for a price decrease of only 10 percent.

Sam's next step was to consider the possibility that he might be able to increase profits by raising his price a little. He used the GBE formula to calculate the breakeven sales level for a price increase of 10 percent, to $44 per hour:

$$BE = \{0 - [(\$44 - \$40) \times 1,000 \text{ hours}]\} / (\$44 - \$28)$$

$$= -(\$4,000) / \$16$$

$$= -250 \text{ hours}$$

Sam recognized that a negative breakeven level needed to be interpreted a little differently than a positive one. A breakeven of −250 hours meant that if the price increase caused sales to drop by that amount, to 750 hours per month, Sam's gross profits would be exactly the same as they were before the price change. In other words, Sam would have a 250 hours per month sales cushion. If sales decreased by less than 250 hours per month, then Sam's profits would be greater than before the price change. However, if sales decreased by more than 250 hours per month, then Sam would have exceeded his sales cushion and would have less profit than before the price change.

Sam recognized that there would certainly be some customers who would cut back their hours if his prices increased. But he felt that most of his clients trusted him to do reliably good work and that it seemed unlikely that he would lose 250 hours per month (25 percent of his sales) from a modest $4 per hour price increase.

Since the small price increase seemed promising, Sam wondered if a larger price increase might be even better. He used the GBE formula to calculate the breakeven sales level for a price increase of 20 percent, to $48 per hour:

$$BE = \{0 - [(\$48 - \$40) \times 1,000 \text{ hours}]\} / (\$48 - \$28)$$

$$= -(\$8,000) / \$20$$

$$= -400 \text{ hours}$$

This breakeven sales level meant that if Sam lost anything less than 400 hours per month, his profits would be higher than before the price change. If his sales level decreased by more than 400 hours per month, then his profits would be lower than before the price change. Sam recognized that a sales decrease of 400 hours per month—40 percent—is a lot. However, he also knew that several of his largest clients were particularly price-sensitive. If the $8 per hour price increase caused them to leave, then he would indeed lose more than 40 percent of his sales.

The breakevens for these four price-change possibilities can be seen in Figure 5.4. Although Sam wished he had the resources to carry out some research on the likely price-change response of his market, his intuitive assessment of these possibilities was clear. He felt most comfortable with the prospects of a 10 percent price increase, and that's what he decided to do.

Figure 5.4   Effect of Price Change on Breakeven Sales Levels

Price Change	BE
20% ↓	2,000
10% ↓	500
10% ↑	−250
20% ↑	−400

Note: BE = breakeven units.

This example illustrates the basic logic of using breakeven analysis to assist in price-modification decisions. It involves computing the breakeven sales level for various prospective price changes and comparing this breakeven against an estimate of the likely actual sales response. Both price decreases and price increases should be investigated; each is capable of producing increases in gross profits. Further, it is usually wise to investigate several levels of price change for each of the two price-change directions.

Base Sales

It is very often reasonable, as it was in the previous example, to assume that the current sales level is the sales level that will continue if no price modification is made. In other words, current sales can often be used as an estimate of base sales.

However, situations exist where the base sales will differ from current sales. One example of such a situation is that where there is a predictable change in the size of the market. Returning to the Sam's Cleaning Service illustration, let's say that the amount of office space in his market area will increase by 20 percent next year when several new office buildings will be completed. This gives Sam a reason to expect that, even if he makes no price change, his sales will increase by 20 percent next year. Thus, for a breakeven calculation for a prospective price change that would be implemented next year, the base sales level would be 1,200 hours per month rather than the current sales level of 1,000 hours. If

Sam wanted to consider putting off until next year the 10 percent price increase he was considering, the breakeven calculation would go as follows:

$$BE = \{0 - [(\$44 - \$40) \times 1{,}200 \text{ hours}]\} / (\$44 - \$28)$$

$$= -(\$4{,}800) / \$16$$

$$= -300 \text{ hours}$$

This breakeven sales level would mean that a 10 percent price increase next year would have to cause less than a 300 hour-per-month sales decrease for Sam to see increased profits. Note that this refers to a decrease from 1,200 hours per month—his total sales would have to be above 900 hours for the price increase to be profitable. If a next-year price increase causes sales to drop to 850 hours per month, Sam would have less gross profit than if he kept his price constant.

Another example of a situation where the base sales will differ from current sales is a price change by a major competitor. If Sam's largest competitor implemented a 10 percent price decrease, Sam might estimate that keeping his price unchanged would result in a 20 percent loss of sales, to 800 hours per month. In such a case, the base sales for a break-even calculation would be 800 hours. If Sam was considering matching his competitor's 10 percent price decrease, he could use the GBE formula as follows:

$$BE = \{0 - [(\$36 - \$40) \times 800 \text{ hours}]\} / (\$36 - \$28)$$

$$= -(-\$3{,}200) / \$8$$

$$= 400 \text{ hours}$$

This breakeven sales level indicates that Sam should not match his competitor's price decrease unless he believes that doing so would increase his sales beyond 1,200 hours per month. Even if matching the competitor's price decrease resulted in Sam maintaining his 1,000 hour-per-month sales level, he would still be better off (by the criterion of short-term gross profits) to forego the price change and allow his sales to decrease to 800 hours.

These effects of base sales on the breakeven sales levels for a 10 percent price increase and decrease are summarized in Figure 5.5.

Figure 5.5   Effect of Base Sales on Breakeven Sales Levels

Price Change	Base Sales	BE
10% ↑	1,000	−250
10% ↑	1,200	−300
10% ↓	1,000	500
10% ↓	800	400

Note: BE = breakeven units.

Contribution Margin

Say that one of Sam's competitors is a similar-sized company called JaniTech, Inc. This company has invested in the latest machinery for cleaning offices, and thus, they are able to keep their labor costs to a bare minimum. For the sake of the example, let's assume that, like Sam's company, JaniTech charges customers $40 per hour and has a base sales level of 1,000 units per month. However, unlike Sam's company, JaniTech's variable costs are $16 per hour and its monthly fixed costs are $14,400.

If JaniTech used the GBE formula to consider the four prospective price changes that Sam considered, the breakeven sales levels would be calculated as follows:

A price reduction of 20 percent, to $32 per hour

$$BE = \{0 - [(\$32 - \$40) \times 1{,}000 \text{ hours}]\} / (\$32 - \$16)$$

$$= -(-\$8{,}000) / \$16$$

$$= 500 \text{ hours}$$

A price reduction of 10 percent, to $36 per hour

$$BE = \{0 - [(\$36 - \$40) \times 1{,}000 \text{ hours}]\} / (\$36 - \$16)$$

$$= -(-\$4{,}000) / \$20$$

$$= 200 \text{ hours}$$

A price increase of 10 percent, to $44 per hour

$$BE = \{0 - [(\$44 - \$40) \times 1{,}000 \text{ hours}]\} / (\$44 - \$16)$$

$$= -(\$4{,}000) / \$28$$

$$= -143 \text{ hours}$$

A price increase of 20 percent, to $48 per hour

$$BE = \{0 - [(\$48 - \$40) \times 1{,}000 \text{ hours}]\} / (\$48 - \$16)$$

$$= -(\$8{,}000) / \$32$$

$$= -250 \text{ hours}$$

Note how these breakeven sales levels compare to those Sam had calculated (see Figure 5.6). JaniTech's management would probably shy away from the 10 percent price increase that Sam favored. If the resulting sales decrease was any greater than only 14.3 percent of sales, their gross profits would decrease. On the other hand, JaniTech's management might show interest in the 10 percent price decrease. If it resulted in a sales increase to any degree greater than a modest 20 percent of their base sales, their gross profits would increase.

Figure 5.6   Effect of Before-Change Contribution Margin on Breakeven Sales Levels

Price Change	Sam's BE (CM$_0$ = $12, or 30%)	Janitech's BE (CM$_0$ = $24, or 60%)
20% ↓	2,000	500
10% ↓	500	200
10% ↑	−250	−143
20% ↑	−400	−250

Note: CM$_0$ = old contribution margin; BE = breakeven units.

This difference in likely price-change decision is due to the differences in contribution margins between the two companies. With low contribution margins, such as those of Sam's Cleaning Service, even a small a price increase increases the contribution margin by a relatively large proportion. Thus, with low contribution margins, price increases tend to be more attractive. On the other hand, with high contribution margins, such as those of JaniTech, every additional unit of sales brings in a relatively large chunk of contribution. Thus, with high contribution margins, it is price decreases that tend to be more attractive.

Note that the fixed costs of the two companies have no bearing on the breakeven calculations. Because these fixed costs do not change as a result of the pricing decisions for that product, their level does not affect those decisions. A company's managers can rest assured that if a product's price is set so that it yields the maximum amount of gross profit for that product, then the managers will be doing everything they can to contribute to covering those costs that will not change as a result of the sales level of the product.

The effect of the contribution margin before the price change on breakeven sales levels—low contribution margins favoring price increases and high contribution margins favoring price decreases—is a general one. A handy table, showing the effect the level of CM$_0$ on breakeven levels in percent terms, can be seen in Figure 5.7.[2]

CHANGE-IN-PROFIT FORMULA

As previously mentioned, using breakeven analysis in a price-modification decision involves evaluating the breakeven's critical sales level for the prospective price change against the expected *actual* sales response to the price change. Keep in mind that the expected sales response—like the breakeven sales level—is a *change* from the base sales level. Thus, for example, if a manager calculates that the breakeven sales level for a prospective price decrease is 100 units (an increase over base sales of 100 units) and expects the sales change resulting from that price decrease to be 120 units (an increase over base sales of 120 units), then the manager could conclude that going ahead with the price decrease will increase the gross profits associated with the product.

Figure 5.7   Breakeven Percentages for Different Before-Change Contribution Margins

Percentage Change in Price	Percentage Contribution Margin Before Price Change							
	10%	20%	30%	40%	50%	60%	70%	80%
+25	−71	−56	−45	−38	−33	−29	−26	−24
+20	−67	−50	−40	−33	−29	−25	−22	−20
+15	−60	−43	−33	−27	−23	−20	−18	−16
+10	−50	−33	−25	−20	−17	−14	−13	−11
+5	−33	−20	−14	−11	−9	−8	−7	−6
0	0	0	0	0	0	0	0	0
−5	100	33	20	14	11	9	8	7
−10		100	50	33	25	20	17	14
−15		300	100	60	43	33	27	23
−20			200	100	67	50	40	33
−25			500	167	100	71	56	45

It is often the case that the manager who is evaluating a prospective price change will want to know more than just whether or not an expected sales change would surpass the critical sales level. The manager might also want to know how a particular expected sales change resulting from the prospective price change would change the product's gross dollar profits. This can be calculated by subtracting the breakeven sales level (in units) from the expected sales change (in units) and multiplying this difference by the contribution margin. This will be referred to as the change-in-profit formula:[3]

$$\text{Change in profit} = (\text{Expected unit sales change} - \text{BE unit sales}) \times \text{CM}$$

For example, the manager who calculated the 100-unit breakeven for the price decrease might want to know how much the estimated 120-unit actual sales change would affect profits. If the product's contribution margin after the price decrease is $14, the manager could use the change-in-profit formula to answer this question:

$$\text{Change in profit} = (120 \text{ units} - 100 \text{ units}) \times \$14$$

$$= 20 \text{ units} \times \$14$$

$$= \$280$$

If the sales response to this price decrease turned out to be, as expected, an increase of 120 units, then this product's gross profits would increase by $280.

To further illustrate the use of the change-in-profit formula, consider how Sam Millstone might react in the decision about whether or not to match his office cleaning competitor's price decrease. Although his breakeven calculation indicated that his short-term profits would most likely be greater if he maintained his $40 price rather than matching his competitor's decrease to $36, Sam worries about long-term profits. Perhaps by matching his competitor's price now, he will be able to retain customers who may at some future time become more profitable. To help make this decision, Sam would like to know just how much gross profit per period he would be sacrificing in order to satisfy this more long-term consideration. If his expectation was that matching the competitor's price decrease would result in his maintaining his sales level of 1,000 hours per month, Sam could answer his question by applying the change-in-profit formula. Note that both the expected sales change and the breakeven sales change are changes with respect to base sales—in this case, the 800 hours per month that Sam would sell if he made no price change:

$$\text{Change in profit} = (200 \text{ hours} - 400 \text{ hours}) \times (\$36 - \$28)$$
$$= -200 \text{ hours} \times \$8$$
$$= -\$1,600$$

Based on this calculation, matching the competitor's price decrease would cause Sam to lose $1,600 per month in profit that he would be making if he kept his price at $40 and let 20 percent of his sales fall to his competitor. It is this amount that he would have to weigh against the more long-term considerations of maintaining market share.

USING THE GENERALIZED BREAKEVEN FORMULA WHEN VARIABLE COSTS CHANGE

So far, we have introduced the GBE formula as a tool for making effective price-change decisions and have discussed its use when the prospective price change does not occur along with changes in costs. However, there are many situations where the price change being considered does occur along with changes in costs. To properly use breakeven analysis to help evaluate a price change in such situations, these changes in costs must be taken into account. In this section, we discuss changes in variable costs. In the section that follows, we discuss changes in fixed costs.

Identifying Changes in Variable Costs

To be able to accurately identify *changes* in a product's variable costs, you need to have a clear understanding of how to identify the product's current variable costs. As was mentioned in Chapter 4, variable costs are those that vary directly with the number of units of the product that are sold. The costs of materials and labor are usually components of a product's variable costs. For a manufacturer, these would include the raw materials that go into the production process and the wages of employees directly involved in the assembly or fabrication of these raw materials into a finished product. For a wholesaler or a retailer, these would include the costs of the goods that they sell and the hourly labor involved in handling and selling these items. Other common variable costs include the following:

- Costs of energy used in the manufacturing process
- Costs of packaging the product and shipping it to the buyer
- Royalties and licensing fees
- Selling costs such as commissions

In general, costs that are incurred on a unit-by-unit basis are always variable costs. For costs that are not separately incurred for each unit, you should consider whether the cost varies with the amount of the product that is sold. For example, the question might arise whether the costs of store merchandise that is lost or damaged—retail shrinkage—should be considered variable costs for those items. The answer would involve knowing the reasons for the shrinkage. Merchandise loss due to the use of items in window displays would probably not be directly related to the number of items sold and thus should not be considered a variable cost. On the other hand, merchandise loss due to the number of customers (such as shoplifting) would be more likely to vary with sales levels and thus should be considered a variable cost.

It is relatively apparent that costs such as materials, labor, packaging, and commissions vary with product sales; thus, when they change, the change in variable costs can be clearly identified. However, there are many situations where the level of variable costs is less obvious. In these situations, it is important to ask two questions:

- What additional costs would be incurred for each new sale that will be made?
- What costs would be saved for each current sale that will no longer be made?

Consider the following scenarios:[4]

1. *When an inventory is maintained.* A major battery manufacturer sells batteries to companies that produce a variety of consumer electronics products. Because the manufacturer's customers require firm delivery deadlines, the manufacturer must keep on hand a two-month supply of zinc, a critical battery component. The manufacturer's zinc costs are a major variable cost for the batteries that it sells. The company has been paying $0.48 per pound for zinc and thus has paid $0.48 per pound for its current two-month zinc inventory. Suddenly, the political unrest in zinc-producing countries has caused the price of the metal to jump to $0.75 per pound. Does this cost increase have any effect on the variable costs of the batteries that will be produced from the two-month inventory of $0.48-per-pound zinc?

   Answer: Yes. If a two-month inventory needs to be maintained, then the first pound of zinc used in batteries sold after the zinc cost increase will require the purchase of a new pound of zinc to replace it. Because the sale of these batteries causes the expenditure of $0.75 per pound to replace the zinc used, then it is this $0.75-per-pound materials cost that is the major variable cost for those batteries.

2. *A discontinued product.* A retailer specializing in household items commissioned the production of custom-designed ceramic bowls and has been buying the bowls from the manufacturer at a cost of $6.50 per bowl. Because of their custom design, they were not returnable. Sales of these bowls have recently fallen off, and the retailer decided not to purchase any additional bowls. Currently, the retailer has 200 of the bowls on hand. The retailer can donate these bowls to charity or keep them on sale. If kept on sale, it is estimated that each bowl will incur an average inventory cost of $2.00 before it is sold. What are the variable costs relevant to the price of each of these remaining bowls that are kept on sale?

Answer: Two dollars. Keeping a bowl on sale will cause the retailer to incur the inventory cost but will not cause a $6.50 expenditure for a new bowl to replace it. Disposing of a bowl now would save the inventory cost on it but would not save a $6.50 expenditure. Thus, the $6.50 paid for each bowl is not a component of the variable costs for selling the remaining 200 bowls.

3. *Actual versus nominal variable costs.* A manufacturer of electric motors for small appliances has been producing 500 motors per month and estimates that direct labor costs for assembling the motors are $5 per motor. The manufacturer is under a long-term contract with the plant's unionized workers. The contract stipulates that production increases will be accomplished by current workers who will be paid time and a half for overtime. It further stipulates that all workers who are furloughed or whose hours are reduced because of production decreases will receive 60 percent of their regular wages. What is the direct labor component of the variable costs for these motors?

Answer: For each of the 500 motors currently being produced, the direct labor component of the variable costs is 40 percent of $5—that is, $2. This is because, although the nominal costs of labor per motor (i.e., those costs called "labor") are $5, only 40 percent of that amount will be saved for every motor that is not produced. However, for any motors produced above the current production level, the direct labor component of the variable costs will be 150 percent of $5.00—that is, $7.50—because that will be the new amount incurred for every additional motor that is produced.

Consider How Changes in Variable Costs Are Related to Changes in Price

We have been approaching the task of identifying changes in variable costs by simply examining how to identify variable costs. Once a manager is clear as to what the variable costs are, then it is straightforward to identify any changes that occur in these costs.

At this point, we need to consider how a change in variable costs can be related to the possibility of a change in price. To do this, we can distinguish between two types of changes in variable costs. The first type consists of changes that are *independent* of any possible changes in price. For example, if the price of newsprint goes up, the variable costs of publishing a newspaper will increase. This variable cost increase will occur whether or not the publisher decides to increase the price of the newspaper in order to try to cover it. Thus, the variable cost change is independent of any price change.

The second type of change in variable costs consists of those that are *tied* to a possible change in price. This means that if the variable costs change, then the price changes and vice versa. The two changes—the change in variable costs and the change in price—are essentially part of the same managerial decision.

Typically, such tied decisions involve basic marketing strategies. For example, say the management of a dinner restaurant that has been targeting middle-income consumers is considering changing the restaurant's target market to a more upper-income group of consumers. This might involve increasing the restaurant's value to the customer (VTC) and raising its prices so as to capture most of this increased customer value. Because increasing the restaurant's VTC would include activities such as using higher-quality meats and vegetables in the menu items and hiring more highly skilled chefs and servers, it would cause variable costs to increase. Thus a decision to target the more upper-income consumers would involve an increase in variable costs that would be tied to an increase in prices.

On the other hand, the restaurant's managers could decide to move toward targeting a less affluent segment of the market. This would involve decreasing prices so as to appeal to this segment, but would also most likely require the trimming of variable costs. Cheaper cuts of meat could be purchased, more use could be made of frozen and canned ingredients, and so on. The decision to target the less affluent consumers would involve a decrease in variable costs that would be tied to a decrease in prices.

To carry out a breakeven analysis to help evaluate a prospective price modification in a situation in which variable costs change, it is necessary to be clear as to whether the change in variable costs is independent of the price change being considered or is tied to it.

Changes in Variable Costs That Are Independent of Changes in Price

When the changes in variable costs are independent of any contemplated price changes, then the computation of the breakeven sales level—the sales change that results in the same level of profits after the price change as before the price change—should use the *new* (i.e., changed) variable costs in both of the terms used to determine how the price change will change per-unit profits. Specifically, when calculating ΔCM for the GBE formula,

$$\text{BE} = \frac{\Delta \text{FC} - (\Delta \text{CM} \times \text{BS})}{\text{CM}}$$

the new variable costs should be used not only to calculate the new contribution margin but also to calculate the old contribution margin.

To understand why this should be done, note that what we have been referring to as the "old" contribution margin (see page 3) is, more precisely, the contribution margin that would exist if no price change were made. If variable costs do not change, then the contribution margin that would exist if no price change were made would indeed be the old contribution margin. However, if the variable costs will change irrespective of whether or not the price changes, then the contribution margin that would exist if no price change were made would be the old price minus the new (i.e., changed) variable costs.

For example, consider the newspaper publisher who incurred an increase in the costs of newsprint. Say that this increase changed the variable costs per newspaper from $0.12 per newspaper to $0.22 per newspaper and that the base sales level of one issue of this newspaper is 25,200 copies. If the publisher is considering raising the price of the newspaper from $0.75 to $0.85 in order to cover this cost increase, the ΔCM involved will be only $0.10—the variable costs will be $0.22 whether or not she changes the price. Thus, the breakeven level she should consider can be calculated from the GBE formula as follows:

$$BE = \frac{-[(\$0.85 - \$0.22) - (\$0.75 - \$0.22)] \times 25,200}{\$0.85 - \$0.22}$$

$$BE = -[(\$0.63 - \$0.53) \times 25,200] / \$0.63$$

$$BE = -(\$0.10 \times 25,200) / \$0.63$$

$$BE = -\$2,520 / \$0.63$$

$$BE = -4,000 \text{ copies per issue}$$

This breakeven sales level indicates the critical sales change for the price increase required if the publisher decides to pass along the cost increase to her customers. If newspaper sales decreased by 4,000 copies (a 16 percent decrease), then the price change would have no profit implications. If sales decreased by less than 4,000 copies per issue, then the price increase would lead to an increase in profit. If sales decreased by more than 4,000 copies per issue, then the price increase would lead to a decrease in profit. Note that the reason for this price increase—only to pass along a cost increase—does not necessarily mean that the increase will have no financial consequences for the publisher. The profit effects will be determined entirely by the price-change response of the market.

Changes in Variable Costs That Are Tied to Changes in Price

When the changes in variable costs are tied to a prospective price change, then the ΔCM used in the GBE formula should include the effects of the changes in variable costs as well as the change in price. The computation of the new contribution margin would involve the new price and the new variable costs. Since the variable costs will not change unless the price changes, the old contribution margin—the one that would exist if no price change were made—would be the old price minus the old variable costs.

For example, say the managers of the dinner restaurant (previously mentioned) decided to implement the new strategy of targeting higher-income consumers. Suppose that the quality improvements associated with this strategy change will increase the variable costs for the average entrée from $2.50 to $4.50 and that the price change associated with this strategy will raise the price of the average entrée from $8.00 to $13.00. If the base sales level for the restaurant is 400 entrées per week, then the breakeven level of entrée sales that the managers should be considering can be calculated from the GBE formula as follows:

$$BE = \frac{-[(\$13.00 - \$4.50) - (\$8.00 - \$2.50)] \times 400}{\$13.00 - \$4.50}$$

$$BE = -[(\$8.50 - \$5.50) \times 400] / \$8.50$$

$$BE = -(\$3.00 \times 400) / \$8.50$$

$$BE = -\$1,200 / \$8.50$$

$$BE = -141 \text{ entrées per week}$$

This breakeven sales level would help the restaurant managers evaluate the prospective price increase that would be tied to an increase in variable costs. If entrée sales decreased by less than 141 per week (a 35 percent drop), then the price increase would lead to an increase in profit. If entrée sales decreased by more than 141 per week, then the price increase would lead to a decrease in profit.

USING THE GENERALIZED BREAKEVEN FORMULA WHEN FIXED COSTS CHANGE

As was noted in Chapter 4, fixed costs are those that do not vary with changes in the amount of product that is sold. In practice, however, fixed costs stay constant with sales changes only within a certain range. For example, building and grounds costs of a manufacturing plant would be considered fixed because they would be constant whether the factory was producing few units of the product or many. However, if sales increased so much that the capacity of the plant was exceeded, a new plant would have to be constructed. This would involve new fixed costs—a change in fixed costs in response to the sales level (see Figure 5.8). These incremental

Figure 5.8   The Behavior of Incremental Fixed Costs With Respect to Unit Sales

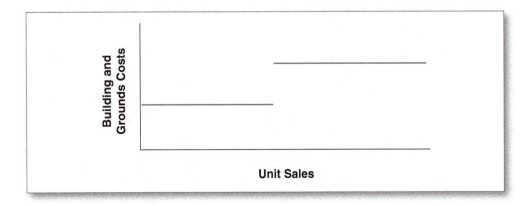

fixed costs would need to be considered in the breakeven analysis of a price change that might result in a sales change sufficient in size to cause such incremental fixed costs.

Identifying Incremental Fixed Costs

As was previously discussed with respect to variable costs, it is important to accurately identify the fixed costs that are incremental—that is, the costs that will be incurred or not in response to sales changes in the range of those that might be caused by the price changes being evaluated. In identifying incremental fixed costs, it is important to consider the following points:[5]

- *Sunk costs are never incremental.* If a fixed cost has been incurred before the prospective price change and cannot be reversed, then it is a sunk cost and should not be considered in the breakeven calculation for the prospective price change. For example, costs of initial product research and development are sunk costs by the time the product is being sold. Thus, these costs are not relevant to decisions concerning price modifications of this existing product.

- *Use changes in real market value to estimate depreciation.* Although tax law and accounting practice have various formulas for calculating the depreciation of an asset, for pricing purposes an asset's depreciation over a particular period is the market value at the start of the period minus the market value at the end of the period. For example, if a tour operator's tourist boat could be sold for $50,000 at the beginning of the season but for only $45,000 at the end of the season, the depreciation cost of the boat for the season would be $5,000.

- *Consider the opportunity costs of capital.* If resources are being tied up in an asset, then relevant costs associated with that asset include opportunity costs—the money that could be earned by an alternative use of those resources. For example, if the tour operator's loan on the boat that was previously mentioned is fully paid off at the start of the season, the use of the boat for giving tours means that it is a $50,000 resource that cannot be used for other money-making purposes. One such purpose would be to sell the boat at the start of the season and invest the $50,000 in, say, a municipal bond fund. If such investment would be the alternative use of the capital tied up in the boat, then the foregone return on this investment should be considered a component of the boat's incremental fixed costs for that tourist season.

In assessing incremental fixed costs, it is often helpful to consider how a company's activities affect the organization's expenses. This is known as activity-based costing. An expenditure that is related to the activities necessary for producing each unit of a product is a variable cost. However, an expenditure that is related to activities that occur only when a new batch of the product is produced is a cost that is fixed within the range of the number of items produced in a batch. Similarly, an expenditure that is related only to activities that occur only when a company gears up for the production of the product is fixed within the range of the number of units of the product that are sold. An example of an activity-based cost hierarchy for a large equipment manufacturer can be seen in Figure 5.9.[6]

Figure 5.9   An Activity-Based Cost Hierarchy for a Large Equipment Manufacturer

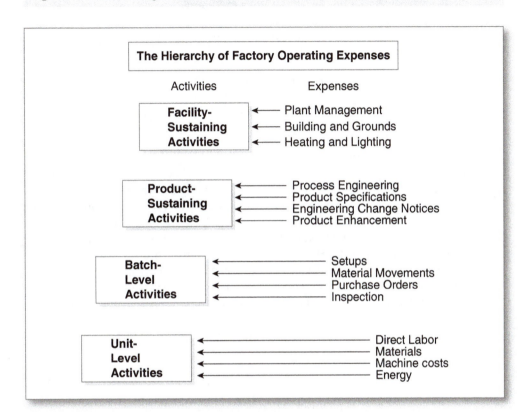

Adding or Subtracting Incremental Fixed Costs

To calculate the breakeven sales level for a prospective price change that involves incremental fixed costs, those incremental costs—whether they are increases or decreases—should be included in the numerator of the GBE formula.

For example, consider a small package delivery company that delivers 3,000 packages per week. The company operates three delivery trucks, each with the capacity to deliver 1,000 packages per week. Thus, the company is currently operating at full capacity. Say that each truck involves a fixed cost of $500 per week and that the variable costs for the average delivered package are $5 per package. Say also that the company is considering lowering its price from $12 per package to $11 per package.

For the company to break even on a price decrease, the price decrease needs to cause an increase in sales. However, because the company's three trucks are already operating at full capacity, any sales increase would require the company to obtain a fourth truck—which would constitute an incremental fixed cost. Assuming that the weekly costs of this fourth truck would be $500, the breakeven sales level for this prospective price change could be calculated from the GBE formula as follows:

$$BE = \frac{\$500 - \{[(\$11 - \$5) - (\$12 - \$5)] \times 3{,}000\}}{\$11 - \$5}$$

$$BE = [\$500 - (-\$1 \times 3{,}000)] / \$6$$

$$BE = (\$500 + \$3{,}000) / \$6$$

$$BE = \$3{,}500 / \$6$$

$$BE = 583 \text{ packages per week}$$

This breakeven sales level indicates that the company would have to deliver 583 more packages per week (a 19 percent increase) just to break even on this price change.

Suppose that in addition to considering this price decrease, the company was also considering a price change in the other direction—say, an increase in the package delivery price from the current $12 to $16. Because breaking even on a price increase would involve a decrease rather than an increase in sales, we need to be thinking about a sales decrease. In a sales decrease situation, there would be no additional trucks needed. Thus, for this prospective price change, the managers would start with the following breakeven calculation:

$$BE = \frac{-\{[(\$16 - \$5) - (\$12 - \$5)] \times 3{,}000\}}{\$16 - \$5}$$

$$BE = -(\$4 \times 3{,}000) / \$11$$

$$BE = -\$12{,}000 / \$11$$

$$BE = -1{,}091 \text{ packages}$$

This result indicates that the company would break even on the $4 price increase if sales decreased by 1,091 packages per week (a 36 percent decrease). Note, however, that at this level of sales decrease, one of the *existing* three delivery trucks would not be needed. Selling or renting out this truck would enable the $500 fixed cost associated with that truck to be avoided. This savings would be an incremental fixed cost—albeit a negative one—and thus should be considered in the breakeven calculation for the $4 price increase:

$$BE = \frac{-\$500 - \{[(\$16 - \$5) - (\$12 - \$5)] \times 3{,}000\}}{\$16 - \$5}$$

$$BE = [-\$500 - (\$4 \times 3{,}000)] / \$11$$

$$BE = (-\$500 - \$12{,}000) / \$11$$

$$BE = -\$12{,}500 / \$11$$

$$BE = -1{,}136 \text{ packages per week}$$

The correct breakeven sales level in this situation would be a decrease of 1,136 packages per week (a 38 percent decrease). Taking into account the savings in the fixed costs due to the truck that will no longer be needed increases the amount of sales that the delivery company could afford to lose as a result of the price increase.

BREAKEVEN ANALYSIS IN PRICE-MODIFICATION DECISIONS

These examples illustrate the wide applicability of the GBE formula. It can be used to help evaluate price changes that do not involve cost changes, for those that involve changes in variable costs, and for those that involve incremental fixed costs. The GBE formula could also be applied to price-change situations associated with more than one type of cost change. In short, the GBE formula makes possible breakeven analysis in the full range of price-modification decisions.

When a Price Modification Should Be Considered

A large survey of corporate pricing practices has found that the average company changes a product's price only about once a year. This finding in itself does not indicate a problem. As we will note in Chapter 7, there can be good reasons for keeping a product's price at the same level over time. However, what may be less than ideal is that it appears that most firms do not carry out regular evaluations of current prices.[7]

A company that is concerned with pricing to maximize profits would be wise to implement a schedule of periodic, and frequent, reviews of the prices of its products. This review could consist of using breakeven analysis to consider a variety of small price increases and decreases. By carrying out this analysis frequently and changing the price when the breakeven analysis indicates that the change is likely to result in a profit increase, a seller can continually track the optimum price point—that is, the item's best price.

Information Needed for Price-Modification Decisions

What makes this approach practical is that breakeven analysis provides a critical sales level. The decision maker needs relatively little information: only whether or not the critical sales level will be exceeded. Types of information that are much more difficult to obtain—such as marginal cost and marginal revenue functions and detailed sales predictions—are not required. It is this simplification of the price-modification decision that makes continual price-change evaluation— and its benefits—a realistic option for virtually any pricing manager.

Note, however, that *little* information does not mean *no* information. Breakeven analysis requires that the price setter have a means to obtain at least an approximate estimate of the market's response to a price change. The understandings and information necessary to accomplish this will therefore be our next concern.

SUMMARY

To help evaluate prospective changes to an existing price, the breakeven formula is generalized to include the contribution dollars that would be gained or lost from the effect of the price change on base sales. When evaluating a price decrease, the breakeven units given by this GBE formula indicate the number of additional units that must be sold to result in no change in gross profits. When evaluating a price increase, the GBE formula gives the number of units of base sales that could be lost to result in no change in gross profits.

The price-change breakeven sales level will be affected by the size of the price change, the base sales level, and the size of the contribution margin. To determine how a particular expected sales change resulting from a prospective price change would change the product's gross profits, the change-in-profit formula can be used.

To consider possible changes in variable costs, look for changes in costs such as those for materials and labor. It can be helpful to ask what additional costs will be incurred for each new sale and what costs would be saved for each sale not made. To use the GBE formula when variable costs change, consider whether the cost change is independent of the prospective price change or tied to it.

To consider possible changes in fixed costs, look for changes in costs such as those for facilities and equipment. When identifying changes in fixed costs, use changes in real market value to estimate depreciation, consider the opportunity costs of capital, and avoid including sunk costs. Changes in fixed costs should be specified in the numerator of the GBE formula.

Breakeven analysis simplifies the price-change evaluation process by providing a critical sales level and helps make frequent price-change evaluation a realistic option.

KEY TERMS

best price

base sales

change in contribution
   margin

new contribution margin

old contribution margin

generalized breakeven (GBE)
   formula

sales cushion

change-in-profit formula

sunk cost

opportunity costs

activity-based costing

REVIEW AND DISCUSSION QUESTIONS

1. Describe the concept of base sales. What would be the base sales level for a new product if a breakeven analysis is used to evaluate whether or not the new product should be offered?

2. Why is it important that a price-change breakeven calculation take into account the effect of the price change on contribution dollars from base sales?

3. If a manager is considering raising a price from $4 to $5 and making no change in variable costs, what would be the change in contribution margin?

4. In the GBE formula, explain why the change in contribution dollars from base sales is subtracted from, rather than added to, the change in fixed costs.

5. Explain why the denominator of the GBE formula consists of the contribution margin after, rather than before, the prospective price change.

6. Does the GBE formula's breakeven sales level for a prospective price decrease represent the total number of units that must be sold in order to break even or the number of units that must be sold over the base sales level in order to break even?

7. The GBE formula gives a negative breakeven sales level for price increases. Explain how such a negative breakeven should be interpreted.

8. If a product has a base sales level of 600 units and variable costs of $12 per unit, what would be the breakeven sales level for a price decrease from $20 to $18? What would be the breakeven sales level for a price increase from $20 to $22?

9. Describe a situation where the base sales level for evaluating a prospective price change for a product would be different than the product's past sales levels.

10. How does a product's contribution margin before a price change affect whether it would be a price increase or a price decrease that would be more likely to increase profits from that product?

11. Assume that the breakeven sales level for a price decrease is 44 units and the product's contribution margin after that price decrease is $4 per unit. If sales were to increase over the base sales level by 50 units, what would be the change in profit associated with this product?

12. Evaluate the following statement: For pricing purposes, all costs that vary with sales on a unit-by-unit basis should be considered variable costs.

13. When identifying variable costs, why is it important to ask about the additional costs that would be incurred for each new sale? How would this apply to a business where an inventory must be maintained?

14. Why is it important to identify costs that would be saved for each current sale that will be no longer made? How would this apply to a manufacturing operation where furloughed workers are guaranteed a portion of their usual wages?

15. What is meant when it is determined that a change in variable costs is independent of a prospective price change? How does knowing this affect the calculation of ΔCM in the GBE formula?

16. Give an example of an increase in variable costs that would be tied to a change in price. Then give an example of a decrease in variable costs that would be tied to a change in price.

17. When setting prices, what is the difference between how you would take into account an incremental fixed cost and how you would take into account a fixed cost that is not incremental?

18. What is meant by the term *sunk cost?* How should sunk costs be treated in the breakeven calculation for a prospective price change?

19. What is the best way to estimate depreciation costs that may be relevant to price setting?

20. Give an example of a situation where the opportunity costs of capital should be considered in a pricing decision. What questions should be asked to estimate these costs?

21. What is activity-based costing? Give an example of how it could be used to identify an incremental fixed cost.

22. If a company is operating at capacity and is now considering a 10 percent price increase, should the cost of increasing the company's capacity be considered in breakeven calculation for this price increase? Explain your reasoning.

23. Describe a situation when the incremental fixed costs used in a breakeven calculation would be a negative amount.

24. Describe how the calculation of a price-change breakeven can take into account changes in both variable costs and fixed costs.

25. Why might it be useful for a company to evaluate its prices more frequently than once per year? How might breakeven analysis help make it practical to carry out more frequent price evaluation?

EXERCISES

1. A manufacturer has been selling 50,000 units per year of a certain product. The price of this product is $20 and the variable costs associated with the product are $12 per unit. The manufacturer is considering decreasing the price of his product to $17 so as to increase sales. If he goes ahead with this price change, the manager will purchase new production machinery, at a cost of $75,000, to accommodate the increased sales.

   (a) The manager intends to evaluate the prospective price change by computing a breakeven sales level using the traditional formula, $BE = \Delta FC/CM$. Explain what is wrong with the logic of doing this.

   (b) Suggest a more appropriate formula for calculating a breakeven sales level. Justify your suggestion.

   (c) Use this more appropriate formula to calculate the breakeven sales level for this prospective price change. How can the manager use this breakeven in his decision about whether or not to go ahead with the price change?

   (d) Use breakeven analysis to help the manager decide whether or not to purchase the new production machinery while keeping the product's price at $20.

2. Eastern Semiconductor is currently selling its most popular microchip for $220. It has been selling 4,000 of these chips per month. The company has learned, however, that next month an overseas competitor will enter the market and start selling a copy of this chip for $200. If Eastern maintains its price of $220 per chip, it expects its sales to decrease to 3,000 units per month.

   (a) Given that Eastern's variable costs for this product are $40 per chip, what is the breakeven sales level for Eastern decreasing its price by $20 price per chip?

   (b) Do you think it is likely that Eastern will achieve this breakeven sales level?

3. Plasiderm, Inc., sells a medical product. The company is currently selling the product for $18/unit and is considering whether it could increase profits by increasing the product's price to $20/unit.
   Plasiderm currently sells 50,000 units per week. Its current weekly operating data are as follows:

Sales revenue	$900,000
Variable costs	$400,000
Fixed costs	$250,000
Pretax profit	$250,000

   You can assume that per-unit variable costs do not vary with the level of production.

   (a) What is the breakeven sales level for the price increase that Plasiderm is considering? Explain what this breakeven sales level means.

   (b) If the sales level for this product decreased by 5,000 units per week after the price increase, what would be the change in Plasiderm's weekly pretax profits caused by the price increase?

   (c) What would be Plasiderm's profit change if, after the price increase, sales remained at 50,000 units per week?

4. A heating oil retailer has been buying heating oil at $2.82 per gallon and keeps a 30-day supply on hand. He sells 5,000 gallons per day and has been charging his customers $3.25 per gallon. The retailer has nonincremental fixed costs of $800 per day. Yesterday the wholesale price of heating oil decreased from $2.82 per gallon to $2.68 cents per gallon.

   (a) What is the per-gallon cost that is relevant for pricing decisions concerning heating oil that the retailer will sell today? Explain your answer.

   (b) If the heating oil retailer is planning to respond to the wholesale price decrease by lowering his $3.25-per-gallon retail price, should he wait 30 days to make that price change? Explain your answer.

5. A leather goods retailer has been buying a popular style of handbag for $12 per bag and selling them for $20 per bag. The retailer has been selling 200 handbags per month. The retailer has been close to bankruptcy for the past year. In response to this threat, the retailer's buyer has found an overseas source for this handbag. The new source results in the cost per handbag

decreasing to $10 per bag, and the new shipments will begin arriving on January 1. The shop's owner feels that the arrival of the new versions of the popular handbag might present a good occasion to carry out a $2 price increase.

(a) What is the change in the retailer's variable costs that will occur on January 1? Is this change independent of the price change that the shop's owner is considering or is it tied to this prospective price change? Explain.

(b) Calculate the breakeven sales level for the price increase that the shop's owner is considering, and justify your answer.

6. A pharmaceutical company has been selling the prescription allergy drug Aquanox to retail pharmacists at a price of $3.20 per tablet, considerably above the company's variable costs of $0.52 per tablet. The company's director of marketing has recently suggested that they consider lowering the price, but the VP of the division rejected this idea. The VP's explanation was that they should not even consider lowering the price until the drug's high research and development costs have been recovered. Do you agree with the VP's reasoning? Why or why not?

7. One year ago, a manufacturer paid $3,000 for a stamping press that can produce only a particular plastic specialty product. The press now has a market value of $2,500 and is expected to continue to lose $500 of its market value each year. If the press were sold, assume that the manufacturer would earn 5 percent annual interest on the proceeds of the sale. The manufacturer is now considering changing this plastic specialty product's price for the coming year. If the manufacturer's pricing decision will affect whether or not this stamping press is retained by the company, what cost associated with the stamping press is relevant to this decision? Explain your answer.

NOTES

1. Thomas L. Powers, "Breakeven Analysis with Semifixed Costs," *Industrial Marketing Management* 16 (1987): 35–41.
2. Adapted from Noel Capon, *Managing Marketing in the 21st Century: Developing and Implementing the Marketing Strategy* (Bronxville, NY: Wessex, 2007), 529.
3. Adapted from Thomas T. Nagle, *The Strategy and Tactics of Pricing: A Guide to Profitable Decision Making* (Englewood Cliffs, NJ: Prentice Hall, 1987), 34.
4. These are adapted from discussions in Thomas T. Nagle and Reed K. Holden, *The Strategy and Tactics of Pricing*, 3rd ed. (Upper Saddle River, NJ: Prentice Hall, 2002), 21–22, 25, 28.
5. Adapted from discussions in Thomas T. Nagle and Reed K. Holden, *The Strategy and Tactics of Pricing*, 3rd ed. (Upper Saddle River, NJ: Prentice Hall, 2002), 25–30.
6. Robin Cooper and Robert S. Kaplan, "Profit Priorities from Activity-Based Costing," *Harvard Business Review* 69 (May–June 1991), 130–135.
7. Kent B. Monroe, *Pricing: Making Profitable Decisions*, 3rd ed. (Boston, MA: McGraw-Hill Irwin, 2003), 19.

CHAPTER 6

Predicting Price-Change Response: Economic and Competitive Factors

To make our breakeven approach to price-modification decisions possible, the manager must have a means of gauging the market's response to a prospective price change. Although a precise sales prediction is not needed, it is essential that the manager be able to judge whether or not the critical sales level from a breakeven calculation will be exceeded. This will require an understanding of the many factors that determine the market's response to a price change. The market's responsiveness to a price change is often referred to as the price sensitivity of the market. When a price change causes very little sales response, the market is said to be "insensitive" to the price change. When a price change causes a very large sales response, the market would be considered "sensitive" to the price change.

In this book, we group the many factors that determine a market's price sensitivity into four categories: (1) economic, (2) competitive, (3) cognitive, and (4) emotional. Economic factors concern the amount of money involved in the price change and in responding to the price change. Competitive factors concern the actions that a company's competitors take in response to the company's price changes. Cognitive factors concern the customer's awareness and knowledge of price levels and price meanings. Emotional factors concern the customer's feelings about prices and price changes.

Each of these categories of price-change response factors will be discussed in some detail. In this chapter, we focus on economic and competitive factors. We first introduce a generally applicable numerical measure of the market's responsiveness to a change in a product's price and then discuss how economic and competitive factors can affect the degree to which a product's price modification increases or decreases the product's sales. In Chapters 7 and 8, we will focus on the cognitive and emotional factors behind the market's price-change response.

THE PRICE ELASTICITY MEASURE

For efforts to predict price-change response, it is very helpful to have a standard numerical measure of this response. Perhaps the simplest such measure would be to calculate a ratio by dividing the size of the sales change by the size of the price change that caused it. An advantage of this measure would be that it is intuitive. If a certain price change caused a small sales change, then their ratio would be a small number. If that same price change caused a large sales change, then the ratio would be a larger number. A larger ratio would thus indicate a greater price-change response.

However, a disadvantage of this measure is that it would be specific to the units used in expressing the sales and price changes. For example, using this measure would make it difficult to compare price-change response measures if one ratio used the sales change for coffee in ounces and another used pounds or if one ratio used the price change in dollars and another used yen.

This measure of price-change response can avoid this disadvantage by a small modification. Rather than using the size of the sales-change, the sales-change *percent* can be used; rather than using the size of the price change, the price-change *percent* can be used. This creates a measure that is independent of how sales and price changes are measured and thus can be compared over various situations. This general price-change response measure has been termed the price elasticity (in the formulas, price elasticity will be referred to as E). Its definition is as follows:

$$E = \frac{\% \Delta \text{ Unit sales}}{\% \Delta P}$$

The denominator in this definition is the size of the price change in percent terms. Note that this is always calculated as the percent change from the old price. Thus, if P is the level of the price after the price change and P_o is the price level before the price change (i.e., the old price), then this percent is as follows:

$$\% \Delta P = [(P - P_o)/P_o] \times 100$$

The numerator in this definition is the percent change in sales units resulting from the price change. Note that this is always calculated as the percent change from the old sales level. Thus, if S is the level of unit sales after the price change and S_o is the sales level before the price change (i.e., the old sales level), then this percent is as follows:

$$\% \Delta \text{ Unit sales} = [(S - S_o)/S_o] \times 100$$

For example, if an increase of a product's price from \$10 to \$12 (a change of +20 percent) results in a decrease in sales from 2,000 units to 1,400 units (a change of −30 percent), then the price elasticity would be calculated as follows:

$$E = -30 \text{ percent} / +20 \text{ percent} = -1.5$$

In words, this price elasticity would indicate that there would be a 1.5 percent sales decrease for every 1 percent increase in price.

Note that a price elasticity can be calculated just as easily from a price decrease as from a price increase. For example, if a product's price is decreased from $160 to $140 (a change of −12.5 percent) and this decrease causes an increase in sales from 340 units to 425 units (a change of +25 percent), then the price elasticity would be as follows:

$$E = +25 \text{ percent} / -12.5 \text{ percent} = -2.0$$

This price elasticity value would indicate that there would be a 2 percent sales increase for every one percent decrease in price.

Interpreting Price Elasticities

Whether a price elasticity is calculated from a price increase or from a price decrease, the elasticity will usually be a negative number. This is because it is generally the case that when a product's price is increased, there is a decrease in the number of units of the product that are sold. When a product's price is decreased, it generally leads to an increase in unit sales. Of course, this inverse relation between price and sales does not always hold. There are occasions when a higher price confers a desirable meaning, such as higher quality or prestige, and this meaning causes price and sales to change in the same direction. For example, a particular pen and pencil set selling poorly at $8 could be seen as more suitable for a gift at $25 and thus sell more briskly at that higher price. However, such examples of positive price elasticity are the exceptions; price elasticities are usually negative.

Given that price elasticities are usually negative, we should note some conventions of speech regarding how they are discussed. If, for example, the price elasticity for dvd rentals among seniors is −3 and the price elasticity among young adults is −1.2, we will say that seniors show "greater" or "higher" price elasticity than young adults. This could be considered a little odd, because −3 is a lower number than −1.2. However, this way of speaking makes sense, because price elasticities are used to measure price sensitivity, and −3 does indicate a *greater* amount of price sensitivity than −1.2. It should also be noted that those who are more technically inclined, such as economists, would speak of the seniors market as being "more elastic" than that of the young adults. You can think of the phrase *more elastic* as indicating more "stretching" of sales in response to a price change and the phrase *less elastic* as indicating sales rigidity, or the market "not bending" in response to a change in price.

Although price elasticity is a price-change response measure that is independent of the way price and sales changes are measured, one should be very careful about generalizing from any particular measured price elasticity. A demand curve shows the relationship between various prices a product can have and the sales that would occur at that price. As can be seen from any demand curve that has been developed from real data (such as the ones in Figure 6.1)[1], the market's sales response to an item's price is not a smoothly varying function of that price. This means that a product's price elasticity measured at, say, low price levels might differ from the price elasticity measured at high price levels. Thus, a

Figure 6.1 Example of Demand Curves Developed From Real Data

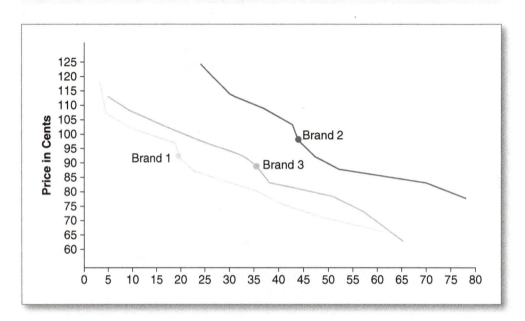

manager should know as much as possible about the situation in which a price elasticity has been measured before using that price elasticity to help predict the market's response to the price change currently being considered.

In fact, because a price elasticity is a ratio of percents, its value can be specific to the particular sales and price levels occurring at the time the price change is being considered. For example, say an item's current sales are 100 units and its current price is $40. If the item's sales rise to 120 units (a change of +20 percent) in response to decreasing the item's price to $30 (a change of −25 percent), this market response would constitute a price elasticity of −0.8 (20 percent / −25 percent). However, say that the seller later changes his mind—he raises the price back to $40 and the sales level of 120 units drops back to 100 units. Because the starting sales level (i.e., S_o) is now 120 units, the sales change would be −16.7 percent. Because the starting price level (i.e., P_o) is now $30, the price change would be +33.3 percent. Thus, the price elasticity for that price change would be −0.5 (−16.7 percent / 33.3 percent). The importance of starting points helps remind us that the exact value of a price elasticity can be very much dependent on the price-change situation.

Using Price Elasticities in Price-Change Breakeven Analysis

In a breakeven analysis for a prospective price change, it is necessary to know whether or not the sales response to a price change will exceed the critical sales level. If you know the elasticity for price changes in situations similar to the one being evaluated, then you can obtain a usable estimate of the market's price-change response. This can be accomplished by rearranging the factors in the definition of price elasticity to arrive at an equation for the percent change in unit sales:

$$E = \%\Delta \text{ Unit sales } / \%\Delta P$$

$$E \times \%\Delta P = (\%\Delta \text{ Unit sales } / \%\Delta P) \times \%\Delta P$$

$$E \times \%\Delta P = \%\Delta \text{ Unit sales}$$

$$\%\Delta \text{ Unit sales } = E \times \%\Delta P$$

In any specific situation, the percent change in sales can be converted into a unit change in the level of sales. This change in unit sales level could then be compared to the price change's breakeven level, which is also a change in the level of unit sales.

Consider the example of a candy company currently selling 2,000 bars per week of a particular product at $0.50 per bar. If the product manager calculates that the breakeven level for a $0.10 price increase is −500 candy bars per week and if he knows that the price elasticity in this situation is approximately −2, then he can answer the question of whether the prospective $0.10 price increase will increase the gross profits associated with the product.

The first step is to convert the prospective price change into a percentage: $(10/50) \times 100 = 20$ percent. The second step is to substitute this value for $\%\Delta P$ in the rearranged definition of price elasticity. The third step is to put in the price elasticity estimate, −2, for E in the equation and carry out the calculation:

$$\%\Delta \text{ Unit sales } = -2 \times 20 \text{ percent}$$

$$= -40 \text{ percent}$$

The calculation tells us that in this situation, a 20 percent price increase will result in a 40 percent sales decrease. The fourth step is to convert this percentage back into units: a 40 percent decrease from the base sales level of 2,000 candy bars per week is a decrease of 800 bars per week $(0.4 \times 2,000)$. This far exceeds the calculated breakeven sales cushion of 500 bars per week. Thus, a price elasticity of −2 indicates that the $0.10 price increase being considered would result in lower gross profits for this product.

It is also possible to evaluate a prospective price change by converting the breakeven sales level into a breakeven price elasticity (in the formulas, breakeven price elasticity will be referred to as E_{BE}). If we continue with the example of the candy company, the breakeven level of −500 candy bars constitutes a −25 percent change from the base sales level of 2,000 candy bars per week. For such a decrease to be caused by the prospective 20 percent price increase, the associated price elasticity would be −1.25 (−25 percent / 20 percent). This, then, would be the breakeven price elasticity. It serves as a critical value—in order for the $0.10 price increase being considered to be profitable, the market would need to show less price elasticity than −1.25.

OBSERVED PRICE ELASTICITIES

Given that the market's price elasticity for a price change provides an indication of whether or not the breakeven sales level will be exceeded, it is important to be able to estimate this price elasticity. One component of a manager's ability to estimate a price elasticity in a price-change situation is to be familiar with aspects of the price elasticities that have already been observed.

Category Versus Brand Price Elasticities

When estimating the price elasticity for a price-change situation, it often makes sense to consider the price elasticity values obtained from previous research, either from the company considering the price change or from published sources. To do this, it is important to understand the distinction between category and brand price elasticities.

The category price elasticity (also known as primary demand elasticity) is the percent change in sales for an entire product category divided by the percent change in the average price for an item in that product category. Category price elasticities in the U.S. market for some selected commodities can be seen in Figure 6.2[2]. Taking, say, tires as an example, the category price elasticity tells us that if the average price of tires increases by 10 percent, overall sales would decrease by about 12 percent. The higher price would lead some customers to replace their tires less often. For a 10 percent price decrease, overall sales would increase by about 12 percent. The lower price would lead to more frequent tire replacement.

Figure 6.2 Some Category Price Elasticities

Commodity	Price Elasticity
Cotton	–0.12
Potatoes	–0.31
Corn	–0.49
Pharmaceuticals	–0.50
Oats	–0.56
Beef	–0.92
Automobile tires	–1.20
Electricity	–1.20
Haddock	–2.20
First-run movies	–3.70

Typically, however, the manager evaluating a prospective price modification is interested in the market's response to a price change in the manager's *brand,* rather than its response to a price change in the entire product category. The market's response to a price change in a brand is known as the brand price elasticity (also referred to as selective or interbrand demand elasticity). The brand price elasticity is the percent change in the sales of a particular brand divided by the percent change in that brand's price.

Note that the brand price elasticity may have little relation to the category price elasticity. For example, if only one tire brand, say Uniroyal, increased its prices by 10 percent, it is possible that many of its customers would switch to Goodyear, Dunlop, Kelly-Springfield, or some other tire brand. This could create a sales decrease for Uniroyal far greater than 12 percent that would be predicted by the category price elasticity.

On the other hand, if the competitive response to a company's price change is such that all of the company's competitors in the industry match the change, then the brand price elasticity and the category price elasticity become equal. For example, if Uniroyal increased its prices by 10 percent, but Goodyear, Dunlop, Kelly-Springfield, and all of the other tire manufacturers followed suit, then there would be no reason for customers to switch from Uniroyal to another brand. In that case, the market response to Uniroyal's price change would be represented by the category price elasticity for automobile tires.

Brand Elasticities Typically Observed

The process of estimating a product's brand elasticity could start by noting the range of brand price elasticities typically observed. In a paper published in the *Journal of Marketing Research,* researchers reported the results of compiling the brand price elasticities found in dozens of marketplace studies published between the years 1961 and 2004.[3] The distribution of the 1,851 brand price elasticities they collected can be seen in Figure 6.3. Although brand price elasticities can vary widely, they typically were found to be around the median elasticity value of −2.22. Over 80 percent of the observed price elasticities fell between 0 and −4. As mentioned earlier, price elasticities are sometimes positive, but this study found elasticities with a positive sign occurred only about 2 percent of the time.

Knowing that the likely range of brand price elasticities is between 0 and −4 is in itself of some value to a pricing manager. Say the breakeven analysis of a prospective price decrease indicates that the brand's price elasticity would have to be greater than −4 for the price change to be profitable. Simply knowing that such a level of price elasticity is unlikely to be observed—without any further information—alerts the price setter to the doubtful wisdom of the price change.

For example, say a manager selling 500 units per month of a product priced at $60 calculates that the breakeven level for a $2.40 price decrease is a sales increase of 120 units per month. Because this breakeven level is a 24 percent sales increase (120/500 × 100) in response to a 4 percent price decrease ($2.40/$60 × 100), the breakeven price elasticity that would have to be surpassed would equal −6 (24 percent / −4 percent). If it is not easy to get further information, knowing the range of likely brand price elasticities would make it reasonable to reject this prospective price decrease on the basis of this consideration alone.

Figure 6.3 Frequency Distribution of 1,851 Observed Brand Price Elasticities

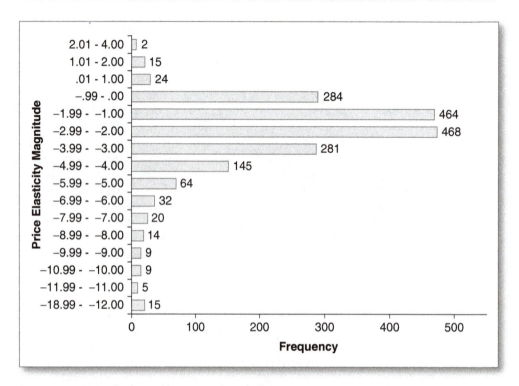

Source: Tammo H. A. Bijmolt, Harald J. Van Heerde, and Rik G. M. Pieters, "New Empirical Generalizations on the Determinants of Price Elasticity," *Journal of Marketing Research*, 42 (May 2005), 141–156.

ECONOMIC FACTORS AFFECTING PRICE-CHANGE RESPONSE

Although knowing the range of typical brand elasticities is of some value, the four-point range between 0 and –4 is still quite large. The evaluation of a prospective price change will always benefit from a somewhat more detailed price elasticity estimate. To arrive at this more detailed estimate, it is necessary to understand the factors that determine the market's response to a price change.

Because a price change involves a change in the amount of money that customers are required to pay, economic factors can have important effects on customers' price-change response. These factors involve the financial implications to the customer of responding to the prospective price change. Consider the following four economic factors:

1. *Amount of money involved in the price change.* Customers can be expected to show a greater response to a price change the greater the amount of money that is involved in the price change. Thus, a $1,000 price increase for a new car is likely to affect customers more than a $0.20 price increase for a jar of mustard.

Also, it is likely that a $0.20 price increase for a gallon of milk or a dozen eggs will affect consumers more than that same price increase for a jar of mustard. Why? Milk and eggs are usually purchased far more frequently than mustard and thus a change in their prices involves a greater amount of money.

If a $0.20 price decrease, rather than increase, is considered, it is likely that the decrease will affect sales of facial tissues or paper towels more than milk or eggs even though all four products are frequently purchased. Why? Facial tissues and paper towels can be stored. Thus, the consumer can stock up in response to a price decrease on these items and save a greater amount of money.

In addition, all of these price-change amounts are likely to have a greater effect on customers who have small incomes than on those who are well-off. The extent of the reaction to the money involved in a price change is likely to be relative to the customer's wealth. Money will tend to be dearer to those who have less.

2. *Amount of the price change that the customer will actually pay.* If we define *customer* as the person who is primarily responsible for making the purchasing decision, there are occasions when this decision maker is not also the person responsible for paying the full amount of a product's price. For example, a product may be tax deductible, covered by insurance, or a customer's employer may reimburse the employee for all or part of the product's price. When the buyer does not pay the full amount of the product's price, the buyer's response to a price change can be expected to be less than if the buyer pays the full price.

An extreme example of this is when an individual has the authority to make the product purchase decision for other individuals. This occurs for products such as college textbooks and prescription drugs. The professor and the physician make the purchase decisions, and the students and patients pay the price. The resulting low price sensitivity has been at least partially responsible for the many years of steady increases in the prices of these products.

3. *Customer's switching costs.* When switching from one brand to another is costly to a customer, then these switching costs are likely to impair a customer from responding to a price change. For example, if the price of new accounting software decreases, a business customer may resist switching from his or her more expensive system because of the necessary costs of retraining personnel in the use of the new system. If a cell phone service increases its price, consumers may be less inclined to switch to another service because such a switch would involve the costs of purchasing a new cellular phone.

4. *Customer's search costs.* When the process of evaluating the price or benefits of alternative brands is costly to a customer, then these search costs are likely to impair a customer from responding to a price change. For consumers, search costs would include the costs of gas, parking, and lost work time a consumer might incur in visiting numerous stores and the costs of discarding or returning items that were tried and deemed unsatisfactory. For business customers, search costs would include the costs of soliciting and evaluating proposals from a number of vendors and the costs involved in resolving the damages created by a new product that did not perform adequately.

One way that understanding price-change response factors can contribute to estimating a price elasticity is to determine the implications of those factors for the prospective price change at hand. For example, one question could be asked for each of the four economic factors previously described:

1. Does the price change involve what the customer would consider a large amount of money?
2. Will the buyer actually incur the full extent of the price change?
3. Are the customers' switching costs low in the product category?
4. Are the customers' search costs low in the product category?

If the answer to each of these questions is yes, then these economic factors would point toward a higher or greater brand price elasticity. If the answer to each of these questions is no, then these economic factors would point toward a lower brand price elasticity.

When a full set of price-change response factors is considered, then the direction of these factors could be applied to the likely range of brand price elasticities. If all or a majority of the factors suggest high price elasticity, then the manager could estimate that the brand price elasticity is likely to be closer to the –4 end of the typical range. If all or a majority of the factors suggest low price elasticity, then the manager could estimate that the brand price elasticity is likely to be closer to the 0 end of the typical range. If there is an equal division of factors suggesting high price sensitivity and factors suggesting low price sensitivity, then the brand price elasticity is likely to be closer to the middle of the typical range.

The four economic factors previously described are particularly useful because they can be easily evaluated in most price-change situations. As we move on to consider other types of price-change response factors, we will encounter some that require more careful understanding and/or more extensive information.

ROLE OF COMPETITORS IN PRICE-CHANGE RESPONSE

One of the key tasks in predicting the market response to a price change is to be able to anticipate how competitors will respond to the price change. The responses of these competitors are important because they determine how the price change will affect the price differentials between the company that initiates the price change and its competitors. The price differential between two competing companies is the difference in their prices for a particular product.

For example, say United Airlines charges $360 for a flight between two cities in the central United States and that there are only two other airlines that fly that particular route: American Airlines and Delta Airlines. If American charges $375 for this flight and Delta charges $388, then there is a $15 price differential between United and American and a $28 price differential between United and Delta (see Figure 6.4).

The customer response to, say, a $15 price increase for this flight by United will be strongly affected by the response of American and Delta. If American and Delta leave their prices unchanged, then the price differentials between these carriers and United will decrease (to $0 and $13, respectively; see Figure 6.5). This will cause United to lose some

Figure 6.4 Price Differentials for a Particular Flight Between Two Cities

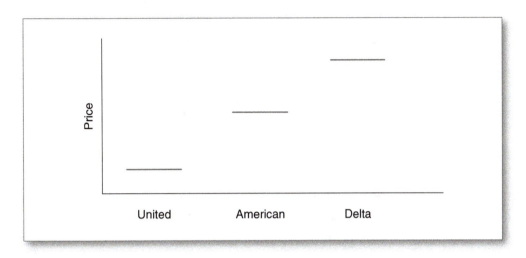

Figure 6.5 An Unmatched Price Increase Reduces the Price Differentials

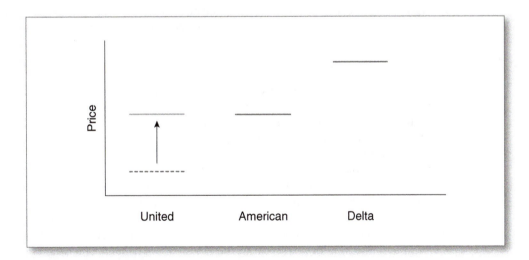

of the customers who had a slight preference for American or Delta but chose United because of its lower price. On the other hand, if American and Delta match United's price increase (raising their prices to $390 and $403, respectively), the current $15 and $28 price differentials will be maintained (see Figure 6.6). In that case, the only sales United Airlines would lose would be its share of those customers who respond to the price increase by deciding not to fly directly between those two cities.

Figure 6.6 A Matched Price Increase Maintains the Price Differentials

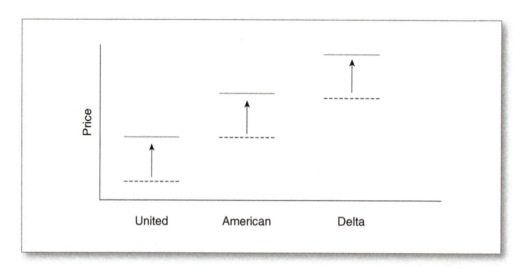

Because of the importance of price differentials to customer behavior, it is impossible to adequately predict the market's response to a prospective price change without some sense of how the competitors in the market are likely to respond to the price change.

Three Basic Competitive Stances

To a large extent, the competitive reaction to a price change is determined by each competitor's general competitive stance toward the organization that considers initiating the price change. A competitive stance is a company's posture, or set of response tendencies similar to an attitude. It can and does change, but companies are often found to hold the same stance for long periods.

There are three basic competitive stances. The competitor who holds a cooperative stance does not want to rock the boat. This competitor is satisfied with the current situation with respect to the price-change initiator and prefers that things remain the same. The competitor who maintains an aggressive stance wants to improve his or her position at the expense of the price-change initiator. This competitor would like to see things change with respect to the initiator, in the direction of the competitor's benefit. The competitor who holds a dismissive stance feels that whatever the initiator does will not substantially affect him or her. This competitor simply ignores the price-change initiator and makes no special response to the initiator's price-change decisions.

The likely price-change responses of competitors holding each of these three stances are summarized in Figure 6.7. The cooperative competitor will be likely to match both the initiator's price increases and the initiator's price decreases. This is what is necessary to maintain the current price differential between the two companies. The attractiveness of the initiator's price relative to that of the cooperative competitor will not change.

Figure 6.7   Competitive Stance and Likely Price-Change Response

Competitor's Stance	Competitor's Likely Response to Initiator's	
	Price Increase	**Price Decrease**
Cooperative	matching increase	matching decrease
Aggressive	no change or smaller increase	matching or larger decrease
Dismissive	no change	no change

The likely response of the aggressive competitor to a price increase by the initiator will be to maintain the competing product's price or to increase it by a smaller amount. Both of these responses will change the price differential between the competitor and the initiator in a way that makes the initiator's price relatively less attractive to customers. The likely response of the aggressive competitor to a price decrease by the initiator will be to match the decrease and to perhaps drop price by a larger amount. This latter response will change the price differential so as to decrease the relative attractiveness of the initiator's price.

The dismissive competitor will most likely maintain the product's price in response to the initiator's price change. As a result, a price increase by the initiator will change the price differential between the two companies so as to decrease the attractiveness of the initiator's price. On the other hand, a price decrease by the initiator will change the price differential between the two companies so as to increase the attractiveness of the initiator's price.

Determining the Stance of Your Competitors

Fundamental to anticipating how competitors will react to a prospective price change is determining the competitive stance of each of your major competitors. Doing this involves collecting relevant information about each competitor. What information to look for and how to find such information are discussed next.

The information that most accurately reveals a company's competitive stance with respect to a price-change initiator is the company's past behaviors. The price-change initiator should note how the competitor has responded to its price changes in the past. If the competitor has usually matched its increases and decreases, it suggests a cooperative stance. If the competitor has usually not followed the initiator's price increases or responded to the initiator's decreases with even larger decreases, it suggests an aggressive stance. If the competitor has failed to respond to the initiator's past price decreases as well as its increases, it suggests a dismissive stance.

If there is little history available regarding the competitor's past responses to the initiator's price changes, the initiator's managers can examine the competitor's past responses to price changes of other, similar companies. For example, a small local pizza shop interested in determining the stance of the local Domino's franchise could look at how the Domino's shop responded to a recent price change of one of the other local pizza shops in the area. It would also be worthwhile to gather data on the past behaviors of key executives in the competing company. Perhaps a competitor's new CEO was responsible for her previous company's consistently aggressive price-change responses.

Because such historical information is rarely sufficient for clearly determining an organization's competitive stance, it is useful to supplement this information with some typical characteristics associated with each general competitive stance. Consider, in particular, the following four competitive dimensions (see Figure 6.8):

1. *Relative size.* Competitors of approximately equal size are likely to feel comparably powerful, which would tend to discourage the perception that an advantage could be gained by changing the price differential between them. For example, United, American, and Delta, along with US Airways, tend to respond cooperatively to price increases or decreases by the others. The resulting tendency for their prices to rise and fall together is an example of what is known as parallel pricing. On the other hand, there is more likely to be instability between competitors of unequal size. A small upstart might take an aggressive stance toward a larger competitor in order to grow, as in AirTran's aggressive stance toward US Airways. It is also possible that a large competitor is likely to feel capable of constraining a smaller competitor and thus may respond aggressively toward that smaller competitor as a means of implementing that power. When one competitor is much larger than another, the larger competitor can feel relatively invulnerable to the actions of the smaller one and thus adopt a dismissive stance. For example, Microsoft is likely to pay little attention to the price-change activities of Corel's WordPerfect product.

2. *Degree of brand differentiation.* Lack of brand differentiation between two competitors (such as between Exxon and Shell gasoline) would mean that changing the price differential between them would be likely to substantially change their relative market shares. This would support a cooperative stance by a competitor satisfied with its market share or an aggressive stance by a competitor interested in increasing its share. A company with a highly differentiated brand, such as Sony televisions, Apple's iPhone, or Hugo Boss clothing, is less likely to be affected by the price changes of competitors. Thus, such companies would be more likely to adopt a dismissive stance toward the price changes of their competitors.

3. *Differences in unit costs.* Competitors with comparable per-unit costs are likely to adopt a cooperative stance toward each other. A dismissive stance will often reward competitors who cut prices, and an aggressive stance will often tempt retaliation. The effect is that both a dismissive and an aggressive stance will tend to encourage price competition. Among competitors with equal per-unit costs, there is unlikely to be a clear victor in price competition, and all of the competitors participating in price competition are likely to see lower profits. On the other hand, having lower unit costs puts a competitor in a better position to win in price competition, and thus reduces that competitor's fear

of it. For example, AMD's foreign manufacturing operations result in considerably lower microchip costs than do Intel's and make possible an aggressive stance toward Intel.

4. *Goals.* A competitor's strategic goals will map onto its likely competitive stance. The goal of a company satisfied with its current sales level in a product category or without the excess capacity to expand will be to maintain its market share. Such a goal fits with a cooperative stance. However, a company intent on gaining share at the expense of a competitor, such as Lowe's goal of taking share from The Home Depot, fits with an aggressive competitive stance. An organization's goals are probably not closely related to its likelihood of adopting a dismissive stance.

Figure 6.8   Competitor Characteristics Associated With Each Competitive Stance

Competitor's Stance	Competitive Dimension			
	Relative size	Differentiated brand	Unit costs	Goals
Cooperative	equal	no	equal	maintain
Aggressive	smaller or larger	no	lower	expand
Dismissive	larger	yes	lower	unrelated

Sources of Competitive Information

Familiarity with the variety of possible sources of information about a competitor can facilitate the process of determining its competitive stance and thus predicting the competitor's likely price-change response. The most accessible of these sources of "competitive intelligence" is the marketplace itself. It is important to shop the competition—be aware of each competitor's prices. In the same vein, be aware of the messages communicated in each competitor's advertising and the products and themes each competitor displays at trade shows.

Other sources of competitive information include trade associations and trade publications. They will often provide accurate data on such key competitive dimensions as relative prices, market share, advertising expenditures, and even costs of commonly purchased components and supplies (see Figure 6.9). The reports of securities analysts in brokerages and investment organizations can also be a valuable source of competitive data. Finally, it is important to keep in mind that your customers can be an important source of information about your competitors. A good salesperson will usually be able to draw from discussions with customers a considerable amount of information about the products, prices, and promotional messages of the other companies that call on those customers.

Figure 6.9   Example of Competitive Price Data Found in a Trade Magazine

Market Basket

An exclusive series on in-store pricing

(*Conducted in conjunction with McMillan/Doolittle in St. Petersburg, Fla, Monday, Sept. 23*)

PRODUCT	SIZE	WAL-MART	WALGREENS	CVS	ECKERD
HEALTH[1]					
Benadryl Allergy	100 ct	$6.94	$7.99	$8.29	$8.59
Actifed Cold & Allergy	24 ct	4.64	6.29	6.49	6.59
Robitussin PE	4 oz	4.30	5.49	4.79	5.29
Q-Tips	300 ct	2.97	2.99	2.79	2.99
Neosporin Max Strength Cream	.5 oz	3.17	6.49	5.89	3.99
Band Aid-SpongeBob Assort.	20 each	1.97	3.29	N/A	2.99
Lamisil–Anti-fungal 1%	.85 oz	7.47	9.99	15.99	9.99
Dr. Scholls Air Cushion Insole–Mens	1 pair	1.57	2.99	2.59	2.49
Aleve	100 ct	7.48	5.99	8.99	8.99
Thermacare–Back	2 pu	6.43	6.99	7.96	7.99
Bayer Caplets	100 ct	5.48	8.99	8.99	8.99
Aspercreme Cream	3 oz	4.48	6.49	5.99	6.29
Ben Gay – Ultra	4 oz	6.83	7.99	7.99	8.99
Advil 200mg	100 ct	6.97	8.99	8.99	8.99
Tylenol Cold-Childrens	4 oz	4.94	6.49	6.49	6.49
Tylenol ES Caplets	100 ct	6.84	8.99	9.49	8.29
Excedrin P.M.	24 ct	3.97	5.99	4.59	4.99
Centrum	100 ct + 30 ct	8.67	8.99	8.99	9.49
SUBTOTAL		**93.15**	**118.13**	**125.30**	**119.43**

Source: Drug Store News, October 21, 2002.

Like any other type of market research, information about competitors will be most valuable if it is collected and stored in a systematic way. Activities such as shopping the competition should be done thoroughly and periodically. Information from different sources should be merged into a common framework. The resulting database of competitive information should be kept up to date and be easily accessible to pricing managers.

COMMUNICATING COMPETITIVE INFORMATION

In addition to appreciating the usefulness of collecting information about competitors, it is also important to recognize and understand the potential consequences of the price information that you communicate to competitors. As will be discussed in Chapter 15, explicit private communication with competitors about pricing—such as sitting down and having a talk—constitutes illegal collusion, an anticompetitive practice that could elicit severe penalties. However, a company cannot avoid at least some public communication of price information. Customers need to have information on the prices of the products they are considering, and both customers and investors can benefit from information from a company concerning its pricing intentions and motives. Because such pricing information is public, it also constitutes communication to competitors.

Price Signaling Strategies

When this publicly available price-related information is intentionally managed to have an effect on competitors, it is known as price signaling.[4] Price signaling typically uses the techniques of publicity, as opposed to paid advertising, to communicate pricing information. For example, the company can signal competitors through news releases, press conferences, giving the media access to company executives, planting articles in op-ed pages of major newspapers, and through blogs and other materials posted on the Internet. The price signaling strategies most often mentioned tend to fall into three broad categories.[5]

The first category includes strategies to signal competitive strength. For example, a company might publicize its intention to match or beat any price cuts initiated by competitors. This might give pause to an aggressive competitor, because such matching would prevent the favorable increase in the price differential that may have been intended by the competitor. Moreover, such a signal raises the possibility that initiating a price cut might lead to price warfare—companies successively exceeding each other's price cuts—which can drastically reduce profits for all of the warring competitors. Such willingness-to-match signals could be supplemented with evidence of the company's ability to carry out such price matching decreases. For example, when its expensive new automated plant was completed, the Goodyear Tire and Rubber Company publicized the plant's capabilities that sharply reduced variable costs and thus communicated the company's formidable ability to lower prices.[6]

A second category of price signaling strategies involves signals to indicate that a company has limited goals for initiating a price decrease. This means that, rather than being an attempt to take market share away from competitors, the goal of initiating a price cut is more limited. For example, the company could communicate that it is using the price cut only to *maintain* its market share, which otherwise would be slipping. Or it could signal that the goal of the cut would be to take advantage of high *category* price elasticity—in other words, to expand the market. Ellisco, Inc., a small supplier of inner-threaded metal caps to consumer packaged goods manufacturers, publicly announced that its price cuts were to compete only for their customers' "second-source" business—the small amount of business that manufacturers allot to small suppliers, as insurance against a disruption of their primary suppliers. In each of these limited-goals signals, the intended message to the company's competitors is "there's no need to match this price cut."

A third category of price signaling strategies involves the use of price signaling to encourage competitors to match a planned price increase. For example, during a speech or media interview, a company executive could interpret a recent event, such as a backlog of orders, as indicating a need to raise prices. This would suggest that competitors interpret any order backlog they may have in a similar way. Another possibility would be to provide justifications for a price increase. For example, publicly noting an industry trend toward higher materials costs could give competitors a justification for also increasing prices. Often a sufficient signal is simply to announce a planned price increase far ahead of time. This would give competitors time to consider the price increase and decide if they will match it. If they do not match it, the initiating company could change its plans and cancel the planned price increase. U.S. airlines have been observed to a post fare increase on a route at the start of a weekend and then retract it Monday morning if competitors who compete on that route do not follow.[7]

Issues Regarding Price Signaling

Because price signaling involves an intention to influence business competitors, the question arises whether or not it is an illegal anticompetitive activity. As will be seen in Chapter 15, price signaling is in a legal gray area. Determinations of its legality have hinged on factors such as the circumstances of the signaling (e.g., Is it seen in a market with only few large competitors?) and its consequences (e.g., Has the profitability of the products in question substantially increased?).

Most regulatory attention regarding price signaling seems to be on signals for price increases, such as those seen in the U.S. airline industry. Signals regarding price decreases appear less often questioned. Indeed, it could be argued that the signal of the limited goals of a price decrease could have procompetitive effects, to the extent that they serve to help protect weaker companies against overzealous stronger competitors.

An important price signaling issue is the question of the degree to which it actually works. Price signaling is sometimes referred to in the economics literature as "cheap talk." There is some evidence from laboratory research that such talk is "likely to fall on deaf ears" unless the competitors are already of one mind concerning goals and strategies.[8] This raises the possibility that pricing signaling could even backfire by raising the awareness of price competition and bringing to competitors' minds the possibility of an aggressive response. In this context, it should be noted that competitors could be reading signals into your pricing communications even if you do not intend them.[9] That in itself is a good reason to be aware of the strategies and issues of price signaling.

APPLYING GAME THEORY TO MANAGING PRICE COMPETITION

In addition to messages that are intentionally or unintentionally communicated about prices and price-related plans and motives, pricing behaviors themselves can communicate information. Game theory involves examining possible patterns of behaviors in order to help predict and manage price competition. A useful tool of game theory is a diagram known as a payoff matrix, the most typical of which contains four cells. The typical payoff matrix is useful because, in a very accessible way, it captures part of the essence of price competition.[10]

It captures this essence by simplifying things. Normally, a seller is faced with many competitors. However, when the seller is considering any particular competitor, there are only two competitors: (1) the seller and (2) the competitor who is being considered. Thus, the typical payoff matrix includes only two competitors, or "players." Normally, there are many price possibilities. However, the seller's decision often comes down to just two prices: (1) one higher and (2) one lower. Thus, the typical payoff matrix includes only two prices. Because each of the two players has two possible prices, there are four possible price situations. These four situations are the four cells of the typical payoff matrix.

Determining the Payoffs

If we examine the matrix in Figure 6.10, we can see how one arrives at the outcomes, or payoffs, for each of the two players in each cell of the matrix. Let's say that Company A and

Figure 6.10   A Game-Theory Payoff Matrix for Price Competition Between Company A and Company B

All amounts in millions	Company A—Maintains Price			Company A—Cuts Price		
Company B— Maintains Price	**Cell 1**			**Cell 2**		
	Co. A	Co. B		Co. A	Co. B	
	$10	$10	Revenue	$13.50	$5.00	Revenue
	− $3	− $3	VC	− $4.50	− $1.50	VC
	$7	$7	Profit	$9.00	$3.50	Profit
Company B— Cuts Price	**Cell 3**			**Cell 4**		
	Co. A	Co. B		Co. A	Co. B	
	$ 5.00	$13.50	Revenue	$9	$9	Revenue
	− $1.50	− $4.50	VC	− $3	− $3	VC
	$3.50	$9.00	Profit	$6	$6	Profit

Source: Adapted from from Nagle (1987).

Company B are approximately equal-sized competitors in a market that supports sales of $20 million per period at current prices. Each company thus has sales of $10 million per period. Suppose each company has variable costs that are 30 percent of current prices. Suppose that neither of the two companies' products are well-differentiated so that a 10 percent price cut by one company will take away half of the sales of the other competitor when the other competitor does not match the price cut. However, if there is a matching 10 percent price cut by the other competitor, then the market's sales will again be equally divided between the two competitors.

When each competitor's variable costs are subtracted from its sales revenue, the resulting payoffs for each price situation can be observed. If both competitors keep the price at current levels, both earn $7 million gross profit. If Company B drops the product's price and Company A does not, then Company B earns $9 million and Company A earns $3.5 million. Correspondingly, if Company A drops the product's price and Company B does not, then it is Company A that earns $9 million and it is Company B that earns $3.5 million. If both competitors drop their prices, then both companies earn gross profits of $6 million.

In most game-theory scenarios, it is assumed that both competitors are aware of the entire matrix and will act rationally (in other words, they will act to maximize profits). Given this, assume that Companies A and B start in Cell 1 of the payoff matrix shown in Figure 6.10. If you were the manager of Company A, what would you do in the next sales period? If you hold price, Company B may cut price and then you would lose profit. If you cut price, you could get more profit—but if Company B cuts also, you get less profit. Clearly, it is a dilemma.[11]

Playing Repeatedly Over Time

Now to capture the dynamics of real price competition, add the knowledge that this game is played repeatedly over time. Because of this, cutting price takes on some new consequences. If, in the next period Company A chooses to cut price, then even if Company B does not cut price in that next round of play Company B is sure to do so after that. Then Company A cannot very well increase price. The two competitors would be relegated to Cell 4, each making $1 million less profit than they would have earned if they had both maintained their prices (which would have kept them in Cell 1). Adding this consideration of repeated play over time makes each competitor think twice about cutting price. It suggests that holding price would be the better move.

However, what if Company A is faced by Company B cutting its price? Then the managers of Company A might feel that their hand is forced. Company A would have to lower its price, thus putting both competitors into Cell 4. Is there anything that Company A could do to help avoid this possibility? The answer is yes—this might be an opportunity for price signaling. Perhaps Company A could use a public form of communication to discourage Company B from initiating a price cut. For example, Company A could state in trade-association presentations and interviews that its policy is to never allow itself to be undersold. By emphasizing to Company B its firm intention to match any price cut, Company A can make the managers of Company B aware that although cutting price will increase their profit in the next period, it will lead to a *decrease* in their profits over the course of repeated play (i.e., in the long run).

What if a signal such as this does not work and Company A finds itself in Cell 4—might it be possible to get back to Cell 1? One approach to attempting this would be to increase price along with a signal to influence Company B to match the price increase. A possible signal of that type would be to publicly note that materials costs in this industry have been increasing and would justify higher prices. The hope would be that such a signal would lead Company B to interpret Company A's price increase as a bid to get both competitors back into Cell 1.

If the managers of Company B find themselves questioning the signal, for example suspecting a trap (i.e., an attempt to get the companies into Cell 2), they should use the payoff matrix to think through that idea. If they were to raise price in the next period and then Company A cut price and took the extra profit of Cell 2, then Company A would have no hope of ever getting Company B to raise price again. If Company A is aware of the payoff matrix and is rational, it will be clear to Company A that trying to trap Company B is not in Company A's long-term interest. By contemplating the implications of the payoff matrix, the managers of Company B can gain reassurance toward acting in a way likely to maximize profits.

Although this is just a bare introduction to game theory, it can be seen how a payoff matrix can be a useful tool. It can help the price setter anticipate, and perhaps influence, the competitive factor in the market's price-change response.

SUMMARY

The breakeven approach to price-modification decisions requires an estimate of the market's sales response that is sufficient to judge whether or not the critical sales level is likely to be exceeded. A standard measure of a market's sales response is the price elasticity: the percent change in unit sales that would occur for every one percent change in price. In a breakeven analysis, a price elasticity can be used to calculate an expected change in the level of unit sales, or a price elasticity can be compared to a critical price elasticity.

Brand price elasticities are more relevant than category price elasticities for price-modification decisions. Research has indicated that brand price elasticities typically fall between 0 and −4. Economic factors that point toward a higher brand elasticity are the involvement of large amounts of money and low switching and search costs.

Competitors' responses are important for predicting how the market will respond to a price change because they determine how the price change affects price differentials. Knowing whether a company's competitive stance is cooperative, aggressive, or dismissive can help in predicting the company's response to a price change. A competitor's stance can be determined from information on its size, brand differentiation, costs, and goals.

Price signaling involves managing publicly available price related information to have an effect on competitors. A competitor could signal competitive strength, limited goals of a price decrease, or the justifiability of a price increase. Price signaling is in a gray area of legality and may not be effective.

A game-theory payoff matrix could be a useful tool for making competitive pricing decisions. It could help estimate whether a competitor is likely to initiate a price cut or aid in a decision of whether or not to match a competitor's price increase.

KEY TERMS

price sensitivity	switching costs	parallel pricing
price elasticity	search costs	price signaling
demand curve	price differentials	publicity
breakeven price elasticity	competitive stance	price warfare
category price	cooperative stance	limited goals
elasticity	aggressive stance	payoff matrix
brand price elasticity	dismissive stance	payoffs

REVIEW AND DISCUSSION QUESTIONS

1. What is meant when it is said that a market is "sensitive" to a price change? What is meant when it is said that a market is "insensitive" to a price change?

2. Give the formula for price elasticity. Explain why the quantities in this formula are percents rather than specific units, such as dollars, euros, or yen.

3. Explain why price elasticities are usually negative numbers. Would a price elasticity calculated from a price decrease be more likely to be a negative number than a price elasticity calculated from a price increase? Explain.

4. What is a demand curve? What is it about the shape of a demand curve developed from real data that indicates the importance of the situation in which a price elasticity is measured?

5. If the breakeven sales level for at 10 percent price decrease is an increase of 14 units over a base sales level of 100 units, would a price elasticity of −1.5 indicate that this price decrease would be profitable? Explain your reasoning.

6. If the breakeven price elasticity for a prospective price increase were −1.2, would an actual price elasticity of −1.3 indicate that the price increase would be profitable? Explain your reasoning.

7. What is the difference between a category price elasticity and a brand price elasticity?

8. Describe a price-change situation where the brand price elasticity is likely to be similar to the category price elasticity.

9. Describe the distribution of brand price elasticities typically observed. Why is it useful for a pricing manager to be aware of this distribution?

10. What is the effect of the amount of money involved in a price change on the market's likely response to the price change? How might this effect be related to the frequency with which consumers purchase the product and the ease of storing the product?

11. Describe a situation in which the product's customer does not pay the product's full price. What are the implications of this for estimating the likely market response to a price change for this product?

12. Describe a product category where it is relatively easy to gather information on alternative brands and to switch purchasing from one brand to another. What is the effect of this easy information gathering and switching on the market's likely response to a price change?

13. Why is it important to know whether or not a price change will change the price differentials between competitors?

14. What is a competitive stance? Why is it useful to know the competitive stance of one's competitors?

15. Describe the three basic competitive stances. Indicate the response to a price increase that each would predict. Then indicate the response to a price decrease that each would predict.

16. How can information about a competitor's past behaviors, or that of its executives, help provide an indication of the company's competitive stance?

17. Explain why a company being of comparable size to competitors would favor its holding a cooperative stance.

18. Explain why a company with a highly differentiated brand would be likely to hold a dismissive stance.

19. Explain why a company with lower unit costs than its competitors would be likely to hold an aggressive stance.

20. What are some of the possible sources of information about a company that could be used for determining the company's competitive stance?

21. What is price signaling? Discuss the legality and effectiveness of price signaling strategies.

22. Describe some signals intended to discourage a competitor from initiating a price decrease. Explain how these signals could accomplish this effect.

23. Give some examples of how a price decrease could have limited goals. Discuss how signaling this could exert competitive influence.

24. Discuss the price signal that might be intended by a company executive giving an interview to a reporter and describing how costs of his product's components have gone up steadily over the past few months.

25. Describe a four-cell payoff matrix. Discuss how it could be useful for pricing decisions even though it considers only two competitors and two price levels.

EXERCISES

1. A company had been selling 250 units per week of a product at a price of $20. When the company decreased the item's price to $16, sales increased to 330 units per week. Calculate the price elasticity that represents the market's response to this price change. Show your work.

2. In an effort to increase profits, the Mid-Central Electric Co. is trying to decide whether to ask the Public Utilities Commission for permission to raise its rates. Some managers feel that a rate increase will not increase profits because higher rates will cause their customers to use less electricity, but other managers disagree.

   Finally, the numbers are in: The director of marketing has determined that the breakeven sales level for a rate increase of 5 percent would be a unit sales loss of 8.6 percent. The market research department has determined that the price elasticity of Mid-Central's market is −1.12.

   Use these numbers to determine whether or not it would increase Mid-Central's profits to raise rates by 5 percent. Show your work.

3. A study by economists has determined that the category price elasticity of the consumer car rental market in the United States is −1.25. National Car Rental is considering lowering its prices by 6 percent.

   (a) If Hertz, Avis, and the other nationwide car rental companies match National's price cut, what is the sales change that National can expect? Show your work.

   (b) If National's competitors maintain their prices and do not match National's price cut, how would that affect the sales-change estimate you gave for Part (a)? Explain your reasoning.

4. For each of the following products, answer each of the four questions relating to economic factors behind price-change response. Be prepared to explain your reasoning for each answer. Then use these answers to rank these products by their likely brand price elasticities.

   (a) A filling by your dentist

   (b) 2012 Honda Accord

   (c) A fender repair by McKenzie's Auto Body

   (d) Box of Q-tip cotton swabs

5. Tropicana is considering raising the price of its 59-ounce container of fresh orange juice by $0.50. Give and justify your view of the competitive stance that Minute Maid orange juice would be likely to take. What would be the implication of this stance for the price-change response that Tropicana could expect?

6. Apex Products is one of three large firms that together share a major proportion of sales in the U.S. market for metal replacement parts for a certain type of industrial machinery. Consideration of costs along with estimates of the category price elasticity for this type of replacement part indicates that a 12 percent price increase would increase Apex's profits.

   (a) Describe how Apex's two competitors would respond to Apex's prospective price increase if they maintained a cooperative stance toward Apex? How would they respond if they held an aggressive stance toward Apex? How would they respond if they held a dismissive stance toward Apex?

   (b) Why should the competitive stance of the two competitors in this market affect Apex's decision concerning whether or not to go ahead with this 12 percent price increase?

   (c) What information should Apex take into account to determine the likely response of each competitor? How might it obtain this information?

   (d) If Apex plans to proceed with the price increase, what information should it communicate to competitors? How might Apex communicate this information?

NOTES

1. John R. Nevin, "Using Experimental Data to Suggest and Evaluate Alternative Marketing Strategies" in Subhash C. Jain, ed., *Proceedings* (Chicago: American Marketing Association, 1978), 209.
2. Edwin Mansfield, *Microeconomics: Theory and Applications,* 6th ed. (New York: Norton, 1988), 142.
3. Tammo H. A. Bijmolt, Harald J. Van Heerde, and Rik G. M. Pieters, "New Empirical Generalizations on the Determinants of Price Elasticity," *Journal of Marketing Research* 42 (May 2005), 141–156. Although this study included elasticities of SKUs (e.g., particular package sizes of a brand) as well as brands, for ease of discussion these elasticities will all be referred to here as brand elasticities.
4. Larry L. Miller, Steven P. Schnaars, and Valerie L. Vaccaro, "The Provocative Practice of Price Signaling: Collusion Versus Cooperation," *Business Horizons* (July/August 1993), 59–65.
5. Thomas T. Nagle, *The Strategy and Tactics of Pricing* (Englewood Cliffs, NJ: Prentice Hall, 1987), 99–101.
6. Ibid., 100.
7. Susan Carey, "Northwest Follows Suit on Fare Rise," *Wall Street Journal,* February 1, 1999.
8. Mariain Chapman Moore, Ruskin M. Morgan, and Michael J. Moore, "Only the Illusion of Possible Collusion? Cheap Talk and Similar Goals: Some Experimental Evidence," *Journal of Public Policy & Marketing* 20 (Spring 2001), 27–37.
9. Oliver P. Heil and Arlen W. Langvardt, "The Interface Between Competitive Market Signaling and Antitrust Law," *Journal of Marketing* 58 (July 1994), 81–96.
10. F. William Barnett, "Making Game Theory Work in Practice," *Wall Street Journal,* February 13, 1995.
11. This basic game-theory scenario corresponds to the situation known as the "Prisoner's Dilemma." Two people arrested for a crime can keep quiet, and the uncertainty concerning their guilt will lead them both to get light sentences. But if one tries to get off completely by implicating the other, it is likely that the other will reciprocate and both prisoners will get long sentences.

CHAPTER 7

Predicting Price-Change Response: Cognitive Factors

Ultimately, the market's response to a price change is determined by what the price elicits in the mind of the customer. In general, mental responses can be divided into three broad categories: (1) cognitions, (2) emotions, and (3) perceptions. Cognitions include thoughts, beliefs, judgments, and ideas. Emotions include pleasure, pain, and the entire range of feelings and moods. Perceptions include the mind's first conscious responses to stimulation from the outside world. Being the first responses, perceptions play an important role in determining both the customer's cognitive and emotional responses.

In this chapter, we look at the effects of price-related cognitions on price-change response. In the next chapter, our focus will be on price-related emotions. In both this and the next chapter, we begin with a discussion of some perceptual factors involved in the mental responses elicited by a price.

PRICE AWARENESS

Economists have often assumed that customers have detailed and accurate awareness of prices. However, this assumption is rarely justified. What customers do know, or believe, about an item's price can have a considerable effect on their response to a price change. The first step in knowing what an item's price is involves the perception of the numbers that represent the price.

Perception of Multidigit Numbers

One might expect that when a printed price is placed in front of a customer—say, on a price tag or in an advertisement—that the customer's first mental response will be an accurate perception of that price. This is probably a safe assumption if the printed price is a one-digit number (e.g., "$6"), but not so in the usual situation where the printed price is a multidigit number (e.g., $0.75, $4.95, $1,350). Because we read multidigit numbers from left to right, our first mental response to the price is the perception of the price's leftmost digit. Although the perception of the subsequent price digits will usually follow quickly afterward, the early perception of a price's leftmost digit creates a "first-impression effect" that tends to bias the consumer's thoughts and feelings about the level of the price.[1]

The price digits to the right of the price's leftmost digit could be referred to as ending digits (see Figure 7.1). If a first-impression effect gives leftmost digits disproportionate price-level potency, then a price change of a given size should be more effective in changing sales when it alters the price's leftmost digit than when it alters only ending digits. A study that developed a demand curve for supermarket sales of Chiffon margarine illustrates just this effect (see Figure 7.2).[2] Sales of Chiffon dropped sharply when the price

Figure 7.1 The Price Digits to the Right of a Price's Leftmost Digit Are Referred to as the Price's Ending Digits

Figure 7.2 Demand Curve for Chiffon Margarine Shows Sharper Sales Decreases When Leftmost Price Digit Increases

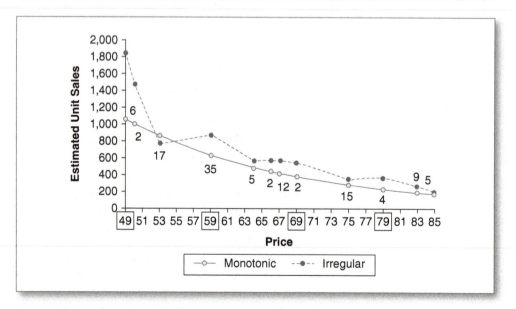

Source: Kirthi Kalyanam and Thomas S. Shively, "Estimating Irregular Pricing Effects: A Stochastic Spline Regression Approach," *Journal of Marketing Research* 35 (February 1998): 16–29.

was higher than $0.49 but then did not drop much until the price exceeded $0.59. Similar sales drops can be seen at $0.69 and $0.79.

This disproportionate potency of leftmost digits suggests that it would be profitable for a seller to increase ending digits until they make the price just below the level where the leftmost digit would change. Further, the high potency of leftmost digits suggests that a seller who is considering round-number pricing (i.e., using one or more consecutive 0s as ending digits) would find it profitable to set a price just below the round number when doing that serves to lower the leftmost digit. Indeed, as was mentioned in Chapter 1, the use of 99, 98, 95, and other ending digits characteristic of just-below pricing has been common in U.S. retailing for well over a century. However, it should be noted that the perceptual effect illustrated in the margarine example has not always been found. Further, as will be seen later in the chapter, there are cognitive effects of using just-below ending digits as well as these perceptual effects, and some of these cognitive effects could oppose the effects of leftmost digit potency and act to discourage, rather than stimulate, consumer purchasing.

Two Types of Knowledge About Prices

After perception of a price's digits, the second step in price awareness involves making the perceived digits meaningful. We will examine two types of such added meaning. The first is price-level knowledge—awareness of the level of a price, for example, knowing that the current price of a haircut at a local barber shop is $15. The second is price-meaning knowledge—awareness of what the price communicates about the product, the seller, and/or the offer. For example, a haircut price of $15 may be interpreted as indicating that the barber shop in question is not very fancy or that this haircut includes only the most basic service.

PRICE-LEVEL KNOWLEDGE

A customer cannot sensibly respond to a price without some price-level knowledge. Without it, the customer would have no basis for evaluating the price. Consider, for example, what you might teach a child to help him understand money: "Twenty dollars is enough to buy this big toy. This candy bar can be had for $0.75." Or consider what you would need to know to make decisions using a totally unfamiliar currency: "This coat is priced at 512 zaglos. Hmm, what does this mean? Well, we paid 96 zaglos for last night's dinner. . . ." An awareness of the price level of at least *some* other objects is necessary for making a reasonable purchase decision.

In general, the more detailed the customer's price-level knowledge, the greater is likely to be his or her response to a price change. There are three prominent sources of a customer's price-level knowledge: (1) awareness of the prices of items that have been purchased, (2) awareness of the prices of items that have not been purchased, and (3) beliefs about the factors that affect the level of an item's price.

Awareness of the Prices of Purchased Items

When a customer makes a purchase, the customer's awareness of the price of the purchased item will contribute to his or her knowledge used for future purchases of the same item and of similar items. Thus, it is interesting that a number of studies have shown that many buyers do not have an accurate awareness of prices that they have just paid.

In one study of supermarket shoppers, it was found that less than half (47 percent) could correctly recall the price of an item that they had just placed in their shopping carts. About one third of the shoppers (32 percent) recalled the item's price inaccurately, with an average error of around 15 percent. Further, about one in five shoppers (21 percent) apparently had so little price awareness that they declined to even offer a price estimate.[3]

Given the limited price recall immediately after the purchase decision, it should not be surprising that later recall of the prices of these items is even lower. Another study looked at what supermarket shoppers know about an item's price before they purchase the item. The researchers interviewed consumers as they were entering the store and asked them to indicate the prices of several items that they usually purchase at the store. The results of this study (which can be seen in Figure 7.3) indicate that only 2 percent of the shoppers were able to correctly recall the prices of items that they purchase. About one-fifth (19 percent) knew the prices within 5 percent. Subsequent questioning indicated that about two-thirds of the shoppers (65 percent) had a rough idea of the prices of supermarket items they regularly purchase, and 14 percent had so little price knowledge that they were referred to as "price oblivious."[4]

Figure 7.3   Price Recall Accuracy of Supermarket Shoppers

Accuracy Level	Percentage of Respondents
Exactly correct	2%
Correct within 5%	19%
Rough idea of price	65%
"Price oblivious"	14%

Source: Based on data from Marc Vanhuele and Xavier Drèze, "Measuring the Price Knowledge Shoppers Bring to the Store," *Journal of Marketing, 66* (October 2002): 72–85.

Although these results illustrate the limited degree of price-level awareness that may be found, it is clear that not all customers are equally unaware of the prices of the items they purchase. Important factors that influence customers' awareness of prices paid include the following:

1. *Price level of the item purchased.* There will be more price awareness for big-ticket items, such as a house or car, than for products that have small per-item prices, such as those purchased at a supermarket. The large amount of money involved in the decision for an

expensive item will tend to motivate customers to pay close attention to what they are paying. The small amount of money involved in any one purchase of an inexpensive item leads to inattention to price. Although this may seem very rational, many consumers fall into the habit of buying the same inexpensive items repeatedly over the course of years, thus in effect making sizable purchases with relatively little attention to price.

2. *Price variation over time.* There will be greater price awareness for items whose prices are relatively stable over time than for items whose prices vary greatly. For example, many canned goods, such as chunk light tuna, have high-price stability and thus relatively high-price awareness among purchasers. Price volatility, particularly if it involves both increases and discounts, makes learning a more arduous task. It is difficult to keep track of a moving target.

3. *Price variation between brands.* There will be greater price awareness for purchased items in product categories where there is little interbrand price variation than for purchased items in product categories where the prices of different brands vary greatly. For example, the tendency for cell phone service providers to offer similar calling plans at relatively similar prices promotes price awareness. If the prices of items in a product category vary little, then it will be easier for customers to use product category price knowledge to facilitate awareness of the price of a purchased item.

4. *Opportunity to learn prices.* There will be greater price awareness the more the customer encounters opportunities to think about the purchased item's price. Thus, when purchases usually involve consideration of price, price awareness will tend to increase with the number of these purchases. For example, a consumer who stays in hotels frequently is likely to become more aware of the prices he or she pays than a consumer who only rarely stays in hotels.

Awareness of the Prices of Items That Have Not Been Purchased

In addition to whatever awareness consumers have for the prices of items they purchase, they also have some awareness of the prices of items that they do not purchase. Some of this knowledge comes from a price information search—activities such as shopping at stores, browsing the Internet, and asking friends and relatives about their purchases in order to investigate alternative possibilities for an upcoming purchase decision. These activities yield information about competing items as well as about the item that is purchased. Awareness of the prices of items that have not been purchased also comes from information encountered passively from everyday activities—seeing media ads and store price displays or having routine conversations with those around us. This is referred to as incidental learning of price information.

Research indicates that the average consumer carries out relatively little price information search. It has been found that even for expensive items such as home appliances, a large proportion of consumers are essentially "nonsearchers"—they will make a purchase after visiting only one retail outlet or examining only one brand (see Figure 7.4).[5]

Figure 7.4 A Large Proportion of Consumers Carry Out Very Little Information Search Before Purchase

Country/Product/Year	Nonsearchers	Limited Searchers	Extended Searchers
America/appliances/1955	65%	25%	10%
America/appliances/1972	49	38	13
America/appliances/1974	65	27	08
Australia/automobiles/1981	24	58	18
America/appliances/1989	24	45	11
America/professional services/1989	55	38	07
Australia/professional services/1995	53	35	12

Source: Del I. Hawkins, Roger J. Best, and Kenneth A. Coney, *Consumer Behavior: Building Marketing Strategy,* 7th edition (New York: McGraw-Hill, 1998).

It appears that consumer motivation to carry out price information search is an important variable in price awareness. For example, it has been found that there is less price awareness among higher-income consumers or among all consumers in periods of economic prosperity. Presumably, high income reduces the perceived need for collecting information about product alternatives. It has also been found that women have greater price awareness than men, perhaps because of a greater interest in shopping and other price information search activities.[6]

In some situations, price information search is constrained by limitations in the consumer's awareness of competitors. For example, travelers staying in a hotel are often unaware of the restaurants and shops other than those that are located in or near the hotel. This makes a price information search difficult and lowers price awareness. Similarly, use of the party plan method of selling, such as done with Tupperware, limits a price information search by encouraging customers to make their purchase decisions during the party. The use of nondescriptive product names can also make price comparison difficult. For example, using only the name "Dr. Pepper" to describe a soft drink tends to obscure which competing soft drinks would be comparable. Such factors that limit knowledge about competitors tend to keep price awareness low.

In product categories where most major sellers list their prices on the Internet, there is likely to be greater consumer price awareness than in categories where such information is not available. All prices listed on the Internet for, say, a particular model of camera or printer can be searched easily and can help consumers learn the prices of alternative retail outlets. However, products sold in supermarkets, drug stores, and clothing stores are unlikely to have sufficient price information posted on the Internet to help improve the consumer's price awareness.

Price-Origin Beliefs

A third prominent source of the buyer's knowledge of price levels does not involve learning specific prices at all. Rather, it involves acquiring price-origin beliefs—beliefs concerning the factors that cause a price to be high or low that can be used as rules of thumb for making price-level inferences. Thus, for example, consumers will judge that the price of a bottle of a particular brand of beer would be higher if purchased at a fancy dinner restaurant than at a grocery store right across the street.[7] Such a judgment is not based on the recall of prices but rather on beliefs concerning how prices originate—that is, on the factors that determine the price levels sellers charge. Here are some examples of common price-origin beliefs:

- Items that show higher-quality materials or workmanship will have higher prices than those that do not.
- Items that have more useful features will have higher prices than items having fewer useful features.
- Prices of items whose production is more labor intensive are likely to be higher than the prices of items whose production is less labor intensive.
- Larger packages of a product will have lower unit prices than smaller packages of the product. A unit price is a product package's price per unit of measure, such as per ounce or per pound.
- The prices in a retail outlet with very simple store fixtures will be lower than prices in a retail outlet with elaborate fixtures.

Note that price-origin beliefs could be more detailed or less detailed. For example, one could have the broad belief that products imported to the United States are generally likely to be lower priced. Or one could have a more detailed set of beliefs, such as that electronics imports are likely to be less expensive than domestic items, but imported wine is likely to be more expensive. Note also that a consumer's price-origin belief may or may not be accurate. For example, it may turn out not to be the case that imported electronics products are less expensive than those manufactured in the United States. The degree to which a consumer's price-origin beliefs are detailed and accurate can have a strong effect on the consumer's price-level knowledge.

The Customer's Internal Reference Price

When evaluating an item's price, a customer will very often make use of what has been termed an internal reference price (IRP). This is a price, or a price range, that is constructed in the customer's mind (and thus is "internal"). It is used as a basis for evaluating an encountered price (and thus is for "reference").[8]

If a customer's IRP for an item is in the form of a specific price, then that specific price is used as a reference point for evaluating the item's price. For example, a consumer considering the $44 price of a deck chair at a garden store might recall that he saw a similar deck chair at Walmart for $38. The recalled price of $38—that consumer's IRP—would serve as his reference point. The consumer would perceive the price of the garden store's chair to be $6 higher than his IRP.

If a customer's IRP is in the form of a price range, then the customer's basis for evaluating the item's price would be, in effect, a very wide "point." Only if an item's price were beyond the IRP range would a difference from the IRP be perceived. Thus, if the consumer considering the $44 deck chair recalled having seen a similar one for "around $40," he would probably perceive the $44 price as consistent with his IRP.

When a customer considers an item's price, information from all three sources of price-level knowledge can contribute to the formation of an IRP. The customer may try to recall the last price paid for the item or the price level he or she had seen for similar items. That estimate may then be modified by noticing relevant aspects of the item (e.g., that it is handmade, imported, sold in a store with elaborate fixtures) and applying price-origin beliefs accordingly. Given that all price-level knowledge will be brought to bear on constructing the IRP, it is clear that the specificity of the IRP will depend on the amount of detail present in the consumer's price-level knowledge. The IRP of a customer with a very high degree of price awareness will tend to be a specific price. The IRP of a customer with very little price awareness will tend to be a broad range.

If an item's price differs from a customer's IRP, then this difference will affect the customer's response to the item's price. The nature of these effects will be discussed in detail in the next chapter. For now, what is important to emphasize is that when a customer's IRP is a range rather than a specific price, an item's price must be outside of this range for there to be a difference that will affect the customer's price response. In fact, when a customer's IRP is in the form of a range, the customer will have very little impetus to respond differently to the various prices within that range. Thus, any price change that stays within that range will elicit little or no change in the customer's purchasing tendencies. In this way, the IRPs of the customers in a market are a key means by which price awareness and knowledge can have effects on the market's price-change response.

MANAGING PRICE-LEVEL KNOWLEDGE

When we understand how price-level knowledge can affect price-change response, we can appreciate why a seller may try to manage what customers know about the seller's prices. When the seller's prices tend to be lower than those of most competitors, it is in the seller's interest to increase the customer's price awareness. When the seller's prices tend to be higher than those of most competitors, it is in the seller's interest to decrease the customer's price awareness.

Increasing Price-Level Awareness

An effective means by which a company can increase price awareness among its customers and potential customers is to simplify its price structure. For example, a department store may make use of a relatively small number of standard price points. Rather than selling men's shirts at many different prices, the store will have a variety of shirts at the $29.99 price point, another assortment at the $39.99 price point, and perhaps a third set of shirts at the $55.00 price point. Having fewer prices to keep in mind, shoppers will be better able to recall these prices. Figure 7.5 illustrates standard price points in a sporting goods retailer with a low-price positioning.

Figure 7.5   Standard Price Points in a Sporting Goods Retailer With a Low-Price Positioning

The extreme of this type of **price simplification** is the retailer who charges a single price for every item sold. For example, the dry cleaning chain AnyGarment Cleaners charges the same price for cleaning any garment that the customer brings in. This price is displayed prominently in storefront signage, such as a large neon sign saying, "$1.99 Cleaners." The "dollar store," the descendent of the "five and dime store," uses the same price simplification strategy. Every item in the store is sold for the same price (usually one dollar), and this policy is communicated prominently, usually in the store's name (e.g., Dollar Tree, 99 Cents Only).[9] The enduring success of this retailing concept indicates the benefits of price simplification for the low-priced seller.

A seller may also increase customer awareness of prices through media advertising. Generally, price advertising increases the role that price plays in the customer's decision process.[10] If your prices are lower than those of competitors, advertising this will increase customers' response to this price differential. If you decrease the price of an item, advertising this will increase customers' response to this price change. Although television and radio are sometimes used for price advertising, most price advertising utilizes the print medium—a large proportion of all newspaper advertising in the United States appears designed to communicate prices to consumers.

Price advertising is not only for low-priced sellers or for price decreases. It can also benefit a seller when customers perceive the seller's price as being higher than it actually is or if they perceive price differentials as less favorable to the seller than they actually are. For example, in the early 1980s, MCI and Sprint were making strong inroads into AT&T's market share based on a low-price appeal. Although MCI's and Sprint's long-distance calls were lower priced than AT&T's, they were lower by only a very small amount. When AT&T's managers carried out some market research to learn why such a small price difference was having such a large effect on sales, they were surprised at the results: Most consumers believed that AT&T's rates for long-distance calls were far higher than they actually were. This was probably because many consumers formed their impression of AT&T's rates years earlier before new technology lowered these rates considerably, and up until deregulation and the entry of competition, consumers had few opportunities to update their price knowledge. AT&T's response to this situation was an extensive advertising campaign designed simply to increase the consumer's awareness of the prices that they were already paying.

Decreasing Price-Level Awareness

Just as simplifying prices is an effective means of increasing customer price awareness, complicating prices can effectively decrease price awareness. One way of doing this is to communicate prices using a price format that makes it difficult to know an item's actual price. For example, many sellers of expensive consumer items such as cars and furniture emphasize per-month payments and de-emphasize discussion of the item's total price. Consumers who remember per-month prices are unlikely to expend the effort to calculate the total amount that must be paid.

As was mentioned in Chapter 1, the practice of using more than one number to express a product's price is referred to as price partitioning. Broadly speaking, price partitioning includes the use of per-month payments as well as the practice of expressing a price as a base price along with separate fees or charges. For example, the price of a product sold on the Internet may be expressed as the price of the item plus a separate shipping charge. The price of cell phone service may be expressed as a monthly base price, plus fees such as a "regulatory cost recovery fee" and a "federal universal service charge" as well as separate charges for both state and local taxes. The many numbers that must be remembered in a partitioned price as well as the effort involved in putting those numbers together makes it difficult for consumers to remember and compare product prices.

Another approach to decreasing price-level awareness is to complicate the product rather than the price. For example, some durable goods manufacturers will produce branded variants—a large array of very similar branded items that are distributed so that no two retailers in a market area will carry the same set of these variants. Thus, consumers shopping for, say, a washing machine may want to compare prices among retailers. They may go to one retailer, select a washing machine brand and model of interest and then visit another retailer to compare prices. What they are likely to find is that the other retailer does not carry the exact same washing machine model. For instance, a consumer looking for the Whirlpool model LSR-2352 might find models LSR-2364 and LSQ-2350 at competing retailers but not the LSR-2352. What's the difference between these models? The store's salespeople are likely to be of little help because they have information about only those models that they carry. Even taking the trouble to compare product brochures leaves open the question of what unmentioned differences there might be. This lack of exact product comparability makes it difficult for consumers to learn and compare prices.[11]

Although the easy search capabilities of the Internet and the many price-comparison websites can facilitate price awareness, the Internet can also be used to complicate pricing and thus decrease the consumer's price knowledge. For example, travelers searching sites such as Orbitz and Expedia for the lowest airline fare to a particular destination will often find that fares change within hours and that the changes are often unpredictable. Further, it has been reported that travelers sometimes miss the lowest fares because they specify coach seats—in some markets for some flights, first-class seats turn out to be cheaper than coach seats![12] This points out that the same technology that can be applied to increasing customers' price knowledge can also be used to keep effective price awareness low.

The Influence of Ending Digits on Price Knowledge

Another aspect of price format that can affect the consumer's knowledge of price levels concerns the choice of ending digits. As mentioned earlier in this chapter, a price's ending digits are those digits to the right of the price's leftmost digit. Because a price's ending digits have a relatively small effect on the level of a price, they can be managed more or less independently of price level. For example, prices such as $30.00 and $29.99 are at virtually the same level, but $30.00 has round-number ending digits and $29.99 has just-below ending digits.

It has been found that prices ending in 0s are more accurately recalled than prices ending in 9s or 8s. Presumably, the perceived simplicity of round numbers enhances the consumer's price learning. Thus, the use of round-number pricing acts to increase price-level awareness, and the use of just-below pricing acts to decrease price-level awareness.

In addition to decreasing price-level awareness, just-below pricing also tends to bias the cognitive processing of price information. Since the use of ending digits such as 99 and 95 rather than 00 increases the perceived complexity of the price, consumers will tend to use their limited attention on the price's most important digit, the leftmost digit. Because there is little attention remaining for just-below ending digits, they will often have to be guessed when price information is recalled. This guessing will lead to biases in price learning. For example, if a price's ending digits are all 9s (i.e., the highest digit), then any guesses of those digits that are incorrect will be lower digits. In this way, the use of just-below pricing will tend to cause prices to be recalled as being lower than they actually were.[13]

PRICE-MEANING KNOWLEDGE

The second aspect of what can be known about a price, beyond price-level knowledge, is knowledge of what the price may communicate about the product, the seller, and/or the offer. Because the effects of a price change may be affected by this price-meaning information, the consumer beliefs and mental associations that can cause a price to have a meaning need to be examined.

The Price-Quality Heuristic

As was mentioned in Chapter 6, there are occasions when the effect of price on sales is influenced by what the price means to the customer. In particular, there is considerable evidence that consumers at least sometimes use the level of a price as a cue to the quality of the product or seller.[14] For example, there may be a tendency to judge a watch priced at $1,200 to be of higher quality than one priced at $50. Many consumers would judge that a clothing store with higher prices will carry better-looking clothes and offer better service than will a clothing store with lower prices. Sellers sometimes even allude in their advertisements to the positive meanings that consumers tend to ascribe to high prices (see Figure 7.6).

Figure 7.6 Advertisement Highlighting the Product's High Price

For customers, such judgments serve as "heuristics," or shortcuts, to simplify the purchase decision process.[15] Rather than investigate the quality of every alternative, it is sometimes much easier to use price as an indication of product quality. This price-quality heuristic is supported by common price-origin beliefs, such as the belief that products that have higher-quality materials or more useful features will have higher prices. When price level is used as a cue to quality, these beliefs are turned around. If high-quality materials and workmanship lead to a higher price, then (as the belief goes) a high price must mean that the product has high-quality materials and workmanship. The price-quality heuristic is also supported by belief in the free market—if a product weren't worth such a high price, how could the company get away with charging that price?[16]

If a substantial proportion of buyers in a market use price level as a quality cue, then the brand price elasticity is likely to be low. Those buyers who are attracted by a lower price will tend to be canceled out by those who find that the lower price raises quality questions. Those who tend to be deterred by a higher price will tend to be counteracted by those who find the higher price reassuring on the product quality issue. If most of the buyers in a market use price level as an indicator of quality, then the brand price elasticity could even become positive. This is a condition that would certainly favor a price increase.

Are Price and Product Quality Related?

It could be asked whether there really is a positive relation between price level and product quality. In one study that addressed this question, the researcher surveyed articles in magazines such as *Consumer Reports* regarding a large group of products such as toasters, hair dryers, trash compactors, and extension ladders. Each published report contained objective ratings of the quality of various brands and models of the product along with each item's price. Based on these data, the researcher found that for 51 percent of the products, there was a positive correlation between the objective quality measure and price. In these products, higher price was indeed associated with higher product quality. However, in 35 percent of the categories, there was no correlation between quality and price, and in 14 percent of the categories there was actually a *negative* correlation between quality and price.[17] These results suggest that price level is very limited in its ability to predict objective product quality.

However, most of the products used in this study were items designed primarily to satisfy consumers' objective performance needs. When it is a product's subjective performance that is critical, the relation between price and product quality could be stronger. For example, if a consumer buys a handbag, a watch, or an automobile largely for social performance needs—increased social acceptance or respect from others—then the high price itself could be considered a benefit. It is the item's high price that would lead those in the consumer's social groups to be impressed that the consumer was able to afford to buy it.

Further, it has been found that a product's subjective performance can be affected by the consumer's expectations concerning that performance. If a high price causes consumers to expect high performance, then these expectations themselves could create the high performance. Thus, for example, it has been found consumers report liking a wine more when they think is priced at $90 a bottle than when that they think it is priced a $10 a bottle. In addition, measures of brain activity suggest that this greater reported liking of the wine believed to be priced at $90 is actually due to greater experienced pleasure rather than merely the idea that one should experience more pleasure when a product's price is high.[18]

Managing Price as a Quality Cue

Customers are particularly likely to use price level as a cue to quality (1) when they find it difficult to evaluate product quality directly, (2) when they believe that large quality differences exist, and (3) when they feel there is a risk of the product being of insufficient quality. Wine is said to be a product category where the price-quality heuristic is often used because the taste of a wine is an experience characteristic that cannot be observed until after the bottle is opened, and many consumers are not knowledgeable about the names and vintage years listed on wine bottle labels. Further, many consumers believe that there are big differences in wine quality and often care strongly about the success of the occasion where the wine will be served. Other product categories where price level is often used as a quality cue include stereo speakers, diamonds, and perfume.

Note, however, that even in these product categories, the consumer's use of the price-quality heuristic is not like giving the seller a license to print money. This is so for two reasons. First, a high price may effectively lead a consumer to like a product, but the consumer's budget constraints could keep the consumer from actually buying the product.[19] Second, it has been found that price can influence the experience of a product's quality only within a certain range. Even in hedonic products such as a wine and dinner restaurants, if the expectation created by a high price is implausible given the actual product, the attempt to use price to influence perceived quality could backfire and cause disappointment and a lower likelihood of purchase.[20]

Price-Ending Meanings

In addition to consumers' use of a price's level as a meaningful cue, there is evidence that consumers may also draw meaning from a price's ending digits.[21] The use of round-number pricing tends to support the image of high quality in a product or retailer. The presence of 0s in a price's ending digits may also suggest an image of classiness. This image may be enhanced by omitting entirely the display of cents digits, such as the upscale restaurant whose menu contains items such as "Tossed salad, $7." The suggestion would be that the seller is above "nickel and diming" customers.[22]

Consumers have been found to interpret the use of just-below pricing as indicating that the item with the just-below price has been discounted or is being sold at a relatively low everyday price. This image effect of ending digits such as 99 and 95 serves to reinforce the low-price perception created by sellers' use of such high ending digits to keep the price's leftmost digit low.

On the other hand, the use of just-below pricing has also been found to suggest lower product or store quality. Further, because a just-below price tends to bring to mind the round-number price a few cents higher, consumers are aware that just-below pricing represents an influence tactic. This "persuasion knowledge" might cause consumers to feel manipulated and lead to questions about the seller's honesty and integrity. Thus, in situations where quality and seller integrity are particularly important, such as the choice of a clinic for vision-correcting eye surgery, the use of just-below prices should probably be avoided.[23]

Walmart, the largest retailer in the United States, has adopted the practice of minimizing the use of both round-number pricing and just-below pricing. This decision produces prices such as $3.17, $8.44, and $176.54. In contrast to round numbers, these prices could be called "sharp" numbers.[24] The use of sharp-number pricing may suggest to consumers that the retailer has engaged in a careful price-setting process in an effort to minimize markups and cut prices "right to the bone." In price negotiation, an impression of the seller's care in price setting might encourage a buyer to accept the seller's price rather than make a lower counter offer. In addition, because sharp numbers are more common among low numbers than among high numbers, they may suggest to consumers smaller magnitudes. In support of this possibility, it has been found that consumers will tend to judge a sharp-number price such as $364,578 to be smaller than the round-number price, $364,000.[25]

SUMMARY

A customer's response to a price is influenced by the customer's price awareness. This awareness is biased by the early perception of a price's leftmost digit and depends on knowledge about both the level of the price and what a price communicates about the product.

When customers have more detailed knowledge about price levels, they will tend to show more response to price changes. Sources of price-level knowledge include awareness of the prices of past purchases, awareness of prices from shopping and other everyday activities, and beliefs about the factors that determine prices. A customer's price-level knowledge is incorporated into an IRP. When a customer's IRP is a specific price, the customer may respond to any price difference from this specific price; when it is a range rather than a specific price, the customer is unlikely to respond to price changes that fall within that range.

When a seller's prices are lower than those of competitors, it is in the seller's interest to increase customers' price awareness. This can be accomplished by price advertising and by simplifying the seller's price structure. When a seller's prices are high relative to competition, it is in the seller's interest to decrease customers' price awareness. This can be accomplished by partitioning prices into per-month terms or into a base price plus additional separate charges, by creating variation among the items in a product line, and by using just-below prices.

When customers find it difficult to directly evaluate the quality of a product or seller, they sometimes rely on prices to communicate such information. This use of price level to communicate quality will tend to reduce customers' price sensitivity. The ending digits of prices can communicate information about the product and/or seller.

KEY TERMS

cognitions	price-level knowledge	internal reference price (IRP)
emotions	price-meaning knowledge	standard price points
perceptions	price information search	price simplification
ending digits	incidental learning	branded variants
round-number pricing	price-origin beliefs	price-quality heuristic
just-below pricing	unit prices	sharp-number pricing

REVIEW AND DISCUSSION QUESTIONS

1. Give some examples of typical retail prices, and divide each one into its leftmost digit and its ending digits. How might the distinction between leftmost and ending digits help explain a greater sales drop when a price increases from $1.99 to $2.00 than when it increases from $1.98 to $1.99?

2. Distinguish between price-level knowledge and price-meaning knowledge.

3. What is the relationship between price-level knowledge and the market's response to a price change?

4. Describe the three prominent sources of price-level knowledge.

5. Give an example of a research method used to measure price-level knowledge. Give an example of what has been found using this research method.

6. Describe how factors such as the amount of money involved, price variation over time, and price variation between brands affects price-level awareness.

7. Explain how price-level awareness can be affected even by products that are not purchased. Give an example of incidental learning.

8. How might consumers differ in their motivation to carry out price information search? How are these differences likely to affect price-level awareness?

9. What is a price-origin belief? Give an example of the effect such a belief could have on the customer's price-level awareness.

10. What should a seller want to know about the IRPs of his or her customers? How could the seller use this information?

11. When would it be in a seller's interest to increase customer price-level awareness? When would it be in his or her interest to decrease customer price-level awareness?

12. What are standard price points? How can standard price points be used to influence the market's response to prices?

13. How is price advertising likely to affect the role of price in the customer's decision process?

14. Describe three methods that a seller can use to decrease customer price-level awareness.

15. Evaluate the following statement: The Internet makes price information more accessible and thus increases price-level awareness.

16. What are just-below prices? What are their effects on price-level awareness?

17. Under what conditions are customers most likely to use price as an indicator of product quality? How does using price to indicate quality affect customer price sensitivity?

18. Describe a meaning that consumers draw from a price's ending digits that is favorable to a seller. Describe one that is unfavorable to a seller.

EXERCISES

1. Consider the following four products:
   Toothbrush
   Electric can opener
   Grandfather clock
   One-gallon container of milk

   (a) Which of these products would you expect to be associated with the greatest amount of consumer price-level awareness before the consumer begins shopping for it? Explain your reasoning.

   (b) Which product would you expect to be associated with the least consumer price-level awareness? Explain your reasoning.

2. Imagine that a market research interviewer asked you to report the price you would expect to pay for some consumer items. For each of the following items, give the price or price range you would expect to pay. Then describe the role (if any) played by each of the three sources of price-level knowledge discussed in this chapter in arriving at each estimate.

   (a) A 15-ounce bottle of Suave shampoo

   (b) An oil change at Jiffy Lube

   (c) A pair of Nike sneakers

   (d) A Weber gas grill

3. A retailer is considering increasing the price of one of her products. She currently sells 80 units per week of this product at $30.00 apiece, and her variable costs for the product are $13.50. A market research study has indicated that, for this product, consumers will show a price elasticity of −1.8 to price changes that they perceive. For price changes that are too small for the consumer to notice, their price elasticity will be 0. The study has indicated that only

50 percent of the retailer's market is aware of the current price for this product. The other 50 percent knows only that the product's current price is somewhere between $22 and $38.

(a) What is the breakeven sales level for a $5 price increase for this product?

(b) Use the price-change response information given in the problem to calculate whether or not this $5 price increase would be profitable for the retailer.

4. A retailer of lawnmowers is considering changing the prices of some of his or her products. A pricing consultant advises him to consider the IRPs of the consumers in his or her market.

(a) Formulate a survey question that the retailer could use to measure consumers' IRPs.

(b) Assume that the retailer is currently selling a particular lawnmower for $269. If the retailer's research determines that the IRP of most consumers for this lawnmower is the range from $250 to $299, what are the implications of knowing this for possible price changes on this product?

5. A computer manufacturer who sells personal computers through catalogs and the Internet has low prices but is frustrated that price awareness in the category is low. What price format and price structure decisions can this manufacturer make to increase price awareness in this product category?

6. For which of the following product categories would you expect consumers to be most likely to use price as a cue to quality: a plastic garbage can, an in-home electronic air cleaner, or a bottle of multiple vitamins? Explain your reasoning.

7. A manager of a stylish gift store plans to set the following prices for three new items:

    Item A $37.00
    Item B $4.50
    Item C $60.00

The manager's partner suggests that it would be better to subtract one cent from each of these prices so that the prices will seem lower to the customer. However, the manager worries that 9-ending prices might give these items a low-quality, "bargain-basement" image. What would you recommend?

NOTES

1. Manoj Thomas and Vicki Morwitz, "Heuristics in Numerical Cognition: Implications for Pricing," in *Handbook of Pricing Research in Marketing,* ed. Vithala R. Rao (Northampton, MA: Edward Elgar Publishing, 2009), 141–142.

2. Kirthi Kalyanam and Thomas S. Shively, "Estimating Irregular Pricing Effects: A Stochastic Spline Regression Approach," *Journal of Marketing Research* 35 (February 1998): 16–29.

3. Peter R. Dickson and Alan G. Sawyer, "The Price Knowledge and Search of Supermarket Shoppers," *Journal of Marketing* 54 (July 1990): 42–53.

4. Marc Vanhuele and Xavier Drèze, "Measuring the Price Knowledge Shoppers Bring to the Store," *Journal of Marketing* 66 (October 2002), 72–85.

5. Del I. Hawkins, Roger J. Best, and Kenneth A. Coney, *Consumer Behavior: Building Marketing Strategy*, 7th ed. (New York: McGraw-Hill, 1998), 532.

6. Hooman Estalami, Donald R. Lehmann, and Alfred C. Holden, "Macro-Economic Determinants of Consumer Price Knowledge: A Meta-Analysis of Four Decades of Research," *International Journal of Research in Marketing* 18 (2001): 341–355.

7. Richard Thaler, "Mental Accounting and Consumer Choice," *Marketing Science* 4 (Summer 1985): 199–214.

8. Gurumurthy Kalyanaram and John D.C. Little, "An Empirical Analysis of Latitude of Price Acceptance in Consumer Packaged Goods," *Journal of Consumer Research* 21 (December 1994): 408–418.

9. Chad Terhune, "In Modest Times, 'Dollar" Stores Remain Upbeat—Stock Market Jitters Don't Hit Home as Much With Lower-Income Shoppers," *Wall Street Journal,* December 22, 2000, B1.

10. Dick Wittink, "Advertising Increases Sensitivity to Price," *Journal of Advertising Research* 17 (April 1977): 39–42.

11. Mark Bergen, Shantanu Dutta, and Steven M. Shugan, "Branded Variants: A Retail Perspective," *Journal of Marketing Research* 33 (February 1996): 9–19.

12. Scott McCartney, "When First-Class Is Cheaper Than Coach," *Wall Street Journal,* January 7, 2004, D1, D4.

13. Robert M. Schindler and Alan R. Wiman, "Effects of Odd Pricing on Price Recall," *Journal of Business Research* 19 (November 1989): 165–177.

14. Akshay R. Rao and Kent B. Monroe, "The Effect of Price, Brand Name, and Store Name on Buyers' Perceptions of Product Quality: An Integrative Review," *Journal of Marketing Research* 26 (August 1989): 351–357.

15. Akshay R. Rao, "The Quality of Price as a Quality Cue," *Journal of Marketing Research* 42 (November 2005): 401–405.

16. George Akerlof, "The Market for 'Lemons': Quality and the Market Mechanism," *Quarterly Journal of Economics* 84 (August 1970): 488–500.

17. George B. Sproles, "New Evidence on Price and Quality," *Journal of Consumer Affairs* 11 (Summer 1977): 63–77.

18. Hilke Plassman, John O'Doherty, Baba Shiv, and Antonio Rangel, "Marketing Actions can Modulate Neural Representations of Experienced Pleasantness," *Proceedings of the National Academy of Sciences* 105, no. 3 (2008): 1050–1054.

19. Ori Heffetz and Moses Shayo, "How Large are Non-Budget-Constraint Effects of Prices on Demand?" *American Economic Journal: Applied Economics* 1 (April 2009): 170–199.

20. Ayelet Gneezy and Uri Gneezy, "Expectations and the Price-Quality Heuristic" (working paper, Rady School of Management, University of California, San Diego, 2010).

21. Robert M. Schindler and Thomas M. Kibarian, "Image Communicated by the Use of 99 Endings in Advertised Prices," *Journal of Advertising* 30 (Winter 2001): 95–99.

22. Robert M. Schindler, H.G. Parsa, and Sandra Naipaul,"Hospitality Managers' Price-Ending Beliefs: A Survey and Applications," *Cornell Hospitality Quarterly* (forthcoming).

23. Anthony Allred, E.K. Valentin, and Goutam Chakraborty, "Pricing Risky Services: Preference and Quality Considerations," *Journal of Product and Brand Management* 19, no. 1 (2010): 54–60.

24. Stanislas Dehaene, *The Number Sense: How the Mind Creates Mathematics* (New York: Oxford University Press, 1997), 108.

25. Manoj Thomas, Daniel H. Simon, and Vrinda Kadiyali, "The Price Precision Effect: Evidence from Laboratory and Market Data," *Marketing Science* 29, no. 1 (2010): 175–190.

CHAPTER 8

Predicting Price-Change Response: Emotional Factors

We have seen in Chapter 7 that price awareness and other price-related cognitions can have a substantial effect on a customer's price-change response. In addition, a buyer's emotions and feelings also play a very important role. Even if a customer has accurate knowledge about the level of a price, that knowledge alone does not tell us how the buyer will feel about that price. The strong effect of price-related feelings on the buyer's response to a price makes it important for the seller to be able to anticipate these emotional factors.

Since a price involves giving up something of value, the feelings associated with paying it will usually be of the negative variety. The pain of paying—how much it hurts to pay a price—is a useful concept for considering the emotional factors in price-change response.[1] Since we cannot know the pain of paying a price from the price level alone, we need to understand what determines how much of this pain a price is likely to evoke in the customer's mind. As we did in Chapter 7, we begin this discussion by dealing with some of the perceptual factors involved in the buyer's mental response to a price.

FRAMING IN THE PERCEPTION OF PRICES

Although the money involved in a price is very concrete and specific, the buyer's perception of this money has a surprising amount of flexibility. Even when a price involves a single sum of money, it does not have to be perceived by the buyer as a single sum. To illustrate that such a thing can occur in perception, consider the drawing shown in Figure 8.1. The same drawing can be seen as either one thing or two things— either a vase or as two profiles facing each other. The perception that dominates will be determined by the available context, or "frame of reference." Figure 8.2 provides an example of how such a frame of reference can change perception. Whether we perceive the ambiguous letterlike character as an *H* or an *A* depends on the context provided by the letters that surround it.

Figure 8.1 A Drawing That Can Be Seen as Either One Thing (a Vase) or Two Things (Facing Profiles)

Figure 8.2 Illustration of How a Frame of Reference (the Surrounding Letters) Can Affect How the Ambiguous Character Is Perceived

TAE CAT

We tend to perceive money in terms of gains and losses—money we get (a gain) or money we lose (a loss). The frame of reference in these perceptions, referred to as the reference point, is often the status quo. For example, if you win $1,000 in a lottery, you would perceive it as a $1,000 gain. Relative to the state of affairs before winning (i.e., the status quo), you are $1,000 richer.

An important aspect of this view is that the reference point that defines gains and losses is entirely in one's mind and thus can quickly change. Such a change is referred to as a reference point shift. For example, imagine that after it was announced that you had won the $1,000 you sit back and think about what you are going to do with the money. This thinking might cause your reference point to shift so that having the $1,000 becomes the status quo. Then, if it is announced that a mistake was made and the winner was actually someone else, you would perceive, and experience the negative feelings of, a $1,000 *loss*.

Because a buyer's feelings can be so strongly related to perceived gains and losses, it is in the seller's interest to consider what can be done to manage how buyers perceive the seller's price. The management of the factors that influence the set of gains and losses that comprise the buyer's perception of a price is referred to as framing. Note that the methods used in framing do not affect the level of the price. They have to do with only the issue of *price format*—how the price is expressed when it is communicated to customers.

THE VALUE OF GAINS AND LOSSES

The recognition that a price is perceived as a set of gains and losses raises the question of how buyers are likely to value each of these gains and losses. Our understanding of this has been advanced by the Nobel Prize-winning work of the psychologists Daniel Kahneman and Amos Tversky. This work is often referred to under the term *prospect theory,* since Kahneman and Tversky referred to possible alternatives in a decision as "prospects."[2] A key result of their research is the prospect theory value function. This is a succinct description of how people feel about gains and losses or, more precisely, the value they place on gains or losses of various sizes.

A graph showing the prospect theory value function can be seen in Figure 8.3. The horizontal axis of the graph represents the size of the gain or loss. At the reference point, there is neither a gain nor a loss. The segment of the horizontal axis to the right of the reference point indicates gains; the farther it is from the reference point, the larger the gain. The segment of the horizontal axis to the left of the reference point indicates losses; the farther it is from the reference point, the larger the loss.

The vertical axis of the graph represents the value that a person places on a gain or loss. At the reference point, there are neither positive nor negative feelings. The segment of the vertical axis above the reference point indicates positive value; the farther it is from the reference point, the greater the pleasure. The segment of the vertical axis below the reference point indicates negative value; the farther it is from the reference point, the greater the pain.

As can be seen in Figure 8.3, the prospect theory value function curves gently upward to the right of the reference point, indicating the degree to which gains of various sizes are positively valued. The value function curves sharply downward to the left of the reference point, indicating the degree to which losses of various sizes are negatively valued. There are two important aspects of the prospect theory value function: (1) the incorporation of the Weber–Fechner Law and (2) the postulation of loss aversion.

Figure 8.3 The Prospect Theory Value Function

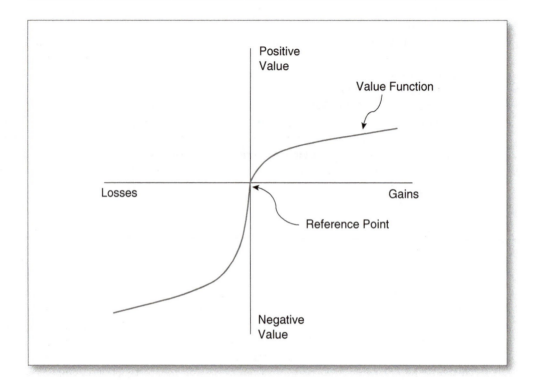

The Weber-Fechner Law

Named after two pioneering researchers of the nineteenth century, the Weber–Fechner Law is one of the oldest and most reliable laws in psychology. It holds that there are "diminishing returns" for the mental effects of a stimulus. In other words, each additional unit of external stimulation will add less to the mental effect of the stimulus than its predecessor. For example, if you hold an object that weighs about one ounce, say a ballpoint pen, you will definitely feel the effects of adding a second ounce to that pen. However, if you add an ounce to an object that weighs 25 pounds, say a full suitcase, you may not even feel the difference. The same ounce has a much smaller effect on our sense of the object's weight if it follows 400 "predecessors" (16 ounces per pound times 25 pounds) than if it follows only one.

Applying the Weber–Fechner Law to pricing would go as follows: Each additional dollar will add less to the pain of paying than its predecessor. Thus, adding a given dollar amount to the price of an inexpensive item will increase the pain of paying more than adding that amount to the price of an expensive item. For example, a $5 increase in the price of a $20 calculator will hurt more than the same $5 increase in the price of a $1,200 computer.

The curved shape of the prospect theory value function reflects the "diminishing returns" effect of the Weber–Fechner Law. From the graph shown in Figure 8.4, it can be seen how the prospect theory value function incorporates the Weber–Fechner Law's implications. The point on the vertical axis that indicates the value of a gain of size A is indicated by the blue arrow in the upper half of the graph. The value of a gain two times the size of A is indicated by the black arrow above it. Note that the pleasure of a gain of size 2A is less than two times the pleasure of a gain of size A. As the Weber–Fechner Law predicts, the second unit of A has less of a mental effect than its predecessor.

Figure 8.4   The Prospect Theory Value Function Incorporates the Implications of the Weber–Fechner Law

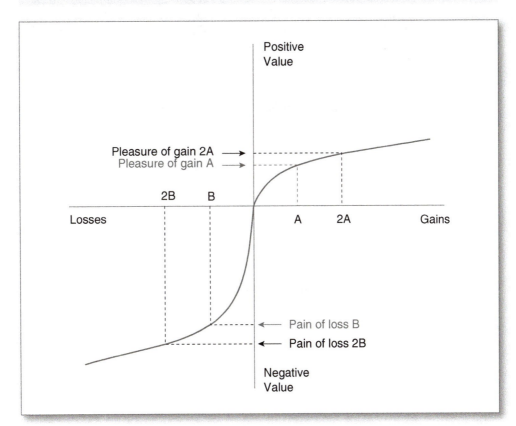

The same pattern occurs for losses. As is shown in Figure 8.4, the point on the vertical axis that indicates the value of a loss of size B is indicated by the blue arrow in the lower half of the graph. The value of a loss two times the size of B is indicated by the black arrow below it. The pain of a loss of size 2B is less than two times the pain of a loss of size B. Prospect theory builds on the Weber–Fechner Law and, as we will see, the Weber–Fechner Law plays a critical role in generating prospect theory's unique predictions.

Loss Aversion

As was previously mentioned, the loss portion of the prospect theory value function curves downward more sharply than the gain portion of the function curves upward. This represents loss aversion—the tendency of a loss to hurt more than an equal-sized gain feels good. This can be illustrated using the example of salaries. If your annual salary is increased by $2,000, you would definitely feel good. However, if your salary is decreased by $2,000, you would not just feel bad but might be downright upset. The $2,000 loss would hurt more than the $2,000 gain would feel good.

Loss aversion in the prospect theory value function is shown graphically in Figure 8.5. If we refer to a certain quantity as A, the value of gaining that quantity is indicated by the blue arrow in the upper half of the graph. The value of losing that same quantity is indicated by the blue arrow on the lower half of the graph. As can be seen in Figure 8.5, losing A causes more pain than gaining A causes pleasure. In other words, losing a quantity causes more emotion than gaining the same quantity.

Figure 8.5 The Prospect Theory Value Function Incorporates Loss Aversion

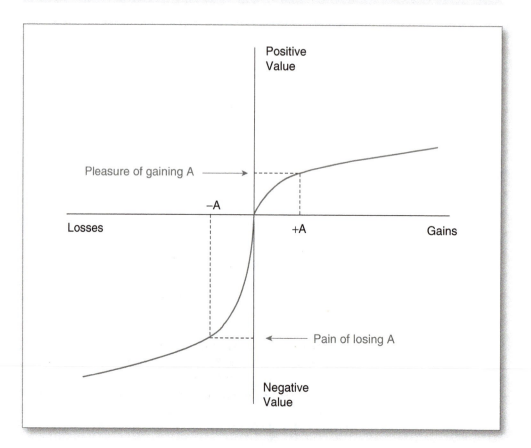

FOUR POSSIBLE PERCEPTIONS OF A PRICE

Prospect theory's description of the value of gains and losses provides guidance as to some fundamental possibilities concerning how a price can be perceived by the consumer. It is easy to appreciate that a price can be perceived as a single loss. However, because of the "behavior" of the consumer's reference point, a price may also be perceived as two losses, a loss and a gain, and even as a gain forgone. Each of these will be discussed in turn.

In this discussion, it is important to recognize that our focus is on price. The consumer's purchase decision of course involves evaluating the product as well as the price. The product can also be perceived as various combinations of gains and losses. To keep our focus here sharply on price, we will consider the consumer's perception of the product to be constant. Given this perception of the product, how the price is perceived will affect the pain of paying and will thus have an effect on the likelihood of purchase.

Perception of a Price as a Single Loss

The simplest perception of a product's price is as a single loss. For example, a consumer considering a living room sofa may perceive its price of $2,200 as simply a loss of $2,200. This is likely to occur when the price is equal to, or within the range of, the consumer's internal reference price (IRP). It will also occur on those occasions when a consumer has an IRP that differs from the product's price, but the consumer does not think about this IRP or bring it to mind. In these situations, the consumer's reference point is the status quo—the state of affairs before the purchase—and the item's price is the loss that must be incurred in order to obtain the product.

When a price is perceived as a single loss, the seller can use the implications of the Weber–Fechner Law to estimate how a price change may affect the pain of paying. A $10 increase on a $25 item would increase the pain of paying more than the same $10 increase on a $250 item. Similarly, a $10 decrease on the $25 price would decrease the pain of paying more than the same $10 decrease on the $250 item. In general, the Weber–Fechner Law suggests that the size of a price change in percent terms will be an important factor in determining the change in the buyer's pain of paying and thus in determining the buyer's response to the price change.

This implication of the Weber–Fechner Law becomes particularly interesting when it is recognized that consumers often consider the products of many sellers as one "item."[3] For example, a young couple may spend $2,400 for their annual vacation at the beach. That would include what they pay to the airline, the hotel, the cab company, the local restaurants, and so on. If one of their favorite restaurants raises an entrée price from $12 to $18, the couple might be unlikely to go elsewhere. They may feel that since they are already paying $2,400 for the vacation, what's $6 more to make it pleasurable. In other words, the couple's tendency to consider the vacation as a single item would lead them to see the 50 percent increase in the entrée price as a one-quarter of 1 percent increase in the price of their vacation. As such, the $6 increase in the price of the entrée would have minimal effect on their pain of paying.

A set of related purchases that consumers consider as one purchase could be referred to as a purchase aggregate. Although consumers often spontaneously think in terms of purchase aggregates, the tendency to do so can also be influenced by a seller. For example, a wedding photographer who is trying to justify his high prices might frame his fees to the couple as being "only a small part of the cost of your wedding."

Perception of a Price as Two Losses

When a product's price exceeds a consumer's IRP, the consumer is likely to perceive the price as two losses. For example, if the aforementioned consumer had expected to pay $2,000 for the $2,200 sofa, she may have perceived the price as a loss of $2,000 and a second loss of $200. In such a case, the first loss perceived could be termed the expected price—the difference between the consumer's initial reference point (the prepurchase status quo, i.e., $0) and her IRP (what she is expecting to pay). When the consumer recognizes that the product's price is not equal to her IRP, her reference point might shift from her prepurchase state to her IRP. The extent to which the product's price exceeds this new reference point would then be perceived as a second loss, which could be termed the perceived surcharge. Such a reference point shift will not always occur, but when a product's price is higher than consumers' IRPs, it will occur at least sometimes and result in at least some perception of the product's price as consisting of two losses.

As can be seen from the graph in Figure 8.6, a price (P) perceived as two losses will be more negatively evaluated than that price perceived as one loss. The size of the first loss, the expected price, is equal to the IRP. The pain of paying this loss is indicated by one of the blue arrows in the lower half of the graph. The size of the second loss, the perceived surcharge, is the difference between the price and the consumer's IRP. The pain of paying this loss is indicated by the other blue arrow in the lower half of the graph. The total pain of paying the price perceived as two losses is the sum of these two amounts of negative feeling. Because of the curved shape of the prospect theory value function (which expresses the Weber–Fechner Law), this total pain of paying the two losses is greater than the pain that would be experienced from perceiving the price as a single loss, which is indicated by the black arrow in the lower half of the graph.

For the seller to avoid the negative evaluations of a price that is perceived as two losses, the key is to monitor the IRPs of consumers. If a product's price is below the IRP of most consumers, then there is some room for an increase. For example, if consumer research indicates that most consumers would expect to pay around $60.00 for a ready-to-assemble wood coffee table currently selling for $45.99, then that product's price could be increased to around $60.00 without considering the negative factor of its price being perceived as two losses. Similarly, when consumers' IRP for a product is a wide range of prices, the product's price can be increased up to the high end of that range without the negative effects of consumers perceiving that they are being asked to pay a surcharge.

In situations where there is high consumer awareness of a product's price, any price increase is bound to be noticed and lead to the negative effects of a perceived surcharge. To deal with this limitation, sellers often find that there will be smaller sales losses from reducing the size of the product or the number of items in the product's package than from increasing the price. This practice is known as downsizing. For example, for a long time, Walmart sold a box of twenty Hefty trash bags for the relatively low price of $2. Because the round-number price and the tendency for this item to be placed near checkout counters or on displays made price awareness high, increasing the price of this item became difficult. Walmart dealt with

Figure 8.6   Perception of a Price as Two Losses

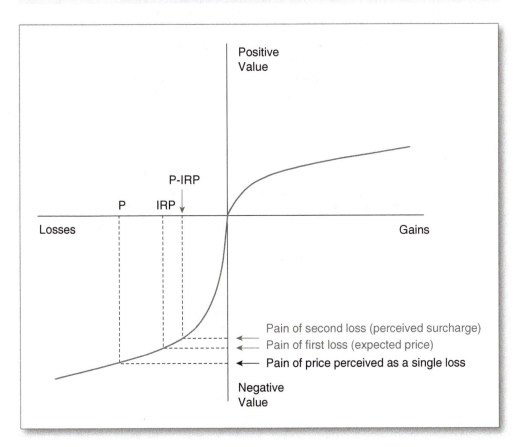

Note: IRP = internal reference price; P = price.

this difficulty by quietly substituting a box of fifteen Hefty trash bags in the same locations where the twenty-count boxes had been displayed and kept the price at $2.

Because downsizing does involve a change in the per-unit price level, is it not, strictly speaking, an example of framing. However, it is a closely related technique in that it relies on consumers' disinclination to adjust their IRPs when a package size decreases. Downsizing strategies have often been used for frequently-purchased consumer packaged goods such as facial tissues, paper towels, coffee, candy bars, ice cream, canned tuna, orange juice, and disposable diapers.

Perception of a Price as a Loss and a Gain

When a product's price is less than a consumer's IRP, the consumer is likely to perceive the product's price as a loss and a gain. For example, if the consumer considering the $2,200 sofa had expected to pay $2,500, she may have perceived the price as a loss of $2,500 and a gain of $300. In such a case, the loss would be the expected price—the difference between the consumer's initial reference point (the prepurchase status quo, i.e., $0) and her IRP. When the consumer recognizes that the product's price is not equal to her IRP, her reference point might shift from her prepurchase state to her IRP. The extent to which this new reference point (i.e., her IRP) exceeds the product's price would then be perceived as a gain, which could be termed the perceived discount.

As can be seen from the graph in Figure 8.7, a price (P) perceived as a loss and a gain will be more positively evaluated than that price perceived as a single loss. The size of the loss, the expected price, is equal to the IRP. The pain of paying it is indicated by the blue arrow in the lower half of the graph. The size of the gain, the perceived discount, is the difference between the consumer's IRP and the product's price. The pleasure of receiving this gain is indicated by the blue arrow in the upper half of the graph. The total pain of paying the price perceived as a loss and a gain is the net pain resulting from the pain of the expected price reduced by the pleasure of the perceived discount. The key prediction of prospect theory (again from the curved shape of its value function) is that this net pain is less than the pain that would be experienced from the perception of the price as a single loss, which is indicated by the black arrow in the lower half of the graph.

Figure 8.7 Perception of a Price as a Loss and a Gain

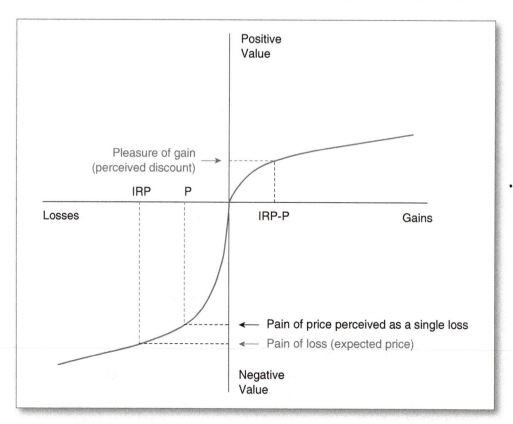

Note: IRP = internal reference price; P = price.

For a seller, the more positive consumer feelings engendered by the loss-and-gain perception of a price make it worthwhile to encourage this perception. The key to doing this is the management of the consumers' IRPs. For example, when a product's price is decreased under conditions of low consumer price awareness, consumers may not recognize that a price decrease has occurred. To create awareness of the price decrease—and thus maximize the likelihood that the price is perceived as a loss and a gain—the seller should communicate the product's former price. Retail ads often carry headlines such as "Was $200.00—Now Only $129.99!" In these ads, the higher price shown is known as an external reference price. Its purpose is to suggest to the consumer the appropriate IRP. To the extent that the suggestion succeeds, consumer IRPs will be higher than the product's selling price, and the likelihood of a loss-and-gain perception of the price will be maximized.

How effective are external reference prices in influencing consumer IRPs? The research evidence suggests that they are most likely to be effective when what is being claimed is a discount of moderate size—that is, a discount of around 20 to 40 percent.[4] It appears that consumers will interpret a discount claim without an external reference price (e.g., "On sale!" "Entire stock reduced!") as indicating a 10 to 15 percent discount. Thus, if the true price decrease is smaller than that, it is not in the seller's interest to specify the former price. On the other hand, it appears that as the claimed discount begins to exceed 50 percent, consumer skepticism increases sharply. Thus, the claim of a 75 percent discount might have a negative effect on the retailer's credibility that outweighs any positive effect on consumers' IRPs.

External reference prices can be used even when a seller's prices have not decreased. In this use, the external reference price would suggest that a high IRP is appropriate because of the higher prices charged by other sellers. Here, research has indicated that the semantic cues—the words used to describe the external reference price—are often critical. Vague semantic cues such as "Compare at . . ." or "Seen elsewhere at . . ." are less effective in influencing IRPs than more specific cues such as "Chain drugstores charge . . ." or "K-Mart's price. . . ."

Perception of a Price as a Gain Forgone

Under certain conditions, it is even possible for a price to not be perceived as a loss at all. For example, if the consumer considering the $2,200 sofa had just inherited about that amount from her great uncle, she might have perceived the $2,200 price as a gain forgone. For such a perception to occur, the consumer's reference point must *not* shift to considering having the gain from her uncle as the status quo. If the consumer's reference point remains at the state of affairs existing before the gain occurred, spending the gain on the sofa would only remove the pleasure that the gain brought. Because of loss aversion, removing the pleasure of a gain decreases happiness less than incurring a loss of the same size (refer again to Figure 8.5). Thus, perceiving a price as a gain forgone will result in a more favorable evaluation of the price than perceiving it as a single loss.

One way for a seller to frame a product's price as a gain forgone is to create a salient link in the consumer's mind between the product's price and something considered to be a recent monetary gain. Some retailers attempt to create such a link by running ads around the time that many consumers receive income tax refunds. "Enjoy your tax refunds" is the kind of message that might encourage consumers to perceive the price of a discretionary purchase in the less painful form of a gain forgone (see Figure 8.8).

Figure 8.8   Advertising Message That Might Lead Consumers to Perceive the Price of a Purchase as a Gain Foregone

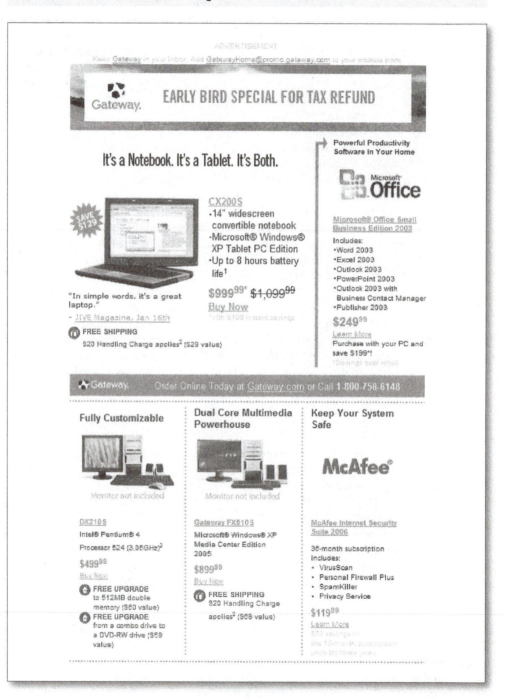

EFFECTS OF FAIRNESS JUDGMENTS ON THE VALUE OF A LOSS

Prospect theory explicitly describes how the value of a loss varies with its size, but it also leaves open the possibility that factors other than size can affect the value of a loss. One such factor is fairness—the degree to which the loss is judged to be in conformance to the rules of acceptable human behavior. For example, seats at popular movies, concerts, or sports events often sell out quickly. Long lines form when the box office opens and latecomers are forced to buy tickets from scalpers. Why don't the producers of the event simply charge prices high enough for demand to be in line with supply? The answer is that doing so would create bad will among consumers. A price sufficient to reduce demand might be as high as $200 or $300 per ticket. Such a price would be considered unfair by many consumers and would lead to anger and perhaps other bad consequences for the actors, orchestra, or teams involved in the event.

Important to fairness is the concept of equity—the sense that both participants in an exchange receive benefits that are, if not equal, at least appropriate to what each participant contributes to the exchange. Consumers recognize that they receive benefits from a purchased product and thus consider it fair for the seller to make a modest profit for providing the product. If consumers see the seller's profit as excessive, as would likely be the case with a $300 concert ticket, they would judge the product's price to be unfair. On the other hand, if the seller is seen as making very little profit, say because of a policy of contributing most profits to charity, the product's price would be considered "more than fair" (i.e., better than average on fairness).

The degree to which a consumer judges a price as fair will influence the consumer's pain of paying that price. A price is most painful when it is judged to be unfair, less painful when it is judged fair, and less painful still when it is judged "more than fair."

This relationship can help explain the phenomenon of shipping charges. As previously discussed, prospect theory predicts that a price perceived as two losses will be less favorably evaluated than that price perceived as a single loss. Despite this, the vast majority of retailers who sell through catalogs or the Internet do not bundle together product's base price with the price of shipping it to the consumer. Rather, they ensure that consumers perceive each product's price as two losses by framing the price for shipping as separate from the price of the product itself. One explanation of how such price partitioning can be advantageous to the seller is that consumers tend to see a shipping charge as just covering the seller's shipping costs and not contributing to profits. This view of a shipping charge as "more than fair" would reduce the pain of paying this charge (see Figure 8.9). When a price is perceived as two losses but the second loss involves relatively little pain, then the sum of the pain of each of the two losses might well be less than the pain involved when the price is perceived as a single loss.[5]

When Is a Price Increase Considered Fair?

When an item's price exceeds a consumer's IRP and the consumer experiences a perceived surcharge (i.e., a second loss), the consumer's feeling about that perceived surcharge will depend on the business situation. If the price is one of long standing and the consumer is

Figure 8.9 Advantage of a Separate Shipping Charge Being Perceived as Only Covering Shipping Costs

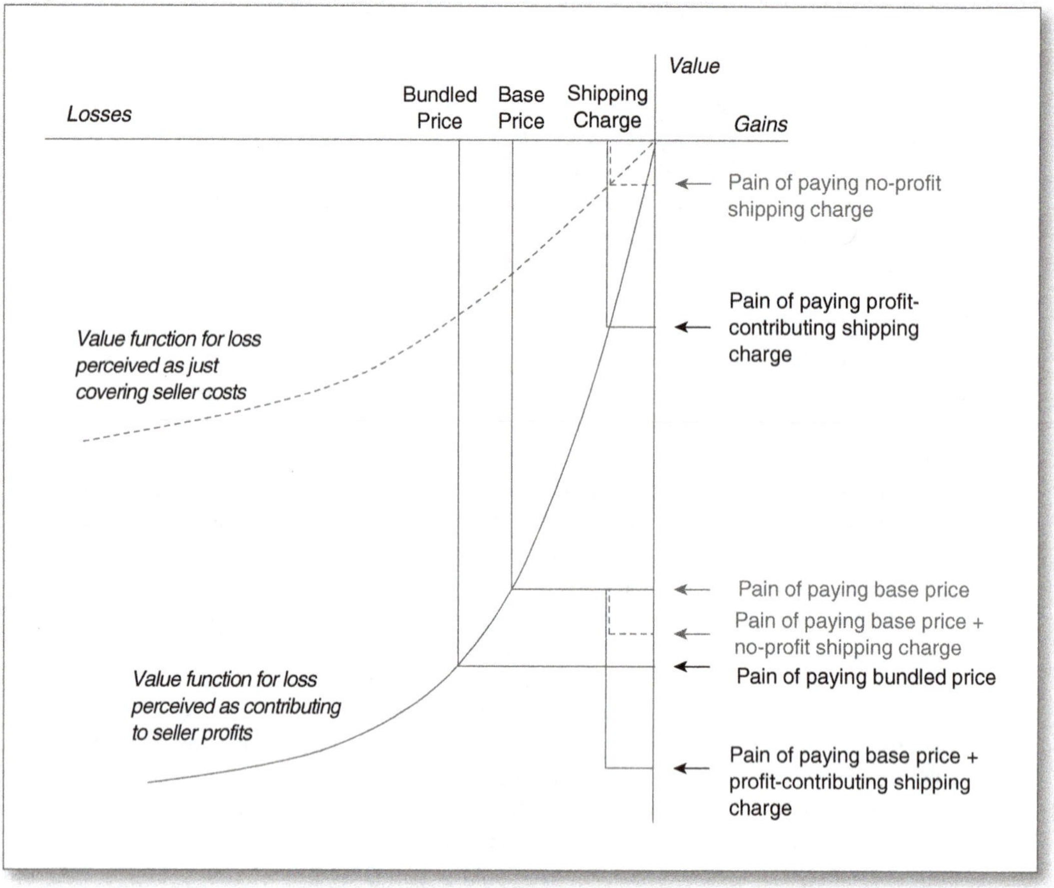

new to the market for such items, then the consumer may well attribute the perception of a surcharge to his or her ignorance and update his or her IRP. In such a situation, there may be consumer disappointment but probably not a perception of unfairness.

On the other hand, if the price has recently been increased, and the consumer has enough price knowledge to be aware of this, then price fairness may well be an issue. If the seller is seen as increasing a product's price in the absence of any increase in the seller's costs, then consumers are likely to feel that the perceived surcharge is unfair.[6] When a shortage creates a price increase, whether it involves concert tickets or the availability of the latest Wii game console, it is clear to consumers that seller costs did not substantially increase, and the price increase is considered unfair. Similarly, when environmental events, such as a large snowfall, cause sudden increases in the prices of items to deal with these events, such as snow shovels, then these increases are likely to be considered unfair.[7]

Given the importance of the seller's costs in the consumer's feelings about a price increase, it is in the seller's interest to accompany a price increase with information about cost increases that could help account for the price increase. One approach to this is to give some transparency to the price-setting process, such as is done in consumer loan products whose interest rates are pegged to a standard financial measure such as the prime lending rate.

Another approach is to provide customers with a price rationale—an explicit price-change explanation which—that highlights the seller's increased costs. Such a statement could draw on media reports of inflation or of price increases in basic product components such as raw materials, energy, or labor. A price rationale for a price increase could also make use of the consumer's price-origin beliefs. For example, if consumers believe that higher-quality materials or a greater number of useful features cause higher prices, then emphasizing such product changes would help make a price increase seem more fair.[8] Note, however, that even though many consumers believe that advertising costs cause higher prices, increased advertising expenditures are commonly perceived as benefiting only the seller and thus are not useful in rationales for a price increase.

A consideration that is perhaps of underlying importance in price fairness judgments is the issue of control. When consumers feel that they have no control as to whether or not they pay a price, they are particularly likely to see a price increase as unfair. Thus, when consumers are faced with persistent parallel pricing by all sellers of a product, consumer resentment of price increases is likely to develop. Further, when a product is viewed as a necessity—for example, important for maintaining life and health and with few alternatives—then the fairness of any price increase will often be questioned.

Other Determinants of Fairness

In making price fairness judgments, consumers also look to what other customers are paying. When they observe that other customers who they see as similar to themselves are paying lower prices for the same product, they will tend to question the fairness of the situation. It is important for managers to take this tendency into account when developing their organization's price structure, and it will be discussed further in Chapters 10 and 15.

Because it is usually difficult for consumers to judge seller costs or be aware of prices that other customers pay, their judgments of price fairness often rely on general impressions of the seller's motives.[9] For example, oil companies and pharmaceutical manufacturers have acquired questionable reputations over the years. For this reason, any increases in the prices of their products are particularly likely to be judged as unfair and thus are likely to be especially painful to consumers. The managers of such companies should keep in mind these consumer impressions when making pricing decisions and, when implementing price increases, they would be wise to pay particular attention to offering price rationales to justify the increases.

FACTORS THAT CAN ENHANCE THE VALUE OF A GAIN

Since a price may be perceived as involving gains, such as perceived discounts, it is useful to understand how the value of a gain can be affected by factors other than the size of the gain. Two such factors, dangling and perceived responsibility, both act to increase the value of a perceived discount.

Dangling

Retail advertising often works hard to draw the consumer's attention to the offered discounts. Headlines loudly proclaim the following:

"Save $$$ now!"

"Don't miss out on storewide savings!"

"Save 40% or more on all camcorders in stock!"

This type of promotion not only helps frame the retailer's prices as discounts but also serves to dangle these discounts in front of consumers. Dangling is the practice of putting a discount or other offer into the consumer's mind in a way that is vivid and immediate.

Understanding the flexibility of price perception can help us explain the benefits of this practice. Although discounts quietly communicated by retailers may catch the consumer's attention, consumers often find it very easy to pass up these potential gains. As we already noted, a gain forgone may not be very painful, especially if the gain is not large. However, through dangling—communicating loudly, in the consumer's face—the motive power of these gains can be increased. As the image of the discount becomes more vivid, the consumer's reference point becomes more likely to shift to the state of having the discount being the status quo. When that occurs, passing up the discount then involves incurring a *loss,* which is more painful than simply forgoing a gain. In effect, then, dangling can be considered a means of enhancing the value of a gain.[10]

Perceived Responsibility

It has been observed that retail discounts are capable of causing some striking extremes of behavior. For example, a story in the *Wall Street Journal* described the effects of the "blue-light specials" in manager Ernest Reed's K-Mart store:

When the blue light starts to flash, mothers sometimes abandon their babies. Shoppers have pushed clerks up onto counter tops and ripped merchandise to shreds. . . . When they miss a special, some shoppers berate the store's employees. Others steal tagged merchandise from the carts of their more successful rivals. In April, two women vying for discounted jelly beans at Mr. Reed's store began throwing punches. Money and keys "went everywhere," marvels Mr. Reed.[11]

Such consumer overreactions illustrate that perceived discounts can take on an emotional potency far beyond that which would be expected given the amounts of money that are typically involved. One reason for this is that consumers often consider themselves responsible for having obtained the discount. Their sense is that they received the discount because they knew where to shop, where to look, when to shop, what to buy, and so on.

Research has shown that when consumers attribute themselves as personally responsible for a discount, the pleasure they feel from this discount increases.[12]

The value-altering effects of perceived responsibility on the prospect theory value function can be seen in the graph shown in Figure 8.10.[13] Note that there is a responsibility effect for losses as well as gains—the pain of a loss increases when one feels responsible for the loss. However, because of our persistent tendency to take personal responsibility for good outcomes and blame other factors for bad outcomes, this is not an important factor in pricing. Consumers tend not to perceive themselves as personally responsible for the parts of prices that they perceive as losses.

Yet feelings of personal responsibility are important when consumers perceive prices as involving gains. One feels a sense of pride—a sense of being worthy, competent, and smart—when one feels responsible for having acquired money. The power of these feelings

Figure 8.10   Effect of Perceived Responsibility on the Value of Gains and Losses

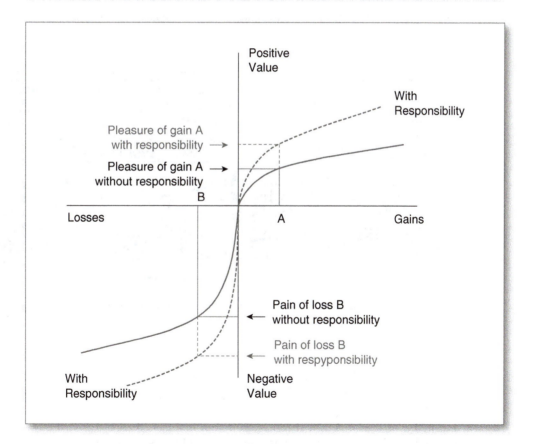

Source: Adapted from Hersh M. Shefrin and Meir Statmen (1984), "Explaining Investor Preference for Cash Dividends," *Journal of Financial Economics,* 13, 253–282.

draws on the deeply rooted value of money in American society. In his book *Money and Class in America,* social critic Lewis Lapham wrote the following:

> Ask an American what money means, and nine times out of ten he will say that it is synonymous with freedom, that it opens the doors of feeling and experience, that citizens with enough money can play at being gods, and do anything they wish. . . . [14]

Thus, we can see how perceived discounts may be capable of sparking feelings strong enough to lead to shopper frenzy at blue-light specials and enduring enough to drive long-term product satisfaction (see Figure 8.11). More typically, these "smart-shopper feelings" can be expected to cause the consumer's response to a price decrease effectively framed as a pride-evoking discount to far exceed sales response expectations based on routine price fluctuations.

Figure 8.11 Illustration of the Enduring Power of the Pleasures of a Discount

Source: CATHY © 1988 Cathy Guisewite. Reprinted with permission of UNIVERSAL UCLICK. All rights reserved.

SUMMARY

A buyer's response to a price is influenced by his or her feelings about the price, known as the pain of paying. Price framing involves managing the set of gains and losses that comprise the buyer's perception of the price, and the prospect theory value function describes how people feel about these gains and losses. There are diminishing emotional effects of the size of gains and losses (Weber–Fechner Law), and a loss hurts more than an equal-sized gain feels good (loss aversion).

The consumer's evaluation of a price depends on how the price is perceived. The alternative perceptions depend on the consumer's IRP and can be influenced by the seller. When the consumer perceives a price as a single loss, then it is the price-change percentage that tends to predict the market's price-change response. When the consumer perceives a price as two losses, then the evaluation of the price is likely to be particularly negative. When the consumer perceives a price as a loss and a gain, then the evaluation of the price is likely to be particularly positive. When the consumer perceives a price as a gain forgone, then the evaluation of the price is also likely to be relatively positive.

Factors other than size affect the value of a perceived losses and gains. Judgments of fairness affect the value of a perceived loss. Making a perceived gain more vivid and immediate to the consumer and leading the consumer to feel personally responsible for a perceived gain can increase the value of the gain.

KEY TERMS

pain of paying	loss aversion	external reference price
reference point	purchase aggregate	semantic cues
reference point shift	expected price	fairness
framing	perceived surcharge	equity
prospect theory value function	downsizing	price rationale
Weber–Fechner Law	perceived discount,	dangling

REVIEW AND DISCUSSION QUESTIONS

1. Distinguish between price awareness and price feelings. What is meant by the phrase *pain of paying?*

2. What is framing? What is the relation between framing and price format?

3. On the graph that is used to show the prospect theory value function, what is indicated on the horizontal axis? What is indicated on the vertical axis?

4. Describe the Weber–Fechner Law. Give an example of it from everyday life.

5. What is indicated by the lines of the prospect theory value function being curved rather than straight?

6. What is indicated by the left-side curve of the prospect theory value function being steeper than the right-side curve?

7. Explain how the consumer's IRP determines whether a price is perceived as a single loss, two losses, or a loss and a gain.

8. What are purchase aggregates? How might a seller use information about them?

9. When might it be particularly appropriate to decrease the size of a product rather than increase its price?

10. What is an external reference price? How can sellers use external reference prices most effectively?

11. What might a seller do to frame a price as a gain forgone?

12. Describe some factors, in addition to size, that can affect the value of a perceived loss or gain.

13. What is the concept of equity? How does it relate to consumer judgments of the fairness of a price?

14. Describe some factors, other than the consumer's impression of the seller's profits, that contribute to judgments of price fairness.

15. Using the terms of perceived gains and losses, describe how dangling an offer of a discount may affect the consumer's response to the discount.

16. How does seeing oneself as responsible for a perceived gain or loss affect the value of that gain or loss? Why is perceived responsibility an important factor in the consumer's response to a discount?

EXERCISES

1. A bar soap manufacturer has lowered prices twice in the past few years. From these price decreases, the manufacturer has calculated the price elasticity of the market to be –0.8. Given that the market has turned out to be so price inelastic, the manufacturer has decided to try a modest price increase. Use what you know about the value of perceived gains and losses to suggest a problem with the manufacturer's logic.

2. A popular brand of organic milk has been selling at local supermarkets for $5.99 per gallon. Recently, the one-gallon jugs (128-ounce) have been replaced by 3/4-gallon jugs (96-ounce), which sell for $4.99.

   (a) Name and describe the pricing tactic that most likely is being used here. What is this technique designed to accomplish?

   (b) Give some reasons why the management of this brand of milk might have judged this pricing technique to be called for in this situation.

3. A large home improvement retailer has run an advertisement for a particular brand-name titanium drill bit set. The headline of the ad is "Was $19.97—Now Only $14.97!"

   (a) What is the external reference price that is mentioned in this ad?

(b) Assume that the external reference price mentioned in this ad causes the advertised selling price (i.e., the price at which the item is being sold) to be perceived by consumers as a loss and a gain. Assuming this, give an example of what that consumer's IRP would have to be.

(c) Given the assumption of Part (b) and the IRP that you gave as an example, what would be the dollar size of the loss that the consumer perceives? What would be the dollar size of the gain that the consumer perceives? Briefly explain your reasoning.

4. Consider the college that has two prices for its services. It charges list price (full tuition) to only a small portion of their students. Everyone else gets a discount (scholarship). This college does not set a low price and charge a tuition premium to those few individuals who are not star students, athletes, or from low-income backgrounds.

   (a) In terms of perceived gains and losses, describe how the recipient of a scholarship is likely to perceive the price he or she pays for college.

   (b) Using what you know about the value of perceived gains and losses, explain why the college prefers to frame its two prices in terms of scholarships rather than tuition premiums.

5. Use the concept of framing and the prospect theory value function to explain each of the following phenomena:

   (a) Gamblers at casino resorts sometimes spend their winnings on lavish luxuries without much concern, considering their winnings to be "free money."

   (b) A popular brand of multiple vitamins finds it advantageous to cancel plans for a slight price decrease and instead wrap the regular vitamin bottle with a small bottle labeled "25 extra vitamins free!"

   (c) A computer magazine finds it profitable to give free one-year subscriptions to young professionals interested in information technology.

NOTES

1. Drazen Prelec and George F. Loewenstein, "The Red and the Black: Mental Accounting of Savings and Debt," *Marketing Science* 17, no. 1 (1998): 4–28.
2. Daniel Kahneman and Amos Tversky, "Prospect Theory: An Analysis of Decision Under Risk," *Econometrica* 47 (1979): 263–291.
3. This is part of what Nagle and Holden have termed the "end-benefit effect." See Thomas T. Nagle and Reed K. Holden, *The Strategy and Tactics of Pricing: A Guide to Profitable Decision Making* (Upper Saddle River, NJ: Prentice Hall, 2002), 94.
4. Robert M. Schindler (1994), "How to Advertise Price," in *Attention, Attitude, and Affect in Response to Advertising,* ed., Eddie M. Clark, Timothy C. Brock, and David W. Stewart (Hillsdale, NJ: Lawrence Erlbaum, 1994), 251–269.
5. Robert M. Schindler, Maureen Morrin, and Nada Nasr Bechwati, "Shipping Charges and Shipping-Charge Skepticism: Implications for Direct Marketers' Pricing Formats," *Journal of Interactive Marketing* 19 (Winter 2005): 41–53.

6. Daniel Kahneman, Jack L. Knetsch, and Richard Thaler, "Fairness as a Constraint on Profit Seeking Entitlements in the Market," *American Economic Review* 76 (September 1986): 728–741.

7. Lan Xia, Kent B. Monroe, and Jennifer L. Cox, "The Price is Unfair! A Conceptual Framework of Price Fairness Perceptions," *Journal of Marketing* 68 (October 2004): 1–15.

8. Lisa E. Bolton, Luk Warlop, and Joseph W. Alba, "Consumer Perceptions of Price (Un)Fairness," *Journal of Consumer Research* 29 (March 2003): 474–491.

9. Margaret C. Campbell, "Perceptions of Price Unfairness: Antecedents and Consequences," *Journal of Marketing Research* 36 (May 1999): 187–199.

10. Stephen J. Hoch and George F. Loewenstein, "Time-Inconsistent Preferences and Consumer Self-Control," *Journal of Consumer Research* 17 (March 1991): 492–507.

11. Melinda G. Guiles, "Attention Shoppers: Stop That Browsing and Get Aggressive," *Wall Street Journal*, June 16, 1987, 1, 17.

12. Robert M. Schindler, "Consequences of Perceiving Oneself as Responsible for Obtaining a Discount: Evidence for Smart-Shopper Feelings," *Journal of Consumer Psychology* 7, no. 4 (1998): 371–392.

13. Adapted from Hersh M. Shefrin and Meir Statman, "Explaining Investor Preference for Cash Dividends," *Journal of Financial Economics* 13 (1984): 253–282.

14. Lewis H. Lapham, *Money and Class in America: Notes and Observations on Our Civil Religion* (New York: Weidenfeld & Nicolson, 1988), 26–27.

Empirical Measurement of Price-Change Response

Chapters 6 through 8 have covered factors that can help the price setter predict and perhaps also influence the market's price-change response. We discussed the likely range of price elasticity values and some economic factors that can tell us where within that range price elasticities are likely to fall. We talked about the importance of the reactions of competitors in the market's price-change response and covered some factors that can help predict the pricing actions of one's competitors. We discussed the important role that the customer's price awareness and price-related feelings play in determining price-change response.

A manager considering a price change should ideally carry out an analysis in all of these areas. However, although such analyses will provide guidance, they may not give a clear enough prediction with sufficient certainty to make the price-change decision. The consequences of a price change may be great. There may be millions of dollars of sales involved, large promotional expenses to communicate the price change, and the possibility of enduring effects on the reputation or image of the company. In situations where the stakes are high, the analysis of economic, competitive, cognitive, and emotional factors affecting response to a prospective price change should be supplemented by more systematic marketing research. In other words, there should be some actual empirical measurement of the market's likely price-change response.

In this chapter, we discuss two market research approaches to predicting the market's response to a price change. The first approach, the analysis of historical sales data, will be referred to as the regression approach. It is possible whenever an organization has access to sufficient past sales data. The second approach, carrying out a controlled experiment, will be referred to as the experimentation approach. It does not require access to past data but typically involves greater costs in time and money. When a price-change decision carries important consequences, either or both of these market research approaches should be applied to the task of market-response prediction.

REGRESSION APPROACH

The regression approach to predicting the market's price-change response involves systematically examining the product's price history—specifically, the product's past prices and past sales levels. The focus of interest is the degree of correspondence that exists between price levels and sales levels. For example, were sales levels lower during those periods when price levels were higher? If so, how much lower were the sales levels?

This analysis would be relatively simple if price were the only variable that affected the product's sales levels. But this is clearly not the case. A large number of variables other than price can affect sales, including for example, changes in the economy, activities of competitors, product advertising levels, in-store promotions, season of the year, and so on. Without taking at least some of these nonprice variables into account, it is unlikely that the analysis of historical data will yield an adequate indication of the nature of the relation between price and sales.

The statistical procedure of multiple regression is well-suited to sorting out the relations between these variables. The form of regression used here is known as "time-series regression," which indicates that the data used are from a number of past time periods. This contrasts with the use of multiple regression in Chapter 3 to carry out conjoint analysis. In that use of regression, the data set was from a survey carried out at a single point in time.

Data Required for the Regression Approach

It is important to have a clear understanding of the type of data that are required for the regression approach to the prediction of price-change response. As with the use of multiple regression in conjoint analysis, it is necessary to base the analysis on a rectangular array of numbers, or data matrix.

Each row in the data matrix consists of data from a particular period of time. That time period could be a week, a month, a quarter, a year, or some other unit of time. Each time period in the series should be of comparable length, and it is usually best if the time periods are adjoining, as in consecutive months of a year.

Each column in the data matrix contains a variable in the analysis. Ideally, there should be a value for each variable in the analysis for each time period in the analysis. Because our overall interest is predicting how sales will change in response to price changes, the dependent variable (DV) in the regression analysis will be the product's sales level. Price and the other variables that may have an effect on sales would each be an independent variable (IV) in the regression.

As an example, consider the data matrix in Figure 9.1. There are thirty-six rows in this matrix, one for each of the months over a three-year time span. There are four data columns in this matrix, one for each of the variables in the analysis. The first three columns are the IVs in this analysis. The first column, labeled "month," is the month of the year (coded 1 = January, 2 = February, etc.). The second column, labeled "price," is the product's price (coded in dollars) during each of the thirty-six months. The third column, labeled "adv $," is the amount that the company spent to advertise the product during each month (coded in thousands of dollars). The fourth column, labeled "sales," is the DV, the product's unit sales for each month (coded in thousands of units).

Figure 9.1   Illustrative Data Matrix for a Multiple Regression Analysis

Month	Price	Adv $	Sales
1	5.35	94	533
2	5.38	112	552
3	6.04	143	543
4	6.47	132	504
5	5.92	122	531
6	5.43	143	563
7	5.10	145	588
8	5.34	130	544
9	5.24	145	569
10	5.18	147	570
11	5.02	147	602
12	4.96	154	633
1	5.13	165	588
2	5.44	145	586
3	5.71	145	566
4	6.03	166	543
5	6.11	145	548
6	6.15	148	535
7	6.15	143	532
8	6.00	155	543
9	5.89	157	566
10	5.78	163	582
11	5.81	165	625
12	5.47	165	624
1	5.82	136	590
2	6.05	140	580
3	6.17	138	558
4	6.32	151	532
5	6.54	146	485
6	6.43	162	522
7	6.80	172	496
8	6.74	154	513
9	6.42	170	515
10	6.35	176	560
11	6.11	180	592
12	6.18	184	638
Means	5.86	149.58	559.75

Note: Price is in dollars, adv $ is in thousands of dollars, and sales are in thousands of units.

For a data matrix to be able to provide a reasonable estimate of a product's price-change response, it must be sufficient in the following three ways:

1. There must be data from a sufficiently large number of time periods. Thirty or forty time periods would usually be sufficient; an analysis of fewer than twenty time periods would be unlikely to produce reliable results.

2. There must be sufficient variation in the price variable over the time span of the analysis. If the product's price does not vary, then it is impossible to observe any relationship between price and sales. In other words, if there is no price change, there can be no measurement of price-change response.

3. There must be sufficient independence between price and the other IVs that affect sales. If there are strong correlations between price and other IVs that affect sales, the effect of price cannot be separated from the effects of these other IVs. For example, if a company tends to advertise a product only when the price of the product decreases, then any sales jump that occurs at the time of the price decreases could just as likely be due to the increased advertising as to the decreased price.

Sources of Required Data

The pricing analyst responsible for assembling a data matrix needs to be familiar with the potential sources of information for the data matrix. A company's internal records should be the first place to look. Data on the past prices for an item will often be available from the marketing department or from others in the organization who are involved in setting prices or monitoring profits. Archived reports from the sales force and customer databases would also be a source of price information. Data on unit sales should be available from similar sources within the company. In addition, inventory records and accounting data would also be sources of sales information. Information on advertising expenditures, displays, and other promotional activities should be available from the marketing department or from whatever unit of the organization is responsible for carrying out those activities.

There are many organizations external to the company that could also provide information for the data matrix. Sometimes trade associations publish the prices and even market shares of various competitors in an industry. For consumer packaged goods manufacturers and other companies that do not sell directly to their end users, there are a number of commercial organizations that track retail sales. For example, AC Nielsen's Scantrack and IRI's InfoScan services obtain information from checkout scanners and in-store audits and sell data on the sales volumes and prices of a wide variety of consumer retail goods. For competitive information, organizations such as TNS Media Intelligence/CMR track advertising expenditures, couponing, and other promotional activities for a large number of consumer brands.[1]

The federal government is a useful source of information on the level of economic activity. For example, in addition to collecting data on population, the U.S. Census Bureau also provides detailed measures of the activity in the major sectors of the economy including agriculture, manufacturing, mining, retail and wholesale trade, services, and transportation.[2] There are also independent organizations that provide data on economic activity, such as the Conference Board, as well as numerous business periodicals, such as the *Wall Street Journal* and *Forbes* magazine.

The Regression Coefficient of the Price Variable

The regression procedure provides an indication of the degree to which price and the other IVs are able to explain the differences that occurred in the product's sales level over the time periods that are included in the analysis. In this use of regression, the sales variable would be considered as a linear combination of price and the other IVs in the analysis. If the analysis were being carried out on the data matrix shown in Figure 9.1, we would be applying the following regression model:

$$\text{Sales} = a + b_1 \text{Month} + b_2 \text{Price} + b_3 \text{Adv } \$$$

The a in the equation is the intercept, which indicates the value of the DV when all IVs equal zero. Because in a pricing study it is not meaningful for the price IV to equal zero, the intercept value is not interpretable. Rather, our interest is in the values b_1, b_2, and b_3, which are known as regression coefficients. The regression coefficient of an IV is the expected change in the DV when the IV is changed by one unit, holding constant the effects of the other IVs.

We could run the regression analysis on the data matrix shown in Figure 9.1 using Excel 2007, as we did for the conjoint analysis in Chapter 3. After bringing the data matrix into the spreadsheet, we would select Data Analysis on the Data tab and then, in the Data Analysis dialog box, select Regression. For the "Y range," we would enter the endpoints for the data matrix column that contains the DV (in this case, the sales variable). For the "X range," we

Figure 9.2 Excel Output for the Regression Analysis of the Illustrative Data Matrix

SUMMARY OUTPUT

Regression Statistics	
Multiple R	0.793
R square	0.629
Adjusted R square	0.594
Standard error	24.198
Observations	36.000

ANOVA

	df	SS	MS	F	Significance F
Regression	3.000	31705.987	10568.662	18.050	0.000
Residual	32.000	18736.763	585.524		
Total	35.000	50442.750			

	Coefficients	Standard Error	t Stat	P-value	Lower 95%	Upper 95%
Intercept	740.509	51.287	14.438	0.000	636.040	844.977
Month	0.649	1.537	0.422	0.676	-2.482	3.779
Price	-57.343	9.041	-6.342	0.000	-75.759	-38.926
Adv $	1.011	0.309	3.273	0.003	0.382	1.639

would enter the endpoints for the rectangle containing the IVs (in this case, the three columns containing the month of the year, price, and product advertising variables).

The output of this analysis is shown in Figure 9.2. Under the heading "regression statistics," we can note that the value of R squared is 0.629. This indicates that our three IVs accounted for 63 percent—a considerable amount—of the variation in our DV: sales. Under the heading "ANOVA" (which stands for "analysis of variance"), we can note that our regression model has a significance of 0.000 (when rounded to three decimal places), well below the standard criterion of 0.05. This indicates that the effects of at least some of our IVs are reliable with respect to random error and indicates that we have used a sufficient number of time periods in this regression analysis.

The lower part of the ANOVA table gives the regression coefficients for the intercept and for the IVs. For the month of the year variable, the regression coefficient is +0.649. The positive sign indicates that sales tended to increase as the months approached the busy winter holiday season. Specifically, according to this regression analysis, every month was associated with an average sales increase of 649 units. However, the p-value of this regression coefficient is greater than the standard criterion of 0.05, indicating that this finding could have been due to random error. For the product advertising variable, the regression coefficient is +1.011, with a p-value low enough to indicate that it is reliable with respect to random error. The positive sign indicates that sales increased with increases in the amount spent on product advertising. Specifically, according to this regression analysis, every $1,000 spent on advertising was associated with a sales increase of 1,011 units.

The regression coefficient of the price variable is the value in this analysis output that is of the greatest interest. The regression analysis indicates that it equals −57.343, with a p-value showing that it is reliable with respect to random error. The negative sign indicates that sales decreased as price increased. Specifically, the regression analysis tells us that, over this three-year period, every $1 increase in price corresponded to a 57,343 unit decrease in sales.

Calculating the Price Elasticity From a Price Coefficient

The regression coefficient of the price variable provides a measure of the relationship between price and sales levels during the period of the analysis. To make this measure more useful for the prediction of price-change response, it should be translated into a measure that is more familiar—brand price elasticity.

As you will recall from Chapter 6, the price elasticity is defined as the percent change in unit sales divided by the percent change in price:

$$E = \frac{\% \Delta \text{ Unit sales}}{\% \Delta P}$$

What is given by the price coefficient is the change in unit sales for each dollar that the price changes (assuming that price is coded in dollars). This can be written as the change in unit sales divided by a $1 price change:

$$\text{Price coefficient} = \frac{\Delta \text{ Unit sales}}{\text{One-dollar } \Delta P}$$

To get to a price elasticity, both the change in unit sales and the $1 price change must be converted to percents. The only problem with doing this is that it is not clear what the base level of sales or price should be—should it be the sales and price levels at the first time period used in the regression analysis, the last, or some time period between? A solution to this problem is to use the average sales level and the average price level for all of the periods included in the regression analysis. Given that the sales-change estimate produced by the regression analysis involves an aggregation of a large number of time periods, it makes some sense that base levels for calculating a price elasticity do so also.[3]

If the mean (i.e., average) sales and price levels are used, the expression to convert a price coefficient to a price elasticity is as follows (S_m = the mean of all of the unit sales measurements used to calculate the regression coefficient; P_m = the mean of all prices used to calculate the regression coefficient):

$$E = \frac{\Delta \text{ Unit sales} \times (1/S_m) \times 100}{\text{One-dollar } \Delta\, P \times (1/P_m) \times 100}$$

By algebraically simplifying this expression (i.e., multiplying it by S_m/S_m and P_m/P_m), we arrive at the following formula for calculating the price elasticity from the regression coefficient of the price variable:

$$E = \text{Regression coefficient of price variable} \times (P_m / S_m)$$

To use this formula to convert the price coefficient shown in Figure 9.2 to a price elasticity, we would multiply the coefficient by the mean of the prices divided by the mean of the sales levels (see Figure 9.1): $-57.343 \times (5.86/559.75)$. The resulting price elasticity, -0.60, constitutes the prediction of the market's price-change response that could be obtained from the regression approach. In other words, given this product's history, our best guess would be that the market would be only moderately responsive to a price change. For example, if the product's price were increased by 10 percent, we might expect sales to decrease by 6 percent; if the product's price were decreased by 5 percent, we might expect sales to increase by 3 percent.

Strengths and Weaknesses of the Regression Approach

The regression approach to price-change response prediction has both strengths and weaknesses. A key strength is that the analysis is often fairly easy to carry out. If the necessary information has been recorded, it might take only a few days or less to assemble. The actual calculations can be completed by a pricing or market research analyst in just a few minutes. This makes it possible to give the pricing decision maker a market-response estimate quickly and at relatively low cost.

An additional strength of the regression approach is that it does not involve interacting with existing customers. It relies entirely on the analysis of past data and does not carry any risk of affecting the responses of, or relationships with, current customers.

There are also weaknesses to the regression approach. One weakness is the requirement of sufficient historical data. As was previously mentioned, the regression approach to price-change response prediction requires the following three things: (1) data from a large number of time periods, (2) sufficient price variation during those time periods, and (3) sufficient independence between price and the other variables that affect sales. Each of these requirements could be difficult to meet. A product might be relatively new, without sufficient sales history. In some markets, there is such a high degree of price stability that there is insufficient price variation to use the regression approach. It is also possible that market conditions have led price and other sales-affecting factors to be highly correlated. For example, higher levels of competitors' advertising may necessitate lower prices, changes in the economy could lead to corresponding price adjustments, or retailers may lower a product's price whenever they put it on display. Such correlations would make it impossible to determine the effect of price on sales, no matter how well the other data requirements of the regression approach are satisfied.

However, even if all the required data are available, there is another weakness of the regression approach. The price elasticity obtained from the regression approach is based entirely on past data. It is completely possible that the price–sales relationships that were shown in the past will not be present during the current time period. This could occur because of changes in any of the many aspects of the marketing environment. For example, there could be changes in the number of competitors in the marketplace, new technological advances, changes in legal or regulatory conditions, or shifts in the preferences and behaviors of customers. If any such changes occur between the time period of the historical data and the present, then the regression approach will do a poor job of predicting how the market will respond to a prospective price change.

EXPERIMENTATION APPROACH

In everyday language, the term *experimentation* could mean any way of giving something a try or learning by trial and error. However, in the context of market research, the term has a very specific meaning. When used to predict the market's price-change response, experimentation involves establishing two or more customer groups that are equivalent. The product's price is then varied between these equivalent groups and the responses of the customers are measured. If the experiment is designed correctly, then these customer responses could constitute an effective test of the market's likely response to changing the product's price.

Designing a Controlled Experiment

To understand the essence of experimental design, let's consider a simple two-group controlled experiment. Designing such an experiment begins with creating two equivalent groups of customers. One way of doing this would be to use a random process to divide a list of the company's customers into two groups. If the dividing process were truly random, then the two groups should look fairly similar—in particular, the two groups should show the same level of product sales.

The next step in designing the experiment is to arrange to change something in one of the two equivalent groups. Since our goal is to test price-change response, the price change that is being considered is what would be changed in one of the groups. This would create the independent variable (IV) in the experiment. The group that receives the price change would be referred to as the test group, and the group that does not receive the price change would be referred to as the control group. It is the presence of a control group that makes this a controlled experiment.

The final step in designing the experiment is to arrange to measure both groups after the change in the test group has occurred. Since this is a test of the market's price-change response, what would be measured in both groups would be the sales of the product whose price was changed in the test group. This sales measurement would be the dependent variable (DV) in the experiment. Because we have designed the two groups so that the only difference between them is the product's price (the IV), any difference between the two groups on the DV must be caused by this IV.

An example of a controlled pricing experiment is presented in Figure 9.3. At time$_1$, a certain frequently purchased consumer packaged good is priced at $5 in both the test and the control groups of customers. Because these two groups were selected so that they would be equivalent, the level of the product's sales in each group should be the same, say 90 units. Then the price manipulation occurs, lowering the price to $4 but only in the test group. At time$_2$ (a period of equivalent length to time$_1$), the customers in the control group purchased one hundred units of the product. Why is this higher than the ninety units they purchased during time$_1$? Perhaps the economy improved or the product became more in season. However, what is important is that whatever caused the control group's sales to rise to one hundred units should have done so also for the test group, since they are equivalent groups. Given this, the finding that the test group's sales are 130 units—30 higher than those of the control group—indicates that the $1 price decrease caused a sales increase of 30 units.

Figure 9.3 Example of a Controlled Experiment to Predict Price-Change Response

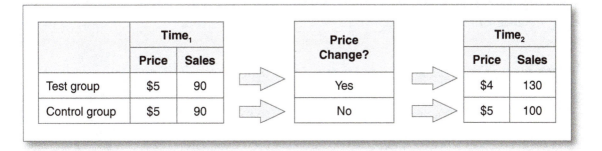

Implementing a Sales Experiment

A controlled experiment in which the DV is the product's actual sales is known as a sales experiment. Because the creation of at least two equivalent groups of real customers is essential for carrying out a sales experiment, we need to look a little further at how this can be done.

It was previously mentioned that a list of a company's customers could be randomly divided into two groups. This can be done whenever the company maintains a customer list. Companies selling in business markets often have few enough customers to be able to keep information on each one. Companies selling to consumers through catalogs, direct mail, or the Internet are also likely to have adequate customer lists.[4] It generally is acceptable to divide such customer lists using what is often called an A–B split. In an A–B split, the first customer in the list is assigned to group A, the second to group B, the third to group A, the fourth to group B, and so on. Assuming that the groups are large (e.g., 50,000 customers per group) and that the customer list is ordered alphabetically or in some other way that that does not make the even- or odd-numbered customers special, then this simple procedure should result in two equivalent groups.

Many companies do not have a list of customers. For example, consumer packaged goods manufacturers will rarely have lists of all the consumers who purchase their products. Retail organizations find it extremely difficult to keep good information on all of their customers, especially since a number of the purchasers of any product for which a price change is being considered could be shoppers who have never before purchased anything from that retailer. Such companies must use an alternative to assigning customers individually to each group.

One such alternative would be to use a random procedure to divide retail outlets into groups. For example, a consumer products manufacturer who distributes a national brand through grocery stores will often base a change in a product's price to retailers on the likely effects of the retailers passing along that price change to consumers. To determine consumers' likely price-change response, a manufacturer could develop a list of every grocery store in a set of representative cities or regions that carried the manufacturer's brand. An A–B split or other random procedure could be used to divide the grocery stores into two groups. One group of stores could then be given incentives to charge a lower price than the others, and the product sales levels of each group of stores could be compared. This alternative would require the cooperation of many retail outlets (e.g., thirty or more per group). It would also be important to take steps to avoid stores in different experimental groups being too close to each other, because this would create undesirable complexities in interpreting the experiment's results.

Calculating the Price Elasticity From a Sales Experiment

If it is well-designed, a controlled pricing experiment will provide an indication of the change in product sales that will result from the price difference that is being tested. To make the results of the experiment more generally useful, these results can be used to calculate a price elasticity for the product in the experiment. This can be done by first calculating the price change and the sales change that resulted from the price change. Then, convert both this price change and sales change into percents, and divide the two percents. Note that when converting the price change and resulting sales change into percents, the price and sales levels in the control group should be used as the base values.

For example, to calculate a price elasticity from the results of the experiment shown in Figure 9.3, we would first calculate the percent price change:

$$\% \text{ change in price } = \frac{\text{Test group price}_{\text{Time2}} - \text{Control group price}_{\text{Time2}}}{\text{Control group price}_{\text{Time2}}} \times 100$$

$$= \frac{4 - 5}{5} \times 100 = -20\%$$

Next, we would calculate the percent by which sales changed in response to the price change:

$$\% \text{ change in sales } = \frac{\text{Test group sales}_{\text{Time2}} - \text{Control group sales}_{\text{Time2}}}{\text{Control group sales}_{\text{Time2}}} \times 100$$

$$= \frac{130 - 100}{100} \times 100 = 30\%$$

Finally, we would divide the percent sales change by the percent price change to arrive at the price elasticity that would be indicated by this experiment:

$$E = \frac{30\%}{-20\%} = -1.5$$

This price elasticity would to some degree increase the generality of the experimental results. It would suggest, for example, that if the product's price were decreased by 8 percent, we might expect sales to increase by 12 percent; if the product's price were decreased by 30 percent, we might expect sales to increase by 45 percent. However, because the experimental price manipulation was a price decrease, one should hesitate in using its results to predict the market response to a price increase. If a price increase is being considered, then the experimental manipulation should be a price increase.

If the researcher desires results that can be applied to both price increases and decreases, then the experiment should be designed to include both a price-increase test group and a price-decrease test group. In such an experiment, there would then be *three levels* of the price variable: (1) the increased price, (2) the decreased price, and (3) the control group. For example, in a paper published in the *Journal of Marketing* by Stephen Hoch and others, the eighty-six stores of the Dominick's supermarket chain were divided into three groups. In the first group, prices of selected items were raised by 10 percent; in the second group, the prices were lowered by 10 percent; and in the third group (the control group), prices remained unchanged. The unit sales decreases in the first group (compared to the control group) were of comparable size to the unit sales increases in the second group. These sales changes indicated a price elasticity of around –0.40.[5]

Multiple Independent Variables in Sales Experiments

In addition to multiple levels of the price variable, a controlled sales experiment could be designed with multiple IVs. Just as price is manipulated in a controlled experiment, there can be experimental manipulation of factors such as presence of an in-store display, level of media advertising, or presence of labeling indicating that the product is made without hurting the environment.[6] An advantage of adding a second IV to price in a controlled sales experiment is that it becomes possible to determine if there are interactions between the two IVs. An interaction occurs when the size of one IV's effect on sales depends on the level of the other IV. A disadvantage of adding a second IV to an experiment is that it doubles the number of equivalent customer groups needed to carry out the experiment.

Examples of controlled sales experiments with multiple IVs can be found in a paper published in the *Journal of Marketing Research* by Gerald Eskin and Penny Baron.[7] One of their experiments looked at the effects of price and advertising on a new snack-food product sold in grocery stores. In each of two test-market cities, thirty grocery stores were randomly divided into three groups of ten stores. In one group, the product was priced at the "base price," the lowest level that the product's managers had seriously considered. In a second group of stores, the product was priced 20 percent above this base price. In the third group of stores, it was priced at 40 percent above the base price. By the use of a total of sixty stores, a test of the price variable was possible.

In these two test-market cities, the plan was to make only low expenditures on advertising. However, in this experiment, the product's managers were also interested in the effect of advertising on the product's sales. In particular, they were considering a high advertising plan that involved 70 percent greater advertising expenditures than the low advertising expenditure plan. To add this advertising variable to the experiment, two additional cities were selected, each one matched in population and other demographic characteristics to the first two cities. Again thirty grocery stores in each of these new cities were divided into the three price-level groups. In these new cities, the advertising expenditures were high, 70 percent greater than those in the low advertising cities. The adding of the advertising variable thus doubled the number of stores that were involved in the experiment, from 60 to 120.

The benefit of adding this second variable to the experiment can be seen from looking at the results, shown in Figure 9.4. There is a clear tendency for sales to decrease as price

Figure 9.4   Example of a Controlled Pricing Experiment With Two Independent Variables

Price level	Advertising Level	
	Low	High
Base price	1.000 (20)	1.525 (20)
20% higher	0.820 (20)	1.066 (20)
40% higher	0.708 (20)	0.710 (20)

Source: Eskin, Gerald J. and Penny H. Baron (1977), "Effects of Price and Advertising in Test-Market Experiments," *Journal of Marketing Research,* 14 (November), 499–508.

Note: The sales numbers in each cell are the units sold in that group divided by the units sold in the base-price/low-advertising group. The numbers in parentheses are the numbers of stores in each group.

increases and for sales to increase as advertising expenditures increase. However, it is also clear that there is an interaction between the price and advertising IVs. At the high level of advertising, there is much greater consumer responsiveness to price than at the low advertising level. Eskin and Baron reported that when the contribution margin of this product is considered, these results suggest to managers that the best strategic alternatives for this product would be the low price along with high levels of advertising or the highest price along with the low level of advertising.

Strengths and Weaknesses of Sales Experiments

Just as there are both strengths and weaknesses to the regression approach to predicting the market's price-change response, there are both strengths and weaknesses to the use of sales experiments. An important strength of controlled experiments in general is that they make it possible to determine the degree to which an IV actually causes a change in a DV. A sales experiment for predicting price-change response isolates the degree to which price actually causes a change in sales. Because price is manipulated in the experiment, it is clear that any differences in sales between the test and control groups must be due to price and not to displays, advertising, or some other variable that might be correlated with price in the marketplace.

A second strength of sales experiments is that they involve the observation of real-world customer purchases. In a well-designed sales experiment, customers will most likely have no awareness that they are part of a study. They will simply respond to marketplace stimuli as they normally do.

These two strengths—the ability to show the causal role of price and the ability to show its effect on naturally occurring purchases—are very important. They give the sales experiment method the potential to be the most accurate means available to obtain a prediction of the market's price-change response. However, that does not mean that sales experiments should always be used. The method has substantial weaknesses that must also be considered.

The first weakness of the sales experiment method is its high cost. There are monetary costs such as the cost of securing the cooperation of a large number of retail outlets, the cost of printing alternative versions of a catalog, the cost of monitoring sales, and the cost of the sales lost in the experimental groups that produce low customer response. There are also time costs. It is often necessary to allow several months for the effects of the price manipulation to become apparent. Although this time period could be longer or shorter depending on the purchase cycle of the product, it is generally the case that the design, execution, and completion of a sales experiment is not something that can be accomplished quickly.

A second weakness of the sales experiment method is that it may have negative effects on the company's existing customers. For example, if an experiment includes a group that is designed to test the market response to a very high price, customers may not only decline to purchase the product during the duration of the experiment but also may form a negative impression that would lead them to avoid any consideration of that product in the future. If there are many customers in that high-price group, such a long-term effect of the experiment could be a serious consequence.

Negative customer effects could also occur if consumers learn of the experiment's price disparities. As mentioned in Chapter 8, observing that other customers are paying lower prices leads to feelings of price unfairness. In the fall of 2000, Amazon.com ran a price test on DVDs. As a result of the A–B split Amazon used, some customers were charged $25.97 for the same movie that other customers could get from Amazon for $23.97.[8] When customers learned of this (and spread the information in online chat rooms), many were angry. The resulting negative publicity was damaging to Amazon. Amazon's CEO, Jeff Bezos, was obliged to appear on national news broadcasts and explain to skeptical reporters than this was only a price test. To minimize future occurrence of such problems, Amazon adopted the policy of refunding the price difference to buyers in the high-price groups of pricing tests.[9]

A third weakness of the sales experiment method is the possibility that changes in the marketing environment could lead current customer behavior to differ from the customer behavior shown during the experiment. Although this weakness is less serious for a sales experiment than for a regression study relying entirely on historical data, it is an issue to consider when a sales experiment runs for months or more. There is also the possibility that a company's competitors will learn of the company's pricing experiment and will run coupons, discounts, or other promotions in an attempt to impair the experiment by reducing the applicability of its results.

Possible Surrogates of Naturally Occurring Sales

Given the high costs and potential for negative customer effects of sales experiments, marketing researchers have developed ways of carrying out controlled experiments without measuring actual sales levels. Instead of naturally occurring sales being the DV in the experiment, a surrogate—some other measure of consumer response—is used instead. Experimental methods using sales surrogates, which are termed sales-surrogate experiments, fall into two categories.

The first category is the artificial-sales experiment. In this type of experiment, a simulated purchase environment is created, and customers make purchases in this artificial setting. For example, an artificial-sales experiment for testing price-change response for a brand of salad dressing might involve setting up a research room in a shopping mall. The room might have a row of supermarket shelves that are stocked with the common salad dressing brands. Consumers would be recruited in the shopping mall, brought to the room, and given an amount of money that is more than would be required to buy a bottle of salad dressing. They would be instructed to consider the salad dressing brands on the room's shelves and then buy one and keep the change. The price of the salad dressing brand of interest could be changed between consumers so as to create two or more equivalent groups that differ on price alone.

The second category of sales-surrogate experiment is the questionnaire experiment. This type of experiment is less elaborate than the artificial-sales experiment. Customers do not make any purchases; they just indicate on a questionnaire their product choice or preference. The key to designing an effective sales experiment is to present different prices to different customers. Thus, the questionnaire for the control group of customers might ask, "How likely would you be to buy this product at $20?" If the price change that is being considered is an increase, the questionnaire for a test group of customers might ask, "How likely would you be to buy this product at $25?"

It is important to avoid questionnaires that ask customers questions like, "How much would you be willing to pay?" or "Which of the following prices would you prefer?" Although some customers would try to answer sincerely, this type of question suggests to the customer that the company is considering a low price and tempts the customer to indicate interest in only this low price. This type of question tends to elicit negotiating or other game-playing behaviors in a customer and is thus unlikely to provide useful information on the customer's likely price-change response.

Managing the Weaknesses of Using Sales Surrogates

Clearly, using a sales surrogate rather than naturally occurring sales as the DV in a pricing experiment involves making a trade-off. On one hand, a sales-surrogate experiment involves lower costs than a sales experiment and is much less likely to cause any negative effects on existing customers. On the other hand, the customer response being measured is an artificial one, which leads to a greater chance that the results of the experiment will be inaccurate.

An approach to dealing with this problem of accuracy is to consider how the artificial aspects of the sales-surrogate experiment are likely to affect the responses of the customers who are participating in the study and then adjusting the experiment's results to account for these effects. One possibility is that the awareness that they are not making real purchases with their own money might lead the customers to show *less* price sensitivity than they would in a natural purchase situation. After all, they have less at stake. However, a second possibility is that the customers take seriously their agreement to participate in the study and therefore give the prices presented in the study more attention than they would have given otherwise. This might lead the customers to show *more* price sensitivity than they would in a naturally occurring purchase of the product in question.

A third possibility is mere knowledge that their behavior is being watched by researchers might affect the customers' responses. They may try to guess what the experiment is designed to find out and then try to "help out" the researchers by making that effect happen. Knowledge that they are being watched may lead customers to become self-conscious and then act according to how they want to be seen. Some would want to be seen as being above caring about price, while others would want to be seen as savvy shoppers who know how to get a good price. Thus, the mere knowledge of being watched could lead customers to show either more or less price sensitivity than they would show in a naturally occurring purchase.

A fourth possibility is that people who agree to participate in a sales-surrogate experiment differ in important ways from most of the product's buyers. Depending on what these differences happen to be, they could make the sales-surrogate experiment show either more or less price sensitivity than actually exists in the marketplace.

Clearly, sorting out and adjusting for factors such as these is difficult, and research studies using sales surrogates have had some highly-publicized failures.[10] Because of this, their role in predicting the market's price-change response is limited. Perhaps sales-surrogate experiments might be most appropriate for comparing the price response between products rather than making absolute price-response predictions. In other words, they might be fairly accurate in determining whether there would be more market response to a 10 percent price cut in one product rather than in another, but of questionable accuracy in determining just how large that market response will be.

CHOOSING A RESEARCH APPROACH FOR PREDICTING PRICE-CHANGE RESPONSE

Given the number of market research methods available for predicting a market's response to a price change, a series of questions to guide the researcher's choice might be helpful. Such a series of questions is presented in Figure 9.5.

Figure 9.5   Questions for Choosing a Research Approach for Predicting Price-Change Response

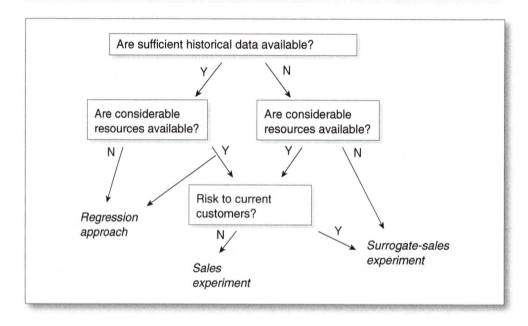

The first question would be whether or not there is available sufficient historical data for a regression analysis of price-change response. If sufficient historical data are available, the next question is whether or not there are sufficient resources of money and time available to conduct a controlled experiment. If such resources are not available, then the research would be limited to a regression analysis of the historical data. If such resources are available, then the researcher could do both a regression analysis and a controlled experiment. The type of controlled experiment to be done would depend on whether a sales experiment is likely to pose a risk to current customers. If a sales experiment is unlikely to pose such a risk, then a sales experiment should be carried out. If a sales experiment is likely to pose a risk to current customers, then the controlled experiment should use a sales surrogate as the DV.

If the answer to the first question is that sufficient historical data is not available, the next question is whether or not there are considerable resources available. If there are, then a sales experiment becomes a possibility. If there is not likely to be a risk to current customers, then a sales experiment should be done; otherwise, a sales-surrogate experiment should be used. If considerable resources are not available, then the only option would be some low-cost form of surrogate-sales experiment, such as a questionnaire experiment.

If the price change being considered is likely to have important consequences, then it is wise to supplement analyses of economic, competitive, cognitive, and emotional factors with some systematic empirical measurement of the likely market response. The review of market research methods presented in this chapter shows that there are many possible ways that this empirical measurement can be done, and not all of them require large amounts of time or large expenditures of money.

SUMMARY

When the stakes of a price-change decision are high, the estimation of the market's price-change response should include systematic market research. Two important market research approaches are the analysis of historical sales data (the regression approach) and carrying out a controlled experiment (the experimentation approach).

The regression approach requires a data matrix where each row consists of a period of time and each column consists of the values of a DV or IV. The key result is the regression coefficient of the price variable, which typically indicates the change in unit sales for each $1 change in price. This coefficient can be converted into a price elasticity. The strengths of the regression approach are that it is easy to carry out and that it does not involve interacting with existing customers. Its weaknesses are that required information might be difficult to obtain and that its predictions are based on past price–sales relationships that may no longer apply.

The experimentation approach typically requires two equivalent customer groups: (1) a test group and (2) a control group. Price is changed in only one group (the test group), and then the level of sales in the test and control groups are compared. A price elasticity can be calculated from these results. Strengths of sales experiments are their ability to show the degree to which price is a causal factor and their use of real-world customer data. Their weaknesses include high costs and possible negative effects on existing customers. The use of experiments on surrogates of naturally occurring sales are attempts to avoid these weaknesses. However, the artificiality of sales-surrogate experiments may cause their results to be inaccurate.

The availability of sufficient historical data, sufficient time and money resources, and the likelihood of negative customer effects determine the type of market research approach that should be used.

KEY TERMS

regression approach	test group	interactions
controlled experiment	control group	sales-surrogate experiments
experimentation approach	sales experiment	artificial-sales experiment
regression coefficients	A–B split	questionnaire experiment

REVIEW AND DISCUSSION QUESTIONS

1. Describe the role of systematic marketing research in predicting the market's price-change response.

2. Distinguish between a DV and an IV in a regression analysis. In the regression approach to predicting price-change response, why is it usually best to have multiple IVs?

3. Describe the data matrix for the regression approach by indicating what is represented in each of the matrix's rows and columns.

4. Discuss the three ways in which the information in the data matrix must be sufficient in order to provide a reasonable estimate of the market's price-change response.

5. What are the most common sources of data for the regression approach?

6. What is a regression coefficient? Describe the meaning of the regression coefficient of a price variable. How would you interpret the sign of a price coefficient?

7. Give and explain the formula for calculating a brand price elasticity from the regression coefficient of a price variable.

8. What are the key strengths and weaknesses of the regression approach?

9. Describe the essential elements in the design of a two-group controlled experiment.

10. In a sales experiment to estimate price sensitivity, what would be the DV? How might a company come up with the equivalent groups necessary to carry out such a sales experiment?

11. Describe how a brand price elasticity can be calculated from the results of a sales experiment.

12. What is a key benefit of having multiple IVs in a sales experiment? What is the main drawback of this?

13. What are some important strengths and weaknesses of a sales experiment?

14. What is a sales-surrogate experiment? What are some commonly used surrogates of naturally occurring sales?

15. Why is a question to consumers such as "How much would you be willing to pay for this product?" inappropriate for a questionnaire experiment?

16. Describe some factors that might lead a sales-surrogate experiment to indicate more price sensitivity than actually exists? What are some factors that might lead it to indicate less price sensitivity than actually exists? How might understanding these factors be helpful to the use of sales-surrogate experiments?

17. For predicting the market's price-change response, what are the key factors determining which market research approach should be used?

EXERCISES

1. The managers of a company that leases trucks to shipping companies and other business customers are considering increasing their leasing fees. In order to evaluate this increase, they have asked you to estimate the price elasticity of their product based on historical data.

(a) By labeling rows and columns, describe the data matrix that would be likely to be sufficient for calculating this estimate.

(b) What would you ask the company's managers regarding past price variation?

(c) Describe how you would go about obtaining the data specified in your data matrix.

2. A manufacturer of fancy scented bar soaps is interested in the price elasticity shown by her popular lilac variety. She assembled data for each of the past twenty months concerning the number of bars sold, the price, and the number of retail outlets that put the lilac soap on display and then carried out a regression analysis on this data. Here are the resulting means for each variable and the Excel output for the regression analysis:

Variable	Mean
Bars of lilac soap sold	2506
Price	1.59
Number of displays	167.9

SUMMARY OUTPUT

Regression Statistics	
Multiple R	0.855
R Square	0.731
Adjusted R Square	0.699
Standard Error	291.738
Observations	20.000

ANOVA

	df	SS	MS	F	Significance F
Regression	2.000	3931151.150	1965575.575	23.094	0.000
Residual	17.000	1446883.800	85110.812		
Total	19.000	5378034.950			

	Coefficients	Standard Error	t Stat	P-value
Intercept	7376.431	1348.809	5.469	0.000
Price	−1261.207	186.770	−6.753	0.000
Displays	−6.361	7.815	−0.814	0.427

(a) Find the coefficient of the price variable in the Excel output. Describe how you would explain the interpretation of this price coefficient to someone who is not familiar with multiple regression.

(b) Calculate the price elasticity implied by these results. Show your work.

3. A manufacturer of beach umbrellas is now considering changing his product's price for this summer's selling season. He would like to use an historical analysis of sales data to estimate the product's price elasticity. Here are the data he has collected:

Year	Sales	Price	Average Advertising Expenditure
2008	42,304	34.99	15,400
2009	54,230	34.99	22,550
2010	65,020	34.99	24,750

(a) Explain to the manager the reasons that the data he has collected are inadequate for determining his product's price elasticity.

(b) If the manufacturer cannot obtain any further historical data, suggest a research approach that would be practical for him to use to help predict the market response to his prospective price change.

4. A manager of a large chain of appliance stores is planning to conduct a pricing experiment to determine the price elasticity of the chain's line of microwave ovens. He plans to measure sales for the month of February, raise prices by 12 percent on March 15, and then measure sales for the month of April. Each sales measurement would take into account the total monthly microwave oven sales for all of the stores in his chain.

He has asked you to evaluate his research procedure and suggest any improvements. What would you suggest?

5. The catalog operation of a large clothing company sends out four regular catalogs per year and one summer sale catalog. Management has recently conducted a pricing test on their line of children's T-shirts. The test was carried out with their annual summer sale catalog. The T-shirts are usually discounted to $12.99 in this catalog. For this test, the first customer on the mailing list received a catalog with the T-shirts priced at $12.99, the second customer on the mailing list received a catalog with the T-shirts priced at $10.99. The third customer received the $12.99 catalog, the fourth received the $10.99 catalog, and so on throughout the entire 500,000 customer mailing list. The sales results of this test are as follows:

Catalog Price	Number of T-Shirts Sold
$12.99	6,743
$10.99	10,757

(a) Based on this price test, calculate the price elasticity for these T-shirts. Show your work.

(b) The price of these T-shirts in the regular catalog has been $16, and the marketing manager is considering raising it to $18. She is planning to use the price elasticity calculated in Part (a) to help her make this decision, and she has asked for your advice con.cerning this plan. How would you respond?

6. The marketing manager of a well-known automobile engine additive suspects that the use of an in-store display affects the price elasticity of his product. Specifically, he suspects that the presence of an in-store display increases the product's price elasticity relative to no in-store display. To test this hunch, he would like to do a sales experiment with the 654 retail stores that carry this product. Currently the additive is being sold for $7.99 a bottle.

Specify the variables and groups that would describe the experiment that this manager could use to test this hunch. Explain your choices.

7. The management of Delicare, a laundry detergent designed specifically for delicate fabrics, decided to test the market's responsiveness to price changes by hiring a market research firm to carry out an artificial-sales experiment. The market research firm intercepted 650 women in shopping malls and brought them to a nearby test room. In the room, they constructed a store shelf with Delicare and a variety of other laundry products on it and gave each woman $10 to buy one of these products. She was allowed to keep the change. For one-third of the women, the Delicare was priced at $3.79 per bottle, which is a typical actual retail price for this item. For another third of the women, the Delicare was priced at $3.29 per bottle. For the final third of the women, the Delicare was priced at $4.29 per bottle.

Describe two factors that would be likely to cause the price responsiveness observed in this experiment to differ from that which would be observed in the market. For each factor, give and justify your view as to whether it would make the price responsiveness appear greater than or less than that which would actually occur in the market.

NOTES

1. Jack Honomichl, "Honomichl Top 50: 2004 Business Report on the Marketing Research Industry," *Marketing News,* June 15, 2004, H1–H15.
2. V. Kumar, David A. Aaker, and George S. Day, *Essentials of Marketing Research* (New York: Wiley, 1999), 120.
3. When a price elasticity is calculated from mean sales and price levels, it represents the elasticity over a segment, or arc, of the demand curve, and thus is known as an "arc elasticity."
4. Eric T. Anderson and Ducan I. Semester, "Effects of $9 Price Endings on Retail Sales: Evidence from Field Experiments," *Quantitative Marketing and Economics* 1 (2003): 93–100. They report that in 1999 over 31 % of catalog retailers used split-sample experiments for pricing research.
5. Stephen J. Hoch, Xavier Dreze, and Mary E. Purk, "EDLP, Hi-Lo, and Margin Arithmetic," *Journal of Marketing* 58 (October 1994): 16–27.
6. See, for example, R.C. Anderson and E.N. Hansen, "Determining Consumer Preferences for Ecolabeled Forest Products: An Experimental Approach," *Journal of Forestry* 102 (June 2004): 28–32.

7. Gerald J. Eskin and Penny H. Baron, "Effects of Price and Advertising in Test-Market Experiments," *Journal of Marketing Research* 14 (November 1977): 499–508. Gerald Eskin went on to become of the founders of IRI, mentioned earlier, a major market research company.

8. "Amazon.com Varies Prices of Identical Items for Test," *Wall Street Journal,* September 7, 2000, B19.

9. Linda Rosencrance, "Outrage Prompts Amazon to Change Price-Testing Policy," *Computerworld* 34 (September 18, 2000): 14.

10. Ted Knutson, "'Marketing Malpractice' Causes Concern," *Marketing News,* October 10, 1988, 1, 7.

PART III

Developing a Price Structure

The Logic of Price Segmentation

$\mathbf{U}$p to this point in the book we have focused on price setting—the seller's decisions about individual prices. We have divided price-setting decisions into two basic pricing tasks: (1) the setting of an initial price for a product and (2) the modification of a product's price. From here on, we will step back and discuss a number of more general pricing issues, which often involve pricing-policy decisions.

In this section of the book, we discuss issues having to do with price structure. As was mentioned in Chapter 1, a company's price structure consists of the pattern of the prices it charges its customers. One aspect of price structure concerns the different prices that a company may charge for the same product. For example, a company may charge customers a lower than usual price for a product when the customers are buying a large number of products or it may charge less than usual for a product if it is purchased during certain times. An important factor behind these differing prices is the presence of differing segments in a market. Pricing practices that enable a company to adapt to market segment differences will be covered in the first three chapters in this section.

A second aspect of a company's price structure concerns the array of prices charged for the different products sold by the company. Because there are often interrelationships between a seller's various products, the pricing of these products should take such relationships into account. An examination of some important types of product interrelations and their pricing implications will be covered in the fourth chapter in this section.

MARKET SEGMENTS AND PRICING

Formally, a market is defined as all customers and potential customers for a product. Potential customers would be those who have needs or desires for a product and have the ability to purchase the product if they so choose.

Most markets are not homogeneous—in other words, they are not made up of customers who are all similar. Rather, most markets consist of individuals or organizations who have widely varying characteristics. Of course, some of these diverse individuals and organizations are going to be similar to each other. These are known as market segments—groups of buyers and potential buyers within a market who have similar characteristics.

It is important for our subsequent discussion to note that dividing a market into segments does not necessarily involve placing an individual or organization into only a single category. A particular individual or organization may be in one market segment when in one purchase situation and in another market segment when in a different purchase situation.[1] For example, suppose the consumer soft drink market is divided into a segment that cares most about the soft drink's taste and another segment that cares most about its thirst-quenching ability. A person could be in the taste segment of this market, say, when consuming a soft drink during a meal and be in the thirst-quenching segment, say, when consuming a soft drink after working out at the gym.

Factors Causing Pricing Differences Between Market Segments

The best price for a product often differs between market segments. As you may recall from Chapter 5, a product's best price is a profitable price that an increase or decrease will not make more profitable. A product's best price is likely to differ between market segments because three factors that determine the best price often differ between market segments. As we have seen in our discussion of price setting, a product's best price is determined by (1) the product's value to the customer (VTC), (2) the costs to the seller of providing the product, and (3) the customers' price sensitivity or responsiveness to price changes. Any or all of these three factors may differ between market segments.

A product may have a higher VTC for customers in one market segment than for those in another. For example, the Sealed Air Corporation sells more durable air-bubble packaging to protect products that are being shipped. For those customers who need to package very large items for long periods, there are few adequate cushioning alternatives. These customers particularly value the differentiating factor of the stronger air bubbles in Sealed Air's protective packaging.

Serving one market segment may involve greater costs than serving another. For example, purchasers of a software product who have never owned an earlier version of the product will tend to require higher levels of costly technical support services than those customers who have owned earlier versions of the software product.

One market segment may be more price-sensitive than another. For example, affluent travelers may consider the price of airline transportation small relative to their income and thus be relatively unconcerned with a $100 difference in round-trip airfare. Some customers may show more price sensitivity for products because they are particularly well-served by sellers who compete on price. For example, a chain of retail stores selling household items may have some stores that are close to a Walmart, Target, or The Home Depot. These stores in the chain would have customers who tend to be more price-sensitive than the customers of those stores in the chain that are not served by such potentially low-priced competition.

Price Segmentation

When one or more of these three pricing factors differs between the segments of a market, this question arises: Which set of factors should determine the price? The bar graphs in Figure 10.1 illustrate the issue. In these graphs, the best product price for a market segment

Figure 10.1   The Problem of Three Market Segments With Different Best Prices

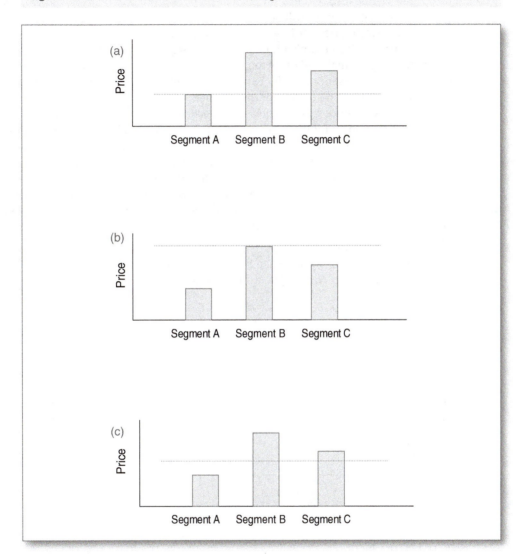

is indicated by the height of the bar for that segment. For the product in question, the best price differs among Segments A, B, and C.

Let's consider the pricing alternatives for this product. If the product's price is set low, say at the best price for Segment A (see Figure 10.1, Part [a]), then the price will be too low for Segments B and C. When a price is too low, potential profits will be lost. If the product's price is set high, say at the best price for Segment B (see Figure 10.1, Part [b]), then the price will be too high for Segments A and C. When a price is too high, sales will suffer and profits will also be lost. If the product's price is set in the middle, say at the average of the three segments' best prices (see Figure 10.1, Part [c]), then the price will be too high for Segment A (and profit will be lost), too low for Segment B (and profit will be lost), and too low for Segment C (and, again, profit will be lost).

Clearly, any single price set in a market such as that illustrated in Figure 10.1 will be flawed. The price will be too high for some market segments and too low for others. Note that a price being too high and being too low *both* cost the seller profits. For this reason, in a market where the best prices differ between segments, it is important to find an alternative to charging only a single price for the product.

This alternative is *price segmentation*—the practice of a seller charging different market segments different prices for the same product. The bar graph in Figure 10.2 illustrates how this would work. A company sells the product to the customers in Segment A for the low price that is best for those customers. It sells the product to the customers in Segment C for a higher price and sells the product to the customers in Segment B for a still higher price. If price segmentation can be accomplished, it relieves the need for a seller to charge a single price in the market and creates the opportunity to gain increased profits from most market segments. The importance of price segmentation for profitable pricing cannot be overemphasized.

Figure 10.2   The Price-Segmentation Solution to the Problem of Three Market Segments With Different Best Prices

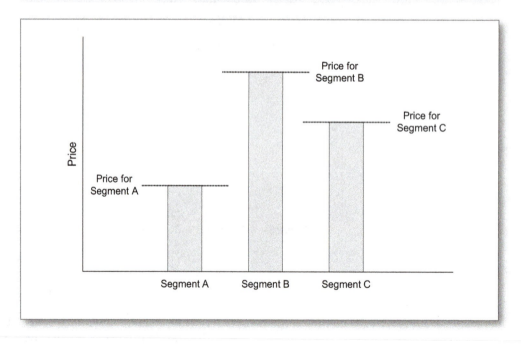

ACCOMPLISHING PRICE SEGMENTATION

There are at least two difficulties in accomplishing price segmentation. The first difficulty is that one cannot expect customers to voluntarily identify themselves as willing pay prices that are higher than those paid by other customers. Imagine, for example, that you were in line for cones at an ice cream stand, and the owner announced that the people who are less price-sensitive should pay $1 more than the others, so he could maximize profits. Clearly, there would be few volunteers.

The second difficulty in accomplishing price segmentation is the possibility of arbitrage. This is the practice of buying a product at a low price in order to sell it to others at a higher price. Those in the segments receiving a low price could make money by reselling the product to those in the segments being charged the higher price. In fact, in some markets, customers would buy products for other customers just as a favor. For example, even if the owner of the ice cream stand had a means of identifying the less price-sensitive customers, these less price-sensitive people would probably be able to find a more price-sensitive fellow consumer to do the buying for them.

To deal with these difficulties in accomplishing price segmentation, it is necessary to establish "fences" to keep the customers in a market segment that pays a higher price separate from those in a market segment that pays a lower price. A price-segmentation fence is a criterion that customers must meet to qualify for a lower price. This criterion could be a characteristic of the customer, such as the customer's age. For example, when a parking garage gives a 10 percent discount to senior citizens, it is using age as a price-segmentation fence. The criterion could also be a characteristic of the purchase situation, such as the quantity of items purchased. For example, when a pizza shop that charges $9.00 for a large pizza also sells two for $15.00 ($7.50 per pizza), it is using purchase quantity as a price-segmentation fence.

A seller who wants to maximize the benefits of price segmentation should be careful— and creative—in establishing price-segmentation fences. It is important to keep in mind the two goals of a price-segmentation fence. The first is that the fence divides the market so that those customers for whom a high price is appropriate are on one side of the fence and those customers for whom a low price is appropriate are on the other. The second goal is to minimize the degree to which the fence can be crossed, say by customers who belong on the high-price side of the fence or by arbitragers who attempt to defeat the fence by buying an item on the low-price side of the fence and reselling it on the high-price side.

Effective management of price segmentation requires a familiarity with the diversity of methods available to accomplish it.[2] We discuss the following six major types of price-segmentation fences:

1. Customer characteristics
2. Purchase quantity
3. Product features
4. Design of product bundles
5. Time of purchase or use
6. Place of purchase or use

Note that only the first of these six types of price-segmentation fences involves characteristics of customers. The other five types involve characteristics of purchase situations. As we will see, this distinction is important for the effectiveness of a price-segmentation fence as a practical means of making price segmentation possible.

We discuss the first four of these six types of price-segmentation fences in this chapter. The remaining two, time of purchase or use and place of purchase or use, are discussed in detail in Chapters 11 and 12.

PRICE SEGMENTATION BY CUSTOMER CHARACTERISTICS

When a product's price differs depending on an observable characteristic of a customer, then this characteristic is being used as a price-segmentation fence. Age is probably the customer characteristic most commonly used for price segmentation. Whether or not a customer is a child is easily observable, and many businesses offer lower prices to children. Seniors also often receive discounts. If their age is not readily apparent, they can document it by showing a driver's license or the membership card for a senior citizen's organization such as AARP.

Examining some examples of the use of age as a price-segmentation fence helps us appreciate the logic of price segmentation. Most AMC movie theaters give ticket discounts of $1 or $2 to children under twelve. A lower price for the under-twelve segment makes sense because they are likely to be more price-sensitive. They tend to have considerably less spending money than teens or adults. Also, children under twelve may assign a lower value to going to the movies. They may not strongly value the getting-out-of-the-house aspect of seeing a movie in a theater, and they may encounter some difficulties in getting transportation to the movie theater.

Modell's Sporting Goods gives senior citizens a 10 percent discount on all merchandise, subject to their showing proof that they are over age sixty-five. Many seniors are more price-sensitive than the average consumer because the often fixed nature of retirement incomes limits their available resources. Also, because people tend to become less active as they age, seniors may have lower valuations of the athletic apparel and equipment sold by this retailer.

The status of being a student is another customer characteristic often used for price segmentation. Upon showing their school ID card, students are able to get discounts for numerous entertainment, travel, and merchandise products. It makes sense for businesses to use student status rather than age as a price-segmentation fence because it is only the young adults who are in school that are likely to have the higher price sensitivity coming from having limited spending money. Customers who are of college age but who are working full-time are likely to have considerably more discretionary income than students and therefore not be especially price-sensitive.

Sellers will sometimes price a product higher when selling to a business or other large organization than when selling to an individual consumer. For example, for many years publishers of academic journals charged university libraries a higher price for a subscription than they charged individual professors for the same subscription. This made sense because professors, the consumers of this product, had a relatively low valuation of a personal subscription. Its benefit was only saving the inconvenience of using the library's copy of the journal. The customer characteristic used for a price-segmentation fence here could be referred to as the customer's commercial status.

Constraints on the Use of Customer Characteristics

If price-segmentation fences could consist solely of customer characteristics, then there would be only limited opportunities to practice price segmentation. The reason for this is that the use of customer characteristics to determine who can pay lower prices is likely to create questions of price fairness. As was mentioned in Chapter 8, customers often perceive a price to be unfair if they observe that other customers are paying a lower price for the same item.

A perception of unfairness is particularly likely when it is perceived that other customers are paying a lower price not because of something these customers choose to do but simply because of who they are. Economists have traditionally referred to price segmentation as "price discrimination." It is indeed discrimination in the sense that sellers make distinctions between customers in setting prices. But when the fence, or criterion that determines who pays what, is an immutable customer characteristic, then price segmentation can also feel like discrimination in the sense of being "discriminated against" or being slighted in favor of other people.

Some legal cases illustrate how strong such feelings can be. In 1996, a woman sued Victoria's Secret for gender discrimination after receiving a catalog offering $10 off a purchase of $75 or more while a man she knew received the same catalog offering $25 off.[3] In California, consumer complaints about women being charged more than men for similar services by dry cleaners and hair salons led the state legislature to pass a law specifically prohibiting gender discrimination in retail pricing.[4] Recently, legal challenges have been raised against bars and clubs having "ladies' nights," where women but not men get free or discounted drinks. For example, a male patron of a popular New Jersey dating bar filed a complaint against its ladies' night with the state's Division of Civil Rights. Although the agency's director ruled that the promotional value of the practice does not override the "important social policy objective of eradicating discrimination," a state legislator quickly introduced a bill to make ladies' nights legal in New Jersey. One columnist suggested that the controversy could be resolved by having "skirt nights," where the discount would be offered to anyone wearing a skirt.[5]

Clearly, the use of a customer characteristic as a price-segmentation fence must be done with care. Use of a characteristic such as gender, race, religion, or ethnic group is very likely to violate customer sensitivities and should generally be avoided. On the other hand, customer characteristics such as age, student status, and commercial status seem to be considered generally acceptable. For other possible customer characteristic fences, it may depend on the specifics of the situation. For example, colleges and universities routinely consider the income of a student's family when setting the price of that student's education. This is done by offering scholarships to accepted students who provide information that they are of limited financial means. This may be considered acceptable because of the recognition of the mission of colleges and universities—that it is beneficial to society for higher education to be widely accessible. One can wonder if the use of the customer's income level to set prices would be as acceptable if practiced by, say, a consumer electronics retailer or a dinner restaurant.

Price Segmentation in Negotiation

As was discussed in Chapter 1, there are many occasions when prices are not fixed but rather are negotiated through a direct interaction between the seller and the customer.

When prices are set through negotiation, the seller has a greater ability to use customer characteristics as price-segmentation fences because it is difficult for customers to recognize that this is being done. For example, a salesperson in business selling may quietly allow some price concessions only to businesses whose public financial data indicate that they are less prosperous than others.

When consumer prices are determined through negotiation, it is often part of a salesperson's job to determine customer characteristics that may be relevant to price segmentation. For example, the salesperson at a car dealership might make some very deliberate small talk to prospective customers interested in going on a test drive. "What type of work do you do?" "Where do you live?" Questions like these can help the salesperson estimate the prospective customer's income, which could help the salesperson decide how firmly to stick to a particular asking price. "What kind of car do you drive now?" "How long have you had it?" Questions like these can provide hints of the customer's brand preference and loyalty, customer characteristics that can also be used for price segmentation.

PRICE SEGMENTATION BY PURCHASE QUANTITY

Because of the fairness issues involved in using observable customer characteristics as price-segmentation fences, it is important to be familiar with an alternative approach to accomplishing price segmentation. This alternative approach involves using a characteristic of the purchase situation rather than a characteristic of the customer as the price-segmentation fence. Having the criterion for a low price involving a purchase-situation characteristic gives customers at least some degree of choice concerning whether or not they obtain the low price. Because of people's greater control over what they choose to *do* than over what they *are*, purchase-situation characteristics tend to be more emotionally acceptable than customer characteristics as price-segmentation fences.

One purchase-situation characteristic that is widely used as a price-segmentation fence is the quantity that the customer purchases. The best price for those customers who buy larger quantities of a product is often lower than that for those customers who buy smaller quantities of the product. When this is so, it makes sense for the seller to offer a lower per-unit price to the customers who buy larger quantities. This lower per-unit price is often termed a quantity discount. When quantity discounts are used for price segmentation, it is the quantity of the product purchased that becomes the fence that enables charging different customers different prices for the same product.

There are a number of ways to offer lower prices to those customers who buy larger quantities of a product. These are among those most commonly used:

- An order-size discount gives customers who purchase larger amounts at one time a lower per-unit price than those making smaller orders.

- A cumulative-purchase discount gives customers who have made many purchases from the seller a lower price for new purchases than customers who have done less business with that seller. Cumulative-purchase discounts often take the form a frequent-user program, such as when collecting enough frequent-flyer miles from traveling on a particular airline entitles the customer to a free trip on that airline.

- Fixed-charge pricing gives open access to a product to customers who pay a single price, such as paying one price for a meal in a buffet restaurant or an annual fee to belong to a health club. The effect of this is that customers who make more use of the product pay a lower per-portion or per-use price than those who make less use of the product.

- Two-part pricing involves both a fixed charge and a per-unit charge, such as paying a fixed amount to rent a car plus an additional amount for each mile driven. These two charges are often set so that customers who buy more units of a product pay less per unit than those who buy fewer units. Two-part pricing is used by retailers such as Costco and BJ's Wholesale Club, who require customers to pay a fixed member fee; the more items a customer purchases, the lower the per-item amount of the member fee.

Why Purchasers of Larger Quantities Might Warrant Lower Per-Unit Prices

Each of the three factors that determine the best price for a market segment—the product's VTC, its costs, and the customer price sensitivity—could all contribute to the profitability of giving lower per-unit prices to those customers who purchase larger product quantities.

The VTC of a product is often governed by what economists refer to as "the law of diminishing marginal utility." For example, at a local Dunkin' Donuts outlet, the posted price for a donut might be $0.79. However, you can also buy six donuts for $3.99 (approximately $0.66 per donut) and a dozen donuts for $5.99 (approximately $0.50 per donut). This has to do with the fact that donuts tend to be rich and filling and don't store well. For the typical donut consumer, the VTC of the sixth, seventh, or eighth donut is likely to be much lower than that of the first, second, and third. The lower per-donut price for those who buy many donuts is thus warranted by the lower average VTC per donut for those customers.

Similarly, the fifth or sixth necktie picked out during a visit to a clothing store is likely to have lower VTC than the first or second. The fourth or fifth running of an ad by a newspaper or television station is likely to have a smaller incremental benefit to the firm being advertised and thus a lower VTC than the first or second appearance of the ad. To a software customer, the upgrade version of a program is likely to have less of an incremental benefit than the original program and thus have a lower VTC. In all these situations, the lower VTC of the last few items in an order creates the need for a lower price for those items.

Cost differences may also play a role in making a quantity discount appropriate. Large orders often involve lower per-unit costs for assembling and shipping the product. This is one reason why order-size discounts are particularly common in the selling of products whose transportation costs are substantial, such as industrial chemicals and machinery.[6] Many magazine publishers offer a lower per-issue price for a two-year subscription than for a one-year subscription. The savings in the costs of renewal appeals is at least part of the justification for this quantity discount.

It is important to keep in mind that lower costs do not by themselves mean that prices should be dropped accordingly. Rather, lower costs are associated with lower prices because they increase the likelihood that a price decrease will be profitable. Recall from Chapter 5 that when variable costs are low and contribution margins are high, the break-even sales increase for a possible price decrease will be small and relatively easy to achieve.

Thus, when costs are low, it is often easier to make more profit by lowering prices than it is when costs are high.

Customer price sensitivity contributes to the profitability of quantity discounts because buyers who purchase larger quantities are likely to be more price-sensitive. One reason for this is that, with larger purchases, more money is involved. This gives the buyer more incentive to switch from a higher-priced seller to a lower-priced one. For example, a business organization with many users of accounting software would be more likely to find it practical to shop around for the best price than would an organization with few users. Thus, it makes sense that the per-user cost of a software site license would decrease as the number of users allowed in the license increases.

Another reason for greater price sensitivity among large-quantity buyers is that larger purchases often involve alternative opportunities that are less available or less practical to smaller-quantity purchasers. For example, Amtrak gives half-fare discounts to children who travel with their parents. This would make sense because when families travel together, alternatives to rail travel such as going by car become more practical options. Similarly, a firm's large customers are likely to be more attractive to competitors than the firm's small customers and are thus more likely to be presented with lower-price offers for their business. The presence of these lower-price offers to switch suppliers makes these customers more price-sensitive and thus more worthy of lower per-unit prices.

Constraints on Use of Price Segmentation by Purchase Quantity

For a quantity discount to be effective as a price-segmentation fence, it needs to be structured to prevent it from being defeated by arbitragers. Particularly if a product is easily stored and transported, it is necessary to keep quantity discounts modest enough so that it would not be profitable for an entrepreneur to buy large quantities of the product for the purpose of reselling the product to small-quantity buyers.

A quantity discount also needs to be structured to discourage purchasing alliances, or associations between groups of buyers of a product. For example, when sellers of heating oil in Europe began giving customers substantial quantity discounts, certain homeowners in a neighborhood would order a large amount of heating oil. When the truck came to deliver it, the homeowner would ask the driver to deliver parts of the shipment to a few of his neighbors. It quickly became necessary for the heating oil companies to establish and enforce rules that prevented the truck driver from doing this.[7] For a similar purpose, frequent-flyer miles and the other types of credits accrued in frequent-user programs have been made nontransferable. Only the person who has earned the credit from using the product is permitted to redeem the credit. The new rules for the delivery truck drivers or for the transferability of frequent-flier miles could be termed segmentation-fence patches that repair the "holes" in the fences that allow high-price segment customers to buy at low-price segment prices.

A different type of constraint on quantity discounts involves the issue of legality. In 1936, the U.S. Congress passed the Robinson–Patman Act, which made it illegal to "discriminate in price between different purchasers of commodities of like grade and quality. . . ." The law was designed to protect mom-and-pop stores from large retail chains, and it has most recently been used by small retailers to try to block the deep discounts manufacturers give to high-volume customers such as Walmart, Best Buy, or Barnes & Noble.[8]

Because the intent of the law is to support business competition, it applies only to differing prices given to business customers, not to consumers. It also applies only to the pricing of goods, not services. Further, there are two important exceptions to the Robinson–Patman Act's restrictions. Charging one business customer less than another for the same good is acceptable (1) if it reflects differences in the costs of serving the two customers or (2) if it is done in specifically order to meet the low price of a competitor. Clearly, the limited reach of this law enables most sellers to retain considerable freedom in using purchase quantity as a price-segmentation fence.

PRICE SEGMENTATION BY PRODUCT FEATURES

A second purchase-situation characteristic that can be used as a price-segmentation fence is the customer's choice regarding the product's features. For example, if customers who value a basic product more than others also tend to choose a certain luxury feature of that product, then it might make sense for the seller to charge a higher price for the basic product to customers who buy the luxury feature. In that case, the buyers of the luxury feature could be said to be paying a feature-dependent premium for the basic product, because the higher price they pay for the basic product is caused by their choice of the luxury feature. When product features are used for price segmentation, it is the choice of the feature that becomes the fence enabling the seller to charge different customers different prices for the same basic product.

The logic of this price-segmentation fence is illustrated in the table in Figure 10.3. The top part of the table indicates a situation where there is one undifferentiated market, and the customers in that market value the basic product at $10 and a particular optional feature at $2. Ignoring (for the sake of simplicity) the importance of setting prices under a product's VTC, the seller would then offer the basic product for $10 and the optional feature for $2.

Figure 10.3   Using a Product-Enhancing Feature for Price Segmentation

	VTC of Basic Product	VTC of Enhancing Feature		Price
No market segmentation	$10	$2	Basic product	$10
			Product with enhancing feature	$12
Segment 1	$10	$0	Basic product	$10
Segment 2	$12	$2	Product with enhancing feature	$14

Note: VTC = value to the customer.

The bottom part of the table indicates a situation where it is recognized that the market consists of two market segments. The customers in Segment 1 value the basic product at $10 and are not interested in the optional feature. The customers in Segment 2 value the optional feature at $2 but also attach a greater value to the basic product than do the customers in Segment 1 ($12 vs. $10). In such a situation, it would make sense to offer the basic product for $10 and the optional feature for $4. Charging $4 rather than $2 for the optional feature would not decrease the likelihood that the customers of Segment 2 purchase the product with the optional feature, because for them the total VTC of the product and the feature is $14. However, in paying this price, the customers in Segment 2 are paying $12 for the same basic product that customers in Segment 1 can purchase for $10—a $2 feature-dependent premium. In this way, the customer's choice of product feature could be used as an effective price-segmentation fence.

Note that we are not talking here about the seller who offers an array of product features that are priced appropriately with respect to their VTCs. For example, sellers will often have fancier versions of a product for more affluent customers. This practice is certainly an instance of market segmentation, but, strictly speaking, it is not price segmentation. Even though the target customer for a fancier version of a product may have a higher income than the target customer for the basic product, pricing the fancy features close to their value to these higher-income customers would mean that the basic product itself has only one price. When product features are used for price segmentation, the result is that different customers pay different prices for the basic product.

Product-Enhancing Features

When the price-segmentation goal is to charge a higher price for the basic product to a segment that has a higher valuation of that product, then it would be appropriate to consider using as a price-segmentation fence a feature that enhances the product.

For example, suppose that market research tells the manufacturer of a particular automobile model that sports-car enthusiasts value the model at $24,000, but that family-car buyers value it at only $20,000. Given the large size of the family-car segment of the market, the manufacturer cannot set the base price of the car above $20,000. However, suppose that the same market research (perhaps a conjoint analysis with the car model and various optional features as independent variables [IVs]) told the manufacturer that the sports car segment of the market would value an optional spoiler at $2,000. The manufacturer could price the spoiler at $6,000. Family-car buyers would not even consider such an expensive option, but the $26,000 total price would be worth it for the sports-car enthusiasts, because they value the car at $24,000 and the spoiler at $2,000. The effect of pricing this product-enhancing feature at $6,000 would be that the sports-car enthusiasts would be paying a $4,000 feature-dependent premium for a car.

A major cell phone service provider in Korea used a product-enhancing feature in a similar way. Although Korean buyers of basic cell phone service for personal use (mostly teenagers and other young people) were highly price-sensitive, buyers of basic cell phone service for business use were not at all price-sensitive. The service provider was able to accomplish price segmentation in this market by offering an optional data transmission line to cell phone users. By setting the price for the data line very high (far higher than costs and even more than business customers would pay for it over their VTC for basic service), the service provider was able to capture the business customer's higher VTC for the basic service without affecting sales to the personal-use segment of the market.

Product-Diminishing Features

When the price-segmentation goal is to charge a lower price for the basic product to a segment that has a lower valuation of that product, then it would be appropriate to consider using as a price-segmentation fence a feature that diminishes the product. In this case, the buyers of the product with the feature that diminishes it could be said to be receiving a feature-dependent discount.

To be effective in price segmentation, a product-diminishing feature should make the product less than fully acceptable to the customers in the market segment that pays the high price. An extreme example of this is in the alcohol market. The best prices for distilled alcohol used for drinking, such as gin and vodka, are generally very high. By contrast, the best prices for distilled alcohol used for medical applications, such as killing germs, are quite low. To make possible low alcohol prices to medical-use customers without concern that arbitragers would resell it to drinking-alcohol customers, products such as rubbing alcohol have an additive (i.e., a "denaturant") to make them so bitter as to be undrinkable. The customer's choice of alcohol that either does or does not include this product-diminishing feature serves as an effective fence to accomplish price segmentation.

In the air-travel market, the Saturday night stay-over has been very successfully used as a price-segmentation fence. Customers who travel by air for business tend to be far less price-sensitive than customers who travel by air for vacations or other personal reasons. To charge personal travelers an appropriate low price without destroying the lucrative business-travel market, the airlines came up with an effective product-diminishing feature. Those traveling for business usually want to be home over the weekend so that they can be with their families. By contrast, those traveling for personal reasons often prefer to be traveling over a weekend. By establishing the feature-dependent discount of a low airfare only for those travelers choosing the Saturday-night stay-over feature of the trip, it became possible to charge a much lower airfare to customers in the personal-travel segment than to those in the business segment.

Combining Price-Segmentation Features

In some situations, it may be appropriate to consider using both product-enhancing and product-diminishing features for price segmentation. For example, the Washington National Opera had been selling all of its seats at three price levels: (1) $47, (2) $63, and (3) $85. Faced with the need to increase revenue, its management looked into the possibility of price segmentation. They found that many operagoers were strong enthusiasts and would pay far more than $85 for a ticket. Once aware of that, it was easy to find product-enhancing features that would be of interest to these people, such as being in the center of the front rows rather than at their ends. The price of these center front-row seats was increased to $150, and they still sold briskly.

On the other hand, management found that there were many people such as students, homemakers, and seniors who would occasionally go to the opera if the price were low enough. These people were offered deep discounts dependent on product-diminishing features that made the seats unacceptable to opera enthusiasts, such as placement in corners or on the upper balconies. They lowered prices for these seats to $29 and brought many new people to the opera.

As a result of these efforts at price segmentation, the Washington National Opera was able to increase its revenue substantially without having to increase the prices for most of the tickets to its performances.

PRICE SEGMENTATION BY DESIGN OF PRODUCT BUNDLES

A third purchase-situation characteristic that can be used as a price-segmentation fence is how a seller's offerings are combined into product bundles. A bundle is any set of products that are offered together as a package. The careful design of product bundles can accomplish price segmentation in a way that is slightly different than that of the previous two types of price-segmentation fences. Quantity discounts (which are sometimes considered a type of product bundle) accomplish price segmentation because some customers choose to buy the higher quantities and others do not. Feature-dependent premiums and discounts accomplish price segmentation because some customers choose the product-enhancing or product-diminishing features and others do not. However, the design of bundles can accomplish price segmentation even if all customers choose to purchase the product bundle.

The key to designing a product bundle to accomplish price segmentation is to identify a set of products that show a VTC "crossover" between at least two important market segments. The logic of this is illustrated in the table in Figure 10.4. The top row of the table indicates that the customers in Segment 1 value Product A at $50 and value Product B at $130. The bottom row of the table indicates that the customers in Segment 2 value Product A at $75 but value Product B at only $100. Note the "crossover" in product valuation: Product A is valued more by customers in Segment 2 than those in Segment 1, and Product B is valued more by customers in Segment 1 than those in Segment 2.

If it is assumed that Segments 1 and 2 are each too important for the seller to ignore, then how should these items be priced? The problem with pricing Product A at $75 is that the customers in Segment 1 would not buy it. For Product A to appeal to both segments, it

Figure 10.4   Value-to-the-Customer Crossover Necessary for a Product Bundle to Accomplish Price Segmentation

	VTC of Product A	VTC of Product B
Segment 1	$50	$130
Segment 2	$75	$100

Note: VTC = value to the customer.

must be priced at $50. Similarly, the problem with pricing Product B at $130 is that the customers in Segment 2 would not buy it. For Product B to appeal to both segments, it must be priced at $100. Thus, when these two items are sold separately, the seller could not receive any more than $150 ($50 + $100) for the two products.

However, if these two products are priced at $75 and $130 when purchased separately but are priced lower when purchased together as a bundle, the situation changes. Since the customers in Segment 1 value Product A at $50 and Product B at $130, they would pay up to $180 for a bundle containing both products. Since the customers in Segment 2 value Product A at $75 and Product B at $100, they would pay up to $175 for a bundle containing both products. This means that both segments would pay up to $175 for the bundle. Thus, when these two items are offered as a bundle, the seller could receive $175 for the pair, $25 more than if they are priced separately to appeal to both market segments.

Note how the revenue benefits of this $175 product bundle result from price segmentation. The customers in Segment 1 value Product A at $50 and could be considered to pay $50 for it. The remaining $125 of the $175 they pay for the bundle could be considered to be for Product B. The customers in Segment 2 value Product A at $75 and could be considered to pay $75 for it. The remaining $100 they pay for the bundle could be considered to be for Product B. In this way, price segmentation is accomplished—each segment pays a different price for each of the two products.

An example of price segmentation by bundle design would be the business market pricing used by a manufacturer of a high-performance computer workstation. Companies engaged in engineering and scientific research value the capabilities of the manufacturer's computer at $1,200 per unit. However, they have less need of a contract for the manufacturer's support services and so would value that product at only $300. On the other hand, companies that use computers for general business purpose would be less likely to appreciate the computer's capabilities; its VTC for them might be only $700. However, these companies are likely to more strongly value the manufacturer's support services, perhaps at $600. If both of these segments are important to the computer manufacturer, then the computer could be sold for no more than $700 and the support contract for no more than $300, for a total of $1,000. By selling the computer and the support service contract together as a bundle, both market segments would buy it for $1,300. The $300 additional revenue is an indication that the design of this bundle has effectively accomplished price segmentation.

CHOOSING A PRICE-SEGMENTATION FENCE

Because of issues regarding customer judgments of price fairness, it is important to be familiar with price-segmentation fences that do not involve a customer's characteristics. Purchase-situation characteristics such as the quantity purchased or choice of product features or bundles can serve very effectively as price-segmentation fences. If designed carefully, quantity discounts, feature-dependent premiums or discounts, and product bundles can create the conditions where different groups of customers pay different prices for essentially the same product.

It should also be noted that a company's price structure may well involve the use of more than one price-segmentation fence. For example, a men's clothing retailer could offer discounts to customers showing proof of being over sixty-five and discounts for high-quantity purchases. The retailer could also charge feature-dependent premiums for services such as monogramming and could offer carefully designed bundles of suits, shirts, and accessories. At times, a seller may need to use more than one fence to effectively separate two segments, as in the symphony orchestra that both offers students discounts for showing an ID card as well as offering feature-dependent discounts for the theater's less desirable seats.

It is a rare company that cannot benefit from price segmentation. An understanding of the possible means for effectively carrying out this important pricing technique is one of the keys to successfully using price to maximize a firm's profits.

SUMMARY

An important aspect of price structure concerns price segmentation, the practice of a seller charging different customers different prices for the same product. Price segmentation could be warranted because some customers value the product more than others, are more or less costly to serve than others, or show more or less price sensitivity than others. When best prices differ between customer segments, using price segmentation can be considerably more profitable than charging all segments a single price.

To accomplish price segmentation, it is necessary to have a fence, or criterion that customers must meet to qualify for a lower price. It is possible to use an observable characteristic of customers, such as age or student status, as a price-segmentation fence, although such use may be considered unfair.

A price-segmentation fence based on characteristics of the purchase situation rather than characteristics of the customer is less likely to be considered unfair. When the best price for a product is lower for customers who buy larger quantities of the product, then it may be profitable to charge them lower per-unit prices. When the best price for a product is higher for customers who are interested in an optional product-enhancing feature or lower among customers who can tolerate an optional product-diminishing feature, then it may be profitable to use a feature-dependent premium or discount. When one product is more valued by one of two segments and another product is more valued by the other, then it may be profitable to sell a bundle containing both products at a price lower than the total charged for the two products purchased separately.

Many firms will be able to simultaneously use more than one price-segmentation fence. Understanding the use of price-segmentation fences is of key importance in a firm's ability to use price to maximize profits.

KEY TERMS

market	commercial status	two-part pricing
market segments	quantity discount	purchasing alliances
purchase situation	order-size discount	segmentation-fence patches
arbitrage	cumulative-purchase discount	feature-dependent premium
price-segmentation fence	frequent-user program	feature-dependent discount
arbitragers	fixed-charge pricing	bundle

REVIEW AND DISCUSSION QUESTIONS

1. Describe two important aspects of a firm's price structure.

2. What are the factors that may lead the best price for a product to differ between market segments?

3. When a product's best price differs between market segments, why is it preferable to use price segmentation rather than to charge a single compromise price?

4. What is a price-segmentation fence? What are the two goals of such a fence?

5. Explain how a price-segmentation fence involving a customer characteristic differs from one involving a characteristic of the purchase situation.

6. Economists refer to price segmentation as "price discrimination." Does this mean that every price-segmentation technique is considered to be unfair?

7. Explain how price segmentation is accomplished when a price is determined by negotiation.

8. Describe four pricing techniques that involve the use of purchase quantity as a price-segmentation fence.

9. What are some constraints on the use of purchase quantity as a price-segmentation fence?

10. Explain the difference between using product features as a price-segmentation fence and offering an array of product features that are priced appropriately with respect to their VTCs.

11. What is a feature-dependent premium? Describe how such a premium is key to the ability of a product-enhancing feature to accomplish price segmentation.

12. Under what conditions might it be appropriate to use a product-diminishing feature to accomplish price segmentation?

13. Describe how offering two products together in a bundle can accomplish price segmentation. What conditions would be necessary for this price-segmentation fence to be effectively used?

EXERCISES

1. Assume you are involved in price planning for a manufacturer of backpacks who sells to consumers through various channels of distribution.

    (a) Describe two market segments that should be charged different prices for these items. Explain why different prices would be appropriate.

    (b) Suggest two types of price-segmentation fences that would make possible charging each segment a different price.

2. A small chain of bagel shops currently prices its bagels at $0.99 apiece. The manager of the chain recognizes the value of price segmentation and is considering how he might charge lower prices to his high-volume customers.

   (a) Design an order-discount pricing structure that could accomplish this price segmentation.

   (b) Design a cumulative-purchase discount structure to accomplish this price segmentation.

   (c) Design a two-part pricing structure to accomplish this price segmentation.

   (d) Would the manager have to choose among the three discount structures described in Parts (a) through (c), or would he be able to do all three? Justify your view on this.

3. A number of group-buying websites, such as Groupon and BuyWithMe, offer consumers a large discount on a popular product if enough other consumers agree to purchase the product.

   (a) Describe the price-segmentation fence being used by the sellers of items offered on these websites.

   (b) Describe an advantage and a disadvantage of this price-segmentation fence over the more traditional ones discussed in this chapter.

4. A company sells two products, Product A and Product B. Assume that the variable costs for each product are $7. In a particular market, men and women value the two products as follows:

	Value to the Customer	
	Product A	**Product B**
Men (50% of market)	$12	$15
Women (50% of market)	$14	$11

   (a) If management is considering offering a bundle containing both products, what is the maximum price that could be charged for this bundle? Justify your answer.

   (b) If the company's goal is to maximize profits, should these products be offered only bundled together, offered only separately, or offered both bundled together and separately? Justify your answer.

NOTES

1. Peter R. Dickson, "Person-Situation: Segmentation's Missing Link," *Journal of Marketing* 46 (Fall 1982): 56–64.
2. Romana J. Khan and Dipak C. Jain, "An Empirical Analysis of Price Discrimination Mechanisms and Retailer Profitability," *Journal of Marketing Research* 42 (November 2005): 561–524.
3. Laura Bird, "Victoria's Secret May Be That Men Get a Better Deal," *Wall Street Journal,* January 3, 1996, B5.
4. Emily Bazar, "Still Making Less, Women Also Paying More," *Salt Lake Tribune,* November 6, 1998, D5.
5. Christopher Halleron, "Raise Up Your Skirts!" *Hudson Current,* June 21, 2004.
6. Robert J. Dolan and Hermann Simon, *Power Pricing: How Managing Price Transforms the Bottom Line* (New York: Free Press, 1996), 164.
7. Ibid., 185.
8. John L. Daly, *Pricing for Profitability: Activity-Based Pricing for Competitive Advantage* (New York: John Wiley, 2002), 66.

Time as a Price-Segmentation Fence

The time at which a product is used or purchased is a type of purchase-situation characteristic that can serve as an effective fence to accomplish price segmentation. For example, sellers of service products often vary prices by time of day, day of week, and season of year. However, the importance of price differences over time goes beyond the marketing of services. The prices of most products can vary over time, and understanding how the time of a customer's use or purchase of a product can be an effective price-segmentation fence is an important part of managing price structure.

We first discuss how the time at which a product is used can be a price-segmentation fence. This discussion focuses on services because, with service products, the time of use is usually known. Services are typically used by customers at the same time that they are "produced" by the service provider. After that, we discuss how the time at which a product is purchased can serve as the price-segmentation fence. Both goods and services can be purchased at times that are different from when they will actually be used.

TIME OF PRODUCT USE AS A PRICE-SEGMENTATION FENCE

One of the distinguishing characteristics of service products is their perishability. Services that are unsold at one time cannot be stored for sale at another time; they are perishable products. This presents a particular problem in dealing with strong fluctuations in demand. For example, a restaurant may have only a modest number of customers during the day, but by evening there may so much demand that customers have to wait to be seated. A bus may run with many empty seats at two o'clock, but around five o'clock, during "rush hour," there may be standing room only.

Peak-Load Pricing

When the demand fluctuations occur during predictable periods, sellers of services often develop a price structure such that their prices are higher during the time periods of peak demand. This is known as peak-load pricing because the practice originated with the price-setting policies of electric utility companies. These companies would set higher electricity prices during the periods when there were heavy loads on their electrical generating capacity and lower prices at other times. Peak-load pricing has since spread to a wide range of organizations that offer service products. For example, many movie theaters will have lower prices for daytime showings than for the same movies shown during the evening, when demand is higher. A list of some of the types of companies that commonly use peak-load pricing can be seen in Figure 11.1.

Figure 11.1 Some Types of Companies Using Peak-Load Pricing

- Electric utilities
- Telecommunication companies
- Hotels
- Restaurants
- Resorts—e.g., ski, beach
- Health clubs
- Transportation—e.g., airline, bus, car rental
- Tax-preparation services
- Retail banking
- Haircutting shops
- Movie theaters
- Bars, night clubs
- Lawn care companies

Peak-load pricing can involve any units of time. The price differences could be between times of the day, days of the week, seasons of the year, or by the timing of special events. Further, the time-of-use price differentials could be complex, taking into account multiple units of time. For example, consider what the rate sheet might look like for a resort hotel located in western Virginia (Figure 11.2). The room rates likely to be higher on weekends than on weekdays during the winter and spring seasons. However, the rates would increase for both kinds of days of the week in the summer and during the fall season, when many tourists come to the wooded mountains of western Virginia to enjoy the autumn foliage.

Peak-Load Pricing as Price Segmentation

One reason for the popularity of peak-load pricing is that it is an effective means of accomplishing price segmentation between groups of customers who are likely to differ in each of the three factors that determine a product's best price: (1) value to the customer (VTC), (2) costs, and (3) price sensitivity.

If we consider customers in the off-peak segment of the market, each of these three factors could contribute to a product's best price being lower than that for peak-period customers. Off-peak customers are likely to value the product less than do peak-period customers. For example, a restaurant's pleasant or entertaining atmosphere and good service, which may be very valuable to customers in the evening who want to relax from the day's pressures, may be of less value to lunchtime or afternoon customers. Incremental

Figure 11.2

Virginia Mountain Inn 2012 Rate Sheet

	Low	Medium	Peak
Standard room	$129	$149	$169
Premium room	$179	$199	$219
Suite	$249	$279	$299

January

S	M	T	W	T	F	S
1	2	3	4	5	6	7
8	9	10	11	12	13	14
15	16	17	18	19	20	21
22	23	24	25	26	27	28
29	30	31				

February

S	M	T	W	T	F	S
			1	2	3	4
5	6	7	8	9	10	11
12	13	14	15	16	17	18
19	20	21	22	23	24	25
26	27	28	29			

March

S	M	T	W	T	F	S
				1	2	3
4	5	6	7	8	9	10
11	12	13	14	15	16	17
18	19	20	21	22	23	24
25	26	27	28	29	30	31

April

S	M	T	W	T	F	S
1	2	3	4	5	6	7
8	9	10	11	12	13	14
15	16	17	18	19	20	21
22	23	24	25	26	27	28
29	30					

May

S	M	T	W	T	F	S
		1	2	3	4	5
6	7	8	9	10	11	12
13	14	15	16	17	18	19
20	21	22	23	24	25	26
27	28	29	30	31		

June

S	M	T	W	T	F	S
					1	2
3	4	5	6	7	8	9
10	11	12	13	14	15	16
17	18	19	20	21	22	23
24	25	26	27	28	29	30

July

S	M	T	W	T	F	S
1	2	3	4	5	6	7
8	9	10	11	12	13	14
15	16	17	18	19	20	21
22	23	24	25	26	27	28
29	30	31				

August

S	M	T	W	T	F	S
			1	2	3	4
5	6	7	8	9	10	11
12	13	14	15	16	17	18
19	20	21	22	23	24	25
26	27	28	29	30	31	

September

S	M	T	W	T	F	S
						1
2	3	4	5	6	7	8
9	10	11	12	13	14	15
16	17	18	19	20	21	22
23/30	24	25	26	27	28	29

October

S	M	T	W	T	F	S
	1	2	3	4	5	6
7	8	9	10	11	12	13
14	15	16	17	18	19	20
21	22	23	24	25	26	27
28	29	30	31			

November

S	M	T	W	T	F	S
				1	2	3
4	5	6	7	8	9	10
11	12	13	14	15	16	17
18	19	20	21	22	23	24
25	26	27	28	29	30	

December

S	M	T	W	T	F	S
						1
2	3	4	5	6	7	8
9	10	11	12	13	14	15
16	17	18	19	20	21	22
23/30	24/31	25	26	27	28	29

costs are likely to be lower during off-peak periods. For example, when a bus travels its route with many empty seats, the costs that would be incurred to serve additional riders at that time are extremely low. Customers may also show greater price sensitivity during off-peak periods. Although the mountain scenery might attract tourists to a ski resort hotel in the summer, the price sensitivity of these tourists is likely to be great since there are many vacation alternatives available (e.g., the beach), and there are likely to be many other unfilled ski resort hotels competing for their business.

If each time-period-defined market segment has a different best price, then, in practical terms, these best prices may be arrived at by successively considering small price increases or decreases until there are no longer any that would produce higher profits. For example, an airline considering a decrease in the fare for a late-night flight would tend to find that the sales increases resulting from these price decreases are profitable. On the other hand, for a popular morning flight, the airline would tend to find that increases in price are profitable despite some loss of customers on these flights. The result of these price changes would be, in effect, a shifting of demand from the peak periods to the off-peak periods. The benefits of using time as a price-segmentation fence are often expressed in terms of the desirability of such demand shifting.

Relevant Costs in Peak-Load Pricing

The differences in costs between peak and off-peak periods could benefit from some further explanation. It was previously mentioned that there are low variable costs for filling empty bus seats. However, we should keep in mind that the relevant costs for a price change include not just variable costs but also fixed costs that are incremental—that is, those fixed costs that will be incurred because of the new sales created by a price decrease or saved because of the sales lost by a price increase (see Chapter 5). For example, if any increase in the unit sales of a manufacturing company requires the purchase of a new machine, the change in fixed costs resulting from purchasing this machine would be incremental for any price decrease and thus must be included in the breakeven calculations for evaluating the price decrease.

Typically, service providers operate at the limits of their capacity during their peak periods. As a result of this, capacity costs, the costs of maintaining or adding capacity, are relevant for pricing decisions during peak-demand periods. This means that evaluation of possible price decreases during times of peak demand must include consideration of the incremental fixed costs of adding capacity. This leads to high breakeven sales increases for such prospective price decreases, and a lower likelihood of the price decrease being profitable. Thus, peak-period prices will tend to stay high.

On the other hand, off-peak prices are driven only by operating costs, which will usually be only the variable costs for providing the service. The equipment or facilities acquired for serving peak-period demand will be underutilized when demand is low and thus their costs are not relevant to the pricing of services provided during those off-peak periods. This means that consideration of price decreases during off-peak periods should not take into account any of the fixed costs that are incurred to support peak-period demand. This leads to relatively low breakeven sales increases for such prospective price decreases and a higher likelihood of the price decrease being profitable. As a result, prices during off-peak periods will tend to be low.

This emphasis on the costs that are actually incremental to a sale has implications for how costs should be allocated in service industries. The costs of maintaining the organization's capacity are incurred for the purposes of peak-period demand and should thus be entirely allocated to peak-period sales. Off-peak sales do not affect whether or not these capacity costs would be incurred and thus need bear no share of these costs. Such a cost-allocation concept suggests that new capacity should be built only when it is estimated that profits from peak-period sales can cover the new expenses. This makes sense, because to subsidize new-capacity expenditures with off-peak profits is to risk being underpriced at off-peak times by a competitor who does not have peak-period capacity to support. Having uncompetitive prices during the off-peak times that are intended to subsidize the peak times could then cause the whole operation to become unprofitable.[1]

It should be noted that the practice of peak-load pricing is capable of causing a peak reversal. This occurs when a lower price in the off-peak period stimulates so much demand that the off-peak times become the peak times. For example, an electric utility's night rates could be so low that it becomes profitable for large industrial customers to move to night-time operations, thus causing the level of nighttime demand to rival that of the daytime peaks. When this happens, capacity costs begin to become relevant to pricing in the off-peak period. For the electric utility, any further nighttime price decreases would need to consider the incremental fixed cost of adding capacity. Because these incremental fixed costs will increase the breakeven sales level for a price decrease, it makes further decreases in off-peak prices more difficult to justify. It is likely then that the off-peak prices that keep sales during those periods just below the amount necessary for adding new capacity are the best prices for those off-peak periods.

TIME OF PRODUCT PURCHASE AS A PRICE-SEGMENTATION FENCE

The techniques for using time of purchase (rather than time of use) as a price-segmentation fence are usually framed as discounts, or lower prices, that the customer can receive by purchasing the product at certain times. These discount-purchase times can be grouped into four categories:

- Those that occur periodically
- Those that occur irregularly
- Those that involve making the purchase earlier than other customers
- Those that involve making the purchase later than other customers

We will consider the characteristics and rationales for each of these four types of time-of-purchase discounts. In the next section, we will discuss periodic discounts. Then we will discuss irregularly occurring discounts used for promotional purposes. After that, we will discuss early-purchase discounts and then late-purchase discounts.

PERIODIC DISCOUNTS

One common means by which time of purchase is used as a price-segmentation fence is by offering items at recurring discounts that are more or less predictable over time.[2] This practice is often known as high/low pricing because there is an alternation of high-price periods with low-price periods.[3] During the high-price periods, the item is sold at what is framed as its "regular" price. During the low-price periods, the item is sold at a discount from the regular price, which is often referred as a "sale" price (see Figure 11.3). This pricing practice is used often in specialty stores, department stores, and supermarkets. For example, a department store might put its line of women's casual sportswear on sale two or three times a year. A supermarket might periodically run a sale on Breyers ice cream or Chicken of the Sea tuna.

Figure 11.3 Price Variation in High/Low Pricing

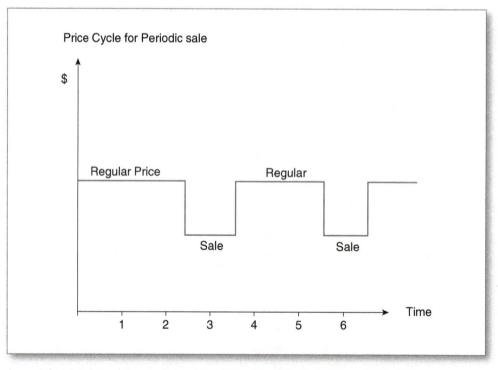

Source: Robert J. Dolan and Hermann Simon, *Power Pricing* (New York: The Free Press, 1996), 256.

High/Low Pricing as Price Segmentation

To understand how high/low pricing accomplishes price segmentation, consider how the potential buyers for a particular brand of coffeemaker might vary over time (see Figure 11.4).[4]

Figure 11.4   Illustration of How High/Low Pricing Can Accomplish Price Segmentation

Period	Number of Potential Customers: This Period Valuing At		Contribution	
	$60	**$40**	**P = $60**	**P = $40**
1	100	100	$2,800*	$1,600
2	100	200	$2,800*	$2,400
3	100	300	$2,800	$3,200*
4	100	100	$2,800*	$1,600
5	←		Same as period 2	→
6	←		Same as period 3	→

*= profit contribution of the preferred price.

Source: Robert J. Dolan and Hermann Simon, *Power Pricing* (New York: The Free Press, 1996), 256.

Say that in each period one hundred customers whose VTC for this coffeemaker is just above $60 will come into the market, and one hundred customers whose VTC for the coffeemaker is just above $40 will come into the market. If we assume that the seller's costs are $32 per unit, pricing the coffeemaker during the first period at $60 will result in $2,800 profit ($28 per-unit contribution times 100 units sold) whereas pricing it at $40 will result in only $1,600 profit ($8 per-unit contribution times 200 units sold). It thus makes sense to charge the high $60 price during the first period.

During the second period, one hundred new $60 customers and 100 new $40 customers come into the market. Because there are now 200 customers in the $40 segment of the market, selling the coffeemaker at $40 to these customers and to the 100 new $60 customers would lead to a profit of $2,400 ($8 per-unit contribution times 300 units sold). However, $2,400 is less than $2,800, so it still makes sense for the seller to price the coffeemaker at $60.

During the third period, when another one hundred customers of each type enter the market, the picture changes. Because there is now a buildup of 300 customers in the $40 segment of the market, selling the coffeemaker at $40 to these customers and to the 100 new $60 customers would lead to a profit of $3,200 ($8 per-unit contribution times 400 units sold). This would make it profitable for the seller to reduce the coffeemaker's price to $40. Note, of course, that after this accumulated low-price demand has been satisfied by the sale, it becomes again more profitable for the firm to price the item at $60. This continues until low-price demand again builds up, thus creating a continuing high/low pattern.

Factors Determining the Success of High/Low Pricing

For high/low pricing to be an effective price-segmentation technique, it is necessary that the market segment with the low VTC be willing to wait around for the seller's next discount. If a sizable proportion of the low-VTC segment is willing to pay just a little more for the convenience of not waiting for a sale, then the opportunity is present for the technique of everyday low pricing (EDLP). This is the setting of a consistent price that is somewhere between the two price levels of the competitor who is using high/low pricing (see Figure 11.5).[5] Often, users of EDLP are able to set their consistent prices relatively close to the high/low retailer's sale (i.e., low) prices because of the lower inventory costs of having a constant sales level and because there is no need for large expenditures to advertise periodic sale prices.

Figure 11.5 Comparison of High/Low Pricing With Everyday Low Pricing

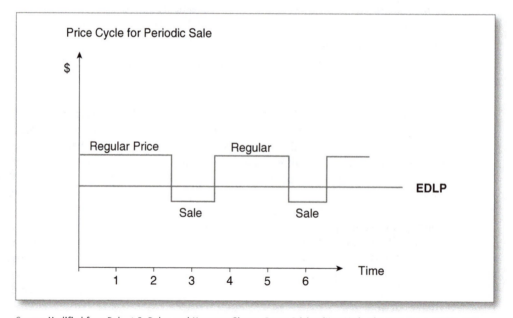

Source: Modified from Robert J. Dolan and Hermann Simon, *Power Pricing* (New York: The Free Press, 1996), 256.

Note: EDLP = everyday low pricing.

General merchandise discounters, such as Walmart or Dollar General, have been very successful with the EDLP approach. Specialty retailers such as Staples and The Home Depot also make heavy use of EDLP. These latter stores are sometimes referred to as "category killers," because their combination of extensive product assortment and low price tends to overwhelm competitors in their retailing categories. In an environment with EDLP competition, there are at least two factors that are important for making high/low pricing successful:

1. The regular (i.e., high) price of high/low pricing can help set a high-quality image for the merchandise. Seeing an item actually sold for a high price tells customers that it is worth that much to at least some people and helps raise their internal reference prices. This is particularly important when the item's quality is difficult to assess or ambiguous as, for example, in fashion goods.

2. Whereas EDLP retailers can offer the low-VTC customer the convenience of not having to wait for a relatively low price, the high/low retailer can offer the excitement of obtaining a perceived gain. The pleasures of this excitement could, paradoxically, make it more (not less) desirable to wait for the low price! As we saw in Chapter 8, the pleasures of a discount are greater when consumers feel personally responsible for obtaining the discount. Waiting patiently for the sale could support such a feeling of responsibility. Note, however, because it may be hard to feel responsible for a discount that is completely predictable, the high/low seller might benefit from putting at least a little variation into the timing of the periodic discounts.

PROMOTIONAL DISCOUNTS

Sellers often set lower prices for brief, irregularly occurring time periods in order to communicate to customers and potential customers information about the existence of products and the benefits of these products. Because marketing communication is known as "promotion," these temporary low prices are termed promotional discounts. When promotional discounts are simple price decreases, they are often referred to as "sales." Cents-off coupons and rebate offers are slightly more complicated forms of promotional discounts. Promotional discounts to product resellers, such as wholesalers and retailers (i.e., "the trade"), are examples of what are known as trade promotions.

Promotional discounts are very widely used, particularly for consumer products. For example, in an average year, over 300 billion cents-off coupons are distributed to consumers in the United States. That is over 1,000 coupons for every man, woman, and child in America.

How a Discount Can Communicate

To fully understand promotional discounts, it is important to appreciate how a discount can communicate information. The diagram in Figure 11.6 is an illustration of a model of the communication process. A source, in this case the seller, desires to communicate an intended message to the receiver, in this case the customer or potential customer. A temporary low price can provide a means for this communication by leading the receiver to take a target action that will have the effect of getting across the intended message. A common target action is the purchase of the product. For example, when Fuji wanted to communicate that its 35mm film was equal in quality to the accepted market leader, Kodak, it offered generous promotional discounts to encourage product trial. Fuji's management calculated that once consumers tried Fuji film, they would see for themselves that it

Figure 11.6   Model of Communication by Promotional Discounts

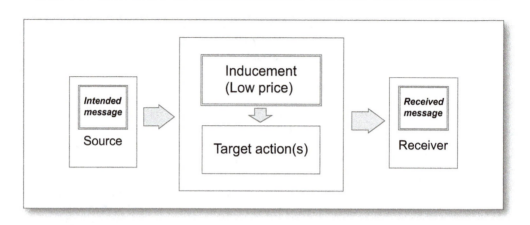

worked as well as Kodak film. By means of this discount-induced trial, the intended message would be communicated.

The target action of a promotional discount need not be product trial (i.e., a buyer's first purchase of a product). The target action could also be the consumer's purchase of more units of a product than usual. This action is often referred to as "pantry loading." It might be appropriate to for communicating the intended message, say, that a product that is known as a bathroom cleaner can also do a good job with other cleaning needs. Having a lot of the product around the house would tend to lead to its use for a greater variety of household tasks and thus get the message across. For expensive, high-involvement products, the target action could be an information-gathering activity. An automobile dealer, for example, might offer a promotional discount in order to lead consumers to read his advertisement or come in to the showroom to learn more about his line of vehicles.

Targeting the Poorly Informed Segment

Promotional discounts are usually thought of as incentives, or rewards, for behaviors that the seller wants to encourage.[6] It does not contradict this viewpoint to recognize that promotional discounts are also a form of price segmentation. In general, the market for a product consists of a segment of consumers who are well-informed of the product's existence and its benefits and a segment that is poorly informed. Because the members of the poorly informed segment do not fully appreciate the product's VTC, the product's best price for them is likely to be substantially lower than the best price for the members of the segment that is well informed about the product. Promotional discounts are a means of using time of purchase as a fence to charge a lower price to the less informed market segment.

Clearly this fence is an imperfect one—nothing stops a well-informed consumer from buying the product on sale. However, it is likely that the well-informed consumer has already purchased the product (perhaps picking it up right after he learned about it) and wasn't planning to purchase again until the original purchase wore out or was used up. If the occurrence of a promotional discount is unpredictable and of short duration, it is unlikely to be offered at just the right time for the well-informed consumer to buy. By contrast, it could be expected that almost none of the poorly informed consumers will have already purchased the product and would thus all be in a position to respond to the suddenly occurring incentive of an attractive price.

By this logic, a discount must be unpredictable and of short duration to be an efficient means of communicating about a product. The longer or more repeatedly a promotional discount is offered, the weaker is its ability to serve as a fence that keeps the well-informed consumers away from the low price. When unwise managers overuse promotional discounts, the price reductions could become a different type of discount, such as a periodic discount, which may not be appropriate for the product in question. Even worse, an overused promotional discount could lower the consumer's internal reference price for the product, and, in effect, become a permanent price decrease. Over the past few years, this has occurred with the supermarket sales of 2-liter bottles of Coke and Pepsi.

Note that many promotional discounts are not only limited in their timing but also require the consumer to present some type of "token," such as a cents-off coupon or rebate form. Such discount tokens can help limit the discount to the poorly informed segment. For example, Catalina's system of printing coupons at the checkout counter offers a packaged goods manufacturer the ability to give a promotional discount to only those consumers who purchase a competing brand (who are presumed to be poorly informed of the benefits of the manufacturer's brand). However, even such precise targeting has to be time-limited, because the use of checkout coupons can soon lead poorly informed consumers to become members of the well-informed segment. The necessity to present a token to get a discount also tends to increase the feeling of personal responsibility for the discount and thus increase the perceived value of the discount. Ideally, the amount of consumer effort required for presenting such discount tokens should be relatively small or else their use may make it too difficult for consumers to try the promoted product and thereby receive the intended message.

Trade Promotions

When manufacturers offer promotional discounts as trade promotions, there are at least two possible price-segmentation rationales. One is that the discount will be passed along to the consumer to create a consumer promotional discount. Such consumer pass-through would occur, for example, when a product's temporary low price to a retailer would lead the retailer to put the product on sale. The other rationale is that the temporary discount leads a reseller to buy more of a product and thus discover that it is possible to quickly move such a larger product inventory. This would be a reseller form of pantry loading.

For each of these two rationales, there are challenges for the manufacturer. If consumer pass-through is expected, then there needs to be some means to determine that it actually occurs. If the communication value of pantry loading is the goal, then the promotional discount needs to be structured so that the reseller cannot use the discount to simply stock up on the product without taking any steps to learn whether this larger inventory could be quickly sold. Manufacturers sometimes address this problem by adding conditions to the trade-promotion discount, such as a requirement to grocery retailers that they put the product on an end-aisle display.

EARLY-PURCHASE DISCOUNTS

In many markets, there are some customers who are more willing than others to make an early commitment to purchase a product. When these customers who are willing to purchase early value the product less or are more price-sensitive than other customers, then it is possible to use the requirement of early purchase as a price-segmentation fence.

Advance-Purchase Discounts for Service Products

A discount for early purchase, also known as an advance-purchase discount, is often used in the pricing of service products. For example, in the hotel industry, customers traveling for leisure activities (such as a vacation or visiting friends) are more price-sensitive than customers traveling for business activities. As it turns out, leisure travelers are also more willing than business travelers to make an early purchase commitment. Thus, to accomplish charging different room prices to these two market segments, a hotel can offer a lower price—a discount—to customers who are willing to book a room several weeks in advance of the date that the room will be provided. Those customers who are unwilling to make such an advance purchase must pay full price for the room.

Clearly, for days when a hotel can fill all of its rooms with business customers, there is no need to appeal to the more price-sensitive leisure customers. However, for those days when the hotel will not be entirely filled with business customers, it could be very important to fill those rooms with leisure customers. Empty rooms produce no revenue. This points to the key challenge in early-purchase discounting: to offer only enough discounts to fill the capacity that will not be used by full-price purchasers. For the hotel, the goal is to offer advance-purchase discounts on only those rooms that will not be booked by full-price business customers.

What makes this a challenge is that the hotel's management does not know how many rooms business customers will purchase on a particular day until that day arrives. Historical data can be used as guide, but such data are likely to show considerable variation. Only the statistical probabilities can be known with any certainty.

Using Probabilistic Historical Information

The key to using probabilistic historical information to make pricing decisions is the concept of expected value. We saw in Chapter 3 how the expected value of a variable—the average value of that variable in the long run—could be useful in assessing a product's VTC. This important concept can also play a role in price segmentation. As mentioned in Chapter 1, revenue management is a set of price-setting techniques that are increasingly used to enhance profitability in service industries. Work in revenue management has led to the development of methods by which information that is relatively easy for a business to obtain can be used to calculate the expected value of a product's revenue—the product's expected revenue. These expected revenues can be very helpful in guiding decisions regarding advance-purchase discounts.[7]

To illustrate revenue management methods, let's say that a hotel with eighty rooms is trying to determine how many rooms on a particular upcoming Monday should be kept for sale at the full price of $150 and how many should be offered at an advance-purchase discount price of $100. To estimate the number of full-price business customers who are likely to book rooms on that day, the hotel's management would construct a table showing the number of rooms that were booked on, say, one hundred similar Mondays when no discounts were available (see Figure 11.7). The first column of the table is each possible

Figure 11.7   Historical Hotel Room Demand Data for Managing Advance-Purchase Discounts

Level of Full-Price Demand, Q	Number of Days at Demand Q	p(Q) Probability that Full-Price Demand ≤ Q	1 − p(Q) Probability that Full-Price Demand > Q	Expected Revenue of Room at Full Price of $150
0-62	3	0.030	0.970	
63	6	0.090	0.910	$ 145.50
64	11	0.200	0.800	$ 136.50
65	9	0.290	0.710	$ 120.00
66	5	0.340	0.660	$ 106.50
67	8	0.420	0.580	$ 99.00
68	10	0.520	0.480	$ 87.00
69	13	0.650	0.350	$ 72.00
70	5	0.700	0.300	$ 52.50
71	3	0.730	0.270	$ 45.00
72	5	0.780	0.220	$ 40.50
73	7	0.850	0.150	$ 33.00
74	6	0.910	0.090	$ 22.50
75	2	0.930	0.070	$ 13.50
76	4	0.970	0.030	$ 10.50
77	3	1.000	0.000	$ 4.50
78	0	1.000	0.000	$ 0
79	0	1.000	0.000	$ 0
80	0	1.000	0.000	$ 0

Source: Adapted from Serguei Netessine and Robert Shumsky, "Introduction to the Theory and Practice of Yield Management," *INFORMS Transactions on Education* 3, no. 1 (2002).

level of demand for full-price rooms (which we will call Q). The second column is the number of days that each level of Q occurred. The third column is the cumulative proportion of days that full-price demand was equal to or lower than Q. This proportion represents the probability that full-price bookings occurred at demand Q or below, and will be referred to as p(Q).

Note how this cumulative proportion information makes possible the calculation of expected revenues. If p(Q) for any row is the probability that full-price demand will be equal to or lower than Q, then 1 − p(Q) is the probability that full-price demand will be higher than Q (see the fourth column of the table). If full-price demand is higher than Q, then the room represented by the following row will be purchased at full price. Since we now know the probability that this following-row room will be purchased at full price (i.e., 1 − p[Q]), we can calculate the expected dollar revenue of this room. It is equal to the full price times the probability that the room will be purchased at full price (see the fifth column of the table).

For example, there were eighty-five Mondays out of one hundred when seventy-three or fewer full-price rooms were booked, so there is a 0.85 probability that full-price Monday demand will be equal to or less than seventy-three rooms. That means that there is a 0.15 probability that demand will be greater than seventy-three rooms and the seventy-fourth room would be purchased at full price. Thus, the expected revenue of the seventy-fourth room equals $150 × 0.15, or $22.50.

To understand how this expected revenue information can be useful, consider the hotel management's question concerning how many rooms should be offered at an advance-purchase discount price of $100. If the expected revenue of a room is greater than $100, then revenue will be lost (in the long run) by selling the room for only $100. However, if a room's expected revenue is less than $100, then selling that room at an advance-purchase discount of $100 will (in the long run) lead to increased revenue. Thus, based on the data shown in the fifth column of the Figure 11.7 table, the sixty-seventh room and all remaining rooms (fourteen in all) can profitably be offered at the $100 advance-purchase discount.

This table of cumulative proportions could also help the hotel's management consider other options. For example, the managers may have found that an advance-purchase discount price of $100 is still too high to attract many of the leisure customers in the hotel's market, and are thus considering lowering it to, say, $75. The information in the fifth column of the Figure 11.7 table would tell them that it would not be profitable to sell the sixty-seventh and sixty-eighth rooms for $75 because they both have expected revenues higher than $75. Thus, an advance-purchase discount price of $75 could be offered profitably for a maximum of only twelve rooms. It certainly makes sense that the deeper the advance-purchase discount, the smaller would be the number of discounts available to be sold.

Using Information on How Demand Accrues Over Time

Information about past customer demand, such as that shown in Figure 11.7, is very useful in forecasting the level of demand for an upcoming service event. However, the predictive ability of such past data can be improved if it is noted how demand for the service event typically accrues over time. An historical booking curve is a graph showing the cumulative number of purchases of a service product as a function of the amount of time before the service is performed.

Consider, for example, a daily airline flight that, on average, flies 82 percent full.[8] If the booking curve for this flight is as shown in Figure 11.8, then at sixteen days before a particular day's flight departs, it could be expected that 20 percent of that flight's seats will be sold. If a pricing manager considering the flight that will depart in sixteen days observes that only 15 percent of the seats have so far been sold, the manager could take action, such as, for example, increasing the number of discount seats available on that flight. This is why it is sometimes the case that a customer who finds himself closed out of discount seats on a particular flight can call back a few days later and succeed in booking a discount seat.

Figure 11.8   Example of an Historical Booking Curve for an Airline Flight

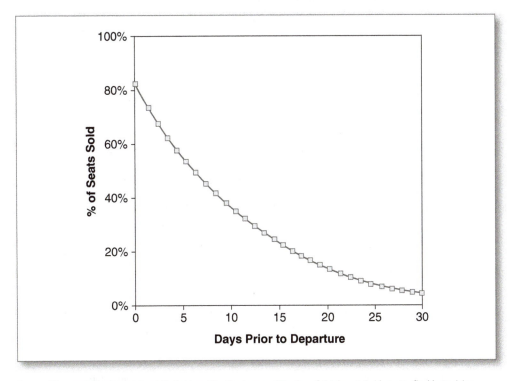

Source: Thomas T. Nagle and Reed K. Holden, *The Strategy and Tactics of Pricing: A Guide to Profitable Decision Making* (Upper Saddle River, NJ: Prentice Hall, 2002), 238.

LATE-PURCHASE DISCOUNTS

Just as early purchase can be used as a price-segmentation fence, so can purchasing a product later than other customers. For example, airlines have long offered deep discounts, known as standby fares, to travelers who can delay their purchase of a ticket until just before the flight takes off. To more effectively keep full-price passengers from receiving these discounts, airlines typically strengthen the time-of-purchase fence by restricting these fares to certain types of customers.[9] For example, AirTran Airways has been offering "U fares"—one-way fares as low at $49 to anyone between the ages of eighteen and twenty-two who books an available seat within two hours of the flight's departure.

Retail Markdowns

Retailers commonly use a late-purchase price-segmentation fence by offering markdowns. Markdowns are decreases in the price of a retail item that occur after the item has been carried by the store for a certain period of time. Markdowns are sometimes known as "clearance prices" because they are used to stimulate sales of items that are slow-moving, obsolete, shopworn, or at the end of their season. Some retailers who specialize in selling merchandise that is at the end of its purchase cycle will even have an "automatic mark-down" policy, such as the one made famous by Filene's Basement (see Figure 11.9).[10]

Figure 11.9   Filene's Basement "Automatic Markdown" Policy

Price of an item put on the selling floor is marked down as follows:

— *After fourteen selling days, it is marked down 25 percent.*

— *After twenty-one selling days, it is marked down 50 percent.*

— *After twenty-eight selling days, it is marked down 75 percent.*

— *After thirty-five days, it is given to charity.*

It makes sense for retailers to offer markdowns on a seasonal item because the item's VTC will decrease as the end of the season approaches. For example, a bathing suit in this year's style is worth much less to a customer in August than in May. Even for items that are not seasonal, markdowns often make sense for retailers because customers who value an item less or are more price-sensitive are likely to be more willing than other customers to wait to purchase the item. Markdowns are widely used in retailing, particularly in department stores. It has been estimated that 20 percent of department store sales come from marked-down items.[11]

Adapting Gross-Margin Pricing to Markdowns

When it is expected that markdowns will be used in selling an item, retailers will typically set the item's initial price high enough to take these markdowns into account. If the retailer's pricing is guided by gross margins (see Chapter 2), then the retailer would calculate an initial gross margin that is large enough so that, after markdown reductions, the final gross margin achieved will be in line with the retailer's profit goals. This final gross margin will be referred to as the maintained gross margin.[12]

To illustrate the calculation of an initial gross margin, let's assume that a retailer has purchased a product at a cost of $42 per item and intends to achieve a maintained gross margin on this product of 30 percent. If there were no price reductions due to markdowns, then the product's price would be $60 ($= \$42/[1 - .30]$). This would equal the retailer's intended revenue per item and would involve an $18 per-item gross margin. However, if it were estimated (say, from historical data) that markdown price reductions on such a product will equal $10 per item, then to achieve the desired profit level, this amount must be added to the $60 to yield an initial price of $70. Thus, for this product, the initial gross margin ($\% GM_i$) would be

$$\% GM_i = [(\$18 + \$10)/(\$60 + \$10)] \times 100 = 40\%$$

If each of the dollar amounts in the expression, ($18 + $10)/($60 + $10), is divided by $60 and multiplied by 100, the value of the expression does not change:

$$\% GM_i = [(30\% + 16.7\%)/(100\% + 16.7\%)] \times 100 = 40\%$$

Note that the 30 percent is the maintained gross margin and the 16.7 percent equals the markdown reductions as a percentage of the product's intended per-item revenue. If the former quantity is designated as $\% GM_m$ and the latter as $\% R$ (for "reduction"), then the general formula for determining the initial gross margin can be expressed as follows:

$$\% GM_i = \frac{\% GM_m + \% R}{100 + \% R} \times 100$$

This general formula can be used to facilitate the incorporation of markdowns into the procedures of gross-margin pricing. For example, say that a retailer whose profit goals require a maintained gross margin of 37 percent estimates that markdown reductions for a line of seasonal items are likely to equal 12 percent of intended revenue. The retailer could then easily calculate the initial gross margin for this season's items:

$$\% GM_i = [(37 + 12)/(100 + 12)] \times 100$$

$$= (49/112) \times 100$$

$$= 43.75\%$$

As with early-purchase discounts, a key challenge in managing markdowns is to decrease the prices of only those items that would not have been sold at full price. Simple markdown rules, such as the one illustrated in Figure 11.9, are unlikely to be profit-maximizing. Rather, there are benefits to using expected-value techniques, such as those used for determining the maximum number of advance-purchase discounts for a service product, to help the retailer decide on markdown timing. These methods combine information about the size of the markdown being considered on an item with an estimate (from historical data) of the probability that the item will not be sold at full price. Companies such as Cambridge, Massachusetts, based ProfitLogic, provide retailers with computer software to implement such methods.

Sequential Skimming

It is not just service providers and retailers who offer discounts to later purchasers. Under some conditions, manufacturers of a product can also use late-purchase discounts as a price-segmentation device. Consider, for example, the simplified demand curve shown in Part (a) of Figure 11.10.[13] It indicates that for a hypothetical new product all the customers in the market would buy it for $10. Further, some customers would pay more than $10,

Figure 11.10   The Logic of Sequential Skimming

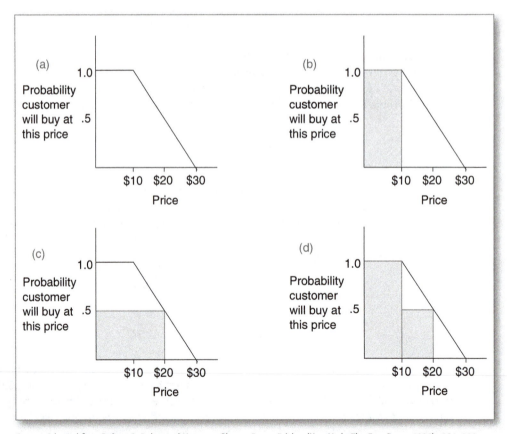

Source: Adapted from Robert J. Dolan and Hermann Simon, *Power Pricing* (New York: The Free Press, 1996), 264, 266.

perhaps as much as $30. Because we do not know how many customers would pay each particular price over $10, we assume an even distribution. Note that the area under the simplified demand curve represents the revenue that could potentially be obtained from the product.

In this situation, what are the manufacturer's pricing alternatives? If the manufacturer priced the product low, at $10, a good deal of potential revenue would be left uncollected. This is indicated by the white area under the simplified demand curve in Part (b) of Figure 11.10. If the manufacturer priced the product high, at $20, there would also be a large amount of revenue left uncollected (white area under the demand curve in Figure 11.10, Part [c]). If the product in question were a frequently purchased consumable, then these might be the only pricing options. But if the product is an item that customers usually purchase only once, then a third pricing alternative becomes possible. The manufacturer can set the price at $20 until most of those in the segment willing to pay $20 or more have purchased it and then lower the price to $10 to appeal to the rest of the market. As can be seen by the smaller amount of white area under the curve in Part (d) of Figure 11.10, this pricing sequence substantially reduces the amount of potential revenue that is left uncollected.

Because it begins with a high price to a small segment of the market, like the skimming strategy discussed in Chapter 4, this pricing technique is often known as sequential skimming.[14] It is particularly appropriate when most customers purchase the product only once (or at least at very long interpurchase intervals) and when the product has some degree of protection against direct competition. For example, the patented Polaroid instant-photography film camera satisfied both of these criteria, and the Polaroid Corporation very effectively used sequential skimming for this product over the period from 1948 to 1977 (see Figure 11.11).[15] Entertainment-related products often satisfy these criteria. Books and movies are protected by copyright laws and tend to be purchased only once. Museum exhibits, symphony performances, and Broadway plays are also examples of products with the uniqueness and onetime appeal that support the viability of the sequential-skimming technique.

The logic of sequential skimming that is illustrated in Figure 11.10 might suggest the benefit of a manufacturer making not just one or two substantial price decreases over time, but rather making numerous small price decreases so as to leave very little white area under the hypothetical demand curve. The problem is that this would enable customers to observe the price-decrease pattern and thus would tempt them to hold off purchasing the product in anticipation of further price decreases. Further, if sequential-skimming price decreases occur too quickly, it could evoke feelings of unfairness in customers who purchased the item at the higher price. This occurred with the introduction of Apple's iPhone when the price of the popular 8G model decreased from $599 to $399 in less than ten weeks.[16]

In addition to maintaining sensible restrictions in the timing and frequency of late-purchase price decreases, the sequential-skimming price-segmentation fence can be strengthened by being combined with a product-features fence. For example, the latest novel by a popular author will appear as a hardcover book, priced perhaps at $30. Over time, the book will be offered at a much lower price (e.g., $4.95) but only in the less durable paperback format.

Figure 11.11   Sequential Skimming in the Pricing of the Polaroid Instant-Photography Film Camera

Dates of Sales	Lowest-Priced Model	Price	
		In Current Dollars	In 1975 Dollars[a]
Black-and-White Cameras			
1948–1953	Model 95	$ 89.75	$200
1954–1957	Model 95A	89.75	181
1957–1959	Model 80A	72.75	139
1959–1961	Model 80B	72.75	133
1961–1963	Model J33	74.95	134
1965–1970	Model 20	19.95	35
1974–1977	Zip Land	13.95	15
Color Cameras			
1963–1966	Model 100	$ 164.95	$290
1964–1967	Model 101	134.95	234
1965–1967	Model 104	59.95	103
1969–1972	Color Pack II	29.95	44
1971–1973	Big Shot Portrait[b]	19.95	26
1975–1977	Super Shooter	25.00	25

Source: Thomas T. Nagle and Reed K. Holden, *The Strategy and Tactics of Pricing: A Guide to Profitable Decision Making* (Upper Saddle River, NJ: Prentice Hall, 2002), 169.

[a]Current dollars converted to 1975 dollars using Consumer Price Index.

[b]Fixed-focus portrait camera that took only flash pictures at a fixed distance (approximately 39 inches from subject).

SUMMARY

The time at which a product is used or purchased can serve as an effective price-segmentation fence. For many service products, the time when the consumer uses the product is known. For such products, it is likely to be profitable to set higher prices during periods of peak demand and lower prices during off-peak periods. Best prices are higher during periods of peak demand because customers are likely to value the product more during those times and are likely to be less price-sensitive. Seller costs are also higher during peak-demand periods because capacity costs in addition to operating costs are incremental to changes in demand during those times.

The time of a product's purchase can be used as a price-segmentation fence for both goods and services. When the segment of customers with a low best price builds up steadily over time, the use of periodic discounts may be an appropriate method of price segmentation. Brief, irregularly occurring discounts can communicate the existence and benefits of a product by providing an incentive to try a product or stock up on it. Such discounts provide an appropriate lower price for the segment of the market that is poorly informed about the product.

Early purchase commitment can be a useful price-segmentation fence when the best price is low for those willing to purchase early. Successful management of advance-purchase discounts often depends on the ability to use historical information about purchase probabilities. Late purchase is also widely used as a price-segmentation fence, particularly in service industries. In retailing, late-purchase discounts are known as markdowns. Manufacturers use this price-segmentation fence by setting a high initial price for a product and then lowering it over time. This technique is most appropriate for products that are purchased only once and that have some protection against direct competition.

KEY TERMS

perishability	trade promotions	historical booking curve
peak-load pricing	intended message	standby fares
capacity costs	target action	markdowns
operating costs	product trial	initial gross margin
peak reversal	pantry loading	maintained gross margin
high/low pricing	discount tokens	sequential skimming
everyday low pricing (EDLP)	consumer pass-through	
promotional discounts	advance-purchase discount	

REVIEW AND DISCUSSION QUESTIONS

1. What is peak-load pricing? What characteristics of market demand make a service product an appropriate candidate for this price-segmentation technique?

2. Use the concepts of VTC, costs, and price sensitivity to explain why a service product's best price is likely to be higher during periods of peak product demand.

3. Distinguish between capacity costs and operating costs. What is the argument against using off-peak sales to subsidize new-capacity expenditures?

4. What is a peak reversal?

5. Explain how high/low pricing can be an effective method to accomplish price segmentation.

6. What is EDLP? What are the factors that can help high/low pricing be successful in the presence of EDLP competition?

7. Describe how a promotional discount can communicate information about a product.

8. Explain how promotional discounts are a form of price segmentation. Why is unpredictability important for the price-segmentation effectiveness of a promotional discount?

9. What are some examples of promotional discounts that require the consumer to present a token? How can tokens be used in the targeting of promotional discounts?

10. What are trade promotions? What are two price-segmentation rationales of trade promotions?

11. Describe the conditions that would make the use of advance-purchase discounts appropriate.

12. Explain the concept of expected revenue. Describe how historical data on full-price demand can be used to calculate expected revenues.

13. How can expected revenue information be used to help determine the number of units that could be sold at an advance-purchase discount?

14. What is an historical booking curve? How can it be used in decisions concerning how many advance-purchase discounts to offer?

15. When an airline offers standby fares to travelers with a military or student ID, what price-segmentation fences are being used?

16. What are retail markdowns? How can the expected level of markdown reductions be used to calculate a product's initial gross margin?

17. Explain how sequential skimming is an example of price segmentation.

18. What are the two main criteria for the appropriateness of sequential skimming? Why should the number of price decreases in sequential skimming be sharply limited?

EXERCISES

1. A dance studio currently charges customers $25 for a half-hour dance lesson. The studio employs a large number of dance instructors who are paid only for the lessons they give and receive $10 per lesson. The studio currently spends $18,000 per month for rent and could increase its dance space by renting an adjoining unit in its building for an additional $8,000 per month. The studio's current space is sufficient to give ten lessons per hour.

Currently the studio is open for forty hours during evenings and weekends and gives an average of 390 lessons per week during those times. However, during its thirty weekday hours, the studio gives only an average of 100 lessons per week.

(a) Calculate the breakeven sales level for a 20 percent decrease in the price of a dance lesson.

(b) Calculate the breakeven sales level for a 20 percent dance lesson price decrease for only those lessons during the studio's weekday hours.

(c) Use the breakeven calculations in Parts (a) and (b) to explain why it would be preferable to restrict the price decrease to the studio's weekday hours. If the price decrease were restricted to the studio's weekday hours, what type of price-segmentation fence would be involved?

2. In 1989, Sears, Roebuck and Co., then America's largest retailer, announced it was adopting an EDLP policy. Over the next year, sales and profits dropped, and Sears returned to its previous pricing policy. What are some reasons why EDLP may have failed for Sears?

3. Ed Oakley is interested in expanding his successful lawn service into a neighboring town. Several competing services are well-entrenched in this town, charging $25 to $30 for each mowing of an average-sized lawn and $300 to $350 per season for fertilizing and lawn treatments. Most customers use the same lawn service throughout a season and there is a considerable amount of repeat business from year to year.

(a) Ed is considering offering low introductory prices to gain the attention of homeowners in this town. What might these low prices be? Describe an advertisement that would effectively communicate these introductory prices.

(b) What factors would determine whether the use of promotional discounts would be an appropriate strategy for Ed's business?

4. Consider again the description of the eighty-room hotel in the chapter and the table in Figure 11.7.

(a) Using the information in Figure 11.7, determine the maximum number of advance-purchase discounts to allow for the Monday in question if the discount price were $125 rather than $100.

(b) Given your answer to Part (a), explain the direction of the difference between the maximum number of $125 advance-purchase discounts and the maximum number of $100 advance-purchase discounts.

5. A buyer for a chain of garden stores is deciding on prices for the chain's extensive line of potted plants. Management has indicated that the target gross margin for these items should be 40 percent. Last year, markdown reductions amounted to 17 percent of the total dollar sales revenue received from potted plants.

(a) If the buyer assumes this year's markdown reductions as a percentage of intended revenue will be similar to last year's, what initial gross margin should she apply to make the maintained gross margin match management's target gross margin for these items?

(b) Use your answer to Part (a) to suggest an initial price for each of the following items:

> Orchids, cost: $8.75/unit
> Chrysanthemums, cost: $3.50/unit

6. A manufacturer is about to introduce into the market a new type of upright vacuum cleaner with a patented curved handle that makes housework easier on the homemaker's back. The limited market research available has indicated that the VTC for this product ranges from $46 to $70.

   If the manufacturer plans to use a sequential-skimming strategy, what would be the best initial price for the product? What would be the next price? How frequently should the price of this item be changed?

NOTES

1. Thomas T. Nagle and Reed K. Holden, *The Strategy and Tactics of Pricing: A Guide to Profitable Decision Making* (Upper Saddle River, NJ: Prentice Hall, 2002), 26–27.
2. Gerard J. Tellis, "Beyond the Many Faces of Price: An Integration of Pricing Strategies," *Journal of Marketing* 50 (October 1986): 146–160.
3. Michael Levy and Barton A. Weitz, *Retailing Management,* 5th ed. (New York: McGraw-Hill/Irwin, 2004), 479.
4. This illustration is from Robert J. Dolan and Hermann Simon, *Power Pricing* (New York: The Free Press, 1996), 255–258.
5. Michael Levy and Barton A. Weitz, *Retailing Management,* 5th ed. (New York: McGraw-Hill/Irwin, 2004), 478.
6. Walter R. Nord and J. Paul Peter, "A Behavior Modification Perspective on Marketing," *Journal of Marketing* 44 (Spring 1980): 36–47.
7. Serguei Netessine and Robert Shumsky, "Introduction to the Theory and Practice of Yield Management," *INFORMS Transactions on Education* 3, no. 1 (2002).
8. Example from Thomas T. Nagle and Reed K. Holden, *The Strategy and Tactics of Pricing: A Guide to Profitable Decision Making* (Upper Saddle River, NJ: Prentice Hall, 2002), 238.
9. Jeffrey I. McGill and Garrett J. Van Ryzin, "Revenue Management: Research Overview and Prospects," *Transportation Science* 33 (May 1999): 233–256.
10. David E. Bell and Dinny Starr, "Filene's Basement," Harvard Business School Case 9-594-018, Boston: Harvard Business School Publishing.
11. Amy Merrick, "Priced to Move: Retailers Try to Get Let Up on Markdowns with New Software," *Wall Street Journal,* August 7, 2001, A1.
12. In retailing, this is traditionally referred to as the "maintained markup." See Levy and Barton A. Weitz, Retailing Management, 5th ed. (New York: McGraw-Hill/Irwin, 2004), 483–485.
13. Illustration based on discussion in Robert J. Dolan and Hermann Simon, *Power Pricing* (New York: The Free Press, 1996), 264–267.
14. Economists sometimes refer to this technique as "sliding down the demand curve." See, for example, Charles W. Lamb, Joseph F. Hair Jr., and Carl McDaniel, Marketing, 4th ed. (Cincinnati, OH: Southwestern College Publishing, 1998), 605.
15. Thomas T. Nagle and Reed K. Holden, The Strategy and Tactics of Pricing: A Guide to Profitable *Decision Making* (Upper Saddle River, NJ: Prentice Hall, 2002), 169.
16. Katie Hafner and Brad Stone, "iPhone Owners Crying Foul Over Price Cut," *New York Times,* September 7, 2007.

Place as a Price-Segmentation Fence

The place where a product is used or purchased is another type of purchase-situation characteristic that can serve as an effective price-segmentation fence. For example, when sellers pay shipping costs for products that are expensive to ship and customers vary greatly in the location at which they use the product, it often makes good sense to charge higher prices to the more distant customers.

Price segmentation based on geography can also make sense when it is the place of the product's purchase that serves as the price-segmentation fence. Different purchase locations may involve differences in the product's value to the customer (VTC), the product's costs, and/or the customer's price sensitivity. For example, consumers might value a newspaper sold at a commuter railroad station more highly than the same newspaper sold at a shopping mall or a drugstore. Selling at some locations may involve higher costs than others, for example, because of taxes, fees, or the expenses of distribution. Customer price sensitivity for a purchase location might vary because of differences in competitive intensity. There may be many competitors selling the product at some locations but few at other locations.

In this chapter, we discuss how geographic segmentation can be accomplished in the selling of industrial products, in retailing, and in international commerce. Following that will be a discussion of how location-based price segmentation can be adapted to the "geography" of the Internet—a seller can charge different prices for the same item depending on the website that the customer uses to find out about the product.

SHIPPING COSTS FOR INDUSTRIAL PRODUCTS

For many industrial products, the costs of shipping them from the manufacturer's plant to the location where they will be used by the purchasing firm is a substantial portion of what the buyer must pay to acquire the products. Steel, gasoline, automobiles, wheat, sugar, coal, lumber, and cement are examples of such products.

Some sellers will set prices that cover only the product. The buyer is responsible for arranging to ship the product from the seller's plant to the buyer's location and the buyer pays for this shipping. This practice known as FOB-origin pricing, a traditional term indicating that the product is "free on board"—that is, free of the seller's responsibility—where it is produced. The product becomes the buyer's property—and the buyer's concern—when the seller loads it onto the buyer's carrier.

Delivered Pricing

Despite the simplicity of FOB-origin pricing, it is more common for sellers of industrial products to use some form of delivered pricing.[1] In delivered pricing, the price that the seller quotes to the customer includes the transportation of the product to the customer's location.[2] Delivered pricing gives the seller a greater degree of pricing control. As we will see, the bundling of a product's shipping along with the product can provide the product's producer with an additional means of managing the price that the customer pays for the product.

Typically, delivered pricing involves using location of product use as a price-segmentation fence. Those customers whose use of the product requires it to be shipped to a location farther from the producer will be charged more for the product than those customers who use the product at a location closer to the producer. The seller's higher costs—in this case, higher shipping costs—would make the product's best price higher for these more distant customers.

There are a number of alternative formats for communicating a delivered price. The issue of price partitioning, mentioned in Chapter 1 and discussed further in Chapters 7 and 8, comes up again here. If the seller chooses to quote a single product price that includes shipping, then the seller would indicate that this price is "FOB destination." Alternatively, the seller could quote a price for the product along with a separate freight charge to cover shipping. For example, a seller could quote the price as "$100, FOB destination" or use price partitioning and quote the price as, "$60 plus a $40 freight charge."

A quoted freight charge need not be the shipping charges from the producer's location. In basing-point pricing the freight charges quoted to the buyer are the costs of shipping the product from a place other than the producer's location. For example, a manufacturer in a remote Nevada location might use the location of a more accessible competitor—say, San Francisco—as a "basing point." Customers would be quoted a product price plus freight charges from San Francisco, which would make it easier for the customers to compare prices.

Because the markets for industrial products often involve a relatively small number of large customers, it is usually practical for sellers to specify FOB-destination prices or freight charges individually for each customer. However, for sellers who want to use publicly posted prices, it is possible to use industrial price zones. These are contiguous areas within which all FOB-destination prices or freight charges would be equal. For example, the London Brick Company has specified price zones in the form of concentric circles around its plant.[3]

Absorption of Shipping Costs

The use of delivered pricing helps make it possible for a seller to address a common problem resulting from high shipping costs. Shipping costs can make it difficult for a seller to successfully compete at the more distant customer locations. For example, a chemical plant in Kansas City could have difficulty obtaining customers in Chicago. For those customers, buying the chemical product from Chicago-area competitors of the Kansas City plant would not involve the high charges for shipping the product from Kansas City to Chicago.

To deal with this problem, a company may set delivered prices that do not fully cover the costs of shipping the product. In other words, the seller absorbs part of the freight shipping costs. When delivered prices are set so as to absorb at least some of the shipping costs, it is referred to as freight absorption pricing. For example, with industrial price zones, the price differentials between zones would be set smaller than the actual interzone differences in shipping costs. That way, companies become able to sell the delivered product at a price closer to what would be the best price for the customers in the more distant markets.

Note that when delivered prices involve partial seller absorption of shipping costs, there are two price-segmentation fences in use. The place-of-use fence allows the delivered product to be sold at a higher price to the more distant purchasers. But it is the pricing of the product in a bundle that includes both the product and its transportation to the buyer that allows the seller to be competitive at the farther locations. Because of this bundling, the more distant buyer in effect pays a lower price for the product itself than does the buyer whose location is closer to that of the seller.

Some companies accomplish this price segmentation between different geographic areas by the bundling fence alone. They will include shipping in the product's price and charge the same price—a uniform delivered price—to all customers, regardless of location. This is sometimes called "postage-stamp pricing" because it has long been used by the U.S. Postal Service. Uniform delivered prices are common in consumer products sold by mail order and online. However, for sellers of industrial products, use of uniform delivered pricing is more questionable. If the uniform prices involve the seller absorbing all shipping costs, then it could be prohibitively expensive. If, alternatively, the uniform prices are accomplished by shifting some of the shipping costs from farther customers to closer customers rather than by absorbing them, then it may make local customers vulnerable to competition by local sellers who use FOB-origin pricing.

RETAIL PRICE ZONES

Geographic price segmentation in retailing is called zone pricing (also called variable pricing or local pricing). The management of a chain of retail outlets will classify the chain's outlets into zones based on their location. The prices charged by any particular outlet in the chain will depend on its zone. The zones may accomplish price segmentation between different types of locations (such as shopping centers, office buildings, or college campuses), between different towns or neighborhoods, or between different national regions, such as New England or the southeastern United States.

The use of zone pricing is widespread in retailing. It is used in gasoline retailing, fast-food outlets, clothing stores, grocery retailing, drugstores, discount stores, and in many other types of retailing. For example, Dominick's, a large supermarket chain in the Chicago metropolitan area, has divided its stores into 16 price zones (see Figure 12.1). The zone-pricing recommendations that the management of a large chain of sandwich shops might make to its franchisees are shown in Figure 12.2. The prices of all the items sold by a retailer can vary between zones, or zone-specific prices can be used for only a few of the items carried by a retailer. In some retail categories, the size of the price differences between zones can be large, sometimes in the range of 40 percent. In other retail categories, the differences between price zones tend to be small. In supermarkets, for example, the price differences between zones are usually less than 10 percent.[4]

Figure 12.1   Numbers Indicate the Price Zones of Chicago-Area Dominick's Supermarkets

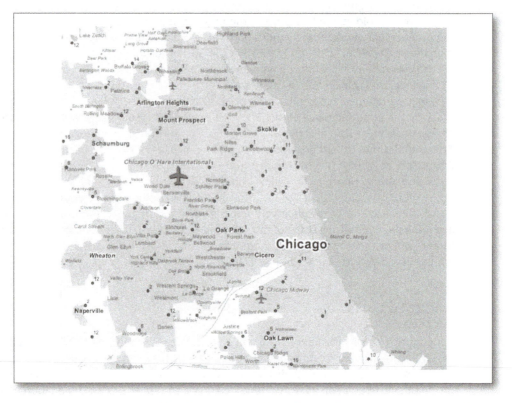

Source: Pradeep Chintagunta, Jean-Pierre Dube, and Vishal Singh, "Balancing Profitability and Customer Welfare in a Supermarket Chain" *Quantitative Marketing and Economics,* 1 (2003): 111–147.

Figure 12.2   Example of Zone Pricing in a Chain of Sandwich Shops

SANDWICH WORLD, INC.			
Pricing Recommendations for Franchisees			
Price Zone	Basic Sandwich	Deluxe Sandwich	Triple-decker
Zone 1: Neighborhood and highway locations with nearby price competition	$2.99	$3.49	$3.99
Zone 2: Neighborhood and highway locations without nearby price competition; downtown locations	$3.29	$3.89	$4.49
Zone 3: Regional shopping malls; colleges; hospital locations; military base locations	$3.69	$4.29	$4.99
Zone 4: Beach and ski area locations; tourist sites	$4.29	$4.89	$5.59
Zone 5: Sports stadiums and theme parks	$4.99	$5.69	$6.49

Convenience-Based Price Zones

In some types of retailing, the use of zone pricing is based on differences between retail outlets in the convenience they provide to customers. The goal here would be to capture the value created by locating an outlet in places that are easily accessible to customers as they pursue activities that bring up the need for the outlet's products. For example, consumers are likely to want a cold drink when they are at the beach and a hot cup of coffee when they are traveling to work. Pricing cold drinks higher when they are sold at locations convenient to the beach and hot coffee higher when provided at locations convenient to people's trip to work makes sense for profit-maximizing pricing.

Higher prices for products sold at convenient locations are appropriate not only because the convenience gives the products a higher VTC but also because selling at convenient locations is likely to involve higher costs. For example, gas stations at highway exits often charge higher prices than gas stations selling the same brand of gas but at locations a few miles away from the highway.[5] The costs of commercial properties in close proximity to highway exit ramps are likely to be higher than those farther away and thus provide another reason for higher prices at those locations. Fast-food chains often charge higher prices at airport or train station locations. This reflects their higher rents for those locations in addition to the convenience they offer.

Sometimes the higher costs of the more convenient locations result from their smaller scale. Chains of stores that maintain locations close to where customers live, such as

7-Eleven, Wawa, and White Hen Pantry, typically have high facilities and labor costs relative to the number items they sell. A soft drink bottler will typically incur higher per-item costs to supply and maintain vending machines—retail outlets designed to be conveniently located—than to provide the same products to supermarkets, which are usually at less convenient locations. Fast-food and other companies that set up operations at outdoor sports events, concerts, and festivals have higher costs from both higher location rents and their smaller scale of operation.

Designing appropriate convenience-based price zones for a product depends on gaining an understanding of the places where customers are likely to be when they have needs for the product. This involves knowing where potential customers live and work and knowing the locations of their shopping centers, churches, hospitals, and entertainment activities. Attention to detail here could be important. For example, if the morning pattern of foot traffic in a commuter train station is different than the evening pattern, then a coffee stand that seeks to achieve high convenience must be in the path of the morning pattern. Note that convenience-based price zones are not contiguous areas but rather categories of locations that offer comparable levels of customer convenience.

Price Zones Based on Other Factors

Retail price zones are often defined by factors that are important in determining customer price sensitivity. One key factor in determining price sensitivity is the customer's income level. Customers in affluent neighborhoods are often less price-sensitive than customers in more middle-income neighborhoods. Retailers such as supermarkets, drugstore chains, and hardware stores will often achieve a comparable level of convenience to all customers by establishing neighborhood locations. However, they will often have higher prices in high-income neighborhoods simply because the low customer price sensitivity makes such prices profitable. Doctors, dentists, lawyers, and other providers of professional services also often establish convenient neighborhood offices and also often use income-based zone pricing in setting their fees.

A second important price-sensitivity factor that is used in defining retail price zones is the intensity of the competition. Prices are likely to be lower in those outlets of a chain that are close to low-price competitors. For example, a grocery chain might classify stores according to their distance from a Walmart or other large grocery retailer with an everyday low pricing (EDLP) strategy. An oil company might classify its gas stations as being in a low-price zone based on whether they are near a large convenience-store gas retailer or near the border of a state with lower retail gasoline taxes. On the other hand, prices are likely to be higher in those locations where there is little close-by competition. Note that high prices due to artificial restrictions on competition, such as occurs with the concession operations of sports stadiums or movie theaters,[6] are over and above the higher prices warranted by convenience alone.

A third price-sensitivity factor is the consumer's ability to engage in price information search in order to take advantage of the price competition that does exist. For example, groups such as retirees or the urban poor may be less mobile and thus less likely to shop around for a low price. The resulting lower price sensitivity may lead some retailers to set higher prices in neighborhoods with large numbers of such people. As was noted in Chapter 7, the inability to price shop and the resulting low price sensitivity, could also be due to lack of knowledge about the competition. For example, at tourist resorts, the prices of restaurants in or near the major hotels will tend to be higher than the prices of equivalent restaurants only a little farther away. One explanation for this is that the out-of-town tourists who stay in the major hotels usually lack awareness of the restaurant alternatives out of the immediate area. Their price sensitivity is thus lowered by their limited ability to compare prices. By contrast, the local residents are likely to be aware of the full range of restaurant alternatives and are thus more able to do enough price information search to become highly price-sensitive.[7]

Research has demonstrated that responding to locational differences in customer price sensitivity can substantially increase a retailer's profits. Given the availability of scanner data on sales and prices in many retailing operations, it is often practical to base these zones on empirical measurement of customer price sensitivity. Further, if an outlet's customer price sensitivity is tracked separately for different products, then a retailer can set a zone's prices higher for some products but lower for others. For example, a supermarket might find it profitable to increase the gap between national brands and store brands in more affluent neighborhoods because the national-brand buyers there may show very little price sensitivity, but the store-brand shoppers there might be highly price-sensitive.[8]

Constraints on Zone Pricing

There are several difficulties that may need to be dealt with in order for zone pricing to be used successfully. One important constraint concerns consumers' judgments of fairness. When consumers observe that the prices in a store are higher than the prices in another store of the same chain just a few miles away, they are likely to feel that they are being treated unfairly. A trade association executive noted that such price differences make the manager of the higher-price store "look like a thief."[9] Fear of negative consumer reactions leads many retailers to be reluctant to talk about their use of zone pricing. When they do talk about it, they often try to give the impression that the price differences are mostly due to differences in the costs of doing business at various locations.[10]

Consumer judgments of fairness are likely to be related also to broader factors such as judgments about the retailer's motives. These are important to consider in decisions about zone pricing. For example, customer awareness of an organization's zone pricing may give the organization a profit-seeking image. A large supermarket company or chain of discount retailers might not be harmed by such an image. But an organization such as Gymboree, which provides goods and services for toddlers and other preschoolers, may find such an image to have more serious effects. A profit-seeking image that could result from customer awareness of zone pricing might detract from the image of caring about children, which would be essential for the success of such an organization.

In addition to the issue of fairness, there are three other possible constraints that may need to be addressed in a retailer's consideration of zone pricing:

1. *Difficulty of managing price zones.* The use of price zones greatly increases the complexity of pricing databases and other systems needed to manage prices across a retail chain. Managing price zones can be particularly costly in product categories such as clothing, where prices are marked on each item. In gasoline retailing, prices often change quickly and there needs to be constant attention to the boundaries of zones and the sizes of the price differentials between them.[11] There is an increasing use of computer software to

help in the managing of price zones, but this use has been criticized. Errors in zone-pricing decisions could cause the failure of retail outlets, which could then be hard to reestablish.[12] If the optimum price differences between zones are not large, then the added costs of managing them may not be worth it.[13]

2. *Conflicts with advertised prices.* Zone pricing may be difficult to accomplish when retail prices are widely advertised. Large metropolitan newspapers have accommodated the retailers using zone pricing by printing separate editions for different areas of the newspaper's readership and by putting price advertising in separate sheets known as free-standing inserts. These inserts can be easily varied between the newspaper's delivery locations. Retailers can also avoid the difficulties created by price advertising by simply refraining from using zone pricing on the particular items that are being advertised.

3. *Conflicts with Internet pricing.* Displaying prices on Internet sites also presents a problem for zone pricing. This not only increases consumer awareness of zone pricing but also undermines it unless the online price is as high as that in any of the zones. Retailers, such as Staples and AutoZone, deal with this problem by requiring a website visitor to enter his or her zip code before any pricing information is displayed. This then allows the retailer to give online prices that agree with the prices that the consumer will find in nearby stores.[14]

PRICING IN INTERNATIONAL COMMERCE

When a product is sold in more than one country, it is commonly sold at prices that differ between the countries. This is often true for goods, as can be seen in the survey of prices of a Big Mac in different countries, shown in Figure 12.3. It is also common in the pricing of services, as can be seen in the prices of a movie ticket in different countries, shown in Figure 12.4. This geographic price segmentation is accomplished by using country of sale as the price-segmentation fence. We first discuss some of the factors that make these differing prices appropriate. We then review some of the factors that constrain the use of country of sale as a price-segmentation fence.

Factors Supporting International Price Segmentation

A product may have a different best price in different countries because of any or all of the three factors that determine best price: (1) VTC, (2) costs, and (3) price sensitivity.

There are innumerable aspects of the cultures, lifestyles, attitudes, and tastes of the consumers in a country that could lead those consumers to value a product more or less than those in other countries. For example, Russian consumers' tastes in chocolate calls for more cocoa and a grittier texture than that of American brands such as Hershey and Mars and leads these American brands to be priced lower in Russia than Russian brands such as Red October.[15] Japanese consumers place a particularly high value on the esthetic aspects of products, such as package quality and style, and are thus willing to pay more

Figure 12.3   Prices of a Big Mac in Various Countries

	Big Mac Prices		Implied PPP* of the Dollar	Actual Dollar Exchange Rate 23/04/02	Under (−)/over(+) Valuation Against the Dollar, %
	in Local Currency	in Dollars			
United States†	$2.49	2.49	-	-	-
Argentina	Peso 2.50	0.78	1.00	3.13	−68
Australia	A$3.00	1.62	1.20	1.86	−35
Brazil	*Real* 3.60	1.55	1.45	2.34	−38
Britain	£1.99	2.88	1.25‡	1.45‡	+16
Canada	C$3.33	2.12	1.34	1.57	−15
Chile	Peso 1,400	2.16	562	655	−14
China	Yuan 10.50	1.27	4.22	8.28	−49
Czech Rep	Koruna 56.28	1.66	22.6	34.0	−33
Denmark	Dkr24.75	2.96	9.94	8.38	+19
Euro area	£2.67	2.37	0.93§	0.89§	−5
Hong kong	Hk$11.20	1.40	4.50	7.80	−42
Hungary	Forint 459	1.69	184	272	−32
Indonesia	Rupiah 16,000	1.71	6,426	9,430	−32
Israel	Shekel 12.00	2.51	4.82	4.79	+1
Japan	¥262	2.01	105	130	−19
Malaysia	M$5.04	1.33	2.02	3.8	−47
Mexico	Peso 21.90	2.37	8.80	9.28	−5
New Zeland	NZ$3.95	1.77	1.59	2.24	−29
Peru	New Sol 8.50	2.48	3.41	3.43	−1
Philippines	Peso 65.00	1.28	26.1	51.0	−49
Poland	Zloty 5.90	1.46	2.37	4.04	−41
Russia	Rouble 39.00	1.25	15.7	31.2	−50
Singapore	S$3.30	1.81	1.33	1.82	−27
South Africa	Rand 9.70	0.87	3.90	10.9	−64
South Korea	Won 3,100	2.36	1,245	1,304	−5
Sweden	SKr26.00	2.52	10.4	10.3	+1
Switzerland	SFr6.30	3.81	2.53	1.66	+53
Taiwan	NT$70.00	2.01	28.1	34.8	−19
Thailand	Baht 55.00	1.27	22.1	43.3	-49
Turkey	Lira 4,000,000	3.06	1,606,426	1,324,500	+21
Venezuela	Bolivar 2,500	2.92	1,004	857	+17

Source: "Big MacCurrencies," *The Economist,* April 27, 2002, p. 76.
*Purchasing-power parity: local price divided by price in Unites States
† Average of New York, Chicago, San Francisco and Atlanta ‡ Dollars per pound § Dollars per euro

Figure 12.4   Prices of a Movie Ticket in Various Countries

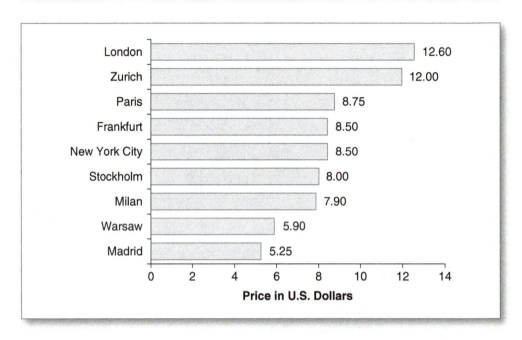

Source: Adapted from "Price of a Movie Ticket in Major Metropolitan Areas" from "Prices at the Europlex," *The Economist,* March 27, 1999, p. 110.

than consumers in other countries for attractively designed products and packages.[16] National pride may be a factor behind the higher price of the Volkswagen Passat in Germany than in neighboring Denmark.[17] There might also be international differences in the recognizability of brand names, which would give them differing abilities to command price premiums.

There are also a number of reasons for differing costs of providing the same product to customers in different countries. One reason is that distribution costs may differ between countries. This may occur either because of differences in the efficiency of the physical movement of goods or because of the necessity of hiring extra middlemen such as importing agents. A second reason for differing costs is that there may be differences in the taxes to carry out operations in a country or in the costs of complying with governmental regulations. For example, automobile manufacturers selling in the United States have to incur the costs of complying with safety and exhaust emissions regulations that are more stringent than those in many other countries. A third reason for differing costs is that the risks of doing business in the country may differ. For example, the costs due to the risk of losses from currency exchange rate fluctuation or political instability may differ between countries.

Consumers in different countries may also differ in price sensitivity. Economic factors play a major role in these price-sensitivity differences. Consumer buying power—a combination of their income and wealth—differs greatly between countries. For the average consumer in a developing nation, the prices of many common products are such a large proportion of their incomes that they will show a higher degree of price sensitivity than will consumers in developed nations. For example, in contrast to the relatively low price sensitivity of snack foods in the U.S. market, Frito-Lay has found that there was so much snack-food price sensitivity in Mexico that it was important to offer some snack foods at prices as low as 1.5 pesos, or around $0.15.[18] Even among countries with a generally high standard of living, differences in how the currency in the producing country translates into the currency of the buying country could have enough of an effect on the expensiveness of a product to affect its price sensitivity. This is particularly important when competitive factors are also involved. For example, the price of Heineken beer in Japan is limited by particularly strong competition from domestic beer producers, such as Kirin, Asahi, Sapporo, and Suntory.[19] In some cases, price competition from local competitors is made more difficult to handle because of subsidies given to those competitors by local governments.

Gray Market Importing

There are several factors that constrain a seller's use of country of purchase as a price-segmentation fence. The first is the possibility of gray market commerce. This is the practice of selling products through unauthorized international distribution channels. For example, a Swiss watch manufacturer might sell watches to an authorized U.S. retailer for a high price, reflecting the prestigious image of Swiss watches in the United States. The manufacturer might also sell the same watches for considerably less to a retailer in Italy, where there is less prestige to Swiss brand names. The Italian retailer might find it profitable to quickly unload the watches by selling them to an unauthorized U.S. retailer at price low enough to enable this unauthorized retailer to undercut the authorized U.S. stores.[20]

The term *black market* refers to commerce that is illegal. Gray market commerce is not illegal in most countries but is unauthorized and ethically questionable. It violates the manufacturer's intentions and often violates contracts with a country's authorized distributors. Thus, it is commerce that, while not "black," is in a gray area. Gray market importing, also called "parallel importing," is responsible for billions of dollars of annual sales worldwide and is expected to increase.[21] Although usually unaware of it, U.S. consumers are often exposed to gray market merchandise not only in watches but in product categories such as jewelry, perfume, liquor, cameras, crystal ware, ski equipment, and batteries.[22] Gray market commerce is a form of arbitrage that makes country of purchase a leaky price-segmentation fence.

Managing the Gray Imports Problem

There are two general approaches to dealing with the problem of gray market imports. The first approach is to take steps to make gray importing more difficult. The seller can modify the product and its packaging, selling in each country a version designed to appeal more specifically to the customers of that country. The producer can sell the product under a different model name or even a different brand name in each country and can vary the language used on the packaging and in the product instructions. The seller can also develop after-sale support-service aspects of the product, such as warranties, technical support, and periodic updates, and promote to consumers that these are available only to purchases made at authorized retail outlets. The ad in Figure 12.5, for example, points out the benefits

Figure 12.5   Promotion Urging Consumers to Buy at Only Authorized Retail Outlets

We "authorize" our TAG Heuer dealers for a good reason. You.

We at TAG Heuer, the leading Swiss Sports Watch, want to remind you, at this time of giving, to purchase our products only from authorized TAG Heuer dealers. This is the only way to be assured of buying a genuine TAG Heuer watch and of being completely satisfied with your timepiece now and in the future.

What defines an authorized TAG Heuer dealer?

There are about 1300 of them in the US, comprised of fine jewelry and watch stores and select department stores. They are experts in our product, selling authentic watches and providing professional servicing. No discount stores and no website vendors are authorized dealers.

What are the risks of purchasing a TAG Heuer watch from an unauthorized dealer?

The watch you purchase may be counterfeit, damaged or tampered with . . . and although an altered serial number is one indication of product tampering, there are others that are less obvious. In addition, TAG Heuer USA will not provide service to a watch purchased at an unauthorized store and will never service a watch without a serial number. Purchasing a watch from an authorized dealer provides you with exclusive access to TAG Heuer's special parts and expertise.

If you are unsure as to whether or not your jeweler is an authorized dealer, please call us at 1-800-268-5055, or check our website at www.tagheuer.com. Thank you for your patronage and have a healthy holiday season.

Source: Warren J. Keegan and Mark C. Green, *Global Marketing,* 2nd ed. (Upper Saddle River, NJ: Prentice-Hall, 2000), 440.

of going to an authorized dealer if one is interested in buying a TAG Heuer watch. These measures make gray importing more difficult by decreasing the consumer appeal of gray merchandise. However, these measures also work against the seller's economies of scale and increase the seller's costs.[23]

The second approach to reducing the problem of gray market imports is to decrease the size of the price differential between countries. Because it is this price differential that makes gray importing profitable, reducing its size can be expected to decrease the amount of gray imports into the countries with the higher product prices. Hermann Simon and his colleagues have used the judgments of experienced managers to estimate the specifics of the relationship between the price differential between two countries and the proportion of gray imports in the more expensive country.[24] An example of the relationship they typically find can be seen in Figure 12.6. This type of research has indicated that gray importing will often disappear completely when price differentials are less than 20 percent (of the upper price). It has led Simon and his colleagues to recommend that managers reduce prices in high-priced countries

Figure 12.6   Effect of Price Differentials on the Amount of Gray Importing

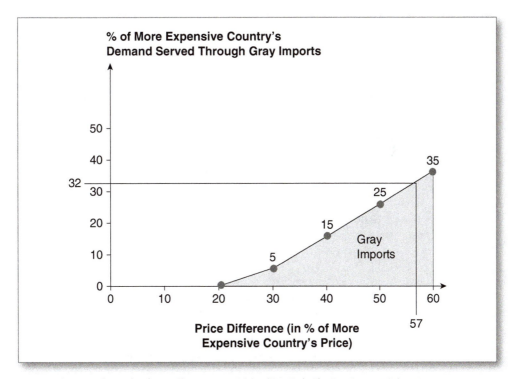

Source: Robert J. Dolan and Hermann Simon, *Power Pricing* (New York: The Free Press, 1996), 158.

and raise prices in low-priced countries so as to keep the price differentials for a product close to being within this 20 percent range. They termed this price range a price corridor (see Figure 12.7).[25]

To illustrate how a company can move its international pricing toward a 20 percent price corridor, let's look at how the existence of gray market commerce can affect the profitability of a price change. A company with a pattern of international product prices like that shown in Figure 12.7 might begin movement toward a price corridor by considering increasing the product's price in the country where it is the lowest, Country C in the Figure 12.7 example. It is likely that a portion of the product's sales in Country C are diverted for gray market resale in the other three countries—Countries A, B, and D—because the prices of the product's authorized sales in those countries are more than 20 percent higher than the product's price in Country C. A price increase in Country C can be expected to not only

Figure 12.7   A Set of International Product Prices and the Possibility of a Price Corridor

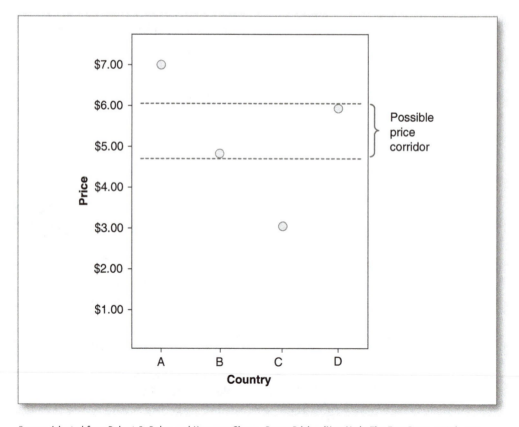

Source: Adapted from Robert J. Dolan and Hermann Simon, *Power Pricing* (New York: The Free Press, 1996), 157.

decrease sales in Country C but also decrease the amount of product sold in Country C that is diverted to replace sales from authorized outlets in the other three countries. Thus, the profit lost from a lost sale in Country C should be adjusted to reflect that some of this profit will be recovered from an increased likelihood of an authorized sale in the other three countries.

To include such an adjustment in the breakeven calculation for the considered price increase in Country C, we can bring an additional term into the denominator of the GBE formula:

$$BE = \frac{\Delta FC - (\Delta CM \times BS)}{CM - \$Adj_{GI}}$$

The term $\$Adj_{GI}$, the contribution-margin (CM) adjustment for gray imports, is the change in contribution dollars from authorized sales in high-priced countries that is caused by each unit change in product sales in the country where the price change is being considered. This change in contribution dollars is calculated by multiplying an estimate of the number of authorized sales created or lost by the number of contribution dollars produced by each authorized sale. Specifically, $\$Adj_{GI}$ is the product of the following two measures:

1. the absolute value of the change that occurs in the number of authorized purchases in high-priced countries per one-unit change in sales of the item in the country where the price change is being considered

2. the average dollar contribution margin of an authorized purchase that has been created or lost

For example, say the company selling a product in the four countries shown in Figure 12.7 has been selling 5,000 units per year in Country C at a price of $3.20 per unit with per-unit variable costs of $2.50. Say also that the average of the product's authorized-purchase prices in the other three countries is $6.00, the average per-unit variable costs in the other three countries is $3.00, and each unit change in sales in Country C is associated with a total change of 0.20 units of authorized sales in the other three countries because of changes in the number of gray imports in those countries. If the company is considering raising the product's price in Country C by $1.30, to move it closer to the product's price corridor, the breakeven sales level could be calculated from the GBE formula as follows:

$$BE = \frac{-\{[(\$4.50 - \$2.50) - (\$3.20 - \$2.50)] \times 5,000\}}{(\$4.50 - \$2.50) - [0.20 \times (\$6.00 - \$3.00)]}$$

$$BE = -[(\$2.00 - \$0.70) \times 5,000] / [\$2.00 - (0.20 \times \$3.00)]$$

$$BE = -(\$1.30 \times 5,000) / (\$2.00 - \$0.60)$$

$$BE = -\$6,500 / \$1.40$$

$$BE = -4,643 \text{ units}$$

This breakeven sales level of −4,643 is rather large (93% of base sales)—a considerably larger sales cushion than there would be without an effect of the prospective price change on authorized sales in the other three countries (−$6,500/$2.00 = −3,250, 65% of base sales). It indicates that it is very likely that the price increase being considered in Country C would be profitable for the company. Even if sales in Country C dropped to almost nothing, the resulting decrease in gray market sales that replace authorized sales in the other three countries would help make the price increase profitable. Also, including consideration of gray imports indicates that it is very unlikely that a *decrease* in the product's Country C price would be profitable. The Adj_{GI} term would cause the sales increase needed to break even from a price decrease to be considerably larger than what the price cut's breakeven sales level would be if no gray market sales were involved.

Note that both of these approaches to dealing with the gray imports problem are limited. The second approach, setting all international prices to be close to a 20 percent price corridor, is likely to lead to lower profits than leaving these prices free to respond to the environment of each country, assuming there were no gray imports. Using the first approach, making gray importing more difficult, would have the advantage of increasing the width of the price corridor, but as previously mentioned, would also be likely to increase costs. Neither of these approaches is entirely able to remove gray importing or its profit-eroding effects, but they serve as useful means to help manage this potentially serious source of leakage in the country-of-purchase price-segmentation fence.

Other Constraints on International Price Segmentation

Gray importing is a marketplace-related constraint on a seller's ability to use country of purchase as a price-segmentation fence. In addition to the marketplace, the actions of governments often limit the ability of an international marketer to sell a product at the price that is best considering the product's VTC, costs, and customer price sensitivity in each country. One type of government action consists of price controls, the government mandating of maximum prices. Price controls could cover all products, such as those imposed by the Brazilian government during its period of excessive inflation, or could be more selective, covering only certain products.[26] It is usually the case that price controls apply equally to local and foreign companies.

A country's government may also impose protective tariffs. These are schedules of import taxes, known as duties, that are designed to protect the local sellers of a product against low-priced competition from foreign producers. Protective tariff duties have declined considerably due to wide international acceptance of the General Agreement on Tariffs and Trade (GATT) and its successor, the World Trade Organization (WTO). However, in recent years, there has also been a rise in actions to counter what has been termed dumping.[27] Dumping is judged to occur when an imported product is sold at a price that harms local competitors and is lower than the imported product's price in the producing country. The typical antidumping action is for the importing country to impose a duty on the dumped product that raises its price enough to make it comparable to its price in its home country and closer to the prices of local competitors.

The rise in antidumping actions highlights the strength of the political forces that can drive a country's government to impose protective duties. An international seller who lowers a product's price to counter the effect of a protective duty, thereby absorbing some or all of it, might simply be inviting the government to increase the duty. A company selling a product in more than one country would be wise to consider political factors in developing the pricing strategy used for each country. For example, the efficient, large-scale U.S. growers of rice should consider the importance in Japan of domestic rice and the small, relatively inefficient farmers who produce it.[28] Rather than try to overcome Japan's protective tariffs on rice, the U.S. growers might adopt a skimming strategy—let prices stay high and focus on competing only within the limited import market.

Just as the Internet presents problems for zone pricing, it also creates difficulties for the use of country of purchase as a price-segmentation fence. These difficulties involve the increasing pervasiveness of online retailing. For example, many seniors in the United States buy cheaper prescription drugs from online pharmacies in Canada and other countries.[29] Although there are U.S. laws against this buying practice, these laws are difficult to enforce. For some products sold online, it is very apparent that the seller's costs do not differ between countries. This tends to lead consumers to judge price differences between countries as unfair. For example, Apple's iTunes music downloading service requires consumers to enter a billing address as part of their means-of-payment information. This has enabled Apple to charge customers in the United Kingdom $1.40 per song, while customers in France and Germany were charged only $1.20. Not surprisingly, British consumers have protested loudly.[30]

Pricing to Base-of-the-Pyramid Consumers

One of the challenges of pricing in international commerce is the issue of how to set prices low enough to appeal to the large number of people in developing nations who have very little buying power. The huge size of this market segment has led it to be referred to as "the base of the pyramid."[31] It is estimated that four billion people—almost two-thirds of the world's population—earn less than $2,000 per year. Such limited buying power appears to be beyond the abilities of price segmentation. How can a product's price be set low enough in developing countries to enable such low-income people to buy and yet still be profitable?

One approach to doing this is to manage a product's nominal price, which is its price in currency (e.g., dollars) as opposed to, say, its unit price (e.g., price per pound). By keeping a product's nominal price extremely low, the product can become affordable to the poor. For consumable products, this can be done by selling the products in small, single-use package sizes. In India and China, for example, Procter & Gamble sells single-use versions of its shampoo products. For durable products, low nominal prices can be achieved by what has been called "the shared-access model," where access to the product is separated from ownership. For a few pennies, the poor can buy, on a per-use basis, the services of a cell phone, computer, or refrigerator owned by a village entrepreneur. For services, low nominal prices can be accomplished through advances in automation and telecommunications. Thus, through local automated kiosks, banking, business advice, and other services can be offered to the poor at very low single-transaction prices.[32]

Note that a very low nominal price will not usually correspond to a very low unit price. Rather, it is likely that the per-ounce price of the single-use shampoo package is higher than if one buys it by the 10-ounce bottle. However, minimizing nominal prices has the benefit of giving the poor access to high-quality products that would otherwise be unavailable to them. As a form of price segmentation, it involves the use of both purchase quantity and country of purchase as fences to separate the segments.

THE GEOGRAPHY OF CYBERSPACE

The vast computer network known as the Internet is also often referred to as "cyberspace," which indicates that it is comprehended as a realm with a spatial aspect. Each webpage is a specific location in this space, all of the pages of a company's website are an area in this space, and the websites of similar types of companies comprise a region in this space. Given this, the website where a customer commits to a purchase could be considered the cyberspace location of his or her purchase. Selling the same item for different prices when purchased at different Internet locations would constitute using the Internet place of purchase as a price-segmentation fence.

One type of web-location price segmentation is between a seller's branded site and a shopping site. A branded website is the Internet location of a product's manufacturer (e.g., Sony.com) or of an online retailer (e.g., Amazon.com). For a particular product, a branded site gives only one price. By contrast, shopping websites (also called "shopping agents"), such as PriceScan.com, PriceGrabber.com, and Shopzilla.com, show the prices of many sellers of an item in a format that facilitates price comparison. Because it is likely that visitors to shopping sites are more price-sensitive than visitors to branded sites, retailers or manufacturers who sell directly to consumers will sometimes list an item at a lower price on shopping sites than on their branded sites.

For travel services, one of the largest categories of online commerce, finding a low price for an airline trip, a hotel, or a rental car can be somewhat complex. In addition to the branded travel sites (e.g., American.com), there are "transparent" shopping sites (e.g., Expedia.com, Orbitz.com), which act as online travel agencies, and "opaque" shopping sites (e.g., Hotwire .com, Priceline.com), which promise very low rates but do not provide the identities of the travel suppliers prior to booking.[33] Because travel service companies often offer the same product on each type of site at different prices, consumers tend to visit multiple websites to try to get the lowest rates. One study indicated that the typical consumer who buys travel services online visits an average of four websites before booking.[34] This suggests that the ease of movement between websites might make Internet location rather leaky as a price-segmentation fence.

SUMMARY

The location where a product is used or purchased is another important type of price-segmentation fence. Most sellers of industrial products use some form of delivered pricing, where the price that the seller quotes to the buyer includes shipping. As a result, sellers typically charge distant customers higher prices than they charge nearby customers. Sellers who want to be more price competitive to their distant customers will often absorb some shipping costs by setting the price differentials between distant and nearby customers to be smaller than the actual differences in shipping costs.

Location-based price segmentation is very common in retailing and is known as zone pricing. Higher retail prices may be warranted at selling locations that offer greater convenience to customers, involve higher costs, or serve customers who have lower price sensitivity because of high income or the lack of nearby price competition.

Products that are sold internationally are often sold at different prices in different countries. This makes sense because of differences between countries in a product's VTC, in the costs of doing business, and in customer price sensitivity between countries. Gray market importing may constitute a serious challenge to the effective use of country of purchase as a price-segmentation fence. Modifying the product for each country and/or decreasing the size of the price differentials between countries can reduce the amount of gray importing and yet still allow some price segmentation.

Because sites on the Internet can be considered locations, this type of geography can be also used as a means to accomplish price segmentation. When a seller offers a lower price to customers who are brought in by a shopping site than to customers who directly access the seller's branded site, then the seller is using Internet place of purchase as a price-segmentation fence.

KEY TERMS

FOB-origin pricing	uniform delivered price	price controls
delivered pricing	zone pricing	protective tariffs
FOB destination	free-standing inserts	duties
freight charge	buying power	dumping
basing-point pricing	gray market commerce	nominal price
industrial price zones	price corridor	branded site
freight absorption	contribution-margin (CM)	shopping site
pricing	adjustment for gray imports	

REVIEW AND DISCUSSION QUESTIONS

1. What is FOB-origin pricing, and how is it distinguished from delivered pricing?

2. What are some of the possible formats for communicating a delivered price?

3. What is freight absorption pricing? Explain how it uses bundling, as well as location of use, as a price-segmentation fence.

4. What is zone pricing? What types of retailers are most likely to use it?

5. Explain why selling a product at a location that is particularly convenient to customers is likely to warrant a higher product price. How might a seller learn which locations are most convenient?

6. How might factors such as customer income and competitive intensity be used in defining retail price zones?

7. Discuss how customers' judgments of fairness might affect the use of zone pricing.

8. When might zone pricing be particularly difficult to manage?

9. How can zone pricing be used by companies that engage in price advertising over a wide area or have a large amount of price information available on the Internet?

10. Explain why a product may have a different best price in different countries.

11. What is gray market importing? Why can it be a problem for the use of country of purchase as a price-segmentation fence?

12. Describe the two general approaches to dealing with the gray imports problem.

13. Indicate how the GBE formula can be modified to consider gray imports when evaluating a price change. Explain why this modification is appropriate.

14. What are protective tariffs, and how do they differ from governmental price controls?

15. What is dumping? How might considering the political forces behind antidumping actions be used in developing international pricing strategies?

16. How can the management of nominal prices help products reach the large numbers of poor people in developing countries? What are some means to manage nominal prices?

17. Describe the difference between a branded website and a shopping site. How can a seller use Internet location as a price-segmentation fence?

EXERCISES

1. A gravel works near Albany, New York, offers #7 pea gravel at $47 per ton, FOB-destination, in New York City. The FOB-destination price for the same product in Albany is $42 per ton.

   (a) What price-segmentation fence is being used here? What is the most likely factor that supports this price segmentation?

   (b) If it is the case that transporting a ton of gravel between Albany and New York costs approximately $10, what additional price-segmentation fence is being used? What is the most likely factor that supports this additional level of price segmentation?

2. The management of a large chain of convenience stores has noticed that customers in affluent neighborhoods are substantially less price-sensitive than customers in middle-income neighborhoods and is considering moving to zone pricing.

(a) If the chain were to institute zone pricing, give a few examples of how the prices of some convenience-store items would differ between the chain's price zones.

(b) What are some of the constraints on zone pricing that the management of this chain should consider?

3. Sales of digital cameras have been growing rapidly. However, most of this growth has occurred in the United States, Europe, and Japan. In anticipation of sales growth in other areas of the world, digital camera manufacturers are considering their strategies for international pricing.

(a) What are some factors that would lead the best price of a digital camera to differ between different countries?

(b) How might a digital camera manufacturer deal with the problem of gray importing in responding to these international differences in best prices for digital cameras?

4. The Duracell Company has been selling 20,000 two-D-cell packages per year to retailers in Brazil for $0.58 per package. The company sells the same packages to retailers in the United States for $1.20 per package. Assume that the company's variable costs for producing these batteries is $0.40 per package and all selling prices are FOB-origin.

(a) Calculate the breakeven sales level for a $0.10 increase in the price of this battery package in Brazil.

(b) Say it is discovered that several of the Brazilian retailers have been carrying out unauthorized resale of these battery packages in the United States. Market research has determined that each one-package decrease of battery sales in Brazil results in a 0.15-package increase in authorized battery sales in the United States. Given this information, recalculate the breakeven analysis described in Part (a).

(c) Explain the implications of the difference in the breakeven levels calculated in Parts (a) and (b).

5. A large U.S. company operates highly efficient cane sugar production facilities in Louisiana and Florida. Consideration of variable costs, the very low income of residents of the country of Guatemala, and the high prices of sugar produced by domestic Guatemalan sugar suppliers have indicated a very low best price for the company's sugar sold in Guatemala (lower than the price charged to U.S. customers). Why might it be impractical for the company to set such a low sugar price to Guatemalan customers?

NOTES

1. M. L. Greenhut, "Spatial pricing in the United States, West Germany, and Japan," *Economica* 48 (1981): 79–86.
2. Kent B. Monroe, *Pricing: Making Profitable Decisions* (New York: McGraw-Hill/Irwin, 2003), 459.
3. Louis Philips, *The Economics of Price Discrimination* (Cambridge: Cambridge University Press, 1983), 25.
4. Dan Scheraga, "One Price Doesn't Fit All," *Chain Store Age,* March 2001, 104–105.

5. Pradeep Chintagunta, Jean-Pierre Dube, and Vishal Singh, "Balancing Profitability and Customer Welfare in a Supermarket Chain" *Quantitative Marketing and Economics* 1 (2003): 111–147.

6. Kent B. Monroe, *Pricing: Making Profitable Decisions* (New York: McGraw-Hill/Irwin, 2003), 302.

7. Thomas T. Nagle and Reed Holden, *The Strategy and Tactics of Pricing* (Upper Saddle River, NJ: Prentice Hall, 2002), 84.

8. Alan L. Montgomery, "Creating Micro-Marketing Pricing Strategies Using Supermarket Scanner Data," *Marketing Science* 16, no. 4 (1997): 315–337.

9. Keith Reid, "In the Zone," *National Petroleum News* 96 (March 2004): 26–36.

10. Dan Scheraga, "One Price Doesn't Fit All," *Chain Store Age,* March 2001, 104–105.

11. Keith Reid, "In the Zone," *National Petroleum News* 96 (March 2004): 26–36.

12. Ibid.

13. Dan Scheraga, "One Price Doesn't Fit All," *Chain Store Age,* March 2001, 104–105.

14. Ibid.

15. Maria Atanasov, "In Moscow, 'Red October' Means Chocolate," *Fortune* 135 (June 9, 1997), 40.

16. Philip R. Cateora and John L. Graham, *International Marketing* (New York: McGraw-Hill/Irwin, 1999), 371.

17. Gerald Albaum, Jesper Strandskov, and Edwin Duerr, *International Marketing and Export Management* (Upper Saddle River, NJ: Prentice Hall, 2002), 454.

18. Steven Van Yoder, "Global Soft Drink Giants Coke and Pepsi Embrace Local Tastes and Customers South of the Border," *Brandmarketing* 7 (May 2000): 52.

19. Warren J. Keegan and Mark C. Green, *Global Marketing,* 3rd ed. (Upper Saddle River, NJ: Prentice Hall, 2003), 446.

20. Michael Levy and Barton A. Weitz, *Retailing Management,* 5th ed. (New York: McGraw-Hill/Irwin, 2004), 467.

21. Matthew B. Myers, "Incidents of Gray Market Activity Among U.S. Exporters: Occurrences, Characteristics, and Consequences," *Journal of International Business Studies* 30, no. 1 (1999): 105–126.

22. Michael Levy and Barton A. Weitz, *Retailing Management,* 5th ed. (New York: McGraw-Hill/Irwin, 2004), 467.

23. Hermann Simon and Eckhard Kucher, "Pricing in the New Europe—A Time Bomb?" *Pricing Strategy and Practice* 3, no. 1 (1995): 4–13.

24. Robert J. Dolan and Hermann Simon, *Power Pricing* (New York: The Free Press, 1996), 154–159.

25. Hermann Simon and Eckhard Kucher, "Pricing in the New Europe—A Time Bomb?" *Pricing Strategy and Practice* 3, no. 1 (1995): 4–13.

26. Warren J. Keegan and Mark C. Green, *Global Marketing,* 3rd ed. (Upper Saddle River, NJ: Prentice Hall, 2003), 458.

27. Ibid., 466.

28. Roger A. Kerin et al., *Marketing,* 7th ed. (New York: McGraw-Hill/Irwin, 2003), 176. Also Philip R. Cateora and John L. Graham, *International Marketing,* 10th ed. (New York: McGraw-Hill/Irwin, 1999), 107.

29. Laura Johannes, "Canadian Web Drugstores Offer Deep Discounts and Legal Quandaries," *Wall Street Journal,* January 18, 2001, B1.

30. James Niccolai, "British Music Fans Decry iTunes Pricing," *PC World,* September 17, 2004.

31. V. Kasturi Rangan, Michael Chu, and Djordjija Petkoski, "Segmenting the Base of the Pyramid," *Harvard Business Review,* June 2011, 113–117.

32. C. K. Prahalad and Allen Hammond, "Serving the World's Poor, Profitably," *Harvard Business Review,* September 2002, 48–57.

33. William J. McGee (2003), "Booking and Bidding Sight Unseen: A Consumer's Guide to Opaque Travel Web Sites," accessed June 27, 2005, www.consumerwebwatch.org.

34. Peter C. Yesawich, "Consistent pricing will give consumers booking confidence," *Hotel & Motel Management,* March 1, 2004, 18.

CHAPTER 13

Pricing of Interrelated Products

We have seen how the pattern of a firm's prices is affected by the use of various fences to accomplish price segmentation. A second aspect of price structure is the pattern of prices over the array of products offered by the firm.

Up until now, we have talked about the pricing of products considered individually. However, most sellers offer more than one product. Often there are interrelations between these products such that a price that is set for one item affects the sales levels of one or more other items. There are at least two general means by which the price of one item can affect the sales levels of others:

- In image interactions, an item's price affects the sales levels of other items by influencing the consumer's perception of the seller's other prices. For example, a grocer's low price on paper towels may increase sales of other items by enhancing the store's low-price image.

- In product interactions, an item's price affects the sales levels of related items by affecting its own sales. For example, if consumers usually use salad dressing when they use lettuce, then this product interaction may lead an increase in lettuce sales caused by lowering its price to also cause an increase in the sales level of salad dressing.

In this chapter, we discuss each of these two means by which the price of one item can affect the sales levels of other items.

PRODUCT INTERRELATIONS THROUGH IMAGE INTERACTIONS

The ability of an item's price to affect the sales levels of other items by virtue of its effect on the consumer's perceptions of the seller's other prices could have to do with the item's price being high or its being low. We first look at some image interactions that suggest benefits of pricing an item high and then some image interactions that suggest benefits of pricing an item low.

Image Effects of a High Price

Some sellers try to maintain an overall high-price image in order to help communicate high product quality and to encourage the sense that owning their products is a sign of affluence and good taste. This practice is known as prestige pricing. De Beers diamonds, Rolls-Royce automobiles, Rolex watches, and Gucci leather goods are just a few examples of manufacturers who practice prestige pricing.[1] Nordstrom and Tiffany are examples of retailers who engage in prestige pricing.

Prestige pricing can be weakened by even a few products or product lines that include items at low price points. For example, Gucci would not be wise to offer a handbag for less than $400. When Mercedes-Benz introduced its C-Class cars, designed to appeal to a lower-priced segment of the automobile market, its management ran the risk of diluting the company's valuable prestige image. Thus, prestige pricing puts constraints on a company's ability to *ever* use low price points.

As we saw in Chapter 7, the endings of prices can communicate information to customers. Thus, in prestige pricing, it is important to rely on 0- and 5-ending numbers and on prices that avoid the display of cents digits in order to maximally communicate classiness and high quality. The use of 9s in ending digits suggests to consumers prices that are discounted or, for other reasons, are low.[2] In addition to this, the negative connotations of 9-ending prices—impressions of lower quality and questionable honesty and integrity—should result in such price endings having little or no place in the context of a prestige pricing policy.[3]

Sometimes the ability of an item's high price to affect customer price perceptions does not involve the overall price image of a manufacturer or store but rather customer price impressions of only a few specific items. One example of this type of effect is the tendency for an item to gain in sales when it is a middle-priced item rather than highest-priced item in the consumer's choice set.[4] For example, the study results shown in Figure 13.1 indicate that, when

Figure 13.1 Results Indicating That the Presence of a High-Priced Alternative Can Affect Choice of a Middle-Priced Alternative

	Share %	
Category: Microwave Oven	**Set 1 (n = 60)**	**Set 2 (n = 60)**
Emerson (0.5 cu. ft.; regular $109.99; sale price 35% off)	57	27
Panasonic I (0.8 cu. ft.; regular $179.99; sale price 35% off)	43	60
Panasonic II (1.1 cu. ft.; regular $199.99; sale price 10% off)	—	13

Source: Itamar Simonson and Amos Tversky, "Choice in Context: Tradeoff Contrast and Extremeness Aversion," *Journal of Marketing Research* 29 (August 1992): 281–295.

given a choice between two microwave ovens, 43 percent of respondents chose the $179.99 model. However, when a more expensive $199.99 oven was added to the choice set, the proportion of respondents who chose the same $179.99 oven increased to 60 percent.[5] Although part of this effect involves people's general tendency to find safety in the middle option, part of it is also likely to involve the use of the high price as a reference point so as to make the middle price seem more reasonable. As we saw in Chapter 7, prices observed during shopping can affect the level of the consumer's internal reference price for a product.

This effect of a high price suggests the benefits of offering customers at least one very high-priced alternative, even if it is known that few customers will purchase this high-priced item. This could be done by introducing a new high-priced item or by raising the price of one that is currently being sold. Such a high-priced item, offered to enhance consumers' perceptions of other items, could be termed a "price decoy." This effect of high price also suggests the benefits of presenting consumers with the higher-priced items of a product line before presenting them with the lower-priced items.[6] This is perhaps a reason why many mail order and other retail catalogs show their most expensive offerings in the first few pages.

Image Effects of a Low Price

In marketing environments characterized by aggressive price competition, such as grocery retailing, it can be important for a seller to maintain an overall low-price image. To do this, it is usually not necessary to have a lower price than competitors on all items. One finding from consumer research is that a low-price image is determined more by the number of products sold at a lower price (which could be termed a frequency cue) than by the size of the price differences (which could be termed a magnitude cue).[7] For example, although the two price lists shown in Figure 13.2 have the same totals, the prices at Clark's are lower than those of Taylor's on twenty of the thirty items. Consumers who viewed these lists tended to see Clark's as being a lower-priced store. This finding suggests that a low-priced seller would be better off having a small price difference on a large number of items than a large difference on a small number of items.

It has also been found that not all items are equal in contributing to a retailer's price image.[8] Items that are particularly powerful in influencing a retailer's price image are known as price exemplars.[9] Because a consumer must be aware of an item's usual price to know if the item's price at a particular store is high or low, price exemplars are likely to be the items that show the highest levels of consumer price awareness. As we saw in Chapter 7, prices of items that are frequently purchased and that are more stable both between brands and over time are more likely to be known by consumers. Thus, the 6-ounce can of chunk light tuna, the half-gallon container of ice cream, or the 14-ounce package of hot dogs would be more likely to serve as price exemplars than the 1-ounce bottle of parsley flakes or the three-pack of plastic coat hangers.

PRODUCT INTERRELATIONS THROUGH PRODUCT INTERACTIONS

When an item's price influences the sales levels of other items through an image interaction, it is the influencing item's price rather than its sales that is having the effect. For example,

Figure 13.2 Two Price Lists That Add Up to the Same Amount—But Clark's Prices Are Lower Than Taylor's on Twenty of the Thirty Items

	Clark's	Taylor's
12 oz. Oscar Mayer bologna	1.89	1.95
7. oz. Banquet chicken pie	.73	.78
10.5 oz. Progresso calm sauce	1.49	1.34
15.5 oz. Ragu pizza sauce	1.28	1.35
32 oz. Wesson corn oil	2.18	2.21
15 oz. Quaker cinnamon Life	2.03	1.85
18 oz. Welch's grape jelly	1.25	1.32
100 ct. Red Rose tea bags	2.88	2.91
6.25 oz. Starkist light tuna	.73	.62
48 oz. Kraft mayonnaise	2.44	2.53
15 oz. Kellogg raisin bran	2.35	2.44
32 oz. Heinz ketchup	1.25	1.14
32 oz. Vlasic Polish dills	2.03	2.12
24 oz. Log Cabin lite syrup	2.44	2.57
48 oz. Ocean Spray cran-raspberry juice	2.09	1.93
24 oz. Hershey's chocolate syrup 1.80	1.80	1.65
22 oz. USDA Grade "A" Cornish hens	2.07	2.22
46 oz. HI-C Drinks-assorted flavors	.91	.96
1 lb. Farmland-Smoked sliced bacon	2.34	2.17
16 oz. Mueller's spaghetti	.90	.95
20 oz. Tide detergent	1.25	1.28
50 oz. Musselman's apple sauce	1.97	1.83
7 oz. Uncle Ben's Minute Rice	.98	1.06
26.5 oz. Nestea ice tea mix 2.79	2.79	2.62
12 oz. Lysol disinfectant spray	3.19	3.05
48 ct. Dixie-9" paper plates 1.74	1.74	1.87
10 oz. Wheat Thins crackers	2.22	2.29
12 oz. Thomas' English muffins	1.69	1.75
10.5 oz. Jergen's liquid soap	1.27	1.38
46 oz. V-8 vegetable cocktail juice	1.18	1.22

Source: Joseph W. Alba, Susan M. Broniarczyk, Terence A. Shimp, and Joel E. Urbany, "The Influence of Prior Beliefs, Frequency Cues, and Magnitude Cues on Consumers' Perceptions of Comparative Price Data," *Journal of Consumer Research* 21 (September 1994): 219–235.

keeping a particular Gucci handbag at a high price will help the sales of other items by supporting the price image of the Gucci brand. This will occur whether or not the handbag that is kept at the high price sells poorly or sells well.

By contrast, when an item's price influences the sales levels of other items through a product interaction, the sales of the influencing item do matter. This is because of the connections between the various products that are sold by a company, which are based on how these products are purchased or used by customers. As a result of these connections, a price change that affects the sales of one product will also affect the sales of others. There are two possibilities concerning the direction of the effect that a product's sales can have on the sales of another product.

Substitutes

When a change in the sales level of one item causes the sales level of another item to change in the opposite direction, then the two items are referred to as substitutes. This relation means that when the sales level of the first item increases, the sales level of the second item will decrease, or when the sales level of the first item decreases, the sales level of the second item will increase. In other words, if one item is a substitute of another, then their sales levels are negatively correlated.

Usually, such negative sales correlations are caused by the purchased items being alternatives to each other. For example, on a given occasion, a motorist will buy regular gasoline or premium but not both. Thus, there will be a tendency for increases in the sales of premium to be associated with decreases in the sales of regular. In general, different brands or varieties of the same product offered by a retailer will tend to be substitutes. For example, an electronics retailer is likely to observe that as sales of Toshiba TVs increase, sales of RCA TVs decrease. Different items in a manufacturer's product line will also tend to be substitutes. For example, Procter & Gamble is likely to observe that as sales of their Pampers brand of disposable diapers increase, sales of their Luvs brand of disposable diapers decrease.

Let's say that the electronics retailer decreases prices on Toshiba TVs in hopes of increased profits due to an increase in Toshiba sales. The retailer should also recognize that if this sales increase of Toshiba TVs also causes a decrease in the sales of the retailer's RCA TVs, then the loss of profit from the unsold RCA TVs will have to be subtracted from whatever increased profits are made from selling more Toshibas. In general, if a seller offers substitutes of an item, it makes it more difficult for the seller to profit from a price decrease on the item.

On the other hand, an increase in the prices of the Toshibas is likely to decrease their sales. If this sales decrease of Toshiba TVs has the effect of also causing an increase in the sales of the RCA TVs, then the added profits from the RCA TVs will tend to offset whatever decreased profits result from selling fewer Toshiba TVs. In general, if a seller offers substitutes of an item, it makes it easier for the seller to profit from a price increase on the item.

Complements

When a change in the sales level of one item causes the sales level of another item to change in the same direction, then the two items are referred to as complements. This relation means that when the sales level of one item increases so will the sales level of the other item, or when the sales level of one item decreases so will the sales level of the other item. In other words, if one item is a complement of another, then their sales levels are positively correlated.

Usually, such positive sales correlations are caused by the items being purchased or used together. For example, many consumers use peanut butter and jelly together in sandwiches containing both items. Thus, there will be a tendency for increases in a store's sales of peanut butter to be associated with increases in the sales of jelly, and sales decreases in peanut butter will tend to be associated with sales decreases in jelly. Peanut butter and jelly are used together because of taste or habit. Other products are complements because the two together are necessary for a functional product. For example, what good is a video game console without video games? What good is a razor without blades? Some products are complements because customers find it convenient to purchase them together. For example, while at a drugstore to get a prescription filled, a consumer may find it convenient to also purchase a bottle of shampoo or hand lotion. Other products are complements because there are practical advantages to purchasing them together. For example, a man who has selected a new suit may find having the suit there increases his ability to pick out just the right matching ties.

The same logic that indicates that offering substitutes makes it more difficult for a seller to profit from a price decrease and easier to profit from a price increase also indicates that the opposite is true for complements. For example, a camera shop operator considering a price increase on digital cameras would need to take into account the profits that would be lost on the memory cards, rechargeable batteries, and other items whose sales are likely to decrease as a result of decreases in the sales of digital cameras. On the other hand, the profitability of a price decrease on digital cameras would benefit from the added sales of memory cards and the other complementary items that would result from increased camera sales. Thus, in general, if a seller offers complements of an item, it makes it harder for the seller to profit from a price increase on the item but easier for the seller to profit from a price decrease on the item.

Loss-Leader Discounts

This ability of complements to help make a price decrease profitable leads many sellers to offer loss-leader discounts. These discounts are often called "promotional," but they differ from promotional discounts in that their main purpose is not to communicate information about a product or even about a store. Rather, the main purpose of offering a loss-leader discount on an item is to lead customers to make the purchases that are complementary to the purchase of the discounted item. The discounted item is known as a *loss* leader because its discounted price may be less than its variable costs. For example, cell phone shops will often deeply discount cell phones or even offer them for free in order to attract customers to their very profitable complementary product, the cell phone service.[10]

The success of a loss-leader discount is dependent on two factors. The first is that the prospective loss leader should have a sufficient number of complements that provide sufficiently high contribution margins. The second factor is that the prospective loss leader's low price is able to attract a large number of customers to purchase the loss-leader item. Drugstore chains, such as CVS and Rite-Aid, often find it profitable to offer loss-leader discounts because they carry a large number of shampoos, lotions, vitamins, and other high-margin items that can serve as complements. For the loss-leader items, these chains tend to use products such as facial tissues or soft drinks, because they are widely purchased and their sales levels tend to be price-sensitive. By varying over time the particular items used as loss leaders, the drugstore chains are able to increase the attention-getting ability of these offers. Supermarket chains, such as the New York area's Shop-Rite, often offer loss-leader discounts on turkeys at Thanksgiving. These discounts are successful because there is wide interest in getting a low-price (or free) turkey at that time, and when the customers come to the store to get their turkeys, they are likely to buy there many of the high-margin items they will need to complete their preparations for the Thanksgiving dinner.

Identifying Product Interactions

To effectively take product interactions into account when pricing interrelated products, it is necessary to be able to identify the relevant interactions that occur within any particular group of products. The task of identifying these interactions should be based on an understanding of the customer's needs and behaviors. For example, understanding that consumers typically use lettuce to make salads indicates that other common components of salads—such as tomatoes, onions, croutons, and salad dressing—are good candidates for being complementary products relevant to the pricing of lettuce. Observing the items that salad-eating consumers would use if lettuce were not available—such as spinach or coleslaw—would provide possible candidates for relevant substitutes of lettuce.

Note that it is important to understand the causal order in the customer's activities. For example, consumers are more likely to make a decision to use lettuce that will cause them to need salad dressing than they are to make a decision to use salad dressing that causes them to need lettuce. This is of particular importance for product interactions that are based on purchase convenience. For example, a liquor store owner might know that most of the store's customers come in primarily for beer, but some buy wine also while there. In that situation, it would be more likely that lowering the price of beer would cause increased sales of wine than lowering the price of wine would cause increased sales of beer. On the other hand, if most customers go to the store primarily for wine but some also buy beer then it would be more likely that beer would be the complementary product.

In looking for product interactions, the manager should consider the full range of possibilities. For identifying possible substitute items, we saw how a manager should look for products that are considered by consumers to be alternatives. But, to be complete in identifying possible product substitutes, the manager might also consider the broader effect of one purchase on the customer's ability to make other purchases. For example, a young husband and wife who have just purchased an expensive sofa may have little left in their budget to purchase any other decorating item sold by the store. In a situation of such a budget constraint, all of the store's other products could be considered substitutes of the sofa.

For identifying possible complementary items, we saw how a manager should look for products that are purchased or used together. But, to be complete in identifying possible product complements, the manager should also consider the following:

- *Products purchased at different times.* For example, if first-time car buyers, who often purchase small cars, are likely to purchase larger cars from the same company in subsequent years, then these larger cars could be considered complements of the company's small cars.

- *Products sold through different distribution channels.* For example, if attending a rock band's concerts lead consumers to purchase CDs of the band's music, then the band's CDs could be considered complements of the band's concert tickets.

- *Products purchased by other customers.* For example, if increases in the number of women patrons of a dating bar lead to increases in the number of male patrons, then the drinks purchased by the men could be considered complements of those purchased by the women.[11]

QUANTIFYING PRODUCT INTERACTIONS

To take product interactions into account in price setting, it is necessary to quantify these interactions. In practice, the size of the interactions between products is often estimated intuitively. For example, from observation of customer behavior, a camera shop operator could estimate that the average purchaser of a digital camera buys $40 worth of memory cards during the same visit to the store. This, then, could serve as the camera shop operator's estimate of the degree to which memory cards are complements of digital cameras.

However, if the necessary data are available, it is possible to more accurately quantify product interactions, as well as verify their existence, through the use of statistical techniques such as multiple regression. The starting points for determining what data are needed are reasoned guesses, or hypotheses, concerning how products may be interrelated. For each product or product group whose sales level is hypothesized to be caused by another one—in other words, a "candidate" substitute or complement—there must be several pieces of information. There must be a measure of the sales level of the candidate substitute or complement, a measure of the sales level of the product that is hypothesized to be affecting the candidate's sales, and measures of any other variables that might have an affect on the candidate's sales.

If we focus on time-series regression, as we did in Chapter 9, we would require these measures in the form of a data matrix where each line of the matrix would consist of a value for each measure for one time period. The data matrix should have (1) a sufficiently large number of time periods, (2) sufficient variation over time in the affecting-product's sales level, and (3) sufficient independence between the affecting-product's sales level and the other variables that might affect the sales level of the candidate substitute or complement.

Illustrative Data Matrix

A data matrix that illustrates what would be needed is shown in Figure 13.3. This matrix shows what some data might look like for a small chain of men's clothing stores whose manager is interested in quantifying some key product interactions. There are thirty-six rows in this matrix, one for each of the months over a three-year time span. There are eight columns in this matrix, one for each of the variables that will be used in this analysis of product interactions.

Figure 13.3   Illustrative Data Matrix for Using Regression to Quantify Product Interactions

Month	Suit sales	Coat price	Coat adv $	Coat sales	Accessory price	Accessory adv $	Accessory sales
1	360	124	5.8	409	24.07	3.4	21.9
2	419	145	4.2	469	52.11	2.6	18.5
3	339	156	10.4	489	58.99	2.9	15.8
4	434	178	20.7	435	35.27	3.8	17.4
5	413	182	9.7	464	38.81	2.7	17.1
6	334	158	8.6	482	26.31	2.5	19.0
7	432	193	7.8	447	44.50	3.2	15.3
8	568	168	7.6	414	24.71	2.6	22.1
9	501	177	11.4	407	44.60	2.8	26.8
10	389	175	15.9	514	44.38	2.7	18.1
11	305	189	14.9	505	50.15	2.6	16.5
12	392	156	16.0	554	52.17	3.1	17.0
1	504	187	11.8	382	38.91	1.0	16.5
2	468	148	6.8	380	26.50	2.6	19.5
3	572	203	12.1	410	57.20	1.2	20.2
4	597	138	8.1	373	48.55	2.9	23.5
5	506	167	10.0	433	59.57	2.7	21.0
6	511	189	7.9	437	45.37	3.4	21.5
7	533	155	16.3	420	33.83	2.0	23.4
8	519	189	8.7	401	49.06	3.0	21.7
9	592	167	7.7	403	22.38	4.5	27.8
10	538	202	9.3	438	51.19	3.7	21.7
11	501	168	18.5	363	35.74	2.5	27.6
12	682	199	14.7	404	42.05	3.0	22.7
1	485	181	12.0	305	55.74	1.5	22.3
2	661	216	9.5	337	67.47	3.5	24.2
3	516	135	5.8	383	21.47	3.9	25.9
4	497	188	5.4	344	59.53	3.0	22.0
5	524	146	12.4	407	19.12	2.7	25.3
6	612	201	6.7	205	52.40	3.1	24.7
7	589	147	6.1	416	34.01	3.5	28.8
8	597	222	7.8	257	51.40	3.2	28.3
9	405	186	7.4	292	43.38	3.9	18.8
10	540	176	4.8	380	52.90	4.1	26.1
11	585	213	10.7	265	18.24	2.9	26.7
12	498	211	10.4	279	27.07	1.9	22.7
Means	497.72	175.97	9.40	397.31	41.92	2.9	21.90

The first column, labeled "Month," is the month of the year (coded 1 = January, 2 = February, etc.). The second column, labeled "Suit Sales," is the number of suits sold chain-wide in each of the thirty-six months. The manager hypothesizes that shoppers who don't buy suits often buy sport coats instead. In other words, he suspects that sport coats are substitutes of suits. To verify and quantify this hypothesis, the manager has included in the data matrix information on the sales levels of sport coats (fifth column, labeled "Coat Sales," coded as the number of sport coats sold) and information on two variables other than sales of suits that might affect sales of sport coats: the average price of sport coats (third column, labeled "Coat Price," coded in dollars) and the average amount spent by the chain on sport coat advertising during each month (fourth column, labeled "Coat Adv $," coded in thousands of dollars).

The manager further hypothesizes that shoppers who buy suits will often also buy items such as belts, ties, socks, hats, scarves, cuff links, and handkerchiefs. In other words, he suspects that these items are complements of suits. The manager does not have detailed data available on each of these items but does have data on these items combined together, which form the category that the manager calls "accessories." The data on the sales levels of accessories for each month can be seen in the eighth column of the data matrix shown in Figure 13.3 (labeled "Accessory Sales," coded in thousands of dollars). As with sport coats, the manager has information on two variables other than sales of suits that might affect sales of accessories: the average price of an accessory item (sixth column, labeled "Accessory Price," coded in dollars) and the average amount spent by the chain on accessory advertising during each month (seventh column, labeled "Accessory Adv $," coded in thousands of dollars).

Regression Analyses

To use regression to verify the existence of product interactions and to quantify the size of these relations, it is necessary to carry out a separate regression analysis for each candidate substitute and complement that has been hypothesized. When a candidate substitute or complement is being examined, it is the sales level of this item that is the dependent variable (DV) in the regression analysis. The independent variables (IVs) in the regression analysis are the sales level of the item that is hypothesized to affect the candidate's sales and the other available measures that may have affected the candidate's sales level over the time period included in the analysis.

As an example, let's imagine we are helping the men's clothing store manager use regression to test and quantify his hypothesis that sport coats are substitutes of suits. If the available data are included in the data matrix shown in Figure 13.3, then the formal model for this regression analysis would be as follows:

$$\text{Coat sales} = a + b_1\text{Month} + b_2\text{Suit Sales} + b_3\text{Coat Price} + b_4\text{Coat Adv \$}$$

This regression analysis provides an indication of the degree to which the four IVs— (1) Month, (2) Suit Sales, (3) Coat Price, and (4) Coat Adv $—are able to explain the differences that occurred in the sales level of sport coats over the observed time periods. The regression coefficients, b_1, b_2, b_3, and b_4, provide the quantitative measure of the effects of each of these IVs. Because sport coats are a candidate substitute of suits, our primary interest is in the relationship between Suit Sales and Coat Sales. This means we will want to know b_2, which is the size of the expected change in Coat Sales when the Suit Sales variable is changed by one unit, holding constant the effects of the other IVs.

We could run this regression analysis on sport coats sales using Excel 2007, as we did for the conjoint analysis in Chapter 3 and for the determination of price elasticity in Chapter 9. After bringing the data matrix into the spreadsheet, we would select Data Analysis on the Data tab and then, in the Data Analysis dialog box, select Regression. For the "Y range," we would enter the endpoints for the fifth column of the data matrix, which contain the DV, Coat Sales. For the "X range," we would enter the endpoints for the rectangle comprising the first through fourth columns of the data matrix, which contain the IVs, Month, Suit Sales, Coat Price, and Coat Adv $.

The output of this regression analysis is shown in Figure 13.4. The lower part of the output's analysis of variance (ANOVA) table gives the regression coefficients for the four IVs, and their level of statistical significance (the "P-value"). There were positive effects of month of the year (b_1 = +2.831) and sport coat advertising (b_4 = +4.442) on sport coat sales, but these effects were not statistically significant (which means that they could have been due to random error). There was a negative and statistically significant effect of sport coat prices (b_3 = −1.159) indicating that, as would be expected, sport coat sales decreased as sport coat prices increased. However, the number in this analysis that is of the greatest interest is the regression coefficient of the suit sales variable (b_2 = −0.334). This coefficient has a negative sign and is statistically significant, thus supporting the hypothesis that sport coats are substitutes of suits. Specifically, the regression analysis quantifies this substitute relationship, indicating that, over this three-year period, every suit sold resulted in the loss of 0.334 units of sport coat sales. In other words, it appears that about every third suit was purchased instead of a sport coat.

Regression analysis can be used in a similar way to test and quantify the men's clothing store manager's hypothesis that accessories are complements of suits. However, for testing this relationship, a separate regression is needed, this time with the sales level of accessories as the DV. Assuming again that the available data are included in the data matrix shown in Figure 13.3, the formal model for this regression analysis would be as follows:

$$\text{Accessory sales} = a + b_1\text{Month} + b_2\text{Suit Sales} + b_3\text{Accessory Price} + b_4\text{Accessory Adv \$}$$

To run this analysis using Excel, it is necessary to make a slight modification of the data matrix. One way to do this to make a copy of the spreadsheet used to do the sport coat analysis. On this copy, we would delete the sport coat variables, columns 3 through 5, in order to make the four IVs of this analysis of accessory sales lie in a contiguous block. Then we would proceed as with the sport coat analysis. For the "Y range," in the regression dialog box, we would enter the endpoints for the fifth column of the modified data matrix, which contains the DV, Accessory Sales. For the "X range," we would enter the endpoints for the rectangle comprising the first through fourth columns of the modified data matrix, which contain the IVs, Month, Suit Sales, Accessory Price, and Accessory Adv $.

The output of this regression analysis is shown in Figure 13.5. From the lower part of the output's ANOVA table, we see that there were positive but nonsignificant effects of

Figure 13.4 Excel Output for the Regression Analysis—How Sales of Suits Affect Sales of Sport Coats

SUMMARY OUTPUT

Regression Statistics	
Multiple R	0.681
R Square	0.464
Adjusted R Square	0.395
Standard Error	59.132
Observations	36.000

ANOVA

	df	SS	MS	F	Significance F
Regression	4.000	93721.252	23430.313	6.701	0.001
Residual	31.000	108394.387	3496.593		
Total	35.000	202115.639			

	Coefficients	Standard Error	t Stat	P-value	Lower 95%	Upper 95%
Intercept	704.007	82.443	8.539	0.000	535.862	872.152
Month	2.831	3.170	0.893	0.379	-3.635	9.298
Suit sales	-0.334	0.118	-2.818	0.008	-0.575	-0.092
Coat price	-1.159	0.464	-2.501	0.018	-2.105	-0.214
Coat adv $	4.442	2.682	1.656	0.108	-1.029	9.912

Figure 13.5 Excel Output for the Regression Analysis—How Sales of Suits Affect Sales of Accessories

SUMMARY OUTPUT

Regression Statistics	
Multiple R	0.772
R Square	0.596
Adjusted R Square	0.544
Standard Error	2.621
Observations	36.000

ANOVA

	df	SS	MS	F	Significance F
Regression	4.000	314.624	78.656	11.446	0.000
Residual	31.000	213.036	6.872		
Total	35.000	527.660			

	Coefficients	Standard Error	t Stat	P-value	Lower 95%	Upper 95%
Intercept	7.434	3.217	2.311	0.028	0.873	13.995
Month	0.090	0.131	0.683	0.500	-0.178	0.358
Suit sales	0.028	0.005	5.859	0.000	0.019	0.038
Accessory price	-0.071	0.034	-2.119	0.042	-0.140	-0.003
Accessory adv $	0.942	0.604	1.559	0.129	-0.291	2.175

month of the year ($b_1 = +0.090$) and accessory advertising ($b_4 = +0.942$) on accessory sales, and a negative and statistically significant effect of accessory prices ($b_3 = -0.071$). As with the sport coat regression, the key number in this analysis is the regression coefficient of the suit sales variable ($b_2 = +0.028$). This coefficient has a positive sign and is statistically significant, thus supporting the hypothesis that accessories are indeed complements of suits. Specifically, the regression analysis quantifies this complement relationship, indicating that, over this three-year period, every suit sold resulted in an average of $28 (i.e., 0.028 thousands of dollars) of additional accessory sales.

PRICE SETTING IN THE PRESENCE OF PRODUCT INTERACTIONS

When setting prices on products that interact with other products, it is important to take these product interactions into account. The process of determining the best price for an item can be made more accurate by considering the profits that are gained or lost through changes in the sales of the item's substitutes and/or complements.

Pricing in the Presence of Substitutes

When evaluating a price change on an item that has one or more substitutes among the seller's array of products, the price setter should recognize how the price change would affect the profits obtained from the substitute items. If the price change being considered is an increase, then some of the profit lost from a decrease in the item's sales would be offset by profits from increased sales of a substitute. We saw this in the discussion of gray market imports in Chapter 12: Some profit lost from raising an item's price in one country can be recovered through the increased likelihood of an authorized purchase, instead of a gray market purchase, in another country. On the other hand, if the price change being considered is a decrease, then some of the profit gained from an increase in the item's sales would be lost through lower sales of a substitute.

This profit gained or lost from sales of a substitute can be taken into account by bringing in an additional term to the denominator of the generalized breakeven (GBE) formula. In Chapter 12, this term was written as $\$Adj_{GI}$, the contribution-margin (CM) adjustment for gray imports. More generally, it can be referred to as $\$Adj_S$, the CM adjustment for substitutes. With this term included, the GBE formula becomes this:

$$BE = \frac{\Delta FC - (\Delta CM \times BS)}{CM - \$Adj_S}$$

Note that subtracting $\$Adj_S$ from the new contribution margin of the item for which the price change is being considered affects a prospective price increase and decrease in opposite ways. By decreasing the size of the denominator of the GBE formula, this adjustment increases the size of the sales cushion, the sales decrease that can be endured before a price increase has the effect of lowering profits. However, decreasing the size of the GBE formula's denominator also increases the size of the sales increase necessary before a price decrease has the effect of raising profits. Thus, this adjustment makes it easier for a price increase to be profitable and harder for a price decrease to be profitable.

The CM adjustment for substitutes can be defined more specifically in terms of the "price-change item"—the item for which the price change is being evaluated:

$$\$Adj_S = |\text{change in contribution dollars from sales of a substitute}$$
$$\text{for each unit sales change of the price-change item}|$$

The absolute value indicators in this definition tell us that, independent of the direction of the change in the substitute's contribution dollars, the value of $\$Adj_S$ is always positive. Note that this change in the substitute's contribution dollars can be calculated from either of two quantifications of the product interaction—(1) a unit-change measure or (2) a dollar-change measure:

$$\$AdjS = |\text{unit change in sales of a substitute for each unit sales change}$$
$$\text{of the price-change item}| \times \$CM \text{ of the substitute}$$

$$\$AdjS = |\$ \text{ change in sales of a substitute for each unit sales change of the}$$
$$\text{price-change item}| \times \text{proportion CM of the substitute}$$

For example, using a unit-change measure, an electronics retailer may observe that every Toshiba TV sold leads to the sale of 0.2 fewer RCA TVs. If the $\$CM$ on the average RCA TV is $130, then $\$Adj_S$ equals 0.2 times $130, or $26. Using the dollar-change measure, the retailer would observe that every Toshiba TV sold leads to an average decrease of $65 in the retailer's sales revenue from RCA TVs. If the proportion CM on the average RCA TV is 0.40 (i.e., 40 percent), then $\$Adj_S$ equals $65 times 0.40, or $26.

Example of Calculating a Breakeven With Substitutes

The manager of a dinner restaurant is evaluating the possibility of changing the price of the restaurant's popular chicken entrée. The variable cost per unit of the chicken entrée is $7, its current price is $12, and the restaurant currently sells fifty-four chicken entrées per day. The restaurant also sells a beef entrée, with a variable cost of $10 per unit and a current price of $15. The manager uses his past experience to estimate that every chicken entrée sold leads to the loss of half of a beef entrée. Given this, the breakeven sales level of a $1 price decrease on the chicken entrée, without considering the substitute, would be as follows:

$$BE = \frac{-[(\$11 - \$7) - (\$12 - \$7)] \times 54}{(\$11 - \$7)}$$

$$BE = -[(\$4 - \$5) \times 54] / \$4$$

$$BE = -(-\$1 \times 54) / \$4$$

$$BE = \$54 / \$4$$

$$BE = 13.5 \text{ entrées per day}$$

The breakeven sales level of a $1 chicken entrée price decrease, *with* consideration of the substitute, would be as follows:

$$BE = \frac{-[(\$11 - \$7) - (\$12 - \$7)] \times 54}{(\$11 - \$7) - [1/2 \times (\$15 - \$10)]}$$

$$BE = -[(\$4 - \$5) \times 54] / [\$4 - (1/2 \times \$5)]$$

$$BE = -(-\$1 \times 54) / (\$4 - \$2.50)$$

$$BE = \$54 / \$1.50$$

$$BE = 36 \text{ entrées per day}$$

Note that considering the substitute substantially raises the breakeven level for the price decrease. If the manager had calculated the breakeven for this price decrease without considering the relation between the chicken and beef entrées, then a sales increase of, say, twenty chicken entrées per day would have seemed to lead to an increase in profits. In reality, given the presence of the substitute item, it would have represented a decrease in profits.

In addition to considering a $1 price decrease in the chicken entrée, the manager might also consider the possibility of a $1 price increase. The breakeven sales level of a $1 price increase on the chicken entrée, without considering the substitute, would be as follows:

$$BE = \frac{-[(\$13 - \$7) - (\$12 - \$7)] \times 54}{(\$13 - \$7)}$$

$$BE = -[(\$6 - \$5) \times 54] / \$6$$

$$BE = -(\$1 \times 54) / \$6$$

$$BE = -\$54 / \$6$$

$$BE = -9 \text{ entrées per day}$$

The breakeven sales level of a $1 chicken entrée price increase, *with* consideration of the substitute, would be as follows:

$$BE = \frac{-[(\$13 - \$7) - (\$12 - \$7)] \times 54}{(\$13 - \$7) - [1/2 \times (\$15 - \$10)]}$$

$$BE = -[(\$6 - \$5) \times 54] / [\$6 - (1/2 \times \$5)]$$

$$BE = -(\$1 \times 54) / (\$6 - \$2.50)$$

$$BE = -\$54 / \$3.50$$

$$BE = -15.4 \text{ entrées per day}$$

Note again that considering the substitute substantially changes the breakeven level. If the manager had calculated the breakeven for this price increase without considering the relation between the chicken and beef entrées, then a sales decrease of, say, twelve chicken entrées per day would have seemed to lead to a decrease in profits. In reality, given the presence of the substitute item, it would have represented an increase in profits.

Pricing in the Presence of Complements

When evaluating a price change on an item that has one or more complements among the seller's array of products, the price setter should recognize how the price change would affect the profits obtained from the complementary items. If the price change being considered is an increase, then the profits lost from a decrease in the item's sales would be compounded by the loss of profits from the decreased sales of complementary items. On the other hand, if the price change being considered is a decrease, then the profits gained from an increase in the item's sales would be further increased by profits from higher sales of the complements.

The profit gained or lost from sales of a complementary item can be taken into account by bringing an additional term to the denominator of the GBE formula. This term can be referred to as $Adj_c, the **CM adjustment for complements**. With this term included, the GBE formula becomes this:

$$BE = \frac{\Delta FC - (\Delta CM \times BS)}{CM + \$Adj_c}$$

Note that $Adj_c is added to the new contribution margin of the item for which the price change is being considered, rather than being subtracted. By increasing the size of the denominator of the GBE formula, this adjustment decreases the size of the sales increase that must be achieved before a price decrease has the effect of raising profits. However, increasing the size of the GBE formula's denominator also decreases the size of the sales cushion, the sales decrease allowable before a price increase has the effect of reducing profits. Thus, this adjustment makes it easier for a price decrease to be profitable and harder for a price increase to be profitable.

The CM adjustment for complements can be defined in terms of the price-change item as follows:

$$\$Adj_c = |\text{change in contribution dollars from sales of a complement for each unit sales change of the price-change item}|$$

As with $Adj_s, the value of $Adj_c is always positive and can be calculated from either a unit-change measure or a dollar-change measure of the product interaction:

$$\$Adj_c = |\text{unit change in sales of a complement for each unit sales change of the price-change item}| \times \$CM \text{ of the complement}$$

$$\$Adj_c = |\$ \text{ change in sales of a complement for each unit sales change of the price-change item}| \times \text{proportion CM of the complement}$$

For example, using a unit-change measure, a camera shop operator may observe that on average each digital camera sold leads to the sale of 1.2 memory cards. If the $CM on the average memory card is $30, then $\$Adj_c$ equals 1.2 times $30, or $36. Using the dollar-change measure, the retailer would observe that every digital camera sold leads to an average increase of $72 in the shop's sales revenue from memory cards. If the proportion contribution margin on the average memory card is 0.50 (i.e., 50 percent), then $\$Adj_c$ equals $72 times 0.50, or $36.

Example of Calculating a Breakeven With Complements

Say that the manager of the small chain of men's clothing stores who used regression to quantify some product interactions is evaluating the possibility of changing the price of suits. The average variable cost per suit is $180, the average current price of a suit is $300, and the chain currently sells an average of 498 suits per month. The chain also sells ties, belts, and other clothing accessories that have an average contribution margin of 75 percent. As shown in the earlier section, the manager's regression analysis indicates that every men's suit sold leads to an additional $28 in sales of accessories. Given this, the breakeven sales level of a $30 price decrease on suits, without considering these complements, would be as follows:

$$BE = \frac{-[(\$270 - \$180) - (\$300 - \$180)] \times 498}{(\$270 - \$180)}$$

$$BE = -[(\$90 - \$120) \times 498] / \$90$$

$$BE = -(-\$30 \times 498) / \$90$$

$$BE = \$14,940 / \$90$$

$$BE = 166 \text{ suits per month}$$

The breakeven sales level of a $30 men's suit price decrease, *with* consideration of the complements, would be as follows:

$$BE = \frac{-[(\$270 - \$180) - (\$300 - \$180)] \times 498}{(\$270 - \$180) + (\$28 \times 0.75)}$$

$$BE = -[(\$90 - \$120) \times 498] / (\$90 + \$21)$$

$$BE = -(-\$30 \times 498) / \$111$$

$$BE = \$14,940 / \$111$$

$$BE = 135 \text{ suits per month}$$

We can see here that consideration of the complements decreases the breakeven level for the price decrease. If the manager had calculated the breakeven for the $30 price decrease without considering complements and had estimated that sales would increase by 150 suits per month, he might not have gone forward with the price decrease. By contrast, considering the complements indicates that a sales increase of 150 suits would have actually increased profits.

If the manager considers increasing the price of suits by $30 rather than decreasing it, then the breakeven sales level, without considering the complements, would be as follows:

$$BE = \frac{-[(\$330 - \$180) - (\$300 - \$180)] \times 498}{(\$330 - \$180)}$$

$$BE = -[(\$150 - \$120) \times 498] / \$150$$

$$BE = -(\$30 \times 498) / \$150$$

$$BE = -\$14,940 / \$150$$

$$BE = -100 \text{ suits per month}$$

The breakeven sales level for a $30 price increase, *with* consideration of the complements, would be as follows:

$$BE = \frac{-[(\$330 - \$180) - (\$300 - \$180)] \times 498}{(\$330 - \$180) + (\$28 \times 0.75)}$$

$$BE = -[(\$150 - \$120) \times 498] / (\$150 + \$21)$$

$$BE = -(\$30 \times 498) / \$171$$

$$BE = -\$14,940 / \$171$$

$$BE = -87.4 \text{ suits per month}$$

These last two breakeven calculations again illustrate how consideration of complements changes the breakeven level. If the manager had calculated the breakeven for the $30 price increase without considering complements and had estimated that sales would decrease by ninety suits per month, he might have gone ahead with the price increase. By contrast, considering the complements indicates that a sales decrease of ninety suits would have actually decreased profits.

The GBE Formula, Further Generalized

We have seen how the term $\$Adj_S$ adjusts the GBE formula for a substitute product and the term $\$Adj_C$ adjusts the GBE formula for a complementary product. It is entirely possible that a product for which a price change is being considered can have both substitutes and complements among the seller's other products. In this case, the formula for calculating the breakeven sales level for a prospective price change would be as follows:[12]

$$BE = \frac{\Delta FC - (\Delta CM \times BS)}{CM - \$Adj_s + \$Adj_c}$$

Recall that bringing the term ($\Delta CM \times BS$) into the traditional breakeven formula enables it to apply more generally, not just to the pricing of new products but also to price changes for products that are already being sold. Bringing in the terms $\$Adj_s$ and $\$Adj_c$ represents a further generalization of this GBE formula. These terms are always there, but when there are no substantial substitutes or complements, they equal zero and thus need not be written in the formula.

QUANTITATIVE CONSIDERATION OF IMAGE INTERACTIONS

The preceding discussion of quantifying product interactions and taking them into account in calculating breakeven sales levels of prospective price changes raises the question of how this could be done for product interrelationships that are based on image interactions. Although we won't cover the procedure for this in detail, we can give an overview of it. Regression can be used to verify and quantify image interactions, but it should be noted that the causal factor in the starting hypotheses is the price of the affecting product rather than its sales. For example, if it is suspected that a product serves as a price decoy, then it would be hypothesized that its price would be positively related to sales of the associated lower-priced items; as the price of the decoy increased, so would sales of the lower-priced items. On the other hand, if it is suspected that a product serves as a price exemplar, then the hypothesis could be that its price would, at least to some degree, be negatively related to sales of all of the other products in the store; as the price of the price exemplar decreased, sales of the store's other products would tend to increase.

The regression analysis can provide an estimate of how any particular change in the price of the affecting item would be expected to affect the sales levels of the interrelated products. This estimate would be multiplied by a measure of the profitability of the interrelated products to form an image-interaction adjustment, the additional contribution dollars from the interrelated products that result from the change in price of the affecting item. Because these contribution dollars are due to the price change and not to the number of affecting items that are sold, these contribution dollars can be expressed in aggregate (versus per-unit) terms and should be placed in the numerator of the GBE formula. This adjustment should be subtracted from the numerator of the GBE formula, because the direction of its affect on breakeven sales levels would be similar to that of the numerator's ($\Delta CM \times BS$) term. This illustrates the possibility for yet another generalization to the GBE formula.

SUMMARY

In addition to price segmentation, price structure involves the pattern of prices over the array of products sold by a firm. This pattern is important because there may be interrelations between the products that can cause the price of one item to affect the sales levels of others.

One means by which an item's price can affect the sales of other items is through an image interaction, where the item's price influences the consumer's perception of the seller's other prices. When sellers use price to communicate a prestigious and high-quality image, then there may be negative sales effects of using any low price points. When it is important to maintain a low-price image, then it may be helpful to set prices only a little below those of competitors on a large number of items and include low prices on items that are frequently purchased.

A second means by which an item's price can affect the sales levels of other items is through a product interaction, where an item's price affects its sales, which in turn affects the sales of related products. Product interactions can be identified by considering how the products are used and can be quantified through multiple regression. For each hypothesized candidate substitute or complement, its sales would be the DV of the regression and the sales of the influencing product would be one of the IVs in the analysis.

To use breakeven analysis to help set prices for products that interact with other products, each quantified product interaction can be used to calculate an adjustment term. The CM adjustment for substitutes is subtracted from the GBE formula's denominator, and the CM adjustment for complements is added to its denominator. These adjustments comprise a further generalization of the GBE formula.

KEY TERMS

image interactions	magnitude cue	hypotheses
product interactions	price exemplars	CM adjustment for substitutes
prestige pricing	substitutes	CM adjustment for
price decoy	complements	complements
frequency cue	loss-leader discounts	image-interaction adjustment

REVIEW AND DISCUSSION QUESTIONS

1. What do image interactions and product interactions have in common? What makes them different?

2. What is prestige pricing? How does this practice constrain the price setting of a retailer or manufacturer? What price endings are most consistent with prestige pricing?

3. What is a price decoy? How does it exert its effect? How could a manager create a price decoy?

4. What are magnitude and frequency cues? Which is more important in the formation of a retailer's price image?

5. What are price exemplars? Give some examples of items that are likely to serve as price exemplars.

6. Describe what is true when two products interact as substitutes.

7. Describe a consumption or purchasing behavior that is likely to produce substitutes. Give an example of a product that is a substitute of another.

8. Describe what is true when two products interact as complements.

9. Describe a consumption or purchasing behavior that is likely to produce complements. Give an example of a product that is a complement of another.

10. What is the goal of a loss-leader discount? Discuss what is necessary for a loss-leader discount to be effective.

11. How can a product be a complement of another even if it is purchased at a different time, through a different channel of distribution, or by a different customer?

12. What is the role of hypotheses in the use of multiple regression to quantify product interactions?

13. In a regression analysis to quantify the most likely product interaction between a camera shop's sales of digital cameras and memory cards, what would be the DV?

14. In the regression described in Question 13, which variable's regression coefficient would be of most interest? Would you expect the sign of that coefficient to be positive or to be negative? Why?

15. Give and explain the formula for calculating the breakeven sales level for a prospective price change on a product that is known to have substitutes among the other products sold by the firm.

16. Is it possible for a product to have both substitutes and complements? Explain why or why not.

17. Describe what would be represented in an image-interaction adjustment, and indicate where this adjustment should go if included in the GBE formula.

EXERCISES

1. Here is a copy of a 1997 newspaper advertisement for Preferred Hotels and Resorts. How do the managers of this hotel chain appear to have considered image interactions between their products in setting the prices displayed in this ad?

An Exclusive Offer for American Express® Cardmembers from Preferred Hotels® & Resorts Worldwide

Languish in the Scenes of Summer

Preferred Hotels & Resorts Worldwide and American Express invite you to take advantage of our exclusive Summer Scenes packages. Stay 2-7 nights at one of our participating hotels or resorts and receive one free night when you charge your stay with the American Express Card.

In addition, you will receive one of the following: Complimentary Upgrade, Breakfast or Activity (please see additional details below). And, as always, the American Express Card offers the added travel security of Assured Reservations.

No matter which unique Preferred hotel or resort you choose, you will find unforgettable service, comfort and undeniable charm. It's the Preferred Way to languish in the scenes of summer.

Cards

City	Hotel/Package	City	Hotel/Package
Alexandria, VA/ Washington, D.C.	Morrison House $320 for 2 nights/3rd night free	New Orleans, LA	Le Pavillon Hotel $492.40 for 4 nights/5th night free
Birmingham, AL	The Wynfrey Hotel at Riverchase Galleria $405 for 3 nights/4th night free		Windsor Court Hotel $816 for 3 nights/4th night free
Charleston, SC	Charleston Place $470 for 3 nights/4th night free	Oakland/ San Francisco, CA	The Claremont Resort, Spa & Tennis Club $477-$642 for 3 nights/4th night free
Charlotte, NC	The Park Hotel $278 for 2 nights/3rd night free	Orlando, FL	The Peabody Orlando $555 for 3 nights/4th night free
Dallas, TX	Hotel Crescent Court $585 for 3 nights/4th night free	Richmond, VA	The Jefferson $331.50 for 2 nights/3rd night free
	The Mansion on Turtle Creek $705 for 3 nights/4th night free	San Antonio, TX	La Mansión del Rio $556-$636 for 4 nights/5th night free
Lana`i City, HI	The Manele Bay Hotel $1976.27* for 6 nights/7th night free (Garden Room)	St. Martin, French West Indies	La Samanna $3500-$6300 for 7 nights/ 8th night free
	The Lodge at Koele $2082.02* for 6 nights/7th night free (Koele Room)	Toronto, Canada	Metropolitan Hotel $477* for 3 nights/4th night free
		Vail, CO	Lodge at Vail $820 for 4 nights/5th night free
Miami, FL	Grand Bay Hotel $820 for 4 nights/5th night free	Washington, D.C.	The Hay-Adams Hotel $645-$855† for 3 nights/4th night free

The Preferred Way   PREFERRED HOTELS & RESORTS WORLD WIDE   1-800-323-7500
http://www.preferredhotels.com/summer.html

For reservations, call your travel professional or Preferred Hotels & Resorts Worldwide.

Rates are per room, single or double occupancy, exclusive of local taxes and service charges at participating hotels and resorts May 23, 1997 through September 13, 1997. Rates are subject to availability and accessible only when you charge your stay with the American Express Card. Complimentary services and amenities are not changeable or exchangeable. Offers are not combinable with any promotion, group, or convention rates. Some blackout dates apply. * Includes tax. † Weekday rates, Weekend rates also available. ‡ Rate in Canadian currency. ©1997 Preferred Hotels & Resorts Worldwide.

2. The managers of a washing machine manufacturer are considering introducing a new super-premium model to the company's product line. They recognize that the high price of this new model will cause its sales to be so low that this model is unlikely to ever recover its development costs. Explain how (and why) the introduction of this new model could have a positive effect on the company's profits.

3. Suppose you are the marketing manager for an independent supermarket whose positioning is that of a low-price competitor in the market. At a meeting on the topic of pricing policy, the store's operations manager suggests that it is not necessary to have low prices on most of the store's items. He argues that it is sufficient to price most of the store's items in line with the prices charged by competitors as long as you substantially beat the competition on a very small number of items that customers use to form their opinion of a supermarket's overall price level.

   How would you respond to the operations manager's suggestion?

4. The manager of a prosperous bicycle shop is considering modifying prices on her line of Trek mountain bikes. She would like to identify products at the shop that are substitutes and complements of the Trek mountain bikes.

   (a) Give an example of a product that the manager might plausibly hypothesize to be a substitute of the Trek mountain bikes and one which might plausibly be a complement.

   (b) For one of the hypotheses that you give in Part (a), describe how multiple regression on past sales data could be used to test the hypothesis. Specify the DV and some reasonable IVs, and describe the type and amount of data that would be necessary to carry out this analysis.

5. A convenience store buys whole milk for $2.17 per gallon and sells it for $2.99 per gallon. It sells an average of 150 gallons per day. By tracking past changes in sales of whole milk with changes in sales of other grocery products, the manager has discovered that each one-gallon increase in the sales of whole milk is associated with a $1.00 increase in the sales of other grocery products. Every $1.00 increase in the sales of other grocery products yields a contribution margin of $0.38.

   The manager is now considering a promotion where the price of whole milk will be lowered to $2.59 per gallon. If this past relationship between sales of whole milk and sales of other grocery products holds, by how many gallons must whole milk sales increase in order for the store to break even on this price promotion? Show your work.

6. The manager of a chain of electronics stores is considering running a sale on a Lexmark printer model that contains many popular features. The store buys these printers for $60 apiece, and at the regular price of $160, has been selling forty-eight of them per week. The manager is considering discounting the printer so that it sells for $120. Although this promotion would involve incremental advertising costs of $3,300, the manager has observed

that each Lexmark printer sold generates increased sales of Lexmark ink cartridges (the store's average contribution margin for Lexmark ink cartridges is 64 percent).

A regression analysis on this was carried out by the chain's research department. The analysis used sales of Lexmark ink cartridges (in dollars per week) as the DV. The sales level of Lexmark printers (in units per week) was an IV, and the coefficient of this IV equaled 18.750.

(a) Given this information, calculate the breakeven sales level for this promotional discount. Show your work.

(b) Give an example of a product interrelationship that the manager has failed to consider that might make this breakeven level overly optimistic

NOTES

1. John C. Groth and Stephen W. McDaniel, "The Exclusive Value Principle: The Basis for Prestige Pricing," *Journal of Consumer Marketing* 10, no. 1 (1993): 10–16.
2. Robert M. Schindler and Thomas M. Kibarian, "Image Communicated by the Use of 99 Endings in Advertised Prices," *Journal of Advertising* 30 (Winter 2001): 95–99.
3. Robert M. Schindler, H. G. Parsa, and Sandra Naipaul, "Hospitality Managers' Price-Ending Beliefs: A Survey and Applications," *Cornell Hospitality Quarterly* (forthcoming).
4. Ran Kivetz, Oded Netzer, and V. Srinivasan, "Alternative Models for Capturing the Compromise Effect," *Journal of Marketing Research* 41 (August 2004): 237–257.
5. Itamar Simonson and Amos Tversky, "Choice in Context: Tradeoff Contrast and Extremeness Aversion," *Journal of Marketing Research* 29 (August 1992): 281–295.
6. Albert J. Della Bitta and Kent B. Monroe, "The Influence of Adaptation Levels on Subjective Price Perceptions," in *Advances in Consumer Research,* Volume 1, ed. Scott Ward and Peter Wright (Ann Arbor, MI: Association for Consumer Research, 1974), 359–369.
7. Joseph W. Alba, Susan M. Broniarczyk, Terence A. Shimp, and Joel E. Urbany, "The Influence of Prior Beliefs, Frequency Cues, and Magnitude Cues on Consumers' Perceptions of Comparative Price Data," *Journal of Consumer Research* 21 (September 1994): 219–235.
8. Kalpesh K. Desai and Debabrata Talukdar, "Relationship Between Product Groups' Price Perceptions, Shopper's Basket Size, and Grocery Store's Overall Store Price Image," *Psychology & Marketing* 20, no. 10 (2003): 903–933.
9. Anthony D. Cox and Dena Cox, "Competing on Price: The Role of Retail Price Advertisements in Shaping Store-Price Image," *Journal of Retailing* 66 (Winter 1990): 428–445.
10. David Schwab, "(Not) Free," *Star-Ledger,* June 30, 2005.
11. Thomas T. Nagle and Reed K. Holden, *The Strategy and Tactics of Pricing: A Guide to Profitable Decision Making* (Upper Saddle River, NJ: Prentice Hall, 2002), 257.
12. It is of course also possible that there exist multiple substitutes or multiple complements. The term Adj_S can be understood to refer to the adjustment for all substitutes and the term Adj_C can be understood as the adjustment for all complements just as the term ΔFC represents all changes in fixed costs.

PART IV

Broader Considerations in Pricing

CHAPTER 14

Interactive Pricing: Auctions and Negotiation

In Chapter 1, we introduced the issue of buyer–seller interactivity in determining prices. When prices are set through interactions between buyers and sellers, the process is known as interactive pricing. The alternative of interactive pricing is for the seller to unilaterally establish a schedule of fixed prices. These are posted prices that must be paid by a customer regardless of any interaction that the customer might have with the seller. Since Chapter 1, we have focused entirely on situations where fixed prices are involved.

However, there are many situations where fixed prices are not used. In fact, despite their greater familiarity, fixed prices may not be the most prevalent type of pricing, at least in terms of the number of dollars being spent.[1] Interactive pricing is widely used for transactions that involve large amounts of money and is used most of the time in business-to-business transactions. Further, interactive pricing has been spreading more widely with the rise of Internet commerce, and this trend can be expected to continue. Thus, we need to consider some of the issues and challenges involved in managing this alternative to the fixed-price policy.

Interactive pricing can be divided into two broad categories based on the number of parties involved in the interaction. When prices are determined by many-to-one interactions, the price setting is by auction. In what most people think of as a typical auction, the price is determined by one seller interacting with numerous buyers. However, auctions can also have many sellers interacting with one buyer, as when a number of providers of equipment maintenance services bid for a contract with a large manufacturing organization. When prices are determined by the interactions between one buyer and one seller, the price setting is by negotiation.

We first discuss price setting by auction. Then we discuss price setting by negotiation.

PRICE SETTING BY AUCTION

Although there are many possible mechanisms by which an auction can be carried out, the following four mechanisms cover the vast majority of business auctions:

1. In an English auction, ascending bids from numerous buyers are entertained by the seller. If the bid prices exceed the seller's reservation price—the minimum that the seller is willing to receive for the item—then the auctioned item will be sold to the last remaining bidder. This bidder will pay the highest bid amount. This is illustrated in Figure 14.1 for the case where there are three bidders: A, B, and C (note that "knocks lot down to" is a traditional auction term for "sells to"). The English auction mechanism is used, for example, by producers when selling commodities such as meat, fish, and tobacco and by auction houses such as Sotheby's, Christie's, or Heritage Galleries when selling antiques or other rare or unique items. The English auction, also known as an "ascending-bid auction," is the most familiar auction mechanism to most people.

Figure 14.1   Sequence of Events in an English Auction

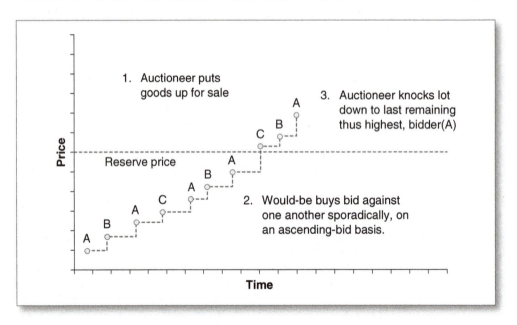

Source: Ralph Cassady Jr., *Auctions and Auctioneering* (Berkeley: University of California Press, 1967), 58.

2. In a Dutch auction, the auctioneer sets a high initial price and starts a clock. At regular intervals, the price of the item is lowered until the first bid is made, which stops the clock. The bidder who makes the first bid purchases the item and pays the amount of

his or her bid. This is illustrated in Figure 14.2. The Dutch auction mechanism, also known as a "descending-price auction," received its name from its long use in tulip auctions in the Netherlands. It is much less commonly used than the English auction mechanism.[2] Note that in market trading venues such as the New York Stock Exchange, prices are set by a combination of ascending bids and descending-price offers. This is known as a double-auction system.

Figure 14.2   Sequence of Events in a Dutch Auction

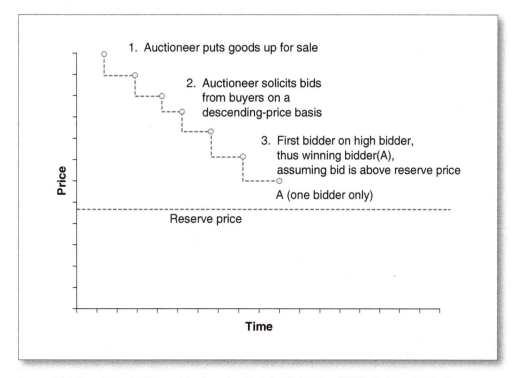

Source: Ralph Cassady Jr., *Auctions and Auctioneering* (Berkeley: University of California Press, 1967), 61.

3. In a first-price sealed-bid auction, all bidders submit bids without any awareness of the bids of others. Bids are accepted for a specified time period. At the end of the time period, the bidder who submitted the highest bid purchases the item and pays the amount he or she bid. Although first-price sealed-bid auctions are sometimes carried out by sellers, this auction mechanism is most often used in auctions carried out by buyers. An auction that involves a buyer seeking bids from a number of sellers is known as a procurement auction. Procurement auctions will be discussed further in a later section of this chapter.

4. A second-price sealed-bid auction differs from a first-price sealed-bid auction in only one respect. The bidder who submits the highest bid purchases the item, but pays the

price bid by the second highest bidder raised only by the smallest allowable bidding increment. Note that choosing this procedure over the first-price mechanism does not necessarily involve the seller giving away revenue, because anticipation of not having to actually pay the amount they bid could lead some customers to bid higher than they otherwise would. This auction mechanism is sometimes called a "Vickrey auction," after the economist who noted that having the winning bidder pay an amount just above the second highest bid serves to make a sealed-bid auction equivalent to the English auction mechanism. To understand why this is so, consider a situation in an English auction where an item has a value to the customer (VTC) of $40 to the second highest bidder and $50 to the highest bidder. The second-highest bidder can be expected to stop bidding at $40. The highest bidder then need bid only the minimum increment over $40.00, say a bid of $40.50, to obtain the item. Thus, the price paid by the highest bidder is just above the second highest bid.[3]

When to Set Prices by Auction

The main reason that sellers choose to use an auction mechanism to set prices is because they believe that the use of auctions will result in higher revenues for the items they sell. This is interesting, because a large part of the appeal of an auction to customers is the sense that they will be able to get items at prices much below their true value!

Traditionally, an auction has been a relatively slow and expensive way to sell something. For example, when holding an English or a Dutch auction, a large number of potential buyers would have to be present in the same place, an auctioneer would have to be employed, and a process taking at least several minutes would have to be devoted to each item or lot to be sold. Because of these high transaction costs, the auction was practical only for commercial transactions that involved large amounts of money. And even within large transactions, there had to be some particular reason to use an auction to set an item's price.

One such reason for an auction would be situations where there is considerable uncertainty about the best price for an item. There is often such uncertainty when selling items that are used. The exact condition of each item must be evaluated by buyers, and it is hard to predict how any particular sign of usage will affect the value of an item to buyers. There is also uncertainty about the best prices for many commodity items. For example, fresh fish have long been sold by auction because of the rapid fluctuation of value-related factors, such as the size and quality of the day's catch and the level of demand for fish on that particular day.

A second reason for an auction would be when there are large differences among potential buyers in a product's VTC. This reason is particularly relevant for the pricing of items that are rare or unique. As we saw in Chapter 4, a seller who has many units of an item available for sale should consider the trade-off between selling at high prices to the few customers with high VTCs or at low prices to penetrate the market. By contrast, a seller with only one rare item for sale need not consider this trade-off; only one buyer is needed. It then makes sense to set the price close to the VTC of the potential customer who values it most, and auctions can be an effective means of doing that. For example, the light saber used by Luke Skywalker in the 1977 movie *Star Wars* is of little value to most people. However, there is likely to be at least one collector who was a particular fan of that movie and would be willing to pay $60,000 or perhaps much more for this item.[4]

A third reason for an auction involves the impression that it is a fair price-setting method. There is often a transparency in the auction process that leads people to judge that a selling price, even if it is a high one, was arrived at fairly. Indeed, research has shown that losers of an auction tend to blame the other bidders rather than the seller.[5] This aspect of auctions makes them particularly appropriate when price legitimacy is particularly important. Thus, we often see auctions used for setting the selling prices of public assets, such as the rights to conduct logging on government land or licenses for the use of frequencies on the radio spectrum.

The Rise of Internet Auctions

Along with the development of the Internet has come the introduction of websites, such as eBay.com, that offer sellers the ability to carry out electronic auctions for the items they want to sell. Being the largest of these sites, eBay has over 100 million registered users who in 2004 placed 1.4 billion listings that resulted in the sale of over $34 billion worth of merchandise.[6]

A seller can auction an item on eBay by posting a description of the item, perhaps setting a minimum bid or a reservation price and a time when bidding will end. As potential customers make their bids, these bids are shown on the item's listing. Each bid must be higher than the previous one, and the person who makes the last bid before the bidding closes buys the item and pays the amount that he or she bid. In this sense, eBay uses the English auction mechanism.

However, eBay also uses a procedure known as proxy bidding. In proxy bidding, a bidder submits to eBay a maximum bid—the highest amount that the bidder is willing to pay for the item. If this maximum bid is higher than the current bid, the eBay proxy raises the bidder's bid just above the current bid by the minimum bid increment. If a new bid is later received, the eBay proxy will raise the bidder's bid to just above that new bid. This will continue until no new bids are received or until the bidder's reservation price is reached. If a bidder submits what would truly be his or her maximum bid, then this proxy bidding procedure becomes, in effect, a second-price sealed-bid mechanism. This makes the eBay system a combination of two auction mechanisms.

There are several important consequences of the ability to conduct auctions online. First, because it is automated, an Internet auction is much less costly to the seller than a traditional live auction. For example, eBay's basic fees for auctioning an item that sells for $20 come to only $2.30. It would clearly be impossible to carry out a live auction for that low an amount. Second, an Internet auction brings access to far more potential bidders than a traditional auction. Because there is no need to be present together at the same time and place and because of the ability to easily search electronically for auction items of interest, it becomes very easy to participate as a bidder in an auction. These two consequences of Internet auctions have greatly expanded the viability of auctions.

Given these consequences of Internet auctions, it is not surprising that we find that items offered in Internet auctions are not limited to expensive items or to items whose value is uncertain or widely varying. Rather, it is common to see mass-produced items that are new rather than used, such as digital cameras and video game consoles, offered on auction sites. In fact, some online retailers offer the same items at a fixed price or at an auction-determined price, and they sometimes do so even in the same listing (as in eBay's Buy It Now option).

It appears then that the Internet has made possible some new uses for auction price setting. One such new use might be as a means of offering promotional discounts. For example, an Internet retailer could conduct auctions for items also available at fixed prices, as a means of generating traffic to its main website.[7] Online auctions could be used to dispose of excess inventory, alternative to offering end-of-season markdowns. Although this is not a new use of auctions— Filene's Basement's automatic markdown policy, discussed in Chapter 11, could in fact be considered a type of slow Dutch auction—this use could be greatly expanded in the online setting. It has also been suggested that many of the bidders in online auctions do so to satisfy needs for excitement, community, or the thrill of winning. Online auctions could be a means by which a retailer could, through the choice of a price-setting mechanism, appeal to the emotional needs of this segment of consumers.[8]

Understanding Bidder Behavior

To effectively use auctions for price setting, it is necessary to have some understanding of the factors that drive the behavior of bidders. A key idea in this regard is the critical importance of getting a first bid on an item. One reason a first bid is important is that a bid from one bidder encourages bids from other bidders. This tendency could be called the herd effect. The herd effect can be at least partly explained by the evidence that bidders value the information they get from observing the bids of others. For example, research has found that the herd effect is particularly noticeable when the product's quality is difficult to evaluate or when the seller does not have a well-established reputation.[9] This importance of observing other bidders could also help explain why the Dutch auction mechanism is far less popular than the English mechanism. The ascending bids of an English auction are open to all potential bidders—the number, size, and timing of the early bids provide a considerable amount of possibly useful information to later bidders. By contrast, in a Dutch auction, the first bid is the winning bid. Losers may feel surprised, and winners may fear that they paid too much; both groups thus may find the Dutch auction mechanism not completely satisfying.[10]

A second reason that a first bid is important is what could be called the momentum effect. A person who begins the bidding process is likely to feel some urge to follow it through. This could occur even in the face of negative feedback such as an increasing number of bidders or an increasing price.[11] The urge to follow through could be driven by a desire to have something to show for the time and energy expended in the early bidding. It is also possible that bidders might feel a need to justify, at least to themselves, that making an early bid on the item was not a bad idea.[12]

In a bidding situation when herd effects and momentum effects combine, there is the possibility of creating what has been called bidding frenzy. This is a state that occurs in the minds of the bidders that is characterized by a high level of competitive arousal and excitement and a desire to win that is so strong that it can lead bidders to lose sight of their intended bidding limits. These feelings may be ego-related—connected to a sense of being worthy, competent, and smart, like the feelings behind the shopper frenzy discussed in Chapter 8.[13] Research indicates that time pressure and bids coming in rapid succession set the stage for bidding frenzy to occur. Note that for these conditions to occur, there must be real-time interaction between bidders such as occurs during a live auction or during the "sniping," or rapid arrival of bids, that often occurs during the last few minutes or seconds of an online auction.[14]

If getting bidders to make a first bid increases the chances of getting the high closing prices produced by bidding frenzy, then the auction seller should consider what can entice a first bid. Because, as previously mentioned, a large part of an auction's appeal to buyers is the hope of getting an item at a price below its value, then it is likely that bidders can be enticed with the promise of a bargain. Setting a low minimum starting bid or reservation price, or even none at all, could effectively indicate to potential bidders that a bargain is possible. This presents the counterintuitive idea that a low starting or reservation price could have the effect of creating a high closing price.

Unfortunately, the research on this question does not provide a clear picture. Low starting or reservation prices do seem to attract more bidders and result in a greater likelihood that the auctioned item is actually sold.[15] However, it has not been shown that low starting or reservation prices lead to higher average closing prices, and some results suggest that they could be used by consumers to infer lower item quality or value.[16] The results of a survey of 350 online auctions shown in Figure 14.3 illustrate several points.[17] First, although the average

Figure 14.3   Distribution of the Results of 350 Online Auctions

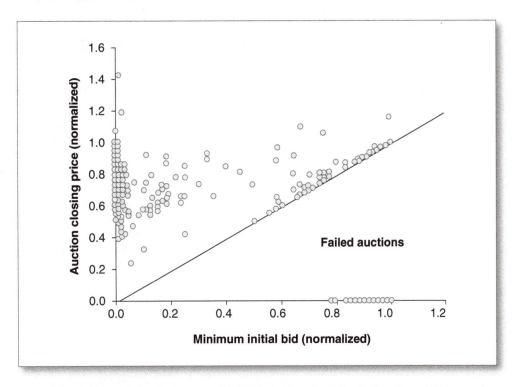

Source: Edieal J. Pinker, Abraham Seidmann, and Yaniv Vakrat, "Managing Online Auctions: Current Business and Research Issues," *Management Science*, 49 (November 2003), 1468.

closing price increased with minimum initial bid, the higher minimum bids also resulted in more auctions where the item was not sold. Second, the highest closing price occurred in an auction where there was no minimum bid. This price, which was over 1.4 times the fixed price for the item posted at retail websites, was most likely the result of a lively bout of bidding frenzy. Although these results are inconclusive, the proliferation of Internet auctions has created new opportunities for carrying out auction research, so we can expect to learn a lot more about these interesting phenomena in the future.

SELLING TO ORGANIZATIONS THAT PURCHASE BY AUCTION

Although auctions are often conducted by sellers, they are also often conducted by buyers. For example, a homeowner who wants to get his or her house painted may ask several local painters to bid on the job. An automobile manufacturer may contract out the manufacture of taillight assemblies and ask potential auto parts suppliers to make competing bids. Because the bids made by painters, auto parts suppliers, and numerous other businesses are an essential part of their price-setting activities, it is important to consider how this bidding process can be managed.

As mentioned earlier in this chapter, auctions carried out by buyers are known as procurement auctions and usually involve the use of a first-price sealed-bid mechanism. In this auction procedure, the buyer will send a request for quotes (RFQ) to a number of potential sellers. The RFQ should contain detailed specifications of the goods or services that are needed along with the minimum quality standards that must be met. Each interested seller submits a bid, which is referred to as "sealed" because it is not revealed to any other seller during the auction. At the end of the specified bidding period, the buyer compares all of the submitted bids and awards the business to the seller who made the lowest bid. The winning seller's bid becomes his or her price for this sale. Note that in a procurement auction, the criterion for winning is the reverse of that in a selling auction. In a procurement auction it is the lowest bid, rather than the highest, that wins the auction.

Sellers often make decisions about the level of their bid through an informal and intuitive process. A manager receiving an RFQ might first estimate what it would cost his organization to supply the goods or services in question and then apply a standard markup to arrive at a tentative bid. The manager's next step would be to consider what his competitors are likely to bid. There are likely to be a number of competitors bidding on the job, and if even one underbids him, the entire sale would be lost. The uncertainties and high stakes involved make this decision difficult. The pressures to win a job are sometimes very intense and lead managers to bid prices so close to costs that even a small error in estimating actual costs could cause the firm to lose money on the job. The tendency for a company to win a bid but then lose money on carrying it out is so common that it has a name—the winner's curse.

Being Systematic in Bidding

An organization that is repeatedly faced with making procurement-auction bids can improve the intuitive management of the bid-setting process by developing a system for setting bids. The challenge in developing such a system is that it can never be known for certain whether or not a given bid will be low enough to win the job. As we saw in Chapter 3's discussion of estimating monetary consequences of a differentiating factor and Chapter 11's discussion of revenue management, the concept of expected value—the worth of an option in the long run—can be helpful in dealing with such uncertainties.

A basic bid-setting system might involve estimating the expected value of the profit that would result from each bid in an array of possible bids.[18] An example of such a set of expected profits can be seen in the table in Figure 14.4. The second column of the table shows an estimate of the profit that would be earned if the job were won at each possible bid level. The third column of the table shows, for each possible bid level, an estimate of the probability of winning the job. Because the expected value of an option is equal to the sum of the value of each possible outcome of the option multiplied by the probability of that outcome occurring—and because losing the job would lead to zero profit—the expected profit of a bid can be calculated by multiplying the estimated profit from winning the job with that bid by the probability that the bid will lead to winning the job. The expected profits for each possible bid level, calculated in this way, are shown in the fourth column of the table. For example, winning the job with a $25 million bid would yield $10 million in profit. Since the probability that the job would be won with a $25 million bid is 0.07, the expected profit of a $25 bid is $10 million times 0.07, which equals $700,000.

Figure 14.4   Information for Calculating the Expected Profit of Each Bid of a Set of Possible Bids

Bid Level ($ millions)	Profit at This Bid Level ($ millions)	Probability of Winning the Job	Expected Profit ($ millions)
25	10	.07	0.70
24	9	.13	1.17
23	8	.25	2.00
22	7	.35	2.45
21	6	.57	3.42
20	5	.64	3.20

Source: Adapted from Thomas T. Nagle and Reed K. Holden, *The Strategy and Tactics of Pricing*, 3rd ed. (Upper Saddle River, NJ: Prentice Hall, 2002), 221.

Examination of the expected profits in Figure 14.4 shows that, in this example, the bid of $21 million has the highest expected profit. This indicates that, even if a $21 million bid is not successful in winning this particular job, choosing to bid $21 million now and continuing in future auctions to choose the highest expected-profit bid is likely to result over time in the highest level of accumulated profits. Because constructing this table of the expected profits of possible bids can provide such useful guidance in making bids, it is worthwhile to consider how one can estimate each possible bid level's probability of winning the job.

Estimating the Probability of Winning

As with the estimation of room-booking probabilities in revenue management, the estimation of bid-winning probabilities can be accomplished through the systematic collection and use of bidding history information. This information would typically draw on bids from procurement auctions of widely varying size and possibly occurring over a long time period. To make these bids comparable, a common scale is needed. A convenient common scale is the ratio consisting of the bid for a job divided by an estimate of the seller's cost of supplying the goods or services involved in the job.[19] This will be referred to as the relative bid. For example, if a seller who is collecting historical information notes that a winning bid in a 1995 procurement auction was $800,000, the seller can estimate what it would have cost his firm in 1995 to have carried out that job. If that cost estimate is $615,000, then the winning bid could be recorded in the seller's database as a relative bid of 1.30 (i.e., $800,000/$615,000).

The source of historical bid information would be the announcements by the buyer of the results of the auction bidding.[20] If the buyer reveals the level of every bid submitted, then a seller could convert each of these bids into a relative bid and enter it into the database. Eventually, the seller would create from this database a table such as that shown in Figure 14.5. The first column of this table shows a set of relative bids ranging from those involving the seller losing money on the job (0.90, 0.95) to those involving a markup of 25 or 30 percent (1.25, 1.30). The second column shows the cumulative proportion of the relative bids collected in the database that exceeded each of these relative-bid levels. Each of these proportions represents the probability that an average bidder in these procurement auctions will place a bid above each level of relative bid. For each relative bid level B, this probability can be designated, $p_{avg}(B)$.

If the seller is bidding in a current procurement auction against only one opponent, the second column of the table in Figure 14.5 can be used directly to estimate each bid level's probability of winning a job. In the absence of any additional information, the seller can assume that one opponent will bid like an average bidder. If the seller makes a relative bid of 1.05, the historical data tell him that there is a 0.90 probability that the average bidder's bid will exceed that level. Thus, that seller's probability of winning with a relative bid of 1.05 is 0.90.

If, in the current procurement auction, the seller is bidding against more than one opponent, then estimating the probability of winning is a little more complicated. For example, if the seller is bidding against two opponents, then a relative bid of 1.05 will be successful only if the bid of *both* of the opponents exceeds 1.05. If it is assumed that each of the two opponents are average bidders, then the probability that both will bid higher than 1.05 equals the probability that one opponent will bid higher than 1.05 (which Figure 14.5 tells us is 0.90) times the probability that the other opponent will also do so (this probability is also 0.90). Thus, in this situation, when bidding against two opponents, there is a

Figure 14.5 Historical Relative-Bid Information for Estimating the Probability of Winning the Job

Relative Bid, B	Proportion of Relative Bids That Exceed This Level, $p_{avg}(B)$	Probability of Winning the Job Against		
		Two Opponents, $[p_{avg}(B)]^2$	Four Opponents, $[p_{avg}(B)]^4$	Six Opponents, $[p_{avg}(B)]^6$
0.90	1.00	1.000	1.000	1.000
0.95	.98	.960	.922	.886
1.00	.95	.903	.815	.735
1.05	.90	.810	.656	.531
1.10	.77	.593	.352	.208
1.15	.60	.360	.130	.047
1.20	.42	.176	.031	.005
1.25	.25	.063	.004	*
1.30	.13	.017	*	*

Source: Adapted from John F. Kottas and Basheer M. Khumawala, "Contract Bid Development for the Small Businessman," Sloan Management Review 14 (Spring 1973), p. 35.

* Less than .001

0.81 probability that a relative bid of 1.05 would be successful. If the probability of a relative bid level B being the winning bid is designated $p_{win}(B)$, and the seller is bidding against n opponents, then the general formula is as follows:

$$p_{win}(B) = [p_{avg}(B)]^n$$

Columns 3 through 5 of Figure 14.5 illustrate the use of this formula. For example, if the seller is considering a relative bid of 1.20 and he anticipates four opponents, then his probability of winning the bid would be as follows:

$$p_{win}(1.20) = [p_{avg}(1.20)]^4 = (0.42)^4 = 0.031$$

If the seller is considering a relative bid of 1.10 and anticipates six opponents, then his probability of winning the bid would be as follows:

$$p_{win}(1.10) = [p_{avg}(1.10)]^6 = (0.77)^6 = 0.208$$

Making the Most of Limited Information

The use of this method of estimating the probability of winning with a particular bid requires that the seller estimate the number of opponents who will be bidding against him in the procurement auction. This estimate would be based on specific information about the intentions of competitors as well as on past experience concerning factors such as how the size of the job relates to the number of bidders.[21] If there is uncertainty between two (or more) number-of-opponent estimates, a seller could take an average. For example, if it is considered as likely that there would be three bidding opponents as that there would be four opponents, then the probability of winning with a relative bid of 1.20 could be calculated as an average of the two number-of-opponent possibilities:

$$p_{win}(1.20) = \{0.50 \times [p_{avg}(1.20)]^3\} + \{0.50 \times [p_{avg}(1.20)]^4\}$$

$$= (0.50 \times 0.42^3) + (0.50 \times 0.42^4)$$

$$= (0.50 \times 0.074) + (0.50 \times 0.031)$$

$$= 0.037 + 0.016 = 0.053$$

It is sometimes the case that there is specific information available about one of a seller's bidding opponents. Let's call this competitor Opponent A. The specific information about Opponent A could be obtained from quantitative data on Opponent A's past bids, or it could be more subjective information, such as the knowledge that Opponent A has new management that is more aggressive and therefore more likely than average to make a low bid. Such specific information can be used for estimating the probability of winning by splitting Opponent A out from the group of average bidders. The probability of Opponent A's bid exceeding a bid level B would be designated $p_{Opponent A}(B)$. If a seller is bidding against n opponents, one of which is Opponent A, then the probability of winning the job with a relative bid level of B would be as follows:

$$p_{win}(B) = p_{Opponent A}(B) \times [p_{avg}(B)]^{n-1}$$

For example, say a seller is bidding against Opponent A and three other bidders. If it is estimated that the new management makes Opponent A's probability of submitting a bid higher than 1.20 drop from the average level of 0.42 down to, say, 0.20, then the probability of winning with a relative bid of 1.20 would be calculated as follows:

$$p_{win}(1.20) = 0.20 \times [p_{avg}(1.20)]^3$$

$$= 0.20 \times 0.074 = 0.015$$

In this example, knowing that one opponent is more aggressive than average causes the probability that a relative bid of 1.20 will win the job to decrease from 0.031 to 0.015.

These procedures illustrate an important advantage of being systematic in the bid-setting process. The system does not remove the uncertainty in the bidding process. But what it does do is provide a means whereby whatever limited information is available to the seller can be used to maximum advantage.

PRICE SETTING BY NEGOTIATION

As was mentioned in Chapter 1, the setting of prices through a process of negotiation between a seller and a buyer was, for much of human history, the only means of arriving at a price. In recent centuries, a variety of forces have contributed to the replacement of negotiated pricing with the policy of posting fixed prices. A desire to achieve the maximum amount of honesty and fairness led George Fox and the Quakers to be the first to abandon negotiation, but other factors fueled the trend. For both buyers and sellers, price negotiations tend to evoke strong feelings—sometimes stronger than seems justified by the amounts of money involved. Replacing negotiation with fixed pricing removed a source of emotional stress in the commercial interaction. Finally, as cash registers and other advances in merchandise distribution developed, retailing began to be conducted on a larger scale. It became simply impractical for most sellers to expend the necessary time and effort to carry out price negotiations for most everyday consumer goods.

On the other hand, there are also forces that have supported the continued use of negotiated pricing. Having the opportunity to determine price through a one-on-one interaction with sellers offers buyers the ability to feel that they are paying the lowest possible price. As was mentioned in Chapter 10, sellers see in negotiated price setting an opportunity to very flexibly and effectively carry out price segmentation. For transactions that involve large amounts of money, it is practical for both buyers and sellers to devote the time and effort necessary to set prices through negotiation. Thus, for expensive consumer products—such as automobiles and real estate—and for most business-to-business products, negotiation remains the most common means of price setting.

Some Basic Principles of Price Negotiation

A seller who wants to be successful in using negotiation to set prices must understand how some basic principles of negotiation can be applied to price negotiation. A negotiation typically consists of two phases. The preparation phase involves the collection of information before interacting with the other party in the negotiation. The meeting phase involves communicating with the other party with the goal of arriving at an agreement.

Say an electronics manufacturer has asked one of its current suppliers if it could provide compact transformers for one of the manufacturer's new products. The supplier indicated that it could provide the transformers. Dave, vice president of sales for the supplier, will meet with Cheryl, the product manager for the new product, to try to arrive at a mutually agreeable price.

During the preparation phase of this price negotiation, Dave and his staff should focus on gathering information in three areas:

1. *Estimation of the customer's reservation price for the product.* Here, the key piece of information is the product's VTC. Dave should attempt to gather the information that

would enable him to go through the four steps of VTC estimation described in Chapter 2. As you recall, these steps would involve determining what the electronics manufacturer considers the next closest substitute of Dave's transformers, identifying the factors that differentiate Dave's transformers from the next closest substitute, and so on. The VTC obtained in this manner would be a good candidate for the electronic manufacturer's reservation price for Dave's product.

It would also be useful to estimate the buyer's degree of price sensitivity. This would provide an indication of how much the customer would appreciate a product's price being less than its VTC. For example, if, for the electronics manufacturer, the transformers were a small part of a highly profitable product, then the manufacturer would probably be less price-sensitive than if the transformers were a large part of an only marginally profitable product.

2. *Determination of the seller's own reservation price for the product.* Dave's calculation of his reservation price for selling the product to this electronics manufacturer would be based largely on the costs that would be incurred as the result of this sale. With this cost information, Dave can calculate the contribution dollars that would be earned at any given price level. Dave's reservation price would be the price corresponding to the profit level that Dave's company could make on the compact transformers (or on the capacity to make them) if these items were *not* sold to this electronics manufacturer. This alternative profit level would correspond to what has been referred to as the "best alternative to a negotiated agreement."[22]

3. *Characteristics of the negotiating situation.* Before entering the meeting phase of the negotiation, it is important for the seller to understand the rules of the situation, which are often implicit rather than stated openly. Dave would try to gather some information on Cheryl's negotiating style. For example, does she expect many rounds of haggling, or does she try to arrive at price quickly, with minimal haggling? Does she often bluff in price negotiations, or does she tend to be straightforward? Dave should also gather information on the likely place of his meeting with Cheryl, the amount of time available to reach an agreement, and the individuals who Cheryl may bring along with her to the meeting.

During the meeting phase of this price negotiation, Dave and the other individuals he brings to the meeting will likely engage in most of the following activities:

1. *Stating an asking price.* Dave should state an asking price higher than his estimate of Cheryl's reservation price. This gives him room to lower his price during the haggling and sets an advantageous reference point. There is research evidence that higher asking prices result in higher final negotiated prices.[23]

2. *Making concessions.* Assuming that Cheryl's initial offer is less than Dave's asking price, Dave will probably make one or more concessions. A concession is a movement toward the position of one's negotiating opponent. There is often an expectation that concessions will occur in a reciprocating fashion, with a concession by one side in the negotiation followed by a concession by the other side. Research evidence suggests that people feel better about a negotiation's outcome when the negotiation involves a series

of concessions.[24] Negotiators often interpret the size and frequency of concessions as indications of the amount of movement that can be expected from their opponents.

3. *Providing rationales.* A negotiator will typically offer a rationale for his or her initial position, for his or her concessions, and for requested concessions that are not made. More general than the price rationales mentioned in Chapter 8, a negotiating rationale is any explanation or justification for a proposed action or for declining to take a requested action. These often serve the purpose of helping the customer fully appreciate the product's value, as when Dave might talk about the useful features of his company's transformers when justifying his asking price. Convincing negotiating rationales tend to include specific facts and detailed measurements and make use of any important search characteristics of the product that can be demonstrated. In price negotiations, rationales often involve an argument that a particular price level is one that is fair.

4. *Responding to the rationales of the customer.* A negotiator should be able to evaluate and perhaps counter the rationales of the other side. For example, if Cheryl supports a low initial offer with a rationale about the low costs of producing the compact transformers, Dave might counter by suggesting that Cheryl has neglected to take into account his company's elaborate quality control procedures and then providing details of the high costs of those procedures. If one of Cheryl's rationales presents new information, such as a low price offered by one of Dave's competitors, then Dave must evaluate this claim by considering the context in which is it said and by determining the consistency of this claim with what he already knows.

5. *Dealing with threats.* Sometimes the urge to prevail leads a negotiator to make a threat—a claim that negative consequences will occur if the other side does not give in. For example, Cheryl may threaten Dave with taking her transformer business elsewhere if he does not accept her low-price offer. The influence of a threat has to do with its credibility and with the relative power of each side. If Dave's company is desperate for the transformer contract, then he has low relative power and could be susceptible to the threat. On the other hand, if Cheryl's company is dependent on Dave's company for other products, the relative power of the two sides would be more equal. Dave could choose to make a counterthreat, say, that her failure to award him this contract could weaken his company and increase its likelihood of being acquired by a larger company that does not have his company's culture of high product quality.

6. *Managing the emotional dimension of negotiation.* Because of the powerful negative emotions that can be evoked by the sense of losing in a negotiation, it is useful whenever possible to help a negotiator save face. For example, if Cheryl feels it important to negotiate a low price on the transformers, Dave could help her save face when accepting a higher offer by relabeling the offer's terms to give a low price on the transformers themselves, but a higher price for delivery or for another necessary service aspect of the products.[25]

Although a negotiator may not like the outcome of a negotiation, it is important that he or she feel that this outcome is the best that could be had. A negotiator who feels that he or she has been fast-talked or rushed into accepting a position will tend to look for ways to modify or back out of the agreement and/or avoid future negotiations with the other side. This underlines the importance of providing negotiating rationales that are convincing and, when exerting relative power, doing so in the gentlest way possible.

Keeping in mind that negotiation has two phases, not just one, helps the seller avoid the mistake of putting too much emphasis on the communication skills that come into play during the meeting phase. Although it is helpful to be able to think on one's feet during a negotiation meeting, often what is most important is to go into the meeting with a good, well-researched plan and to stick with it. The quality of the work done in the preparation phase of the negotiation really matters. When the preparation has been done well, a negotiator with even modest communication skills is likely to come away with a satisfactory outcome.

Win-Win Negotiation in Pricing

This outline of the principles of price negotiation leaves out many subtleties of the negotiation process. The negotiation between Dave and Cheryl is an example of distributive negotiation. This is where the goal of the negotiation is to divide up a fixed pie. It involves an essentially competitive, win-lose situation. The price of the transformers determines whether it is Dave's company or Cheryl's that gets the bulk of the profits available with this product. If one company gets more profit, the other company gets less.

It is important to note that alternatives to straight distributive negotiation exist. Consider the following story concerning an individual's pricing of his professional services:[26]

> Rick was graduating soon and had just finished a round of final interviews with several companies. He was very pleased because the company he wanted to work for had made him an offer; he was going to take it. The salary they offered was good, but he had a nagging feeling that it could be better. He wanted to ask them for more money before he accepted the job, but he didn't want to alienate them in any way because he fully intended to accept the job, even if they couldn't or didn't offer him any additional money.
>
> Rick's immediate priority was to be accepted by the people in the firm. The starting salary was secondary: He wanted to deal with it if he could, but he wanted to be very careful. He didn't want the salary issue to interfere with a smooth transition into the job. How could he increase his chances for a better salary without turning off anyone at the company?
>
> Normally, salary negotiations are strictly distributive. . . . But Rick's circumstances were different—salary wasn't the most important issue. As a result, the strategy . . . that was finally accepted was exactly the opposite of the obvious one. Rather than asking for more money before he accepted the job—with the expectation that he would then get involved in potentially difficult negotiations—he simply accepted the job and said how happy he was to be coming to the firm. (That was completely true.) Then he said that there was one thing troubling him—the starting salary. He couldn't help feeling that it was a little low. (That was also true.) Could they do something about it?
>
> This strategy restructured the entire interaction. Rather than taking an aggressive, distributive bargaining stand, as many people think they must in salary negotiations, Rick shook hands first, accepted the job, and then asked the firm, as a matter of good faith, to help on the salary issue. He didn't beg or plead or bargain hard—just the reverse. He agreed

with them on the big issue and left his final salary—the issue he had defined as secondary—up to them. He was already part of the team; it was now their turn. Rick's strategy opened the door for the company to reciprocate. He hoped that they would say to themselves, "Rick accepted, now it's our turn to do something." Rick's strategy also took the burden off his own shoulders and placed it squarely on the firm's: If they didn't come through, they would be the ones who looked bad.

Early the next day Rick proceeded just as planned. Someone from the company called him back a few hours later and said that they could increase his salary by $5,000. Needless to say, Rick was very pleased.

Rick's restructuring of the interaction created the possibility of a win-win negotiation (also called integrative or accommodative negotiation). Rick won the higher salary, but the firm didn't lose. Rather than being forced to make a concession, they won the likelihood of having a more enthusiastic and dedicated employee at what the firm probably regarded as a small cost.

Thinking of such restructurings takes some creativity, and it is hard to give general rules for identifying them. However, the stage can be set for coming up with win-win negotiations by attempting to unbundle the many issues that are often involved in a negotiation and considering the relative importance of each. For example, an item's per-unit price may be an important issue in the negotiation, but there may be subsidiary issues of extra product features, purchase quantity, delivery time, policy on taking returns, training of the buyer's personnel, and so on.

Of particular interest are issues that involve a value asymmetry—a situation where something is more highly valued by one side than the other. For example, price negotiations between a home improvement retailer and a manufacturer of patio tiles might also involve the question of whether the manufacturer can ship the tiles in batches of assorted colors. The labor savings resulting from this packaging could be of considerable value to the retailers, yet it could cost the manufacturer very little to produce this assortment. If so, this packaging issue could be conceded to the retailer in return for something that is more important to the manufacturer than the retailer, thus creating a situation where both parties gain. Value asymmetries are at the heart of the commercial exchange (see Chapter 1) and help provide the basis for win-win outcomes in price negotiations.

MANAGING PRICE NEGOTIATIONS

Given our understanding of some of the basic principles of price negotiation, we can take up some key issues in the seller's day-to-day management of price negotiation. The issues involved in selling to business customers, where negotiated pricing is the norm, are very different from those involved in selling to consumers, where fixed prices are the norm.

Price Negotiations With Business Customers

When negotiating prices with business customers, it is important to appreciate that a business organization is not a monolithic entity. Talking to different people within an organization can lead to very different outcomes. For example, the owner of a small company selling job control and accounting software for printing operations was finding it difficult to negotiate profitable prices with the print-shop managers. A breakthrough in these difficulties occurred when the owner hired an experienced salesperson who pointed out that the owner had been talking to the wrong person in the printing companies. A print shop manager has a relatively small budget to work with and has difficulty appreciating the full benefits of this software product. When the owner and his new salesperson began talking with the VPs of operations and other top executives of the printing companies, they were easily able to negotiate prices five or six times higher than what the owner had ever been able to squeeze out of a print shop manager.

The description in Chapter 3 of the five decision-process roles of an organization's buying center (user, influencer, gatekeeper, decider, and purchaser) can serve as a helpful guide to understanding the differing needs and viewpoints of the individuals who are negotiating for the buyer. In general, it should be the seller's goal to be negotiating with the people in the buying organization who can appreciate the product's value and who have the incentives and power within the organization to authorize the appropriate expenditures.

Up until this point, we have talked about negotiating situations that occur at predictable times. A seller expects price negotiations when the buyer is making a new purchase or when the time comes to renew a contract. However, a seller may be suddenly challenged on price by a regular customer if, for example, the customer is approached by a lower-priced seller or finds out that other customers are paying less for the same product. In the short-notice negotiations that will ensue, it would be beneficial for the seller to provide negotiating rationales that communicate the full extent of the product's VTC. The seller might describe the differentiating factors that make his or her product worth more than that of the lower-priced competitor or might detail the ways in which the higher-paying customer is given greater product selection, better service, or other benefits not available to the customers who are paying less. Because such negotiations can come up suddenly, it would be wise for a seller to routinely engage in some preparation-phase information gathering about all of his or her customers.

As a customer buys from a seller repeatedly, the customer becomes more experienced in negotiating with the seller and thus becomes more able to "beat up" the seller on price. To prevent this kind of difficulty, it may be appropriate to pull back from negotiating and establish a fixed-price policy for business products that tend to be frequently purchased. This can be done while maintaining at least some of the pricing flexibility needed for dealing with diverse customers by the use of price menus.[27] A price menu is a schedule of fixed prices for each of the tangible and service features of the seller's product. An example of such a menu can be seen in Figure 14.6. In the use of price menus, the salesperson does not have the authority to change prices. If a customer wants a lower price, then the customer must decide what product feature(s) he or she is willing to give up.

Although the use of price menus can remove a means by which customers can pressure a seller to lower prices, for it to work, it is necessary that the same menus are used for all customers and that the menu prices are set at the right levels. In an environment where there are many competitors who negotiate individual prices with customers, it may be hard for a seller to effectively implement this or any other form of fixed-price policy.

Figure 14.6   Example of a Price Menu

	Turnaround	Special Processing	Long-Term Contract	On-Site Customer Support
Low price package	3–7 days, when available	Not available	Not available	Not available
Regular package	3 days(+15% for 24 hours)	Service A +3% Service B +7% Service C +5%	–10%	+15%
Full service package	24 hour	A, B, C include with added performance guarantee Service D +9%	1 year minimum	Included

Source: Thomas T. Nagle and Reed K. Holden, *The Strategy and Tactics of Pricing,* 3rd ed. (Upper Saddle River, NJ: Prentice Hall, 2002), 158.

Price Negotiations With Consumers

The vast majority of consumer products are sold at fixed prices. There are only a few product categories—such as real estate and automobiles—where most consumers expect to engage in the back-and-forth haggling of price negotiation. However, it should be noted that there is a middle area between fixed prices and full negotiation. Some retailers have adopted, at least implicitly, what could be called a partial-negotiation policy. This involves the use of fixed prices with some accommodation to those customers who want to negotiate. This policy is characterized by most consumers paying the fixed price—only a minority engaging in nego- tiation. For example, a *Wall Street Journal* reporter did an informal study of retailers such as a furniture store, a lighting store, and a men's clothing store. He picked out an item in each store and attempted to negotiate a lower price. He found that approximately half of the retail- ers were willing to shave something off their fixed prices, sometimes as much as 20 percent![28]

To carry out a partial-negotiation policy, the seller must set the price high enough that it allows for making one concession. The advantage of this policy is that it provides a means for price segmentation. The concession is a possibility for only those customers who ask for it. Further, among those customers, the concession need be granted to only those who the seller judges are so price-sensitive that the concession is likely to make a difference in whether or how much they buy. If, for example, a customer who reveals he absolutely loves the suit that he is trying on asks for a price concession, the salesperson can simply say something like, "I'm sorry, but I can't do anything with the price of this particular suit. It is one of our best sellers."

The disadvantage of a partial-negotiation policy is that it could lead to hard feelings among consumers. A consumer who has received a price concession in the past is likely to feel disappointed if he or she does not receive one during every visit to the store. Customers of a retailer who hear that others have received a price concession from the retailer may consider themselves to have been treated unfairly. They may plan to ask for concessions when they next visit the store. Some may even tend to avoid the store so as to not have to deal with the stress of having to ask for a price concession. In other words, even an only occasional use of negotiation threatens the consumer's trust in the seller's fixed prices. We should not let the commonness of fixed pricing lead us to believe in its sturdiness. Perhaps, like the thin veneer of civilization, negotiation lurks behind fixed-price transactions, ready to rise up whenever the genteel structure of the fixed-price discipline begins to break down.

The risks involved in a partial-negotiation policy may help explain the common retailing practice of advertising a price-matching guarantee. This is the seller's promise to match a lower price offered by any other seller of the same item and to refund the difference if the item has already been purchased from the seller. This device serves to offer a structure for partial negotiation. Those consumers who are seeking a lower price know what to do. They shop for a low price, bring in the competitor's ad or other evidence of the low price, and receive their price concession. Those consumers who are unaware of the policy, too busy to collect the evidence, or who are not sufficiently price-sensitive will pay the regular price. Although it is likely that the vast majority of consumers will pay the regular price, the availability of the price concessions to all who follow the specified procedures will tend to blunt any resentment that they may feel. Price-matching guarantees may have the additional benefit of giving the retailer a low-price image in the minds of consumers.[29]

Compensating the Negotiators

Just as the individuals in an organization's buying center can have differing needs that may impact the outcome of price negotiations, it is also important to consider the differing needs of those on the seller's side of these negotiations. In particular, it is important that salespeople, who are often on the frontline of price negotiations for the selling organization, have negotiating incentives that are in line with the goals of the firm that employs them.

Typically, sales force compensation formulas are based on the dollar revenue of the products that the salespeople sell. Thus, if a salesperson sells 100 units of a product at a price of $5 per unit, a revenue-based compensation method would lead the salesperson's credit for the sale to be based on the $500 of revenue ($5 price × 100 units sold) that would be brought into the company by that sale. Although the typical company rewards salespeople for bringing in revenue, the goals of the company are to gain the profits associated with the revenue. If, for example, a product's contribution margin is 50 percent, then $500 of sales revenue would yield the company $250 of profits.

The consequences of a profit-motivated company using revenue to motivate salespeople in this situation are illustrated in the table in Figure 14.7. If the salesperson doesn't hold firm during price negotiations and lets the product go for $4.50 per unit, then the salesperson's credit would decrease by 10 percent. However, the company's profit from this sale would decrease by 20 percent. If the salesperson sold the product for $4.00, the salesperson's credit would decrease by 20 percent, but the company's profit would decrease by 40 percent. On the other hand, if the salesperson worked hard at communicating to the customer the benefits of the product and sold the item for $5.50 or even $6.00, the

Figure 14.7   Effects of Using a Revenue-Based Salesperson Compensation Method

Selling Price	Revenue-Based Sales Credit	Salesperson's Credit Difference	Company's Profits	Company's Profit Difference
$6.00	$600	20% more	$350	40% more
$5.50	$550	10% more	$300	20% more
$5.00	$500		$250	
$4.50	$450	10% less	$200	20% less
$4.00	$400	20% less	$150	40% less

Assumptions:
   Salesperson sells 100 units
   Target price = $5/unit
   Item's contribution margin at target price = 50%

salesperson's credit would increase, but the company's profits would increase by twice as great a percentage. The revenue-based sales force compensation method puts the salesperson's incentives out of line with the company's goals and gives the salesperson too little motivation to negotiate the highest possible price.

To correct for this disparity, a profit-based compensation method should be used. A simple method for implementing profit-based sales force compensation begins with setting a target price (TP), which is the price at which management expects the item to be sold. The formula for calculating the salesperson's compensation would then be as follows:[30]

$$\text{Sales credit} = \{\text{TP} + [w \times (\text{Actual price} - \text{TP})]\} \times \text{Units sold}$$

The salesperson's credit is calculated by multiplying the units sold by the target price plus the difference between the actual selling price and the target price. This difference is weighted by w, the profitability factor. The profitability factor equals 1 divided by the product's proportion contribution margin at the target price. Note that the profitability factor becomes larger as the product's profit margin gets smaller. Thus, for a product with a 75 percent contribution margin, which is a rather high profit level, here is the outcome:

$$w = 1 / 0.75 = 1.33$$

For a less profitable product, with a 25 percent contribution margin, the profitability factor is much larger:

$$w = 1 / 0.25 = 4$$

Note also that if all sales revenue was treated as profit, then w would become equal to one, and this profit-based formula would become the traditional revenue-based (price-times-units-sold) formula for calculating sales credit.

The sales credit numbers shown in the table in Figure 14.8 illustrate how this profit-based compensation formula can put the salesperson's incentives in line with the company's profit goal. With the profit-based formula, the salesperson's credit for selling the product at $4.50 per unit would not be $450 as with the revenue-based formula, but rather $400:

$$\text{Sales credit} = \{\$5.00 + [(1/0.50) \times (\$4.50 - \$5.00)]\} \times 100 \text{ units} = \$400$$

This is 20 percent less than the salesperson's credit for selling the item at the target price of $5.00, which exactly equals the percentage reduction in the company's profits from selling the item at $4.50 rather than $5.00. Similarly, using the profit-based formula, the salesperson's credit for selling the item at $5.50 would be 20 percent above that for selling it at $5.00, exactly equaling the percentage increase in the company's profits that would result from selling it at $5.50 rather than $5.00.

Figure 14.8   Effects of Using a Profit-Based Salesperson Compensation Method

Selling Price	Profit-Based Sales Credit	Salesperson's Credit Difference	Company's Profits	Company's Profit Difference
$6.00	$700	40% more	$350	40% more
$5.50	$600	20% more	$300	20% more
$5.00	$500		$250	
$4.50	$400	20% less	$200	20% less
$4.00	$300	40% less	$150	40% less

Assumptions:
Salesperson sells 100 units
Target price = $5/unit
Item's contribution margin at target price = 50%

The use of a profit-based sales force compensation method helps give the salesperson the appropriate motivation to do the hard work necessary for negotiating successfully. It increases the negative consequences of selling at a low price, thus reducing the salesperson's inclination to use price to close the deal. It also increases the positive consequences to the salesperson of selling at a high price. In so doing, it points the salesperson toward doing the hard preparation-phase work of understanding and communicating the product's VTC, which, as we have seen, is at the heart of carrying out successful price negotiations.

SUMMARY

There are many situations where prices are not fixed but set through an interaction between buyers and sellers. This may occur through the many-to-one buyer–seller interactions of auctions or the one-to-one buyer–seller interactions of price negotiations.

Sellers choose to use auctions for price setting when there is uncertainty about an item's best price and when there are large differences between buyers in the product's VTC. Traditionally, auctions have been expensive to carry out, but the development of websites that carry out automated auctions has made it practical to also use auctions for the sale of everyday items.

Auctions carried out by buyers—procurement auctions—involve requesting price quotes from a number of sellers. The seller who makes the lowest bid wins the job. Although sellers often use an intuitive process to decide on bid levels, available information can be utilized more effectively if the seller uses a systematic procedure, such as choosing the bid that has the highest expected profit.

Price negotiation can help give buyers the feeling of getting a low price and can help sellers with price segmentation. Before meeting with the buyer, it is important for the seller to gather information on the product's VTC. In the meeting phase of the negotiation, the seller should state a high asking price and be prepared to make concessions. The seller should also give supporting rationales for his or her actions and be prepared to respond to rationales, and possibly threats, from the buyer.

A seller to business customers might consider replacing negotiation with menus of many options at fixed prices. Fixed-price retailers may offer occasional concessions or price-matching guarantees. It is useful to have sales force compensation methods that are based not on sales revenue but rather on the level of profits resulting from the sale.

KEY TERMS

interactive pricing
auction
negotiation
English auction
Dutch auction
double-auction system
first-price sealed-bid
   auction
procurement auction
second-price sealed-bid
   auction
proxy bidding

herd effect
momentum effect
bidding frenzy
request for quotes (RFQ)
winner's curse
relative bid
preparation phase
meeting phase
concession
negotiating rationale
threat
relative power

distributive negotiation
win-win negotiation
value asymmetry
price menus
partial-negotiation
   policy
price-matching guarantee
revenue-based compensation
   method
profit-based compensation
   method
profitability factor

REVIEW AND DISCUSSION QUESTIONS

1. What distinguishes the two types of interactive pricing: auctions and negotiations?

2. Describe the four auction mechanisms that cover the vast majority of business auctions.

3. What are the three types of reasons for using an auction to set an item's price?

4. Describe how eBay uses a combination of two auction mechanisms. How have Internet auction sites such as eBay expanded the viability of setting prices by auction?

5. Explain how setting a low starting price in an auction could have the effect of increasing the level of the closing price.

6. What is a procurement auction?

7. How would one calculate the expected profit of a bid? How would you use information on the expected profits of an array of possible bids?

8. What is a relative bid? Why is it important for the collection of bidding history information?

9. Give and explain the formula for using information about the average bidder to estimate the probability of winning the job. How would this formula be modified if there is specific information about one particular bidder?

10. Describe the forces that have worked against the continued use of price negotiations and the forces that have worked for its continued use.

11. Give some examples of the types of information that should be collected during the preparation phase of a price negotiation.

12. What are concessions? Why are they important in price negotiations?

13. What are value asymmetries, and what is their role in restructuring negotiations so that both sides can come out ahead?

14. How can an understanding of the individuals and roles in an organization's buying center be used in preparing for price negotiations?

15. How could the use of price menus be an effective response to a seller being "beaten up" by regular customers in price negotiations?

16. What is a partial-negotiation policy? How might devices such as price-matching guarantees reduce the risks of such a policy?

17. Describe the formula given in the chapter for profit-based sales force compensation. How might the use of such a formula improve the outcome of price negotiations?

EXERCISES

1. For each of the following items, give and justify your view concerning whether the item should be offered in a catalog for a fixed price or whether an auction would be a more desirable method for determining the item's selling price:

   (a) A Civil War military order actually signed by General Ulysses S. Grant

   (b) Sony's PlayStation 3 video game console

   (c) A 1923 Ford Model T automobile, partially restored

   (d) Government sales of the oceanfront lots at an abandoned naval base

2. It is mentioned in the chapter that (1) auctions are appealing to sellers because they believe that auctions will allow them to sell items at relatively high prices and (2) auctions are appealing to buyers because they believe that auctions allow them to buy items at prices much below their value. Explain how both of these beliefs could be correct, even on the same transaction.

3. Say that you have inherited a sterling silver necklace with a six-carat ruby pendant from a distant relative and you would like to sell it on eBay. What would you take into account when considering what, if any, minimum price to mention in your listing of this item?

4. You are evaluating the possibility that your company bids $150,000 for a particular construction job.

   (a) If a bid of $150,000 corresponds to a relative bid of 1.20, what is the dollar profit that your company would make from winning the job with this bid? Show your work.

   (b) Calculate an estimate of the expected profit of the bid of $150,000 for this job. Assume that, historically, 55 percent of the bids of an average bidder for this type of job would exceed the bid ratio of 1.20. Assume also that you are bidding against three other construction companies. Show your work.

5. Your company, which provides bookkeeping services to municipalities and small businesses, is about to bid on a five-year contact to provide payroll services to a large suburban school district. Your past data indicates that the average bidder for this type of contract will submit a bid higher than a relative bid of 1.10 about 80 percent of the time. However, there is a new, more aggressive competitor in the area, Compu-Pay. You estimate that Compu-Pay will bid higher than a relative bid of 1.10 only 40 percent of the time. If your company will be bidding against Compu-Pay and four other bookkeeping services companies, what is your probability of winning the contract with a relative bid of 1.10?

6. Diversified Production Corp. is a large manufacturer of high-quality plastic parts. A major automobile company is one of Diversified's oldest and largest customers. Annette, one of Diversified's sales

representatives, has recently received a call from Patrick, the purchasing agent for the automobile manufacturer. Patrick told Annette that the price she quoted for the renewal of their contract for front-seat console supports was too high. Her price was $1.52 million. A competitor from Japan had offered to provide these supports for $1.20 million, and a domestic competitor has submitted a proposal for a price only a little higher than that. Patrick tells Annette that he will be unable to renew Diversified's contract unless she offers a "substantial" price reduction. Annette has scheduled a meeting with Patrick to try to work out an agreement on this.

(a) What information should Annette gather in preparation for the meeting with Patrick?

(b) Give and justify your view as to what price Annette should start with when she meets with Patrick.

(c) How should Annette decide what concessions to make? Give some examples of negotiating rationales she could use to support her positions during the negotiation process.

(d) How might this situation be restructured into a win-win negotiation?

7. The management of a packaging materials company has decided to change how the company calculates the sales credit that forms the basis for determining the sales commissions for their sales force. Rather than use a salesperson's sales revenue to calculate his/her sales credit, management now uses the profit-based compensation formula discussed in the chapter. To calculate the profitability factor, management uses the firm's average contribution margin of 25 percent.

(a) For a product with a target price of $500 per unit, calculate a salesperson's sales credit for selling 10 units of the product at a price of (1) $450 per unit, (2) $500 per unit, and (3) $550 per unit.

(b) What are the effects that this change is likely to cause on the behavior of the sales force? How might these effects be beneficial to the packaging materials company?

NOTES

1. Edieal J. Pinker, Abraham Seidmann, and Yaniv Vakrat, "Managing Online Auctions: Current Business and Research Issues," *Management Science* 49 (November 2003): 1457–1484.
2. Ralph Cassady Jr., *Auctions and Auctioneering* (Berkeley: University of California Press, 1967), 66.
3. This predicted equivalence has been supported by the results of an experimental study showing that English auctions and second-price sealed-bid auctions produce comparable amounts of revenue. See David Lucking-Reiley, "Using Field Experiments to Test Equivalence Between Action Formats: Magic on the Internet," *American Economic Review* 89, no. 5 (1999): 1063–1080.
4. "Luke Skywalker's Light Saber Up for Highest Bid," last modified July 6, 2005, http://news.yahoo.com
5. Tracy A. Suter and David M. Hardesty, "Maximizing Earnings and Price Fairness Perceptions in Online Consumer-to-Consumer Auctions," *Journal of Retailing* (2005): 307–317.
6. "eBay Inc. Announces Fourth Quarter and Full Year 2004 Financial Results," last modified July 22, 2005, http://investor.ebay.com/news/Q404/EBAY0119-777666.pdf.
7. Edial J. Pinker, Abraham Seidmann, and Yaniv Vakrat, "Managing Online Auctions: Current Business and Research Issues," *Management Science* 49 (November 2003): 1457–1484.
8. Amar Cheema et al., "Economics, Psychology, and Social Dynamics of Consumer Bidding in Auctions," *Marketing Letters* 16 (2005): 401–413.

9. Utpal M. Dholakia, Suamn Basuroy, and Kerry Soltysinski, "Auction or Agent (or Both)? A Study of Moderators of the Herding Bias in Digital Auctions," *International Journal of Research in Marketing* 19 (2002): 115–130.

10. Amar Cheema et al., "Economics, Psychology, and Social Dynamics of Consumer Bidding in Auctions," *Marketing Letters* 16 (2005): 401–413.

11. James H. Gilkeson and Kristy Reynolds, "Determinants of Internet Auction Success and Closing Price: An Exploratory Study, *Psychology & Marketing* 20 (June 2003): 537–566.

12. Barry M. Staw, "The Escalation of Commitment to a Course of Action," *Academy of Management Review* 6 (October 1981): 577–587.

13. James H. Gilkeson and Kristy Reynolds, "Determinants of Internet Auction Success and Closing Price: An Exploratory Study, *Psychology & Marketing* 20 (June 2003): 537–566. See also Gillian Ku, Deepak Malhotra, and J. Keith Murnighan, "Competitive Arousal in Live and Internet Auctions" (working paper, Northwestern University, Chicago, IL, 2004).

14. Gerald Haubl and Peter T. L. Popkowski Leszczyc, "Bidding Frenzy: Intensity of Competitive Interaction Among Bidders and Product Valuation in Auctions," *Advances in Consumer Research* 31 (2004): 90–93.

15. Patrick Bajari and Ali Hortaçsu, "Economic Insights from Internet Auctions," *Journal of Economic Literature* 42 (June 2004): 457–486.

16. Michael A. Kamins, Xavier Drèze, and Valerie S. Folkes, "Effects of Seller-Supplied Prices on Buyers' Product Evaluations: Reference Prices in an Internet Auction Context," *Journal of Consumer Research* 30 (March 2004): 622–628.

17. Edieal J. Pinker, Abraham Seidmann, and Yaniv Vakrat, "Managing Online Auctions: Current Business and Research Issues," *Management Science* 49 (November 2003): 1457–1484

18. John F. Kottas and Basheer M. Khumawala, "Contract Bid Development for the Small Businessman," *Sloan Management Review* 14 (Spring 1973): 31–45.

19. Murphy Sewall, "A Decision Calculus Model for Contract Bidding," *Journal of Marketing* 40 (October 1976): 92–98.

20. Lawrence Friedman, "A Competitive Bidding Strategy," *Operations Research* 4 (February 1956): 104–112.

21. Ibid.

22. For further discussion of this concept, see Roger Fisher, William Ury, and Bruce Patton, *Getting to Yes,* 2nd ed. (New York: Penguin, 1991).

23. Roy J. Lewicki, David M. Saunders, and John W. Minton, *Essentials of Negotiation* (Chicago: Irwin, 1997), 45.

24. Ibid., 47.

25. Leigh L. Thompson, *The Mind and Heart of the Negotiator,* 2nd ed. (Upper Saddle River, NJ: Prentice Hall, 2001), 46.

26. J. Keith Murnighan, *Bargaining Games: A New Approach to Strategic Thinking in Negotiations* (New York: William Morrow and Company, 1992), 17–19.

27. Thomas T. Nagle and Reed K. Holden, *The Strategy and Tactics of Pricing,* 3rd ed. (Upper Saddle River, NJ: Prentice Hall, 2002), 157.

28. Jeffrey A. Trachtenberg, "A Buyer's Market Has Shoppers Demanding and Getting Discounts," *Wall Street Journal,* February 8, 1991, A1.

29. Joydeep Srivastava, "A Consumer Perspective on Price-Matching Refund Policies: Effect on Price Perceptions and Search Behavior," *Journal of Consumer Research* 28 (September 2001): 296–307.

30. This formula is adapted from the one presented in Thomas T. Nagle and Reed K. Holden, *The Strategy and Tactics of Pricing,* 3rd ed. (Upper Saddle River, NJ: Prentice Hall, 2002), 216.

Law, Ethics, and Social Responsibility in Pricing

We have talked about pricing decisions from the standpoint of the seller, how to be guided by considerations of short-term profitability in setting initial prices or in modifying existing prices. But price setting and the price-setting process must also be guided by a consideration of the consequences of pricing decisions for the community and the society in which the firm operates.

Managing the societal implications of a pricing practice involves considering several different forms of guidance. For the pricing consequences that are most critical to societal functioning, there are laws and regulations. These are governmental rules that are enforced with penalties, such as fines and imprisonment. Laws are rules enacted by the U.S. Congress or by the legislative bodies of states or municipalities. Regulations are more specific rules set out by the government agencies that are empowered to implement the laws, such as the Federal Trade Commission or the Food and Drug Administration.

Pricing practices with negative implications that are less critical to the functioning of society or that are perhaps hard to restrict by law are said to involve ethics, the standards and principles concerning fairness and whether something is considered right or wrong. Among the negative consequences here are that people will be offended and avoid purchasing the item in question and other items from the seller. Prices or pricing practices that have consequences concerning whether society is better off or worse off are said to involve social responsibilities, the obligations of a business to implement policies that are most beneficial to society. This affects the customer's general attitudes toward the seller's products and prices and their trust in the seller.

In this chapter, we discuss the legal, regulatory, ethical, and social responsibility implications of four types of societally questionable pricing practices. The first category of societally questionable pricing practice involves price-setting processes that limit price competition among sellers. The second category involves adopting prices that are too high or too low. The third category involves setting inappropriate price differentials. The fourth category involves inadequately communicating price information to prospective customers.

PRICE FIXING

One of the great societal benefits of a free-market economic system is the ability of price regulation to be accomplished by the market itself. Market regulation helps keep prices low. For example, say that the bakeries in a particular community sold bread at prices that were higher than needed to cover necessary costs and earn an adequate profit. In a free-market system, this situation would attract new bakeries into that community who would sell bread for less and would thereby receive the consumers' business. The offending high-priced sellers would be forced to lower prices or withdraw from the marketplace. This disciplining of prices through competition encourages efficiency in production and other business operations. The savings from these efficiencies result in the members of society benefiting from lower prices.

To have the price competition that enables this to work, the price-setting process of each seller must be independent of the price-setting process of competing sellers. If the independent price-setting process is subverted by prices being "fixed" at a certain level—for example, by a collusive agreement between competitors—then society is likely to be deprived of the benefits brought by what Adam Smith referred to as the "invisible hand" of a free-market economy.[1] A pricing practice that interferes with the independence of the price-setting process among competitors is generally referred to as price fixing.

Because price fixing could be very profitable to sellers, it became apparent very soon after the widespread growth of free-market economies that a society's government needs to play a strong role in preventing companies from making arbitrary or collusive agreements on prices. The results of such agreements were known as "trusts" in the nineteenth century, and to make them illegal, the U.S. federal government has instituted a number of antitrust laws. Key among these laws is the Sherman Antitrust Act, passed in 1890. Its essential restriction is expressed (in its Section 1) as follows:

> "Every contract, combination in the form of trust or otherwise, or conspiracy, in restraint of trade or commerce . . . is declared to be illegal."

Since its passage, this law has been invoked many times in cases of businesses improperly interacting in the price-setting process. These cases could involve only competing sellers or could involve a manufacturer or supplier attempting to control the pricing of those companies that are competing on the resale of the manufacturer's or supplier's product.

These two types of price-fixing situations can be understood within the common conception of product distribution as involving a matrix of companies (see Figure 15.1). On the top row of the matrix are the manufacturers, the originators of the product. The manufacturers typically sell the product to companies on the middle rows of the matrix, middle-men such as wholesalers and retailers, who help the product arrive in the hands of the consumers. Price agreements between companies on the same row—that is, competitors—comprise horizontal price fixing. Price agreements between companies on different rows—that is, those companies who buy and sell from each other—compose vertical price fixing.

Figure 15.1   Matrix of Companies Involved in the Distribution of Products

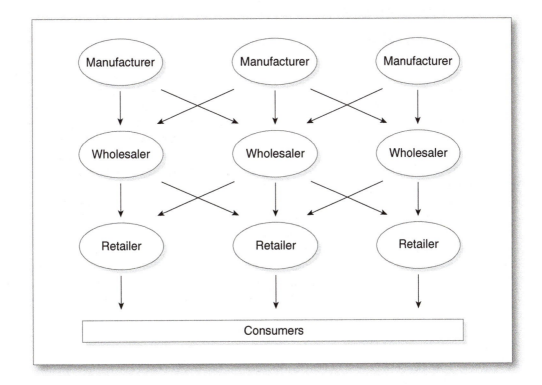

Horizontal Price Fixing

Horizontal price fixing can take a variety of forms. There can be agreements among competing sellers on a common target price, agreements to set a common minimum price, agreements to impose the same mandatory surcharges, agreements to establish uniform costs and markups, or agreements to restrict product supply. Prices set by procurement auctions can be fixed by bid rigging among competing sellers who are bidding for the job. In one type of bid rigging scheme, conspiring companies will agree to withhold bids or purposely bid too high in return for having a designated successful bidder subcontracting to them a portion of the work. Colluding bidders could also decide to take turns winning the business, agreeing to throw the bidding first to one of the conspirators, then the next, and so on.[2]

A business practice that so clearly violates the intent of a law that no conceivable circumstances could justify it would be considered by the courts as illegal by the per se criterion. This means that the business practice is, in itself, a violation of the law. Like murder, robbery, and other criminal actions that are per se illegal, the question in court becomes only, "Did they do it?" On the other hand, a business practice could be illegal or not, depending on the likely consequences of the practice, such as whether or not the practice benefits consumers. Such a practice would be evaluated by the courts by considering these likely consequences. This would constitute the rule of reason criterion of legality.[3]

Explicit price-setting collusion by managers of competing companies has been considered to be a per se violation of the Sherman Act. In other words, if the managers are found to have agreed in a meeting, or by the exchange of email or letters, to hold to a common set of prices, then these managers and their companies would face fines and possible prison time. In 2004, the Criminal Antitrust Penalty Enhancement and Reform Act raised the Sherman Act's maximum penalty to $100 million for companies and up to 10 years in prison for convicted individuals. There has been a constant stream of price-fixing prosecutions over the years, such as the 1996 conviction of the Archer Daniels Midland Company and several of its executives for conspiring with two competing companies to fix the global price of lysine, an important animal feed additive.[4]

Suspicious competitive behaviors short of an explicit price-fixing agreement have been evaluated in the courts by the rule of reason criterion. For example, parallel pricing among competitors (see Chapter 6) has not been judged, in itself, an indication of an illegal activity. It is recognized that competing businesses may make the same pricing choices through independent processes. The legality of parallel pricing is judged by the presence of circumstances, known as *plus factors*, that suggest something other than independent pricing decisions. A list of common parallel-pricing plus factors can be seen in Figure 15.2.[5] To

Figure 15.2   Parallel-Pricing Plus Factors

1. It would be in the parties' self-interest if they all acted the same way (rational-motive test).

2. The price increases in times of surplus.

3. There is an artificial standardization of products.

4. Suspicious reasons are given to explain behavior.

5. There is an opportunity to collude—for example, correspondence or meetings, especially if immediately followed by simultaneous, identical actions.

6. The price uniformity over a long period of time is not caused by rise in cost of a common input.

7. The market structure is conducive to collusion—for example, small number of sellers, high barriers to entry, unsophisticated or last-minute purchasers.

8. There is a stability of market shares over time.

9. High profit margins are present.

illustrate the logic behind these, consider the first two plus factors on this list. A seller would be unlikely to independently choose to increase price when there is a surplus of the product on the market. However, it would be in the seller's interest to do so if all the competitors in the market also raised their price. Thus, if there were uniform price increases in times of product surplus, these two plus factors would support a judgment against the legality of these increases.

The legality of price signaling practices (again, see Chapter 6) have also been judged by the rule of reason criterion. Their evaluation in the courts has relied on a set of plus factors similar to those used in evaluating parallel pricing (see Figure 15.3).[6] Note the importance of the price information being communicated in a public way and the negative regard that would be given to a trade association that, say, published industry price schedules but then threatened to expel any association member who did not adhere to these schedules. It has also been recognized that, in a market that is not highly concentrated in a few companies, public communication of price information could actually have a *pro*-competitive effect, by facilitating free price competition.[7]

Figure 15.3   Signaling/Price-Information Plus Factors

1. There is evidence of anticompetitive intent.

2. The absence of independent business reasons for information exchange is present.

3. Data are not available to the public.

4. Present or future data are exchanged.

5. The data disclose individual transactions or customers.

6. The market is highly concentrated.

7. There is evidence of coercive mechanisms that pressure competitors to adhere to price schedules.

Perhaps the most famous cases of horizontal price fixing have involved international cartels, such as the control of diamond prices by the De Beers Company or of oil prices by the Organization of Petroleum Exporting Countries (OPEC). These pricing practices indeed involve explicit collusion but are able to exist because of the absence of effective international legal constraints corresponding to U.S. laws such as the Sherman Antitrust Act.

Vertical Price Fixing

The typical vertical price-fixing situation involves a manufacturer or other supplier of a product specifying the price that can be charged by the resellers of the product, such as wholesalers or retailers, who compete with one another. For example, the New Balance company might attempt to require its dealers to maintain the company's list prices on its shoes and to avoid offering discounts to consumers. Such practices are designed to accomplish what is referred to as resale price maintenance.

By requiring all resellers to maintain a minimum price, the manufacturer reduces price competition and thus protects reseller margins. Doing this enables the manufacturer to maintain its prices to the resellers and thus also protects the manufacturer's profits. A supporter of resale-price-maintenance practices could argue that these practices benefit society by helping ensure that resellers have the resources to provide information and full product service to consumers. It could also be argued that such practices could actually promote competition by, for example, enabling the manufacturer of a poorly known brand to use price to help communicate a respectable, quality image. On the other hand, an opponent of resale price maintenance could argue that the restriction of price competition among resellers leads to higher prices to consumers.[8]

Arguments for the potential pro-competitive effects of resale price maintenance have led the U.S. Supreme Court in 2007 to soften the prior legal constraints against vertical price fixing. It ruled that even explicit bilateral contracts (i.e., contracts signed by both sides) among a manufacturer and its resellers should be evaluated by the rule of reason rather than by the per se criterion of legality. Thus, whereas a resale-price-maintenance policy of a small-brand manufacturer might be ruled legal, a similar policy by major-brand manufacturer might raise legal questions. This would be particularly so if the major-brand manufacturer appeared to use a resale-price-maintenance policy that provided high margins to retailers as bargaining chip to influence its retailers to not carry competing smaller brands. Because of the remaining possibility that explicit manufacturer–retailer agreements can be ruled illegal, it may sometimes be safer for companies to rely on unilateral actions to accomplish resale price maintenance.[9]

Unilateral actions that work toward accomplishing some degree of resale price maintenance include a manufacturer prominently displaying a product's price on its package or mentioning a particular retail price in the product's advertising and other promotional materials. These practices are considered legal because, although they encourage a reseller to maintain (and, in particular, not exceed) the resale price that the manufacturer desires, they do not involve the reseller in any sort of agreement. Such practices can work together with unilateral actions based on what is known as the Colgate doctrine[10]—the "long recognized right" of a private company to decide what other companies to deal with. This principle makes it possible for a manufacturer to announce prices and then choose to deal with only those resellers who the manufacturer judges are likely to maintain these prices. The key to the legality of this type of practice is that the manufacturer acts on its own, without any threats or discussions with particular retailers that could be interpreted as a bilateral agreement.[11]

Public Utility Regulation

Although it is not called "price fixing," there are industries where the government explicitly sanctions a noncompetitive price-setting process. It is usually the case that such industries are considered to be natural monopolies, which are said to exist when the presence of competing sellers creates inefficiencies. For example, if individual homes were served by many competing water companies, the frequent digging necessary for installing and maintaining all the required underground water lines would be likely to create difficulties that would outweigh the benefits of competition. The tangle of wires shown in Figure 15.4 illustrates the effects of open competition in the early years of telephone service. Other industries that have been considered natural monopolies include sewerage services, electricity, gas, cable television, and railroad transportation.

Figure 15.4   Tangle of Wires in Early Telephone Service Illustrating Why It Was Considered a Natural Monopoly

Source: Brown Brothers.

http://www.nlm.nih.gov/onceandfutureweb/database/seca/case3-artifacts/photoslg/photo1.jpg

In these industries, the government will often give one company a formal monopoly—that is, the exclusive right to provide the service in a given area. Companies that are granted these exclusive rights to serve the public are known as **public utilities**. The benefit to society of giving these companies exclusive rights carries along with it the disadvantage that there can be no price setting by competitive interaction. In its place, price setting in public utilities must be accomplished by government price regulation. What does such a price-setting process look like?

In the United States, most public utility price setting is accomplished through the interaction of the utility company and a state regulatory commission. Typically, the utility company will initiate a "regulatory contest" in which it will claim to the commission that higher rates (i.e., prices) are required, usually because of increases in costs. The company's accountants will then be brought before the commissioners to present the cost-increase documentation. The commission will then rule on which costs are allowable and will apply the return on investment (ROI) that the utility is allowed to earn so as to arrive at a new maximum rate level. State regulatory commissions often differ on the types of costs that are allowable and on how costs should be determined (e.g., original cost vs. replacement cost). They may also differ on allowable profit levels (e.g., ROIs pegged to current interest rates or to the bond market). Regulatory commissions typically do not grant public utilities the entirety of the rate increases they request. However, the companies often ask for larger rate increases than they think they will get, so it is not clear how severely their rate setting is constrained by regulatory commission decisions.[12]

If the goal of public utility regulation is to approach the price levels that would have been produced by price setting through marketplace competition, it is questionable how successful this regulation has been. It is often suggested that the regulatory price-setting process fails to help companies maintain sufficient discipline to minimize costs and operate efficiently. Many observers feel that regulatory commissions tend to be influenced by both labor organizations and utility companies in the industries that they regulate.[13] Further, by focusing utility companies on continually requesting rate increases, the regulatory price-setting process appears to lead utility companies away from examining their typical assumption of low category price elasticity. Utilities rarely consider the possibility that lowering their rates could so stimulate demand as to increase their profits.[14] Recently, there has been experimentation with new models of deregulating services in natural monopolies, such as separating the generation of electricity from the delivery of that electricity to individual homes. It may be only the delivery of the electricity that would need to be a regulated public utility.[15]

INAPPROPRIATE PRICE LEVELS

Price fixing is a type of societally questionable pricing practice that concerns the price-setting process. A second type of questionable pricing practice concerns not so much any particular price-setting process as much as the negative societal consequences of the prices that end up actually occurring. These negative consequences could result from prices being too high, or they could result from prices being too low.

Excessively High Prices

Various factors in the economic environment can cause prices to climb to levels that may have societally undesirable consequences. For example, after World War II, the sudden increase in demand for housing in San Francisco, New York, and other U.S. cities led to rent increases so severe that many longtime residents were becoming unable to afford their apartments.[16] The period of high inflation in the United States following the oil price shocks of the 1970s led the prices of many consumer goods to increase to levels that began to put financial burdens on middle-class citizens. Floods, hurricanes, or other natural disasters often create scarcities that can put severe upward pressure on prices. After the 1994 earthquake that devastated areas of Southern California, it was reported that half-liter bottles of drinking water were selling for as much as $8 per bottle.[17]

When the undesirable consequences of such high prices become apparent, the resulting public outcry may lead the government to take action. As we noted in Chapter 12, one form of governmental action against prices that are considered to be too high is the introduction of price controls—legally mandated maximum prices in a product category. For example, since the 1940s there have been laws in New York City that have placed specific limits on the size of increases that can be made in apartment rents. Another form of governmental action is the enactment of laws against price gouging. Rather than place limits on prices in any particular product category, these laws usually attempt in a more general way to restrain sellers from taking advantage of earthquakes, hurricanes, or other natural disasters. For example, in Florida, one of the twenty-eight U.S. states that have anti-price-gouging statutes, the law forbids prices that represent "a gross disparity" from what was the commodity's average price during the thirty days immediately prior to a declared emergency.[18] Such legal constraints on price levels are controversial, opponents noting the occurrence of negative consequences such as product shortages, rationing, and black markets.[19]

It is not just factors that occur in the economic or natural environment that could lead a price to be excessively high; governmental policies could also be the culprit. For example, the U.S. government grants twenty-year patents to companies that develop new pharmaceutical products. By prohibiting any competitors from selling a product, a patent supports the profitability of setting the product's price very high and accepting whatever sales decrease occurs by virtue of the product's category elasticity. As we saw in Chapter 4, this is known as the skimming strategy—making higher profit margins from fewer buyers.

Although letting price limit the number of buyers may be profitable to the product's seller, it may not be fully acceptable to society. When a high-priced product satisfies an important need and there are no effective alternatives, then ethical and social responsibility issues arise. For example, GlaxoSmithKline and other multinational drug companies have been selling the set of antiretroviral drugs necessary to treat the AIDS infection for $10,000 per year. In African countries where these patents have not been honored, effective generic versions of these drugs have been selling for $300 per year. If, as the generic prices indicate, the variable costs for producing the AIDS drugs are less than $300, the $10,000 price tag indicates an enormous contribution margin. This has led to sharp criticism of the drug companies' skimming strategy. For example, the president of the relief organization Doctors Without Borders has written:

> "The poor have no consumer power, so the market has failed them. I'm tired of the logic that says: 'He who can't pay dies.'"[20]

It is often argued that patent laws benefit society, because by protecting the profitability of useful new products, these laws help motivate companies to develop such products. A basic issue here is how to balance the long-term societal benefits of providing incentives for innovation with the short-term benefits of maintaining widespread access to products that can relieve human suffering. If patent protection is deemed necessary for motivating new discoveries, then governments may have an obligation to subsidize high prices when such patent protection causes undue hardships to consumers. A related issue is how much profit should useful new products be allowed. For example, it has been argued that setting a patent's length so that it yields say $1 billion in profits for a new drug would lead drug companies to make more wasteful expenditures, such as costs involved in racing to be first, than if the patent's length were shortened so that, say, only $800 million in profits could be expected.[21]

Excessively Low Prices

It is not just high prices that could have negative societal consequences; low prices could also be harmful to society. One way that this could occur is when a low price contributes to the consumption of a product that is considered undesirable. Consumer interest in an undesirable product is sometimes referred to as unwholesome demand. For example, the availability of "Saturday night specials"—small, inexpensive handguns—is thought by gun control advocates to increase the likelihood that guns are used in drunken brawls, domestic disputes, and other emotional occasions when guns might not have been used if they had been more costly to obtain.[22] Opponents of products such as alcohol and tobacco have also argued that low prices unnecessarily encourage consumption. The most common government response to the conclusion that low prices increase unwholesome demand is to increase prices on undesirable products by levying taxes on them. For example, the average state cigarette tax in the United States raises cigarette prices by over 20 percent. In some states, such as New Jersey, cigarette taxes raise the price of a pack of cigarettes taxes by almost 40 percent.[23] These "sin taxes" have been criticized for inordinately impacting the poor and for encouraging black markets.

Another way that low prices could have negative societal consequences is if the prices are low because the full costs of producing and/or disposing of the product are borne by the general public rather than by the product's producers and consumers. It could be argued that the prices of products whose production depletes forests or grasslands or pollutes the air or water are low only because society at large pays part of the price of their manufacture. The most common legal approach to raising these prices is to require that manufacturers adhere to environmental protection regulations and to levy tariffs on products imported from countries that do not require environmentally sound manufacturing.

A clever legal approach to raising prices on products whose package disposal unnecessarily contributes to litter or landfills is to add to the item's price a charge for this negative environmental effect and then return the money to consumers who return the package for recycling. Eleven U.S. states currently have "bottle bills" requiring package-return deposits—usually of $0.05—on bottles and/or aluminum cans.[24]

A more market-based approach, part of what is known as green marketing, involves consumers paying a premium for environmentally friendly products. A key to succeeding in this approach is to ensure consumer awareness of the environmental claim either by the product's name, such as Ben & Jerry's naming an ice cream flavor "Rainforest Crunch" to bring to mind the company's contributions to saving the Amazon rainforest or by use of a standard ecolabel such as "Energy Star."[25] Analogous to the environmental concern of green marketing is the concern that a product's manufacturing process reflects social justice. For example, the SweatX brand of sports clothing charged higher prices but with the assurance to consumers that its workers were paid fair living wages.[26]

Excessively low prices could also be harmful if they are used to undermine marketplace competition. The practice of setting prices very low, perhaps even below variable costs, in order to do harm to a competitor is known as predatory pricing. The logic of predatory pricing is that if a seller sets prices low enough to drive out the seller's competitors, the resulting monopoly would give the seller the power to charge very high prices that will provide the strategy's payoff. However, in most markets, the barriers to entry are low enough that it can be expected that new competitors will come in long before the predatory seller could make enough profit to outweigh the profit sacrifices necessary to drive out the original competitors. Although frustration at low-priced competitors often leads firms to accuse those competitors of predation, it is probably a pricing strategy that is rarely used.

A competitor suspected of predatory pricing could be challenged under Section 2 of the Sherman Antitrust Act ("Every person who shall monopolize, or attempt to monopolize . . . trade or commerce . . . shall be deemed guilty of a felony . . ."). However, the Supreme Court has ruled that, in such cases, the burden of proof is on the accuser, who must convincingly demonstrate that the firm accused of predation is likely to be able to recoup the profits lost through future high prices.[27] Successfully attacking a suspected predator under state laws is also very difficult. For example, an association of retail grocers in Oklahoma accused Walmart of violating the Oklahoma Unfair Sales Act by selling items at prices below costs. The court rejected that claim under what could be called "the clean-hands doctrine," by noting that the accusing grocery retailers often used below-cost prices themselves in promotions to compete with each other.[28]

INAPPROPRIATE PRICE DIFFERENTIALS

Sometimes it is not the level of price that creates the problems but rather the differences in price levels between different buyers. A company selling an item at different prices to different buyers is, of course, price segmentation. As we saw in Chapters 10 through 12, when carried out appropriately, price segmentation is a key strategy for maximizing profits. However, when done inappropriately, price segmentation can create societal problems.

Limitations on Consumer Price Segmentation

When a price-segmentation practice is seen by consumers as unfair, the resulting consumer anger is likely to hurt the profits of the offending sellers. If often repeated, impressions of unfairness could even contribute to a demoralizing cynicism about the benefits of free-market commerce. As we saw in Chapter 10, price segmentation is likely to be seen as unfair, and possibly illegal, if it leads to higher prices for groups of consumers who are considered vulnerable or disadvantaged. We also saw that consumers additionally take into account the consequences of a price-segmentation practice, as in the acceptability of using household income as a price-segmentation fence in the prices students pay for a college education.

In 1999, it was reported that the Cola-Cola Company had begun testing a new vending machine that senses the outside temperature and adjusts the prices of its cold drinks accordingly.[29] Although that could be considered a creative idea for a price-segmentation fence, there was immediate negative reaction. One observer said, "What's next? A machine that x-rays people's pockets to find out how much change they have and raises the price accordingly?"and Coke's competitor Pepsi immediately distanced itself from the idea. The sense that this price-segmentation tactic is unfair can be understood in the context of the role of perceived profits in fairness judgments (see Chapter 8). Since consumers are likely to use Coke's current vending machine profits as a reference point, Coke's receiving a higher profit in hotter weather, without the company expending any additional effort, would seem unwarranted and unfair. Note, however, that it is the consumers' consideration of the seller's "reference profit" that is important here.[30] If Coke had proposed using the temperature-sensing vending machines to offer soft drink discounts in cold weather, it seems unlikely that there would any serious objections.

Price Segmentation as a Means of Restricting Competition

Price segmentation can have negative societal effects when it serves to work against marketplace competition. A classic example of this involves John D. Rockefeller's Standard Oil, one of the large nineteenth century conglomerates that led to the Sherman Act and other antitrust laws. After incurring the fixed costs of purchasing the oil wells and building the refining plants, it was transportation of the oil that constituted the main variable costs of the kerosene and other oil-related products sold by Standard Oil. Rockefeller was able keep these transportation costs lower than those of his competitors by obtaining from the railroads freight prices lower than his competitors were able to get. These low costs enabled him to set low consumer prices which, by increasing his sales, gave Rockefeller even more power to obtain low freight prices that were unavailable to his competitors.

Although the Sherman Act set the groundwork, it was the Clayton Act in 1914 that specifically prohibited practices such as the anticompetitive price segmentation practiced by the railroads in Rockefeller's time. In 1936, this law was amended by the Robinson–Patman Act (1936), which was described in Chapter 10's discussion of legal constraints on using purchase quantity for price segmentation. Recall that, because the Robinson–Patman Act is designed to protect competition, it covers price segmentation only in business markets. Price segmentation in consumer markets can be judged as unfair, but it has little to do with the strength of marketplace competition.

The key factor for setting off a lawsuit based on the Robinson–Patman Act is a supplier giving one business customer low prices that are not available to the business customer's competitors. Usually, it is one of these competitors who will bring the lawsuit, claiming that his or her business has been unfairly harmed by the supplier's pricing practices. For Robinson–Patman to be applicable, the accusing competitor must demonstrate that the supplier's different prices were indeed for the same item (i.e., items of "like grade and quality") that were purchased at roughly the same time. Note that service products are considered to be intrinsically adapted to the purchaser and thus unable to be clearly the same product. Thus, the Robinson–Patman Act covers the pricing of only goods, not services.

Further, the practice of giving favorable prices to only some customers has not been considered per se illegal. Rather, the rule of reason criterion has been applied, considering whether the practice in question really harmed competition and whether or not there were justifying circumstances. These potentially justifying circumstances fall into the following two categories:

1. *The cost-justification defense.* If a customer really costs less to serve, then it is legal for the seller to pass those cost savings on to the customer in the form of lower prices. Because handling goods in large quantities often involves lower per-item costs, this defense can make volume discounts allowable. However, with this defense, the burden of proving the lower costs lies with the defendant.

2. *The meeting-competition defense.* A supplier can justify giving one customer a low price not given to other customers by documenting that this low price was necessary to meet the supplier's competition for the customer's business. For example, the Borden Milk Company was not penalized for selling milk to A&P supermarkets for particularly low prices because A&P told Borden that its price quote was "not even in the ballpark" given the prices of the competing milk suppliers who had contacted A&P.[31]

Although the Robinson–Patman Act is well-suited to prohibiting grossly anticompetitive practices, such as those of John D. Rockefeller, it clearly still allows many opportunities for price segmentation in business markets.

INADEQUATE PRICE COMMUNICATION

An important aspect of protecting marketplace competition is ensuring that customers are given sufficient price and product information to enable them to make purchase choices that fit their needs. Without the adequate communication of price information, the price-regulating ability of a free-market economic system cannot operate effectively.

As we saw in Chapter 7, there are many factors that contribute to low price-level knowledge among customers. Sometimes sellers exacerbate these factors by engaging in price-communication practices that appear to have little purpose other than to make it difficult for the customer to become fully aware of the price that he or she will be paying for the product. Here are some examples of common price-communication practices that have been considered ethically—and in some cases legally—questionable.

Manipulation of Price Formats

Managing price format—how a price is expressed—can be important for effective pricing. For example, decisions about two-part pricing (Chapter 10) and charging separately for shipping (Chapter 12) are relevant to price segmentation, and describing products in terms of price-itemized menus can be a useful alternative to negotiation (Chapter 14).

However, when a seller's price-format practices seem to have little purpose other than to obscure what the customer must pay, these practices have been criticized as being exploitive or manipulative. As mentioned in Chapter 7, expressing prices using ninety-nines and other just-below price endings can lead to questions about a seller's honesty and integrity. Many hotels, airlines, and phone service providers generate consumer anger by loudly advertising competitive prices but being quiet about numerous fees and extra charges that often add 10 percent or more to the price of the service.[32] Some new and used automobile dealers so strongly emphasize the price framed in terms of monthly payments that it becomes difficult for customers to be clear on the actual price of the car. Some sellers use price format to mislead by presenting prices in unusual terms, such as carpeting priced by the square foot rather than, as is more customary, by the square yard.

The difficulty of enacting legislation to protect customers from such practices is illustrated by the truth-in-lending provision of the 1968 Consumer Credit Protection Act. Because the actual price of a consumer loan involves various finance charges in addition to the simple interest rate, this consumer protection law required all covered loan and credit offerings to provide consumers with the price of the loan in a standard format—the annual percentage rate (APR). However, for many loans, sellers still advertised the simple interest rate, so the law resulted in consumers being presented with an additional number. Because of that and because of the complexity concerning what is and is not included in the APR, it has been suggested that the law leads credit customers to be less, rather than more, aware of the loan prices that they really will be paying.[33]

Some sellers, overly eager to frame their prices as discounts, create the impression of a price savings, when none really exists. For example, some price advertisements present inflated external reference prices described by phrases such as "compare at." Consumers may interpret these as actual prices of competing sellers and be influenced by them.[34] Other retailers have been suspected of raising prices only to immediately lower them. Recently, a department store advertised an electric percolator for $61.99, "on sale" from its "regular" price of $69.99, which was suspiciously higher than the manufacturer's suggested retail price of $59.99.[35]

Misleading Merchandising

Some questionable price-communication practices concern merchandising issues, such as the display and packaging of products. For example, it has been found that many consumers assume that grocery items featured in end-aisle or other displays are being sold at discounted prices.[36] Sellers who display regularly priced merchandise in this way have been accused of taking advantage of those consumers.

It was mentioned in Chapter 7 that a common price-origin belief is that consumers can get a lower unit price (e.g., a per-ounce or per-pound price) on a product by purchasing a larger package size than a smaller one. In this belief, consumers are presuming the existence of quantity discounts. The reality is that there are often quantity surcharges—higher unit prices for larger package sizes than for smaller ones.[37] Although many retailers provide explicit unit price information on shelf labels that enables consumers to detect quantity surcharges, it has been found that consumers often do not use this information.[38] Companies that sell larger package sizes at higher unit prices have been accused of taking unfair advantage of consumers' quantity discount assumption.[39]

An alternative view of sellers' pricing motivations is offered by researchers who find that there are more quantity surcharges when a brand's small-size package is one of the retailer's fast-moving items, and a larger-size package is not.[40] They argue that when small package sizes are among the store's most frequently purchased items, there is more consumer price awareness and more price competition, which results in greater price sensitivity for these items. Price sensitivities high enough to surpass the critical values in price-decrease breakeven calculations tend to make price decreases profitable and lead to lower item prices. Indeed, as we saw in Chapter 10, high-price sensitivity is one of the factors that leads to a lower best price. In addition, as we saw in Chapter 13, keeping prices low on such fast-moving items is particularly important for maintaining a favorable retail price image. These considerations point out that, rather than necessarily being exploitive in intent, quantity surcharges can result from reasonable business decisions.

Using Fictitious Low Prices as "Bait"

To attract consumer attention, sellers sometimes offer prices that seem very low but may not be as desirable as they appear to be, and may even be fictitious. Sellers sometimes use hedge words in price advertisements, such as "up to" (e.g., "Save up to 50 percent") or "as low as" (e.g., "At prices as low as $19.99"). Although consumers do recognize the ambiguity in these claims, they often assume an equal distribution of values (e.g., as many 50 percent savings as 10 percent savings), which may not reflect the seller's actual prices.[41] Some sellers advertise attractive price deals (e.g., three books for $0.01 each), but include in fine print severe restrictions that are often overlooked by consumers (e.g., "necessary to buy three more books at regular prices during the year").[42]

Credit card offers and other financial service products are sometimes structured with teaser rates—very low fees or interest rates during a brief introductory period that are more than wiped out by higher prices afterward. For example, a very low advertised rate for a home mortgage might involve large upfront interest payments (known as "points"), have a variable interest rate, or even turn out to be a short-term balloon loan. A related misleading use of price as bait is a consumer credit provider advertising, "first month free," when what is meant is that the payment for the first month is added to the amount borrowed on which interest is charged. Teaser rates have been criticized for not making it sufficiently clear to consumers that advertised low initial interest rates are only temporary, that large rate increases are possible, and that the consequences of likely rate increases would have a substantial effect on the size of their payments.[43] For example, in the partial pricing information for a credit card offer shown in Figure 15.5, is it sufficiently clear that your interest rate could more than double if you make a late payment?

Some sellers promote a very low price on an item in order to get consumers to their store or office and then claim that they are sold out of the advertised product and try to persuade the consumer to purchase a more expensive item. This practice, known as "bait and switch," is illegal if the seller refuses to honor the advertised discount to any consumers.[44] However, having only a very limited quantity available of the advertised item is routinely practiced by retailers, especially on "Black Friday" (the day after Thanksgiving) and during the rest of the holiday buying season.

PRIMACY OF ETHICS AND SOCIAL RESPONSIBILITY

From this discussion of four types of societally questionable pricing practices—(1) price fixing, (2) inappropriate price levels, (3) inappropriate price differentials, and (4) inadequate price communication—it can be seen that some pricing techniques often considered unethical and/or socially irresponsible are not illegal. Despite this, it is important that sellers take concerted steps to avoid such practices. The guiding principle of the marketing concept, discussed in Chapter 1, focuses the seller toward using every feasible means to satisfy customer needs. Because customer needs include the feeling of being treated fairly, sellers would be wise to avoid even the appearance of manipulative or deceptive pricing. For example, if a retailer's quantity surcharges offend the retailer's customers, then such surcharges should be reconsidered, even if they were no more than the result of the retailer's routine and reasonable price-setting process. Perhaps moderating the price of a brand's larger package size, despite the low price sensitivity of that item, might be usefully viewed as an investment in building a favorable long-term relationship with customers.

It should be emphasized that, even when legal, pricing practices considered ethically questionable could have serious negative consequences for the seller. It has been found that consumer anger at being treated unfairly leads consumers to take actions far beyond those likely from mere dissatisfaction with a company's product or service.[45] Anger is likely to lead a consumer to switch away from a company's product or away from all of the company's products. Angry consumers are also likely to spread negative word-of-mouth information to other consumers, to start or contribute to "hate websites," and to file complaints to consumer-protection groups and other outside organizations.

Note also that when considering legal, ethical, and social responsibility obligations of price setters, it is the ethical and social responsibility guides that are in a sense primary. To the extent deemed practical, the pricing standards of ethics and social responsibility have been codified into governmental laws and regulations.[46] This codification is a process that is ongoing. Thus, one consequence of engaging in a pricing practice that violates ethical principles and social responsibility obligations is that it could lead to the practice being restricted more forcefully in the future by the imposition of governmental laws and regulations.

Figure 15.5   Pricing Information for a Credit Card Offer

PRICING INFORMATION	
INTEREST RATES AND INTEREST CHARGES	
Annual Percentage Rate (APR) for Purchases	**14.24%** This APR will vary with the market based on the Prime Rate.[a]
APR for Balance Transfers	**14.24%** This APR will vary with the market based on the Prime Rate[a]
APR for Cash Advances	**19.24%** This APR will vary with the market based on the Prime Rate.[b]
APR for Overdraft advance	**19.24%** (not available in some states). This APR will vary with the market based on the Prime Rate.[b]
Penalty APR and When It Applies	**29.99%.** This APR will vary with the market based on the Prime Rate[c] The Penalty APR will apply to your Account if you: • fail to make any Minimum Payment by the date and time due (late payment); • exceed your credit line (if applicable); • make a payment to us that is returned unpaid; or • do any of the above on another account or loan you have with us or any of our related companies. **How Long Will the Penalty APR Apply:** If an APR is increased for any of these reasons, the Penalty APR will apply indefinitely to future transactions. If we do not receive any Minimum Payment within 60 days of the date and time due, the Penalty APR will apply to all outstanding balances and future transactions on your Account; but if we receive six consecutive Minimum Payments when due, beginning immediately after the increase, the Penalty APR will stop being applied to transactions that occurred prior to or within 14days after we provided you notice about the APR increase.
How to Avoid Paying Interest on Purchases	You due date will be a minimum of 21 days after the close of each billing cycle. We will not charge you periodic interest on any portion of new purchases billed to a statement that we allocate such payment to, so long as your current statement shows that we received payment of the entire balance for your previous statement by the time the Minimum Payment was due. You may not be able to avoid interest on new purchases if you have another balance at a higher interest rate, unless you pay balance in full each month, because we generally allocate payments to higher rate balance first. We will begin charging interest on balance transfer, cash advances, and overdraft advances on the transaction date.
Minimum Interest Charge	If you are charged periodic interest, the charge will be no less than $1.50.
For Credit Card Tips from the Federal Reserve Board	To learn more about factors to consider when applying for or using a credit card, visit the website of the Federal Reserve Board at http://www.federalserve.gov/creditcard.

Source: Chase Bank USA, Wilmington, Delaware.

SUMMARY

Pricing decisions should be guided not only by the seller's short-term profits but also by consideration of their consequences for the community and for society. Forms of this guidance include laws, governmental regulations, ethical standards, and the obligations of social responsibility. Societally questionable pricing practices include price fixing, inappropriate price levels, inappropriate price differentials, and inadequate price communication.

Price fixing includes practices that interfere with the independence of price-setting practices among competitors, which limits the disciplining of prices through competition. Horizontal price fixing occurs among competing companies, such as when competitors agree to set common prices or rig bids in a procurement auction. Vertical price fixing involves a supplier specifying the price that must be charged by resellers of the product.

Excessively high prices include rents that long-term tenants can no longer afford and lifesaving drugs that are too expensive for many who are ill. Excessively low prices include prices that support unwholesome demand, prices that do not reflect the costs of the product's environmental damage, and prices designed to drive competitors out of business.

Inappropriate price differentials include practices that give consumers a feeling of being treated unfairly and practices enabling suppliers to restrict competition by giving lowered prices to favored business customers. This latter practice is generally illegal, but lower prices to some business customers can be justified if those customers cost less to serve or if the lower prices are necessary to meet competition.

Inadequate communication of price information to consumers includes manipulation of price formats to obscure prices, misleading product displays and package sizes, and the use of exaggerated or fictitious low-price claims to gain consumer attention or to attract them into stores.

Even when societally questionable pricing practices are not illegal, it would be wise for sellers to avoid such practices.

KEY TERMS

laws	per se criterion	unwholesome demand
regulations	rule of reason criterion	package-return deposits
ethics	plus factors	green marketing
social responsibilities	resale price maintenance	predatory pricing
price fixing	Colgate doctrine	quantity surcharges
horizontal price fixing	natural monopolies	teaser rates
vertical price fixing	public utilities	
bid rigging	price gouging	

REVIEW AND DISCUSSION QUESTIONS

1. Distinguish between ethics and social responsibilities as sources of guidance concerning the societal implications of pricing decisions.

2. Distinguish between laws and regulations and discuss how they tend to relate to the principles of ethics and the obligations of social responsibility.

3. In the context of a free-market system, explain the negative consequences of price fixing.

4. What is horizontal price fixing? Give some examples.

5. Use the distinction between the per se criterion and the rule of reason criterion to discuss the legality of explicit price-setting collusion and the legality of parallel pricing.

6. What are plus factors? Give some examples plus factors relevant to price signaling and how they can be used.

7. Describe vertical price fixing, and make clear how it differs from horizontal price fixing. What does the Colgate doctrine have to do with the legality of vertical price fixing?

8. Describe the typical price-setting process for public utilities. What are the benefits and drawbacks of this price-setting process?

9. Give three examples of situations where price levels were inappropriately high. Use societal consequences to explain why these high prices were considered excessive.

10. Describe how legally requiring package-return deposits is a means of dealing with the excessively low prices of some environmentally sensitive products.

11. Account for why predatory pricing is a strategy that is often mentioned but probably not often successfully used.

12. Describe at least two examples of how consumer conceptions of fairness limit the use of price segmentation.

13. Describe how price segmentation could be used as a means to restrict competition.

14. Describe the products and markets covered by the Robinson–Patman Act. What are two common legal defenses for the practice of giving favorable prices to only some customers?

15. Explain the negative societal consequences of allowing sellers to give consumers inadequate information about prices.

16. Give at least three examples of common price-communication practices that have been considered ethically and/or legally questionable.

17. Explain why it is important for sellers to consider the ethical and social responsibility implications of their pricing practices even if these practices are completely legal.

EXERCISES

1. Several years ago, your firm entered a market in which five large companies had 90 percent of the market share. Your firm attempted to gain some of the market by pricing aggressively, but whenever your firm lowered its prices, all five of the competing firms immediately followed suit.

This behavior seems suspicious to you, and it is definitely hurting your firm's ability to compete in this market. You are planning to sue these companies for violation of the Sherman Antitrust Act. What arguments should you attempt to make so as to give your suit the best chance of succeeding? Be specific.

2. The trade association for cement manufacturers has started a program asking its members to file weekly reports on their levels of production, sales, and prices. The association distributed this information to its members in a monthly newsletter. Describe the information that would most likely be requested in a court hearing to determine whether or not this practice is legal.

3. Suppose you are providing legal advice to businesses on pricing-related practices. For each of the following two companies, describe and explain a circumstance when the practice they are considering would most likely be considered legal and a circumstance when the practice would most likely be considered illegal.

    (a) The manufacturer of the leading brand of vacuum cleaners would like to establish a program of resale price maintenance among the retailers that sell the brand.

    (b) A fresh fish wholesaler located in a large metropolitan area would like to sell flounder fillets at a higher price to some retailers and restaurants and at a lower price to others.

4. Assume that the seller of a product has established the product's best price by considering the product's value to the customer (VTC), costs, and the market's price sensitivity using the procedures discussed in previous chapters.

    (a) Give an example where negative societal consequences would make many people consider this price to be too high. Describe the product, price, and the negative consequences.

    (b) Give an example where negative societal consequences would make many people consider this price to be too low. Describe the product, price, and the negative consequences.

NOTES

1. Adam Smith, *The Wealth of Nations* (1776; repr. New York: Random House, 1994), 485.
2. "Price Fixing, Bid Rigging, and Market Allocation Schemes: What They Are and What to Look For" (accessed November 12, 2010, http://www.justice.gov/atr/public/guidelines/211578.pdf).
3. Thomas T. Nagle, *The Strategy and Tactics of Pricing: A Guide to Profitable Decision Making* (Englewood Cliffs, NJ: Prentice Hall, 1987), 326.
4. Kent Monroe, *Pricing: Making Profitable Decisions* (New York: McGraw-Hill/Irwin, 2003), 512–513.
5. Thomas T. Nagle and Reed K. Holden, 1995, *The Strategy and Tactics of Pricing* (Englewood Cliffs, NJ: Prentice Hall) 371.
6. Thomas T. Nagle and Reed K. Holden, 1995, The *Strategy and Tactics of Pricing* (Englewood Cliffs, NJ: Prentice Hall) 372, 374.
7. John L. Daly, *Pricing for Profitability: Activity-Based Pricing for Competitive Advantage* (New York: Wiley, 2002), 68.

8. Dhruv Grewal and Larry D. Compeau, "Pricing and Public Policy: A Research Agenda and an Overview of the Special Issue," *Journal of Public Policy & Marketing* 18 (Spring 1999): 3–10.

9. Surinder Tikoo and Bruce Mather, "The Changed Legality of Resale Price Maintenance and Pricing Implications," *Business Horizons* (forthcoming).

10. It is known as the Colgate Doctrine because it is based on the outcome of litigation involving a forerunner of the Colgate-Palmolive Company.

11. Virginia G. Maurer and Michael Ursic, "Resale Price Maintenance: A Legal Review," *Journal of Public Policy & Marketing* 6 (1987): 171–180.

12. Edwin Mansfield, *Microeconomics,* 6th ed. (New York: Norton, 1988), 308–310.

13. Clifford Winston, "Economic Deregulation: Days of Reckoning for Microeconomists," *Journal of Economic Literature* 31 (September 1993): 1263–1289.

14. Edwin Mansfield, *Microeconomics,* 6th ed. (New York: Norton, 1988), 310.

15. Gregg Easterbrook, "Power Surge," *The New Republic* 220, May 10, 1999, p. 6.

16. Jack Hirshleifer and David Hirshleifer, *Price Theory and Applications,* 6th ed. (Upper Saddle River, NJ: Prentice Hall, 1998), 218.

17. Benjamin A. Holden, "Quake Price-Gouging Is Tempting but Shortsighted," *Wall Street Journal,* January 27, 1994, Section B, p. 2.

18. "Attorney General Warns Against Price Gouging," accessed December 17, 2008, http://www.dep.state.fl.us/mainpage/em/2005/rita/news/0919_03.htm

19. Edwin Mansfield, *Microeconomics,* 6th ed. (New York: Norton, 1988), 45.

20. Sushil Vachani and N. Craig Smith, Socially Responsible Pricing: Lessons for the Pricing of AIDS Drugs in Developing Countries," *California Management Review* 47 (Fall 2004): 117–144.

21. Richard A. Posner, "Pharmaceutical Patents–Posner," *The Becker-Posner Blog,* accessed April 20, 2006, http://www.becker-posner-blog.com/2004/12/pharmaceutical-patents--posner.html

22. Daniel W. Webster, Jon S. Vernick, and Lisa M. Hepburn, "Effects of Maryland's Law Banning 'Saturday Night Special' Handguns on Homicides," *American Journal of Epidemiology* 155, no. 5 (2002): 406–412.

23. "State Cigarette Prices, Taxes, and Costs Per Pack," *Campaign for Tobacco-Free Kids* (accessed April 18, 2006, http://www.tobaccofreekids.org/research/factsheets/pdf/0207.pdf).

24. "Trails of Trash," editorial, *North Carolina News & Observer,* April 4, 2006.

25. Jill M. Ginsberg and Paul N. Bloom, "Choosing the Right Green Marketing Strategy," *MIT Sloan Management Review* (Fall 2004): 79–84.

26. Carole Winkler, "The SweatX Story," *The Harbus,* March 22, 2004.

27. Thomas T. Nagle and John Hogan, *The Strategy and Tactics of Pricing,* 4th ed. (Englewood Cliffs, NJ: Prentice Hall, 2006), 337.

28. G. Richard Shell, *Make the Rules or Your Rivals Will* (New York: Crown Business, 2004), 139.

29. Constance L. Hays, "Coke Tests Vending Unit That Can Hike Prices in Hot Weather," *New York Times,* October 28, 1999.

30. See the concept of "dual entitlement" in Daniel Kahneman, Jack L. Knetsch, and Richard Thaler, "Fairness as a Constraint on Profit Seeking: Entitlements in the Market," *The American Economic Review* 76 (September 1986): 728–741.

31. Thomas T. Nagle and Reed K. Holden, *The Strategy and Tactics of Pricing,* 2nd ed. (Englewood Cliffs, NJ: Prentice Hall, 1995), 379.

32. Emily Thornton and Michael Arndt, "Fees! Fees! Fees!" *BusinessWeek,* September 29, 2003, 98–104.

33. Jinkook Lee and Jeanne M. Hogarth, "The Price of Money: Consumers' Understanding of APRs and Contract Interest Rates," *Journal of Public Policy & Marketing* 18 (Spring 1999): 66–76.

34. Larry D. Compeau and Dhruv Grewal (1998), "Comparative Price Advertising: An Integrative Review," *Journal of Public Policy & Marketing* 17, no. 2 (1998): 257–273.

35. "5 Holiday Shopping Traps to Avoid," *Consumer Reports,* December 15, 2010.

36. Jeffrey J. Inman, Leigh McAlister, and Wayne D. Hoyer, "Promotional signal: Proxy for a price cut?" *Journal of Consumer Research* 17, no. 1 (1990): 74–81.

37. Stanley M. Widrick, "Measurement of Incidents of Quantity Surcharge Among Selected Grocery Products," *Journal of Consumer Affairs* 13, no. 1 (1979): 99–107.

38. Kenneth C. Manning, David E. Sprott, and Anthony D. Miyazaki, "Unit Price Usage Knowledge: Conceptualization and Empirical Assessment," *Journal of Business Research* 56 (May 2003): 367–377.

39. Omprakash K. Gupta and Anna S. Rominger, "Blind Man's Bluff: The Ethics of Quantity Surcharges," *Journal of Business Ethics* 15 (1996): 1299–1312.

40. David E. Sprott, Kenneth C. Manning, and Anthony D. Miyazaki, "Grocery Price Setting and Quantity Surcharges," *Journal of Marketing* 67 (July 2003): 34–46.

41. Joan Lindsey-Mullikin and Ross D. Petty, "Marketing Tactics Discouraging Price Search: Deception and Competition," *Journal of Business Research* (2009). doi:10.1016/j.jbusres.2009.10.003

42. Indrajit Sinha, Rajan Chandran, and Srini S. Srinivasan, "Consumer Evaluation of Price and Promotional Restrictions—A Public Policy Perspective," *Journal of Public Policy & Marketing* 18 (Spring 1999): 37–51.

43. Elizabeth Warren, "Product Safety Regulation as a Model for Financial Services Regulation," *Journal of Consumer Affairs* 42, no. 3 (2008): 452–460.

44. Ross D. Petty and Joan Lindsey-Mullikin, "The Regulation of Practices that Promote Brand Interest: A "3Cs" Guide for Consumer Brand Managers," *Journal of Product & Brand Management* 15, no. 1 (2006): 23–36.

45. Roger Bougie, Rik Peters, and Marcel Zeelenberg, "Angry Customers Don't Come Back, They Get Back: The Experience and Behavioral Implications of Anger and Dissatisfaction in Services," *Journal of the Academy of Marketing Science* 31, no. 4 (2003): 377–393.

46. William M. Pride and O. C. Ferrell, *Marketing,* 14th ed. (Boston: Houghton Mifflin Company, 2008), 90.

The Role of Price in Marketing Strategy

As was mentioned at the end of Chapter 1, it is important that an organization's everyday pricing activities fit with the organization's strategies and long-term interests. A key variable for achieving this fit is for management to be clear on the strategic prominence of price in the marketing mix. This refers to the degree to which price is the focus of strategic concern and drives the other marketing mix variables. When price is highly prominent—when price is used to attract and keep customers—then it could be said to be a lead variable in the marketing mix. When price is not strategically prominent—when it is the marketing mix variables of product, distribution, and/or promotion that are primary in attracting and keeping customers—then price could be said to be a background variable in the marketing mix.

The strategic prominence of price is likely to be reflected in a company's positioning, or how it is regarded in the minds of customers. For example, Walmart, which uses price as a lead variable, is thought of by customers in terms of price—as a retailer that sells at low prices. On the other hand, Starbucks, which uses price as a background variable, is more likely to be thought of by customers in terms of the product it provides—high-quality coffee offered in a modern, sophisticated atmosphere.

The distinction between using price as a lead variable versus as a background variable is similar to the distinction that has been made between "price competition" and "nonprice competition."[1] However, it is important to appreciate that this lead-background distinction is not related to the discussion in Chapter 2 of cost-based versus customer-based pricing. Using price as a background variable does not mean considering price only after considering product costs. Whichever element of the marketing mix is the focus for attracting and keeping customers, pricing decisions should begin with the consideration of customer needs.

The strategic prominence of price can provide a useful context for reviewing and further developing the important pricing concepts discussed in this book. When price is used as a background variable, almost all of the fundamental pricing concepts come into play. When price plays the role of a lead variable, the fundamental concepts continue to apply, but also other strategic pricing concepts become relevant. Thus, in this chapter, we first discuss price as a background variable and then discuss its use as a lead variable. Because these two sections will assume a fixed price policy, the third section will review how these concepts can apply to interactive pricing and to situations where technological advances have raised problems with traditional pricing models. Finally, we consider pricing in a nonprofit setting and will return to the importance of customer focus in pricing decisions.

PRICE AS A BACKGROUND VARIABLE

It is probably the case that, for most businesses, price is a background variable in the marketing mix. Research has shown that most customers do not base their decision on price alone,[2] and we have seen (in Chapter 6) that brand price elasticities are often found to be low. This relatively low importance of price can be illustrated by considering the brands that come to mind that are considered "premium" or high quality (e.g., Apple, Sony, Sub-Zero, BMW, Rolex, Whole Foods, Pepperidge Farm), the brands that are associated with particular lifestyles (e.g., Harley-Davidson, Calvin Klein, Laura Ashley, IKEA), or the brands that come to mind as convenient alternatives (e.g., 7-Eleven, Amazon, TD Bank). When consumers think about these brands, price is a secondary consideration.

In addition, we can reflect on how many of our everyday purchases are not primarily price-driven because of the economic price-sensitivity factors discussed in Chapter 6. For example, we might buy Morton's salt because the price difference from the generic brand seems inconsequential, we might stick with our current plumber because we know and trust his work, and we might favor a particular local grocery store because we have learned how to find things there.

It has sometimes been said that many corporate and small-business managers do not put enough of their energies into developing prices and pricing policies. While this may be true, it should also be recognized that for most businesses, it makes sense for managers to focus their efforts on the company's products and on the distribution and promotion of these products. Given that price is often not the prime concern of customers, it should often not be the prime concern of managers. Returning to the distinction (from Chapter 1) between creating and harvesting value, price as a background variable means that managers should keep their focus, and most of their attention, on the marketing mix elements that create value.

Managing Price as a Background Variable

To manage price in an environment where the available management time is limited, it is helpful to have checklists.[3] The checklists here are offered to illustrate how, in a fixed price environment, price management can be systematized. They also serve to help review the key pricing concepts discussed in this book.

The following are routine, relatively frequent periodic pricing activities:

1. *Determining initial prices* (see Chapters 2 through 4). When a product is offered for the first time, use an estimate of its value to the customer to set its initial price. Do at least

some investigation of the product's reference value, possible positive and negative differentiating factors, and the value of these differentiating factors to customers.

2. *Determining best prices* (see Chapters 5 through 9). For each product currently offered, periodically consider increasing or decreasing the price by a small amount (i.e., 5 to 20 percent). Calculate the breakeven sales level for each prospective price change, and use an estimate of the market's likely sales response to judge if one of these price changes should be implemented.

3. *Consider new possibilities for price segmentation* (see Chapters 10 through 12). Consider how each of the six major types of price-segmentation fences could be used or how it could be used in a new way.

4. *Consider product interrelations* (see Chapter 13). Investigate the possibility that one or more offered products may have a pronounced effect on the company's price image, and identify products that have strong complements or substitutes among other items sold by the company. For each of these products, return to the determination of its best price, taking its product interrelation(s) into account.

5. *Track price implementation* (see Chapter 1). Track the degree to which the prices, determined by the four steps above, are actually being implemented. Take action to plug up sources of price leakage.

The following are some more complex, less frequent pricing activities:

1. *Review policies on price format* (see Chapters 7 and 15). Consider customer information needs in decisions on price partitioning. Minimize use of just-below prices and other means of price expression that might appear manipulative or tacky or might otherwise potentially detract from the perceived quality of your product and company.

2. *Review policies on price promotion* (see Chapters 8 and 11). It generally makes sense to communicate about prices when they have been decreased and to use price promotions for the purpose of price segmentation. However, when price is a background variable in the marketing mix, most of the communication with the customer should be about the marketing mix elements that create value.

Long-Term Factors in Managing Prices

In our discussions up to now of determining an item's best price, our viewpoint has concerned factors that operate in the short term, which would be the period within, say, six months following the prospective price change. However, effective price management involves also taking long-term factors into account. There are at least three types of such long-term factors.

The first type of long-term factor concerns price elasticities, the key measure in estimating the market's response to price changes. There is considerable evidence that price elasticities measured over a long period of time differ from those measured over a shorter time period. Some examples of these differences can be seen in Figure 16.1. As can be seen from these examples, long-term elasticities are often higher than short-term elasticities. This may be due to the customer's limited knowledge of marketplace prices (as was noted in Chapter 7). It may take some time for many customers to notice that a price has changed. This may also be due to the time necessary to find purchase alternatives. For example, if one of a manufacturer's suppliers increases prices, it might take considerable time for the manufacturer to find an acceptable alternative source. There might be a necessary trial period or the requirement of making new arrangements for the transportation and storage of the new supplier's materials. Another example of this might be the consumer trend away from breakfast cereals toward products such as muffins and bagels, mentioned in Chapter 1.

On the other hand, there may be some instances when short-term elasticities are higher than long-term elasticities. For example, a customer may have a negative emotional reaction to a price that greatly exceeds his or her internal reference price (IRP). However, as time passes, the customer's IRP is likely to shift upward, which will have the effect of lessening the emotional reaction. Thus, a customer who fails to buy or switches brands on hearing of a price increase may come back to the brand after time has allowed some adaptation to the change. When evaluating price elasticity estimates in determining best prices, it would be wise to consider the possibility of such sources of delayed market response.

A second type of long-term factor concerns the tendency of many customers who purchase from a company to purchase from that company again in the future. This is important because these repeat-purchasing customers tend to become more profitable over time. One reason for this is that customers may become confident about the quality of the company's products as in the example, mentioned in Chapter 13, that first-time car buyers may tend to later purchase larger cars from the same company. For service-based products such as insurance and credit cards, professional services, and subscription-based products such as cell phone service and software support, an important source of the greater profitability of repeat customers is that they do not require the relatively high costs of customer acquisition. Further, compared to first-time customers, repeat customers are likely to have fewer problems, make fewer customer-service calls, and in other ways are likely to be less costly to serve.[4]

Because a product's repeat customers tend to become more profitable, the calculations for determining the best price for that product should consider these greater future profit levels. In particular, a sale lost due to a price increase might represent a repeat customer who, along with his or her likelihood of greater future profits, is "lost for good."[5] Thus, a breakeven analysis that indicated that a price increase would be profitable in the current period may indicate that the increase would not be profitable if the likely future higher profits of the lost customers were taken into account. Also, it would work the other way. A breakeven analysis that indicated that price decrease would not be profitable in the current period may show that the decrease is desirable if the likely future higher profits of newly acquired customers were taken into account.

An approach to considering these greater future profits of repeat customers is to use the concept of customer lifetime value—the revenue over time expected from a customer, minus the costs of serving the customer.[6] Estimates of customer lifetime value often make use of historical data on the likely length of time a repeat customer will buy from the company. With such an expected customer duration, the greater customer profitability in future

Figure 16.1   Examples of Short- and Long-Term Price Elasticities

Brand	Price Elasticities	
	Short-Term	**Long-Term**
Captain Crunch	−0.83	−1.79
Cheerios	−2.75	−3.02
Cocoa Puffs	−1.23	−2.07
Country Morning Granola	−0.24	−0.62
Fruite Brute	−2.55	−6.02
Golden Grahams	−0.11	−0.17
Kellogg Apple Jacks	−2.23	−3.28
Kellogg-Corn Krisp	−3.11	−3.17
Kellogg-Corn Flakes	0.95	1.16
Kellogg-Fruit Loops	−3.62	−3.66
Kellogg-Frosted Mini-Wheats	−2.21	−2.88
Kellogg-Product 19	−1.18	−14.42
Kellogg-Raisin Bran	−0.15	−0.25
Kellogg-Rice Krispies	−0.83	−0.99
Kellogg-Special K	−0.12	0.15
Kellogg-Sugar Frosted Flakes	−1.67	−2.26
Kellogg-Sugar Pops	−3.42	−9.57
Kellogg-Smacks	−4.77	−4.57
Life Cereal	−3.14	−6.32
Lucky Charms	−2.32	−3.23
Nabisco Shredded Wheat	1.63	−2.02
Post Alpha Bits	−1.42	−1.43
Post Grape Nuts	−0.47	−0.72
Post Raisin Bran	−0.53	0.70
Post Super Sugar Crisps	−1.64	−3.00
Ralston Purina Chex Cereal	0.65	1.12
Total	−1.81	−2.55
Trix	−3.36	−4.35
Wheaties	−2.90	−2.63

Source: Avijit Ghosh, Scott A. Neslin, and Robert W. Shoemaker, "Are There Associations Between Price Elasticity and Brand Characteristics?" in *1983 Educators' Conference Proceedings,* ed. Patrick E. Murphy et al. (Chicago, IL: American Marketing Association, 1983), 226–230.

time periods can be taken into account by allocating part of the average customer's remaining lifetime value to the current time period.

For example, consider an insurance agent who estimates that each of his seventy-four homeowners insurance customers will remain with him for an average of four more years and will have, at current premium levels, a remaining lifetime value over that time of $1,200 (in present-period dollars). He could spread out customer profitability differences between years by allocating one-fourth of this remaining lifetime value, $300, to the current year. If his customers' current annual contribution margin averages $125, then this allocation adds $175, or in proportion terms, a factor of 1.4 (= $175/$125).

To calculate from this allocation factor a contribution-margin (CM) adjustment for customer lifetime value (Adj_L) that could be used in a breakeven analysis of a prospective price change, the allocation factor could be multiplied by the contribution margin after the price change. This adjustment would be included in the denominator of the generalized breakeven (GBE) formula, as was done for the CM adjustment for complements (Adj_C) discussed in Chapter 13. If the agent is considering a $60 increase in annual premiums, then the CM adjustment for customer lifetime value would be $259 (= 1.4 × [$125 + $60]), and the breakeven sales level would be as follows:

$$BE = \frac{\Delta FC - (\Delta CM \times BS)}{CM + \$Adj_L} = \frac{0 - (\$60 \times 74)}{\$185 + \$259} = -10 \text{ customers}$$

The third type of long-term factor involves the broader marketing environment. This includes social and technological factors that may affect commercial exchanges as well as the ethical, legal, and political issues discussed in Chapter 15. Often, these environmental factors change slowly. For example, gradual lifestyle changes that have led to increased time pressure on homemakers has led to decreased demand for more time-intensive products, such as condensed soup. The Campbell Soup Company has recognized this source of decrease in its condensed soup sales and thus can exclude this source of sales decline from analyses of the effects of canned soup prices on sales.

There are times when it is a long, slow change in prices that causes the environmental change. For example, repeated increases in the prices of health care–related products and services over the years have had the long-term result of providing political support for governmental regulation of the health care industry. An awareness of long-term environmental changes, especially those related to competitive and economic factors, could also be important prompts for considering advancing the strategic prominence of price and making price a more important factor in a company's marketing strategy.

Be Your Own Pricing Consultant

When price is a background variable in the marketing mix, managers' best efforts are likely to be elsewhere, and they are often tempted to hire a consultant or consulting firm to manage pricing. Although there are many business situations when outsourcing is appropriate, pricing decisions are generally too important to be entrusted to people outside of the organization. With an understanding of the concepts of this book, the manager can create his or her own system for automating the management of prices, particularly when price remains of low strategic prominence.

The structure of an automated price management system based on the concepts of this book is illustrated in Figure 16.2. Conceptually, there would be a GBE formula setup for each item (i.e., stock-keeping unit, or "SKU") that the company is currently selling. This setup would receive input from at least four databases:

1. Current estimates of the unit variable costs for producing this item

2. Estimates of additional profit dollars that would be gained from a sale of this item (e.g., from complementary products or from customer lifetime value) or lost from a sale of this item (e.g., from substitute products or from authorized price sales in other countries)

3. Any incremental fixed costs that would be associated with a price change (e.g., cost of communicating a price decrease or fixed manufacturing cost saved for a sales decrease caused by a price increase)

4. Estimate of the item's price elasticity under current conditions, based on a continually updated regression analysis of prices and sales for each period

Figure 16.2   Structure of an Automated Price Management System

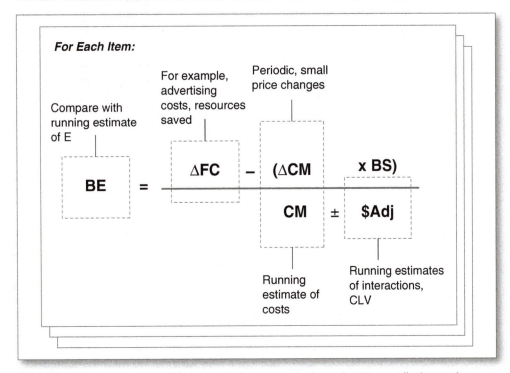

Note: Adj = adjustment to contribution margin, BE = breakeven, BS = base sales, CM = contribution margin, CLV = customer lifetime value, E = price elasticity, FC = fixed costs.

Once this setup is arranged, it will be "worked" periodically to test if the item's current price could be improved. This would be done by calculating the breakeven unit sales for a small (say, 5 percent) price increase and price decrease and evaluating each by the current price elasticity estimate. If this evaluation indicates that a prospective change would lead to more profit, then a succession of larger changes in that direction would be tested until the current best price is determined. For example, if the breakeven price elasticity (E_{BE}) for a 5 percent price decrease for an item were −2.4 and the current price elasticity estimate were around −3.0, then successive E_{BE}s would be calculated. If the E_{BE} for a 10 percent price decrease were −2.8 and the E_{BE} for a 15 percent price decrease were −3.2, then the item's current price minus 10 percent would be deemed the item's current best price.

This price management system could be run in a way that would be completely automatic so that it would periodically scan all of a company's products and change prices to what the system calculates is the current best price. Alternatively, there could be some human oversight of the process, so that the system would propose price changes that a manager would then have to approve or disapprove. An important advantage of at least occasional human oversight is that it makes it possible for the system to improve. If a proposed price change is deemed unacceptable, the system and/or its inputs could be modified so as to make the system less likely to propose such price changes in the future.

In being your own pricing consultant, you would have to take into account the promotional messages of the many consulting companies, both large and small, that offer services using sophisticated, "state-of-the-art" price-optimization algorithms. Although there are certainly more elegant, calculus-based procedures for determining profit-maximizing prices, it would be hard for a provider of such procedures to demonstrate that they are more effective than the simple iterative process described above. Further, by virtue of its simplicity, the system just described enables the manager to understand every component and thus correct, modify, and apply each component as is appropriate. This helps make possible an effective merging of human judgment with numerical systems, a combination that can be more beneficial to business decision making than either of these two processes alone.

PRICE AS A LEAD VARIABLE

When price is of high strategic prominence in the marketing mix—that is, when it is used to attract and keep customers—it could possibly be the *high* price of a product or firm that is bringing in the customers. This occurs in the practice of prestige pricing, which was discussed in Chapter 13. However, in the overwhelming majority of cases, when pricing is used as a lead variable, it is a *low* price that attracts and keeps the customers. Thus, pricing is the lead marketing mix variable in companies that we think of as low-price competitors, such as Southwest Airlines, Walmart, and McDonald's. Also, there are a number of products and companies that may not currently hold low-price positionings but did so at earlier points in their history, such as Ford automobiles, Pepsi-Cola, and Nathan's hot dogs. For these companies, the past use of price as a lead variable was an important factor in their success.

Given that using price as a lead variable usually involves a low price, most of the examples of it are variations of the penetration pricing strategy. The discussion of penetration in Chapter 4 highlighted two factors that are important for a penetration strategy to work. One is the ability to set a price that is low enough to matter to customers, and the other is to have some degree of protection against competitive price matching. For some products, such as consumer packaged goods that are infrequently purchased, it is difficult to find any way to create a meaningful price incentive, and for some companies, their small size gives them at least temporary protection against price competition. But in most cases, it is a company's ability to achieve low costs in production and operations that both makes a sufficiently low price possible and provides a deterrent to and defense against price competition. Thus, it is important to review the possible ways that low costs can be accomplished.

Achieving Low Costs

Work on the topic of "cost leadership" in the field of strategic management has identified at least three general sources of a cost advantage.[7] These are the availability of low-cost resources, economies of scale, and economies of experience.

1. *Availability of low-cost resources.* This could include easy access to raw materials such as lumber or iron, cheap sources of energy such as nearby coal fields or hydroelectric power, or access to a large pool of low-cost labor.[8]

2. *Economies of scale.* Larger business operations can often provide products at lower per-unit costs than can smaller businesses. This could be because large size makes possible the hiring of more highly trained personnel who can be more efficient at their jobs or makes possible the purchasing of more sophisticated machinery or larger, more efficient facilities. It could also be due to large size making it possible to obtain supplies and raw materials at volume discounts such as those discussed in Chapter 10. Walmart's large size provides an example of both sources of low costs. Walmart benefits from an efficient, dedicated distribution system as well as from substantial volume discounts from suppliers.

3. *Economies of experience.* In general, as a business produces a product, learning occurs that can be translated into cost savings. With experience, workers tend to develop more efficient procedures and make fewer mistakes, companies obtain more efficient equipment, and managers discover ways to standardize or otherwise redesign products to obtain production cost savings. Several examples of "experience curve" effects on costs can be seen in Figure 16.3. Whereas economies of scale are created by the amount of current production, economies of experience are created by the amount of cumulative production—the number of units of the product that the company has ever produced.

A fourth source of cost advantage is particularly important given the focus of this book on paying close attention to customer needs. This is the possibility of coming up with a product innovation that serves to make the product less costly to produce. To distinguish this from the usual use of the term *innovation* as something new that makes the product better (see Chapter 4), a new concept or change that does not improve the product, but

Figure 16.3 Some Examples of Experience Curves

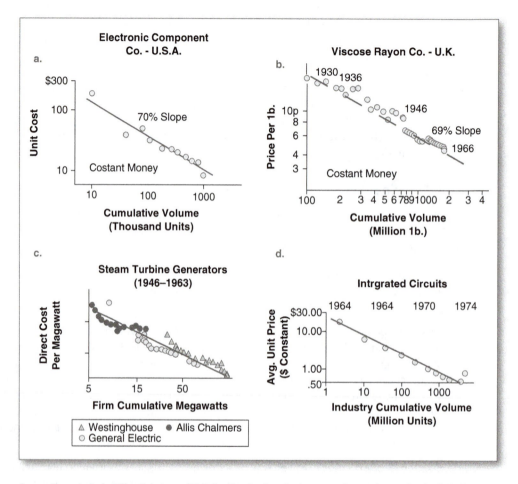

Source: Roger A. Kerin, Vijay Mahajn, and P. Rajan Varadarajan, *Contemporary Perspectives on Strategic Market Planning* (Boston: Allyn & Bacon, 1990), 118.

does substantially decrease its production costs, could be termed a cost innovation.[9] If work on cost innovation involves achieving a specific cost goal, it would be termed *target costing,* and the efforts to make the product reach this cost goal could be termed *cost engineering.*

At the heart of work to achieve a cost innovation is carrying out market research—or at least listening carefully to customer needs. Because it is usually the case that some aspects of product quality will need to be sacrificed to achieve substantially lower costs, it is essential that the aspects that are sacrificed are those that are relatively unimportant to the customer. Thus, the story of the Ford Mustang, mentioned in Chapter 2, provides a classic example of a cost innovation. Customer research enabled Ford to realize that sports car styling and feel was so important to many customers that even if sports car performance were sacrificed, the product would still be of considerable appeal. In the 1970s, the developers of the First Alert home smoke detector achieved great success by sacrificing high-quality hand-assembled metal parts. Their molded plastic smoke detector adequately did the job that customers wanted; because of its low-cost production, it was able to be sold for around $15—much less than competitors' prices of $50 and above.

The Ford Mustang and First Alert examples are important because they illustrate that, if sufficiently insightful, an understanding of the customer can in itself make a cost innovation possible. However, it is probably more often the case that cost innovations involve also the application of new technology. For example, in the 1950s and early 1960s, the Bic company was outstandingly successful in applying the then-new technology of plastics to produce consumer goods such as pens and shavers, so that they could then be sold as disposables at very low prices. In the 1990s, the E-Trade Financial Corporation successfully applied Internet technology to achieve an outstanding cost innovation in securities trading. In both of these cases, it was important that the sellers understood the product attributes that customers viewed as essential. However, neither of these cost innovations would have been possible without the application of new technology.

In the current service-economy environment, one source of cost innovations is the possibility that a service could be "industrialized." This would involve simplifying the service, standardizing it, and providing it with the maximal use of automation.[10] McDonald's and other fast-food restaurants have achieved great success in offering low-priced food service based on this type of cost innovation. Although attempts to industrialize service products more complex than food service have not generally met with success, there have been exceptions. Jiffy Lube is a well-known low-price provider of automobile oil-change services, and Weight Watchers has been successful in providing low-price weight-control services. Perhaps a key to the success of their cost-innovation-based products is that they focus on only one very specific service and avoid offering a wide range of car repair or health care services.

Varying the Strategic Prominence of Price Over Time

In decisions concerning when to make price the lead variable in the marketing mix, it is helpful to be familiar with the concept of the product life cycle. In this view, a product is considered to pass through four stages over time: (1) the introduction stage, a period of slow growth; (2) the growth stage, a period of rapid sales increase; (3) the maturity stage, a period of relatively stable sales; and (4) the decline stage, a period of decreasing sales (see Figure 16.4).[11] For the purposes of marketing strategy, the product life cycle concept is best applied to a type of product, as opposed to a particular company or brand. For example, the stand-alone fax machine was in its introduction stage in the 1970s, experienced rapid sales growth in the 1980s, was a mature product through the early 2000s, and has recently entered the decline stage as it is being superseded technologically by Internet-based alternatives.[12]

A product's introduction stage is an unlikely time for price to be a lead variable. Customer price sensitivity tends to be low during this period, particularly when, as

Figure 16.4 The Four Stages of the Product Life Cycle

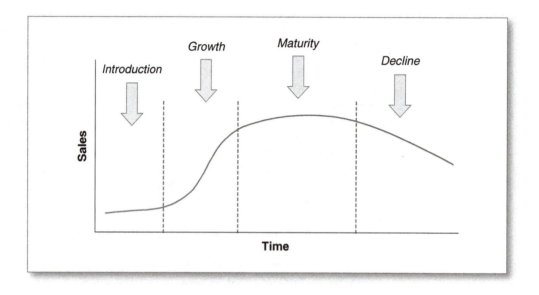

discussed in Chapter 4, the product could be considered an innovation that involves what consumers perceive to be substantial economic, physical, or social risks. However, when a product has spent some time in the introduction stage and has received some consumer acceptance, increasing the strategic prominence of price could be highly appropriate. For example, the automobile had been around for decades when, in 1908, Henry Ford introduced the Model T, at very low price points. Made possible by cost innovations such as the moving assembly line, Ford's low-price strategy took the automobile product into its growth stage and made Ford the preeminent automobile company of that era.

The growth-stage use of price as a lead variable is particularly appropriate in situations where there may be a pioneer advantage, the benefit of being first that was discussed in Chapter 4. For example, Amazon.com positioned itself as a low-price provider of books and other consumer goods during the growth stage of online retailing, even though its low prices impaired the company's ability to be profitable. The consumer loyalty achieved during that period has benefited Amazon as online retailing has entered its maturity stage. During the growth stage of personal computers, Microsoft sold its DOS and Windows operating systems to computer manufacturers at very low per-unit prices. This helped Microsoft software spread so widely that it soon became the worldwide standard in most types of personal computing functions.

The use of price as a lead marketing mix variable during the maturity stage of the product life cycle is common in industries where there is intense competition among sellers. If mass-market retailing is considered a mature industry, the presence of many strong competitors often leads managers to maintain a focus on pricing issues. For example, CVS, Walgreens, Rite-Aid, and other chain drugs stores incessantly communicate with consumers about low-priced items and a seemingly endless variety of price promotions. This is also common among new-car dealerships, supermarket chains, and retailers of office supplies, home improvement products, and consumer electronics. This managerial attention to price helps these companies stay salient in consumers' minds and helps them avoid being seen as overpriced competitors in the crowded retail marketplace.

It is also possible for a mature-product competitor to, at least temporarily, elevate the strategic prominence of price from a background variable to a lead variable in order to grow or revive the company. A classic example of this is Pepsi-Cola. Established in 1903, Pepsi had been a small also-ran to Coca-Cola, and had actually gone bankrupt twice by 1931. To revive the company, its management decided on a low-price appeal—selling a 12-ounce bottle of Pepsi at the same $0.05 price as the familiar 6-ounce bottle of Coke. Perhaps because Coca-Cola found it difficult to change the size of its familiar bottle or lower its even-nickel price, Pepsi was able to retain the price differential, and rose to be a strong and highly profitable brand.[13]

A product's decline stage, like its introduction stage, is unlikely to be the best time for price to be a lead marketing variable. The trend toward declining product sales would make it difficult for a company to obtain the sales increases necessary to make a penetration strategy profitable. Further, as sales decline, the individuals who remain customers of the product tend to be more loyal, and thus less sensitive to variations in price.

Varying the Strategic Prominence of Price Among Market Segments

In the same way that the strategic prominence of price in a company may vary over time, it may also vary across market segments. It is likely that, in most markets, there is a segment of customers who are particularly price conscious.[14] A company that usually uses price as a background variable can make price a lead variable when designing and managing offerings to serve the price-conscious segment of its market. For example, although Pepsi has long-abandoned its low-price strategy, it has returned to a price-centered strategy for the price-conscious segment of the soft drink market. For this segment, Pepsi frequently offers its two-liter bottles at prices as low as $0.99, and in so doing, maintains brisk price competition with Coke and other soft drink producers.

The price-conscious market segment can often be further divided into a "good-buy" segment—those who want a regular-quality product at a lower than regular price—and a "low-price" segment—those who so strongly want a low price that they are willing to sacrifice some aspects of product quality (see Figure 16.5). Appealing to the good-buy segment might involve periodic discounts and other devices, among those discussed in Chapter 11, that enable time to be used as a price-segmentation fence.

Appealing to the low-price segment might involve offering feature-dependent discounts, such as those discussed in Chapter 10. So that products that are somewhat "denatured" in order to make possible a lower price do not hurt the image of a seller's respectable brand name, sellers will sometimes sell the reduced-quality/reduced-price brands under a different name. For example, lower-priced GE appliances are sold under the Hotpoint name; lower-priced Rollerblade skates are sold under the Bladerunner name. Another possibility is that a manufacturer could sell the reduced-quality/reduced-price product to marketers who will retail the product as a store brand (e.g., Sam's Club) or as a generic product.

Figure 16.5   Market Segments Related to the Strategic Prominence of Price

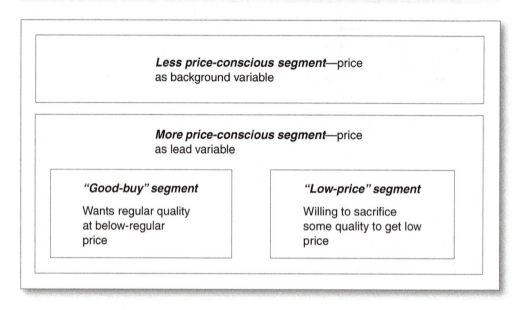

Communicating Low Price

When price is used as the lead variable in the marketing mix, it is typical that the message that the product is low-priced is involved in a high proportion of a company's communications with its customers and potential customers. Such frequent communication about low prices will tend to increase customers' price sensitivity. This will occur at least partially because the price communication will increase customers' price awareness, as discussed in Chapter 7. In addition, the greater price sensitivity could occur for more emotional reasons, as was mentioned in the discussion of dangling and perceived responsibility in Chapter 8. It should be noted that there is here the possibility of a "vicious cycle"—high customer price sensitivity causes management to use price as a lead variable, which in turn creates even more customer price sensitivity.

One challenge in communicating a low-price message is to effectively make the point that the product's price is indeed low. Usually, this is approached by including an external reference price in the low-price advertisement, as discussed in Chapter 8. When a seller communicates low-price messages frequently, then a second challenge arises: explaining to the customer the reasons for these low prices being offered. Like the price rationales for price increases discussed in Chapter 8, a seller could communicate price rationales for price decreases. One study of the price rationales given in retail discount price ads found the following three reasons most common:

1. Store had an inventory overstock
2. Retailer was passing along a discount received from the manufacturer
3. A holiday was being celebrated

The results of this study indicated an advantage of the received-discount rationale over the inventory-overstock rationale, presumably because the overstock rationale suggests something negative about the desirability of the merchandise.[15] In the same vein as the received-discount rationale, a seller could communicate that its low prices are due to the efficiencies of its large size or cost savings from its no-frills services or facilities. The important point is that a seller who frequently makes a low-price claim should pay attention to, and manage, the consumer's perceptions of the reasons why these claims are being made.

When price is a lead marketing mix variable, it is reasonable for price communications to make liberal use of price-ending formats that maximize the perception of low price. As discussed in Chapter 7, there is likely to be a perceptual benefit to using a just-below price ending when such use lowers a price's leftmost digit. However, even when a just-below ending does not lower a price's leftmost digit, the low-price and discount connotations of just-below endings will tend to serve the goals of a low-price communication. Further, the use of sharp-number prices, as is typically done by Walmart, may, by virtue of the association of sharp numbers with low numbers, also contribute to a low-price image.

Avoiding "The Wheel of Retailing"

A well-known observation of the retailing industry is that new retail entrants often attract customers by offering low prices made possible by cost savings from minimizing customer services and amenities. With their success comes competition, which tempts the low-price retailers to add services and amenities that cause them to raise prices. This eventually creates the environment for a new generation of retail entrants to attract customers by low prices that undersell the current retailers. The cyclic nature of this sequence has led it to be termed *the wheel of retailing*.[16]

An awareness of the tendency toward this pattern over time can help a seller avoid becoming trapped by such a cycle. One approach to avoiding the wheel of retailing would be to scrupulously avoid the temptation to add services or amenities—in other words, focus strongly on continuing to keep prices low. Another approach would be to accept that one's low-price position will not last forever and plan to lower the strategic prominence of price after it has had its desired effects, such as establishing the company as a familiar competitor in the marketplace.

INTERACTIVE PRICING AND PRICE CONSTERNATION

The previous discussion of basic pricing concepts in the context of price as a background variable or as a lead variable has assumed a fixed price policy. As was discussed in Chapter 14, interactive pricing—determining price by auction or negotiation—involves procedures that differ substantially from those of setting fixed prices. Next are some suggestions for applying basic pricing concepts in businesses where interactive pricing predominates.

When price is a background variable, the following are some routine interactive pricing activities:

1. *Determining initial prices.* Use an estimate of a product's value to the customer (see Chapters 2 and 3) to determine and support your asking price during price negotiation.

2. *Determining best prices.* When bidding in procurement auctions, be systematic in estimating the expected profit of each possible bid, and choose the bid with the highest expected profit (see Chapter 14). To the extent possible, use a systematic compilation of past data to decide on minimum bids when selling by auction and to set reservation prices when engaged in price negotiation.

3. *Consider price segmentation and product interrelations.* During the price negotiation process, gather information useful for price segmentation (see Chapter 10). Consider the types of product interrelations discussed in Chapter 13 when setting reservation prices in price negotiation.

4. *Implement interactive pricing with profit-based compensation.* Use profit-based compensation methods (see Chapter 14) for salespeople who have negotiating responsibilities and for managers responsible for bidding in procurement auctions.

When price is the lead marketing mix variable in an interactive-pricing environment, the following should receive particular management attention:

1. *Communicating a low-price position.* Advertising a low asking price could help a low-priced seller attract buyers into price negotiations. In procurement auctions, submitting bids lower than those corresponding to maximum expected profit levels could serve to communicate the intention to be a low-price provider. When selling by auction, a low minimum starting bid, or none at all, could be used to attract a high number of bidders (see Chapter 14).

2. *Track effects of low price on sales.* Explicitly estimate the sales benefits of using price as a lead variable, and be prepared to reduce the strategic prominence of price when conditions make that possible.

Price Consternation

It is being suggested in this chapter that a strategic intention to use price to attract and keep customers is good reason for price to be a lead marketing mix variable and be the focus of management attention. However, there are other possible reasons. In particular, there are times when technology, legal factors, or other elements of the marketing environment raise such serious problems with a company's business model that questions of price—that is, "How can we make money in this business?"—cannot help but come to the forefront of the manager's concerns.

A salient example of such price consternation has been occurring recently in the recorded music industry. Technological advances of digitization and the Internet have given music consumers the ability to obtain musical recordings without charge (e.g., by capturing the audio from music videos posted on YouTube) and to easily share these recordings with friends. In response to these changes, there have been lawsuits against music-sharing websites and a rise of iTunes and other services that sell musical recordings inexpensively by the song. One popular band, Radiohead, made their album available for download, allowing consumers to "pay what you want," thus putting price on a voluntary basis.[17] Although gaining a lot of publicity, Radiohead's experiment with voluntary prices does not seem to have caught on. Some musicians have accepted that most consumers will obtain their music without paying and have put efforts into increasing the frequency and prices of concert tours and other live performances as a means of generating revenue.

Although it would be difficult to establish general rules for resolving price consternation, the necessary rethinking of traditional pricing models would benefit from many of the basic pricing concepts discussed in this book. For example, a sensitive assessment of differentiating factors could reveal seemingly small things, such as increasing the convenience of downloading a song or enabling a fan to be among the first to obtain a new song, that could be of considerable value to the customer. Also, it would be good to keep in mind that there might well be segments in the recorded-music market that vary greatly in their price sensitivity.

PRICING IN NONPROFIT ORGANIZATIONS

In virtually all of the discussions of this book, the criterion for good price setting and pricing policy has been the maximization of profits. How then might pricing be different in a nonprofit organization—one whose primary goal is not profits but to accomplish something of benefit to society?

For many organizations in the nonprofit sector of the economy, there would actually be very little pricing differences from for-profit organizations. Nonprofit organizations that provide services such as health care, child care, education, and artistic performances derive the major portion of their revenue from payments for these services. These organizations incur costs to provide these services, and consumers think about the prices of these services largely as they would think about the prices of for-profit goods and services.[18] Although these nonprofit organizations do not pay dividends to shareholders, it makes perfect sense for them to maximize revenues and minimize costs. The larger the revenue-minus-cost surplus, the more money available for providing additional beneficial services. From the standpoint of pricing principles, it does not seem to make a big difference whether or not this surplus is referred to as "profit."

However, despite the relevance of the basic pricing concepts discussed in this book to nonprofit organizations that provide services for payment, these pricing concepts may not fit well in what is by many measures the largest part of the nonprofit sector: organized religion. Although in the past, religions often required payments (i.e., "tithes") from members, currently in the United States approximately 90 percent of the operating revenue of religious congregations is obtained from voluntary contributions from members.[19] If such contributions are considered voluntary prices, then it can be asked why what was considered an unusual experiment in selling musical recordings is a widespread standard practice in religious organizations.

One possible answer to this question would be that religious organizations have found that relying on a member's conscience will lead to more revenue than a tithe. However, another possible answer could lie in how one thinks about the exchange between a religious organization and its members. In the context of the commercial exchange discussed in Chapter 1 (see Figure 1.1), it may be that a religious organization's price—what it wants in return for the religious activities and community it provides—is not primarily money. Rather, a religious organization's price may be most essentially something of a more personal nature, such as a member's openness to change and personal transformation. A required monetary price might tend to evoke the question "If I have to pay, what does the organization have to do?" which would tend to distract the member from an openness to personal change. Further, paying voluntarily would help support intrinsic motivation, leading to attributions such as "I pay because I care about what this organization represents."[20] In this view, even if voluntary payments lead to less monetary revenue, they might help the member give in the exchange what could be called "familiar ways of being"—something often more difficult to part with than money.

THE IMPORTANCE OF CUSTOMER NEEDS

This book's discussion of pricing concepts and practices has been guided by the marketing approach to business. As mentioned in Chapter 1, the heart of this approach is the marketing concept—the idea that the key to business success is to focus on satisfying customer needs. Hopefully, it has been apparent through the chapters following Chapter 1 that there is a benefit to considering customer needs through every pricing step and through every aspect of the pricing decision process.

To review and further illustrate this importance of customer needs, it may be helpful to take the perspective of the manager who is involved with the everyday pricing activities for an organization or a set of products. Consider the following sampling of some common signs that one's pricing practices are not all that they could be, along with a brief description of how considering customer needs could help point to a solution:

- *Many customers, few profits.* If product demand is brisk, look more carefully at the value your product creates for customers. Look for segments of customers for whom this value might be particularly high. This research may identify opportunities to raise prices.

- *Ouija-board price setting.* If your company's price-setting process seems arbitrary and haphazard, consider developing a system to implement the basic concepts discussed in this book. Particularly important is a means to apply all readily available information that can help predict how customers will respond to a prospective change in price.

- *Clients who "beat you up" on price.* If you focus on fully understanding the value that your product creates for your clients, you will be better able to help your clients understand and appreciate that value.

- *Price promotions that don't work.* Discounts or other price promotions used as a quick fix for low sales often amount to unintended, and unprofitable, price cuts. Consider price promotions as a means to satisfy the needs of customers in particular market segments or as a means of supporting price as a lead marketing mix variable.

- *Competitors cutting into profits*. Consider the differentiating factors that might give your product value to customers over competing items. Look for product attributes of low importance to customers to gain ideas for cost innovations.

Although these are only a small sampling of pricing "frustration signs," they illustrate how considering customer needs could help offer a way out. Indeed, if marketing-oriented pricing principles are considered throughout one's business decision making, it will be less likely that such frustration signs will ever appear.

SUMMARY

To effectively manage pricing activities, it is important that an organization be clear on the strategic prominence of price. When price is used to attract and keep customers, it serves as the lead variable in the marketing mix. When it is mainly other marketing mix variables that are used to attract and keep customers, then price has a lower strategic prominence, serving as a background variable in the marketing mix.

Price is appropriate as a background variable in businesses where customers attend primarily to other factors, such as quality, style, or convenience. To facilitate price management with only limited managerial attention, it is helpful to have checklists for pricing activities. It is also important to maintain awareness of long-term pricing factors. By developing these checklists and long-term considerations into a largely automated system, a manager can efficiently retain understanding and control of pricing decisions.

The use of price as a lead marketing mix variable usually involves being a low-price competitor. This is appropriate when price can be set low enough to matter to customers and to offer some protection against price competition. The appropriateness of using price as a lead variable tends to be higher during the growth and maturity stages of the product life cycle, and it may be appropriate to use price as a lead variable for only a segment of the market.

The principles of managing price as a background or a lead marketing mix variable can also be applied to interactive pricing situations, and it is sometimes sharp changes in the marketing environment that raise price to the focus of managerial attention. For-profit pricing principles also hold for many nonprofit organizations, although for some there may be greater use of voluntary prices. In all price management situations, there are important benefits to carefully considering customer needs.

KEY TERMS

strategic prominence	contribution-margin (CM)	cost innovation
lead variable	adjustment for customer	product life cycle
background variable	lifetime value	the wheel of retailing
positioning	marketing environment	price consternation
customer lifetime	economies of scale	voluntary prices
value	economies of experience	

1. Describe the concept of the strategic prominence of a marketing mix variable. How does using price as a lead variable differ from using price as a background variable?

2. Explain the concept of positioning. How is a company's positioning likely to be related to the strategic prominence of price in that company?

3. Give some of the items that would be on a checklist of routine pricing activities. Why are checklists particularly important when price is used as a background variable?

4. Provide an example of a factor that would make a long-term price elasticity higher than a short-term one. Then describe a factor that would make a long-term price elasticity lower than a short-term one.

5. Describe the concept of customer lifetime value. Explain how consideration of this factor could be included in the GBE formula.

6. Give an example of a change in the marketing environment that would have important implications for managing a product's pricing.

7. Describe what could be done to make it practical to "be your own pricing consultant" when price is used as a background variable. Describe the benefits of not outsourcing pricing decisions.

8. Explain why achieving low costs in production and operations is a key factor in the decision to use price as a lead marketing mix variable.

9. What is the difference between an economy of scale and an economy of experience?

10. How does a cost innovation differ from the type of innovation that makes a product better? Explain why carefully considering customer needs is of key importance in developing cost innovations.

11. Describe the concept of the product life cycle. Give an example of a current product that illustrates each of its four stages.

12. In which of the product-life-cycle stages is the use of price as a lead variable likely to be most appropriate. Explain your reasoning.

13. Describe how a pricing plan to serve the "good-buy" market segment might differ from one to serve the "low-price" segment.

14. What are some of the means by which frequent price communication could increase customer price sensitivity? Is higher customer price sensitivity desirable or undesirable?

15. What is the wheel of retailing? What are two approaches that a retailer could take to avoid being trapped by it?

16. Describe an example of an interactive pricing activity that would be appropriate when price is used as a background variable. Then describe an example of an interactive pricing activity that would be appropriate when price is used as a lead variable.

17. What is price consternation? Describe an example of an industry, besides the recorded-music industry, that is currently facing price consternation.

18. Describe how nonprofit organizations where basic pricing principles apply differ from those nonprofit organizations where basic pricing principles may not so well apply.

19. Give two examples of pricing "frustration signs," and describe how managerial attention to customer needs might point to a solution.

EXERCISES

1. Consider the following product categories:

Supermarkets	Smart-phones
Automobiles	Car insurance
Jeans	Hotels

    (a) For each category of product, give an example of a well-known brand that uses price as a background variable and one that uses price as a lead variable.

    (b) Choose one of these background-lead pairs. For each of the two companies in the pair, describe the factors that were likely to have determined that company's decision on the strategic prominence of price.

2. For more than 95 years, Blaine Candies has operated a candy shop in a convenient downtown location in a middle-sized Midwestern city, providing customers a well-regarded assortment of handcrafted chocolates. Blaine sells standard chocolates, such as buttercreams, caramels, peanut chews, and jellies as well as a variety of specialty pieces that are handcrafted, such as almond butter crunch, almond balls, marshmallows, and cashew patties. Chocolates are available in 1/2 lb., 1 lb., 2 lb., 3 lb., and 5 lb. boxes and are priced strictly by multiplying the amount of chocolates being purchased by the price offered for a 1 lb. box.

    The company has relied mostly on cost-based pricing, using a 50 percent markup for chocolates produced at the store and selling purchased goods (e.g., gummy bears, Swedish fish, lemon drops) and tins at a 100 percent markup. Among national companies competing with Blaine Candies is Russell Stover (low-end) and Godiva (high-end). Blaine's tends to set prices to be similar to those of local competitors.

    (a) Describe the strategic prominence of price at Blaine Candies. What are the factors that appear to make this level of strategic prominence appropriate for this company?

    (b) Use the material from this chapter to outline a plan that Blaine's management can use to make routine, frequently occurring pricing decisions.

(c) Give an example of a change in the company, the market, or the marketing environment that might lead Blaine's management to change the strategic prominence of price at the company.

3. The owner of a company that sells job-management software to small construction and contracting businesses is thinking about the long-term implications of a possible price increase. The company sells its customers an annual software license, which includes program installation, maintenance, and technical support.

   (a) Describe some of the factors that would tend to make the repeat customers of this company more profitable than newly acquired customers.

   (b) The owner estimates that, at current price levels, the average remaining lifetime value of the company's 660 customers over the next five years equals $2880 (in present-period dollars). The average contribution margin on the software license for current customers is 30 percent. The owner is considering increasing his company's average price for an annual software license from $1200 to $1380. Calculate the breakeven sales level for this prospective price increase both with and without including the CM adjustment for customer lifetime value. Show your work.

   (c) Describe the effect of considering customer lifetime value on the breakeven sales levels that you calculated in Part (b). How is this effect likely to affect the decision that the owner will make regarding the possibility of raising the software license's price?

4. Here are some common consumer service products:

Personal financial advice	Pest-control services
Home computer repair and software training	Home carpentry services
Plumbing services	Tree-care services

   (a) Choose one of these products and describe how you might come up with a cost innovation by "industrializing" the service. Your plan should involve simplifying it (and perhaps focusing on only one specific part of the whole service), standardizing it, and making maximal use of automation.

   (b) Outline a plan for the business development of the cost innovation you describe in Part (a). In your plan, specify the strategic prominence of price and describe some of the implications of that role of price for the pricing activities involved in managing this product.

NOTES

1. William M. Pride and O. C. Ferrell, *Marketing*, 14th ed. (Boston: Houghton Mifflin, 2008), 578.
2. David A. Aaker and Erich Joachimsthaler, *Brand Leadership* (New York: The Free Press, 2000), 15.
3. Checklists have been found to improve decision making in various types of situations. See, for example, Alex B. Haynes et al., "A Surgical Safety Checklist to Reduce Morbidity and Mortality in a Global

Population," *New England Journal of Medicine* 360 (January 29, 2009): 491–499. See also J. Scott Armstrong, *Persuasive Advertising* (New York: Palgrave Macmillan, 2010), 290.

4. Frederick F. Reichheld and W. Earl Sasser, Jr., "Zero Defections: Quality Comes to Services," *Harvard Business Review* 68 (September-October 1990): 105-111.

5. F. Robert Dwyer, "Customer Lifetime Valuation to Support Marketing Decision Making," *Journal of Direct Marketing* 11 (Fall 1997): 6–13.

6. Paul D. Berger and Nada I. Nasr, "Customer Lifetime Value: Marketing Models and Applications," *Journal of Interactive Marketing* 12 (Winter 1998): 17–30.

7. Roger A. Kerin, Vijay Mahahan, and P. Rajan Varadarajan, *Contemporary Perspectives on Strategic Market Planning* (Boston: Allyn & Bacon, 1990).

8. Ming Zeng and Peter J. Williamson, *Dragons at Your Door: How Chinese Cost Innovation Is Disrupting Global Competition* (Boston: Harvard Business School Press, 2007).

9. Zeng and Williamson's use of this term focuses on a description of how a company can make the most of low labor costs.

10. Theodore Levitt, "The Industrialization of Service," *Harvard Business Review* 54 (September–October 1976): 63–74.

11. George Day, "The Product Life Cycle: Analysis and Applications Issues," *Journal of Marketing* 45 (Autumn 1981): 60–67.

12. "History of the Fax Machine," accessed July 22, 2011, http://faxswitch.com/fax_machine_history.html.

13. "A Brief History of Pepsi-Cola," accessed September 10, 2010, http://gono.com/museum2003/museum%20collect%20info/briefhistoryofpepsicola.htm.

14. Donald R. Lichtenstein, Richard G. Netemeyer, and Scot Burton, "Distinguishing Coupon Proneness from Value Consciousness: An Acquisition-Transaction Utility Theory Perspective," *Journal of Marketing* 54 (July 1990): 54–67.

15. George Bobinski, Dena Cox, and Anthony Cox, "Retail 'Sale' Advertising, Perceived Retailer Credibility, and Price Rationale," *Journal of Retailing* 72, no. 3 (1996): 291–306.

16. Stanley C. Hollander, "The Wheel of Retailing," *Journal of Marketing* 25 (July 1960): 37–42.

17. Josh Tyrangiel, "Radiohead Says: Pay What You Want," *Time,* October 1, 2007.

18. There is interesting evidence for this in the prices used in the public sector of the economy—that is, taxes. It has been found that the rightmost digits of Danish local government income tax rates over a thirty-five-year period showed an overrepresentation of the digit 9, as is commonly found in surveys of retail prices. See Asmus Leth Olsen, "The Politics of Digits: Evidence of Odd Taxation," *Public Choice* (forthcoming).

19. Michael O'Neill, *Nonprofit Nation: A New Look at the Third America* (San Francisco: Jossey-Bass, 2002), 20, 53. In Christian churches, this practice has been influenced by the New Testament passage: "Each man should give what he has decided in his heart to give, not reluctantly or under compulsion, for God loves a cheerful giver" (2 Corinthians 9:7, NIV).

20. See Edward L. Deci, "Effects of Externally Mediated Rewards on Intrinsic Motivation," *Journal of Personality and Social Psychology* 18, no. 1 (1971): 105–115.

Index

Note: Figures are indicated by f after the page number.

CPSIA information can be obtained
at www.ICGtesting.com
Printed in the USA
LVHW051441151222
735252LV00015B/53

9 781412 964746